Behavioral Norms, Technological Progress,
and Economic Dynamics

Behavioral Norms, Technological Progress, and Economic Dynamics

Studies in Schumpeterian Economics

Edited by Ernst Helmstädter and Mark Perlman

Ann Arbor

THE UNIVERSITY OF MICHIGAN PRESS

1999   1998   1997   1996   4   3   2   1

A CIP catalog record for this book is available from the British Library.

Library of Congress Cataloging-in-Publication Data

Behavioral norms, technological progress, and economic dynamics :
   studies in Schumpeterian economics / edited by Ernst Helmstädter and
   Mark Perlman.
       p.   cm.
   Includes bibliographical references and index.
   ISBN 0-472-10730-5 (hardcover : alk. paper)
   1. Evolutionary economics.   2. Technological innovations—Economic
aspects.   3. Economic development.   4. Schumpeter, Joseph Alois,
1883–1950.   I. Helmstädter, Ernst.   II. Perlman, Mark.
HB97.3.B44   1996
330—dc20   96-19399
                                                                CIP

Contents

Introduction

Ernst Helmstädter and Mark Perlman

Starting from the Present

The August 1994 biennial meetings of the International Schumpeter Society in Münster, FGR, were the fifth that the Society has held. After ten years of existence the time has come to look over the Society's figurative shoulder to see where it has been and to see what its personality really seems to be. Accordingly, it makes a certain sense to start by comparing the thrust of the most recent meetings with the comparable characteristics of earlier conference volumes. What do we note?

First, we see evidence that Schumpeterian evolutionary economics increasingly focuses on the perceptions, even "mind-sets," underlying the visions or theoretical foundations of organized economic research.[1]

Second, qualitatively the studies have come to focus on empirical examinations of the effectiveness of "dynamic competition," which Schumpeter clearly saw as the very core of his system. True, Schumpeter wrote in 1942 of creative destruction as being the action at the heart of progress, but by 1947 he had reconsidered his earlier careless slogan and substituted and stressed "the creative response" in the place of destruction. This creative response, not the details of destruction, is the common thread linking the papers; it is to be seen in the relationships between technical change and the growth of firms, in the changing composition of the labor force as modern innovation takes hold, and in the studies of innovation in specific industries involving worker training and the choice of various types of physical capital.

Third, Schumpeterian evolutionary economics focuses on historical experiences with market- as well as welfare-oriented "managed" socioeconomic systems, with regard to product intermediaries, factor intermediaries, and financial intermediaries. Efforts are made to go well beyond the kind of

---

1. One of us wrote in another context, "[A]s we learn more about the process of imagination we will give more order to our understanding of how choices are made. It is in imagining, . . . , where creative thinking and all economic choice processes begin" (Perlman 1990, p. 17).

economic analysis either in place or really dreamed of in the last decade of Schumpeter's life (he died in 1950). That these matters were not on the "profession's plate" during that decade does not mean that they had been previously served and, at best, relegated to the deep freeze until such time as they could either be thawed or (as is so often the case) cooked anew.

To what degree does the present tie to the Society's own past?

Looking at the Record

The 1980s were an era during which a dominant interest in replacing stagnation with some form of economic growth was emerging. In contrast to the depression decade of the 1930s, the decade of the 1980s turned from the short run to the long run, from statics to dynamics. The internationalization of product markets became an established fact, and there was every reason to think that factor markets, too, would become equally internationalized. Economic internationalization renders autarkic decision making increasingly ineffective; the problem is how to adjust one's thinking.

Horst Hanusch described the 1988 situation in his Introduction to the Society's first volume, *Evolutionary Economics: Applications of Schumpeter's Ideas:*

> From the point of view of evolutionary economics, Schumpeter copes with one major problem; dynamic growth of the potential aggregate supply. But contrary to neoclassical theory, he is not at all interested in optimization and pure equilibrium economics. For him, the driving forces of economic development are dynamic entrepreneurs and dynamic competition. (p. 1)

The chapters in this first volume test some Schumpeterian hypotheses: Morishima and Catephores argue, for example, that in addition to seeing the entrepreneur as a dynamic force, the banking system works to develop a dynamic equilibrium. Several writers attempt to explain how a firm becomes dynamic and what changes in the form of ownership have done to affect this process.

Schumpeter, in his time, did not join the professional crowd in condemning monopolistic power; rather, he suggested that both its prospect and its presence might do much to encourage change in the preferred direction. Why? Because research and development, necessary to the process of change, are expensive, and only when there are monopoly profits will there be sufficient funds for that purpose. Nor did Schumpeter join the professional crowd in decrying taxation and public expenditure. However, there is a caveat: social expenditure at the expense of national competitive productivity gains is a major modern danger.

In retrospect, the first (1986) meetings were clearly exploratory—was there a common thread tying disparate groups into a Schumpeterian entity? The 1988 meetings stressed the noncentrality of rational maximizing and market equilibrium. The 1990 meetings identified the hard core of the tradition, interest in technological change, entrepreneurship, and solid, factual research. To these the 1992 meetings added two important rubrics; the product of imagination-turned-into-economic reality and the importance of institutions in shaping and being shaped by both the thought and the economic market processes.

The 1988 meetings in Sienna, of which certain papers were published as *Evolving Technology and Market Structure: Studies in Schumpeterian Economics,* showed a major effort to flesh out the scope of Schumpeterian evolutionary economics, both by way of distinguishing and by prescription. The editors, Arnold Heertje and Mark Perlman, stressed that the fundamental axiom of Schumpeterian economics, unlike the neoclassical variety, was not rational maximization, nor was its preferred analytical goal market equilibration. Rather, the fundamental axiom concerned identifying the parts of the economic evolutionary process, and the preferred analytical goal involved understanding how the spark of dynamic growth was ignited.

> It is a virtual commonplace that there are many in the economics profession who, convinced that we have reached one of the more advanced levels of Walrasian general equilibrium analysis, take controlled pride in the recent achievements of their discipline. What impresses them as much as anything is the beauty of the economists' reasoned thinking, particularly when they can vary assumptions and reason their way to clear conclusions. Typical of those holding this assessment are scholars who subscribe to models such as rational expectations, neoclassical systems with natural rates of unemployment, and disequilibrium models with varying fixed-price assumptions and hold them as intellectual achievements of the highest order.
>
> Yet there remain some who are convinced that no such high plateau (or even peak) has been achieved. They see this vision as illusionary. The perfect apple of theory, they aver, is threatened by worms of many types. . . . (p. 1)

The third biennial meetings were held at Airlie House (Virginia, United States). In the resulting volume, *Entrepreneurship, Technological Innovation, and Economic Growth: Studies in the Schumpeterian Tradition,* the editors (Frederic M. Scherer and Mark Perlman), looking over the papers (presumably representative of the Society's members' interests) and noting their composition, concluded:

> The Schumpeterian tradition of economic analysis . . . embodies several
> themes. . . . the crucial role of technological innovation and technologi-
> cal change . . . in generating economic growth . . . [and] entrepreneur-
> ship [as] . . . a fundamental driving force in the achievement of techno-
> logical innovation. . . . Schumpeter triggered a lively debate over the
> type of economic structure that most fruitfully fosters technological inno-
> vation. Finally, many scholars are fascinated with what Schumpeter
> called the "process of creative destruction." (p. 1)

When the editors of the volumes growing out of the 1992 meetings in
Kyoto prepared their introduction to the first of the two volumes, *Innovation
in Technology, Industries, and Institutions: Studies in Schumpeterian Perspective*,[2] Yuichi Shionoya and Mark Perlman wrote of two distinct aspects:
visions and institutions.

> Schumpeter's thought is characterized not so much by any single theory
> he established, but rather, by the visions he entertained. Visions are our
> sense of how the world works. Visions are the foundations on which
> theories are subsequently built. (p. 1)

> Although innovation has been the central subject of the Schumpeterian
> tradition, the analysis of innovation in institutions and organizational
> structures is still to be developed. (p. 2)

> In connection with the problems of institutions, it can be claimed that the
> discussion of different visions of capitalism and their comparison are
> important. Specifically the logic and modus operandi of the Japanese
> industrial system are now an indispensable subject of serious discussion,
> from a Schumpeterian perspective. Japan's way of organizing its econ-
> omy has often been regarded as merely an exception, or deviation, from
> Western principles of economic management. We can say, however, that
> studies of the Japanese system provide the possibility of discovering a
> rationale that has not yet been noticed or represented in the Western
> historical experience. (p. 2)

Back to the Present

Now at the fifth (1994) set of meetings it seems apparent that the earlier foci
are being linked. Schumpeterian evolutionary economics, as well as the Soci-

---

2. Papers at the Kyoto meetings were published in two volumes. The first has been noted;
the second, *Schumpeter in the History of Ideas*, focused on an important but somewhat peripheral
side of the Schumpeterian legacy: the history of economic thought.

ety, is forging a modern intellectual entity. If ever there was an Age of Keynes, and if ever there is to be another kind of one-thinker-dominated age, the Age of Schumpeter, we see that the personality of the latter is, itself, creative and dynamic. The Keynesian legacy left rival groups claiming the mantle (sometimes taking pride in their legitimacy, while at other times taking a perverse pride in their nonrespectability). The Schumpeterian legacy, besides being much less personality focused, starts from the outside, and even if questions of legitimacy/bastardy are eschewed, the "babies" have a collective personality.

Thinking about This Volume

This volume is organized into three parts. After the introduction, the second part, having seven chapters, deals with Schumpeterian economics and various levels of behavioral norms. The third, reporting on empirical studies of innovation, growth, and technological progress, contains eight chapters. The last, again having seven chapters, focuses on economic dynamics as a general as well as a specific set of topics.

We wish to thank Dr. Charles R. McCann, Mr. Morgan Marietta, and Ms. Kristin Anderson for their help in processing this volume. We also wish to thank Dr. Jürgen Reckfort for his assistance to the Local Organizing Committee. The Society is much indebted to Dr. Detlef Aufderheide, Dr. Uwe Cantner, Dr. Mathias Erlei, Dr. Matthias Göcke, Dip rer.pol. Hans Georg Helmstädter, Dr. Michael Konig, and Dipl.-oec. Georg Westermann for their help in running the 1994 Münster meetings.

The Society is most grateful for financial support given by the Deutsche Forschungsgemeinschaft, the Ministerium für Wissenschaft und Forschung des Landes Nordrhein-Westfalen, the Deutsche Bundesbank, the Gesellschaft zur Förderung der Westfälischen Wilhelms-Universität, the Bayerische Hypotheken- und Wechselbank AG, the Bayerische Motorenwerke AG, the Bayerische Vereinsbank AG, the Kaufhof Holking AG, and the Westdeutsche Landesbank. The Society expresses its continuing gratitude to the weekly *WirtschaftsWoche* for awarding the prestigious Schumpeter Prize during its biennial meetings.

While it is true that the visible products of this conference are the chapters in this volume, they were brought to expression because of all of this outside help. Such help is needed to make a scientific conference possible and fruitful.

REFERENCES

Hanusch, Horst, ed. 1988. *Evolutionary Economics: Applications of Schumpeter's Ideas*. New York: Cambridge University Press.

Heertje, Arnold, and Mark Perlman, eds. 1990. *Evolving Technology and Market Structure: Studies in Schumpeterian Economics*. Ann Arbor: University of Michigan Press.

Perlman, Mark. 1990. The Fabric of Economics and the Golden Threads of G. L. S. Shackle. In [G. L. S. Shackle], *Unknowledge and Choice in Economics: Proceedings of a Conference in Honour of G. L. S. Shackle,* edited by Stephen F. Frowen, 9–19. London: Macmillan.

Scherer, Frederic M., and Mark Perlman, eds. 1992. *Entrepreneurship, Technological Innovation and Economic Growth: Studies in the Schumpeterian Tradition*. Ann Arbor: University of Michigan Press.

Shionoya, Yuichi, and Mark Perlman, eds. 1994. *Innovation in Technology, Industries, and Institutions: Studies in Schumpeterian Perspective*. Ann Arbor: University of Michigan Press.

Shionoya, Yuichi, and Mark Perlman, eds. 1994. *Schumpeter in the History of Ideas*. Ann Arbor: University of Michigan Press.

Part 1. Schumpeterian Economics and Behavioral Norms

Laying Rumors to Rest

Wolfgang Stolper

Schumpeter was dogged throughout his life by attacks on his personal honor while at the same time being denied the opportunity to defend himself. The Government and court archives in Vienna have yielded documentary evidence that the rumors were unfounded and malicious. It is dangerous to draw psychological explanations of Schumpeter's behavior on the basis of inadequate knowledge of the facts.

The honor of giving an address on the occasion of the awarding of the Schumpeter Prize has come to me unexpectedly and I have accepted it gladly but with some trepidation. What is there that I can tell you that you do not know already, and what can be said on an occasion like this? Though tempted to do so, I will not give an analytical talk. To stay within the allotted time I propose to lay to rest, I hope once and for all, the slurs on Schumpeter's character for his actions as minister of finance, bank president, and investment banker. I also believe that it was not jealousy that prompted Schumpeter's sharp review of Keynes's General Theory. For the background to what I have to say I must refer you to Allen's, Swedberg's and my own Schumpeter biographies.

We know that Schumpeter led an intensive life, in which theoretical and political ambitions played a major role. We have heard many scandalous anecdotes, some of which may even be true. There are others that I do not believe, and not only because my parents, who certainly would have known of them, had no memory of them. Schumpeter undoubtedly was a great sinner in the fin de siècle style of Vienna, Berlin, Paris, or London, but he was also something of an aesthete and I do not believe that he would ever have committed an unaesthetic sin.

Moreover, not one story suggests that he was ever less than generous, and all scandalous or scurrilous stories relate to Vienna. The stories of the Cairo or Czernovitz periods all have a good-natured touch, and none survive from the American visit in 1913 or his later visits to America. This itself, I suggest, says something about the nastiness of the postwar atmosphere of

Vienna and amply explains why, after his departure for Bonn, he ceased to follow Austrian events.

We have been told of his many failures and his supposed lack of character; of his frivolity and cynicism; his jealousy of Keynes; and his prejudices, political and personal, with the somewhat grudging admission that while he evidently considered himself above bourgeois limitations of personal behavior and late in life described himself as a big snob during his youth, he also observed the strictest canons of scholarly reasoning and seemed to a remarkable degree to be successful in keeping his prejudices separate from his analysis, and even from many of his policy advocacies. Nobody to my knowledge has ever shown any influence for better or for worse of his sins on his analyses or policy prescriptions (and, I might add, this is also true for Keynes).[1]

Delving into the documents of the time has reminded me that great care must be taken in making a particular interpretation of events, even when the facts can be established with reasonable certainty. This is a generally accepted methodological rule of theoretical interpretations, but it is doubly true when we speak of motives for a man's actions. Only a novelist can be sure of his character's motivations; after all, he controls them. Let me give an example.

Schumpeter's membership in the German Socialization Commission has raised eyebrows: how could he, an ardent monarchist and antisocialist, be a member of a socialization commission? He has also been blamed for the failure of the Austrian socialization attempts in 1919. The accusation is made that he showed a lack of character in suddenly changing his mind. According to one trustworthy account, he infuriated the great Max Weber by calmly saying that he did not know whether the Bolshevik experiment in Russia would work, but that it would be interesting to see what would happen. Max Weber, who clearly saw the monstrous nature of the regime, evidently considered Schumpeter's remarks cynical and complacently immoral.

But consider some facts that may lead to a different view. The members of the German Socialization Commission were not only socialists, and the Coal Socialization Commission was only one of four commissions dealing with specific sectors. It also was the only one that produced an intellectually respectable report. According to the account of Theodor Vogelstein, a bourgeois member, the Report of the Coal Socialization Commission was really a sort of rear-guard action against hasty changes. The Reich Ministry of Economics wanted the Commission to ratify the decisions the ministry had al-

---

1. The relation of Schumpeter's theories to his political and policy analyses and prescriptions is the central focus of my biography, *Joseph A. Schumpeter. The Public Life of a Private Man* (Princeton, N.J.: Princeton University Press, 1994). See also my "The Theoretical Bases of Economic Policy; The Schumpeterian Perspective," *Journal of Evolutionary Economics* 1(1): 189–205.

ready taken. When the commission insisted on its independence, it lost all influence and became essentially an academic enterprise.

Schumpeter did indeed believe for the briefest of moments that socialism in Austria might be politically feasible, but that moment quickly passed. Observe also that what was to be understood by the term *socialism* was at the time quite unclear, and you could then be both in favor of a planned economy and a conservative in good standing. Indeed, many people saw the arrival of socialism in wartime controls and welcomed it as a model for the future. It was only in 1920, when Mises and Schumpeter published lengthy analyses of socialism—both thought that socialism would be a failure, though for very different reasons—that the Mises definition carried the day and the association of socialism with planning and the political Left and of capitalism with the market and the political Right brought some clarity into the discussion.

Otto Bauer, the famous Austro-Marxist protagonist of socialization and head of the Austrian Socialization Commission with cabinet rank, believed that socialized enterprises would not only be more efficient than the existing private ones, but would also be able to contribute their profits to the budget. The decision to pursue socialization was based on the explicit premise that no budgetary funds would be required, and Bauer himself had agreed to that.

But Bauer wanted socialization *à tout prix*. This was really a strange position for a Marxist to take, because the part of the Austro-Hungarian Empire that would become what today is called Austria really inherited very few industries. As a wag had it, the Czechs got the industry, the Hungarians the agriculture, and Austria the landscape, the bureaucracy, and a disproportionate part of the imperial debt. It was only when Bauer changed his position on budgetary subsidies for the day-to-day operations of the enterprises to be socialized that he came into conflict with Schumpeter. Schumpeter, as minister of finance, was faced with enormous deficits. He could hardly agree to anything that would further enlarge the deficits. It was Bauer, not Schumpeter, who changed his mind and used rather roundabout methods, to put it mildly, to try to get his way.[2] Incidentally, Bauer's not quite correct behavior continued under Schumpeter's successor. Besides, Schumpeter pointed out to Bauer in an official letter that the need for current subsidies would justify all the opponents of socialism and would discredit the idea of socialization from the very beginning.

In fact, Schumpeter comes out of this whole controversy smelling like a rose. Bauer published his accusations that Schumpeter had sabotaged social-

---

2. This is documented in detail in my biography. An earlier account appeared in my "Schumpeter and the German and Austrian Socialization Attempts of 1918–1919," in *Research in the History of Economic Thought and Methodology,* vol. 3, ed. Warren J. Samuels (1985). Greenwich, Conn.: JAI Press. The 1985 account was written before I had found the verbatim transcript of the protocols of the Cabinet inquiry into the matter.

ization by preventing the socialization of the Alpine Montan Gesellschaft as late as 1923 and they were taken up in the United States by Gulick,[3] who refused to believe Schumpeter's account. There was a Cabinet inquiry into the matter which exonerated Schumpeter completely. However, the report to the Cabinet with this unequivocal conclusion was inexplicably kept secret. Bauer must have known that his accusations were false. He refused to name the person who had made additional scurrilous accusations against Schumpeter, robbing him of the opportunity to defend himself.

Schumpeter was similarly the victim of anonymous accusations when he was—at the insistence of the Prussian Ministry of Education—considered for a possible appointment to the University of Berlin. The faculty, with the exception of Emil Lederer, suggested not only that he was a shady character, but also that his scientific work was of no value.

Rumors about Schumpeter's supposedly shady behavior were put into circulation, but Schumpeter was refused access to any documents that would have helped him to defend himself. These rumors had already circulated when Schumpeter's appointment in Bonn was discussed, but Spiethoff had defeated them with an insistence on facts. The Berlin faculty, on the other hand, even decided to delete from the record the names of the persons who had supplied the damaging information. Schumpeter contemplated suing the Berlin faculty for libel, but Gustav Stolper advised against it because the faculty could always hide behind an *Amtsgeheimnis,* an official secret. Stolper's advice was based on his own unhappy experience with libel law. Schumpeter, with considerably more charity, never accused Bauer of falsifying history, only of a faulty memory.

So there is the first point: the conflict with Bauer arose not over socialization but over budgetary subsidies. Socialization, incidentally, was a Cabinet-accepted policy also supported by the Christian-Social Catholic conservatives.

But there is here a second important point: is sticking to an ideological position a sign of character (or of intelligence for that matter) when the facts have changed so as to make the original position irrational? Is it really morally superior to stick to a position that has become nonsensical? What justice is there in *Fiat justitia, pereat mundus?* Indeed, Schumpeter defined ideological prejudice as seeing facts not as they are but as one would like them to be. Schumpeter had strong ideological positions as to aims, but he had remarkably little ideological prejudice.

---

3. Schumpeter's letter to Charles A. Gulick dated August 7, 1944 is reproduced in Christian Seidl and W. F. Stolper, eds., *Joseph A. Schumpeter. Politische Reden* (Tübingen: J. C. B. Mohr (Paul Siebeck) 1992) 357–58. Gulick's use and his interpretation of the letter is found in his *Austria from Hapsburg to Hitler* (Berkeley: University of California Press, 1948).

Keynes, too, has been accused of changing his mind so often that it became virtually impossible to know what he really thought. Keynes was luckier than Schumpeter: he was accused only of inconsistency, not of lack of character.[4] I suggest that sticking to a position that has become indefensible is not only stupid, but morally indefensible. Sticking to positions shown to be based on wrong analysis and a faulty assessment of the factual situation virtually guarantees bad results sooner or later.

To err is human. Politicians make mistakes; they also promise many things they know they will not be able to deliver if and when they get into power. As minister, Schumpeter did not do so. He painted the situation in stark colors, and made clear that under the best of circumstances it would take four years to put the economy on a sound footing and to reduce the budget deficit to a level where one could say the situation was under control. He was overoptimistic, but the optimism related to his hope that both the Austrians and the Entente would see where their long-term interests lay.

When the peace conditions of the Treaty of St. Germain became known, Schumpeter pronounced them a death sentence. Schumpeter wanted peace; the Entente wanted revenge. We still suffer the consequences that the Entente did not see their own long-term interest. It has been suggested that this century would be known as "From Sarajewo to Sarajewo."

Now consider the story about Schumpeter and Weber which I mentioned before. There were in 1919 Bolshevik regimes in Budapest and Munich. There were also rumors that alarmed the Entente that the Bolsheviks had large sums of money in Vienna to finance revolutionary activities and install a Soviet regime in Vienna. Schumpeter had defended his policies in Parliament as having preserved social peace despite Budapest and Munich. (This phrase, incidentally, was used by *The Economist* to defend current Czech policies.) While minister of finance, he took an active part in a conspiracy by a bunch of excitable and highly incompetent Hungarian aristocrats to topple the communist Bela Kun regime in Budapest. The whole affair was, in the words of the English journalist who reported on and also participated in it, something of a cross between a tragedy and a musical comedy. Three thousand Hungarians were supposed to invade Hungary; thirty eventually did, with predictable consequences. The Hungarian embassy in Vienna was invaded and robbed of Austrian Crowns and Swiss Francs, and while some of the Crowns were recovered, the Swiss Francs were not. The episode also infuriated Otto Bauer.

The open participation of a sitting minister and a journalist evidently did not at the time present the ethical problems that present sensibilities would

---

4. Any accusations against Keynes's character relate to his sex life, not his political life. Neither in Keynes's nor in Schumpeter's case has anyone even hinted that their private predilections had any relevance to their public activities and positions. The general knowledge of their peccadilloes made any attempt at blackmail impracticable in any case.

see, though Colonel Cunninghame, the British representative, was surprised to come upon Schumpeter with the conspirators in the Cafe Sacher of Sacher Torte fame.

But knowing of Schumpeter's counterrevolutionary activities, is it not possible that when he made the remarks that so offended Max Weber, Schumpeter may have thought: "you get excited but just talk. I actually tried to do something about it." In the absence of a positive witness nobody can know what went on in Schumpeter's head. But surely one should be careful about inferring motivations, and one should eschew the methods of amateur psychology. Perhaps Schumpeter was not as fickle, as uncommitted, as cynical, as he has been painted to be.[5]

So far as jealousy of Keynes is concerned, Professor Musgrave remembers that during one of the famous wartime seminars at the Federal Reserve Board, Keynes held that the postwar problem would not be insufficient demand, but instead a capital shortage, and Professor Haberler remembers that there were, fortunately unsuccessful, attempts to suppress the publication of Keynes's posthumous article on the American balance of payments. In fact, Schumpeter refused to sign an anti-Keynes letter after Keynes had, in his *How to Pay for the War,* changed his attitude toward savings, characterizing Keynes as an intelligent and responsible man.

The only major substantive difference between the two great scholars was that Schumpeter saw the continuous changes inherent in the structure of the economy as *the* problem to be analyzed, while Keynes's approach is in this sense essentially a stationary approach with which he dealt by changing his mind as the facts changed. This is indeed a very big difference in seeing reality, and Schumpeter was indeed very unhappy about the all-pervasive hostility to savings of the *General Theory* and about how things developed in the United States. But Schumpeter did not blame Keynes for creating the antisaving atmosphere in America, only for making it respectable. And he thought this was the basic reason for Keynes's success, something Keynesians would, of course, dispute. But this is a far cry from believing Schumpeter to have been jealous of Keynes.

Time does not permit me to lay many other stories to rest: how a banker appeared during the night at a newspaper to ask the editor not to print a denial of a false story involving Schumpeter. Or how Schumpeter tried in vain to help Ludwig Wittgenstein, the father of the philosopher and left-handed pianist, to save his American fortunes. Or how Schumpeter tried to set up front corporations to save Austrian assets in the "newly foreign countries," as the

---

5. Just as Schumpeter was provably innocent in the socialization failure, the so-called Kola and Alpine Montan Gesellschaft affairs, so he was equally innocent of any scandals involving the Biedermann Bank or his investment activities. I present the relevant documentation in my biography.

successor states of the double monarchy were then called, from being confiscated. I must refer you to my biography of Schumpeter if you are interested. You may like or dislike Schumpeter—and many people could not and still cannot abide him. You may find his many affairs amusing or disgusting. (There is, however, no story to suggest that he ever made any of the ladies unhappy.) It is even possible that E. T. A. Hoffmann's or Soren Kierkegaard's or George Bernard Shaw's interpretations of the Don Giovanni myth may also be applicable to Schumpeter, for he certainly was a fascinating man. But there is no question in my mind that in all other respects his character was above reproach.

REFERENCES

Allen, Robert Loring. 1990. *Opening Doors: The Life and Work of Joseph Schumpeter.* 2 vols. New Brunswick, N.J.: Transaction Publishers.
Stolper, Wolfgang F. 1994. *Joseph Alois Schumpeter: The Public Life of a Private Man.* Princeton, N.J.: Princeton University Press.
Swedberg, Richard. 1991. *Schumpeter: A Biography.* Princeton, N.J.: Princeton University Press.

The Imagined, Deemed Possible

Brian J. Loasby

Schumpeter sets entrepreneurial imagination against the routines of the circular flow of economic activity, but assumes that imagination, though inexplicable, is always correct. This assumption is challenged, and Shackle's theory of decision making is used to introduce routines for testing ideas into the process of Schumpeterian innovation.

The Paradox of Rationality

In his *Theory of Economic Development,* Schumpeter set forth a paradox with which few economists have yet come to terms.

> The assumption that conduct is prompt and rational is in all cases a fiction. But it proves to be sufficiently near to reality, if things have time to hammer logic into men. Where this has happened, and within the limits in which it has happened, one may rest content with this fiction and build theories upon it. . . . Outside of these limits our fiction loses its closeness to reality. To cling to it there also, as the traditional theory does, is to hide an essential thing and to ignore a fact which, in contrast with other deviations of our assumptions from reality, is theoretically important and the source of the explanation of phenomena which would not exist without it. (Schumpeter 1934, p. 80)

In a footnote Schumpeter insists that "the choice of new methods is not simply an element in the concept of rational economic action, nor a matter of course, but a distinct process which stands in need of special explanation."

Schumpeter's paradox implies that rational choice theory, in both its general equilibrium and game theoretic applications, can be used only to model the outcomes of routine behaviour; where there are significant decisions to be made (or significant decisions to be predicted by an observer) something else is required. Moreover, the structure of the theory does not correspond to the structure of routine following, and is therefore no more than

17

an instrument for making predictions; it cannot explain in what circumstances those predictions are most likely to be correct. That, of course, is no more than some economists, including Schumpeter himself (Shionoya 1992), have claimed for it. But the rhetorical question that is sometimes used to defend instrumentalism: "how can we understand, if we cannot predict?" may reasonably be answered by another: "how can we predict, if we do not understand?" To understand how equilibrium is maintained, let alone how it is achieved, we need to examine the institutions—the rules, customs, precedents, and procedures—that cause people to behave in ways that maintain the compatibility of individual plans; for coordination depends on frictions as well as on flexibility. This Schumpeter himself was unwilling to do.

Schumpeter's claim that rational choice theory is an acceptable fiction only when routines are firmly established creates a paradox in his admiration for Walras, for Walras's ambition was to go beyond a model of general equilibrium to a model of an ever-changing economy. Walras (1877, p. 310) compared the market to "a lake stirred by the wind, in which the water continually seeks its equilibrium without achieving it," and invoked the entrepreneur as the essential agent of equilibration, whose role was to bring input and output markets into better alignment. This, he wrote to Francis Walker, was "the key to all economic theory" (Jaffé 1965, letter 800) because fresh changes continually recreated the need for new alignments. But, according to Schumpeter's own argument, this "key to economic theory" was necessarily "a distinct process which stands in need of special explanation," and should not be confused with proofs (or near proofs) of the existence of a general equilibrium, by which Walras earned Schumpeter's accolade. Schumpeter's paradox implies that rational choice theory may replicate the prices and quantities of a Walrasian equilibrium, but is not relevant to the process by which that equilibrium is attained; it is not then surprising that we have no general rational choice theory of equilibration, or that Walras's program has been abandoned.

Walras's simile of the lake disturbed by the wind reminds us of Keynes's rebuke to those economists who are content to tell us that when the storm is past the sea will be calm once more. Keynes had in mind rather larger disturbances than Walras was presumably thinking of, but both believed that any thorough study of the coordination of economic activities had to go beyond an analysis of the conditions of full coordination. As Schumpeter's paradox implies, that means going beyond rational choice theory. Schumpeter did go beyond it—but not to explain how coordination was achieved. On the problem of coordination he was content to assert that, given time, people would fumble their way to a solution, and though he wrote of conduct being formed "through decades and, in fundamentals, through hundreds and thousands of years" (Schumpeter 1934, p. 80), thus providing a charter for both institutional and evolutionary economics (and thereby justifying the hetero-genous membership of this Society), he never asked what would happen if people were not given enough time. That, one might say, is the question that Keynes (1936) asked in his *General Theory,* and we shall return to it.

Schumpeter's chosen problem was the initiation of change and its impact on a stable economy that presented only the appearance of conscious ratio-nality. His solution to that problem was the process of creative destruction. Walras envisaged his entrepreneurs as operating within the system; but Schumpeter saw that they must go beyond the logic of the circular flow in order to inject innovation, and, because he had declared rational choice to be a fiction, he saw that this innovation must be disruptive. "Where the boundaries of routine stop, many people can go no further, and the rest can only do so in a highly variable manner" (Schumpeter 1934, p. 80). In Schumpeter's theoreti-cal system there are only two kinds of behavior: routine following and innova-tive, which is routine breaking. The apparent rationality of the circular flow is incapable of generating or even of responding to novelty; there is no straight-forward transition to a new pattern of coordinated activities. Innovation does not simply change the data to which the decision model is applied; it invali-dates the model itself. As in Kuhn's (1962, 1970) account of paradigm change, the old and the new are not reducible to a common basis; the standard technique of analyzing change by the comparison of equilibrium positions is therefore not applicable. The price of progress, in Schumpeter's theory, is the business cycle.

The Business Cycle

The destruction and reestablishment of the Walrasian equilibrium controls Schumpeter's cycle. It is a real business cycle, aggravated by the expansion and contraction of credit. The flow of entrepreneurial ideas, which we shall examine shortly, is continuous, but their application is not. For the entrepre-neurs are uniquely, self-consciously rational: they will not commit themselves to their innovation unless they can assure themselves of its profitability, and that is possible only in the stable equilibrium of the circular flow. We must not forget that in Walrasian theory prices cannot convey the information that decision makers need unless they are equilibrium prices, and—what is not always recognized—unless they are known to be equilibrium prices. There-fore, routine is a precondition of innovation; it provides the bounds within which entrepreneurs can be rational. But what Schumpeter failed to realize is that the prices that the entrepreneur needs to know are those that will prevail after the innovation, and the derivation of these from current patterns is not obviously compatible with his insistence on discontinuity; however good the data, the future must always be imagined. Schumpeter's analytical structure does not generate the sharp-edged conclusions that are found in his presentation.

For a thorough examination of the problems of establishing a tolerably secure basis for investment decisions, we may turn to Richardson (1960, 1990), but Richardson's (1960, p. 57) observation that "A general profit opportunity, which is both known to everyone and capable of being exploited by everyone, is, in an important sense, a profit opportunity for no one in particular" sanctions an exploration of Schumpeter's theme, which explicitly depends on the entrepreneur's confidence in the uniqueness of his vision. When calculation is possible, such unique entrepreneurial opportunities are taken and create a period of prosperity; but their impact on other people's established routines destroys the initial equilibrium, and so prevents other potential entrepreneurs from making the calculations that must precede further innovation. All these potential entrepreneurs may be confident that their particular vision is unique; none can demonstrate that it will be profitable. Innovation therefore stops and the economy falls into depression, but in the absence of further disturbance time can then begin to hammer logic into men, and gradually a new pattern of coordinated activities emerges. Meanwhile, ideas for further innovations accumulate, and when the new pattern is established, calculation begins again, and inspires a new cycle of progress.

If we compare Schumpeter's theory of business cycles with Keynes's theory of employment, we find that both explain unemployment by uncertainty. The difficulty is not that investment is known to be unprofitable, but that potential investors have no way of knowing whether it is profitable or not, and so do not invest. A reduction in interest rates is therefore unlikely to be very effective in restoring prosperity. Modern theories of equilibrium business cycles explain the cycle by rational choice, but Keynes and Schumpeter deny the possibility of rational choice in a depression: people simply do not know. The crucial factor for both is the changing state of business confidence. But then they part company. Keynes believes that business confidence is subject to kaleidic shifts, as animal spirits are buffeted by items of news and beliefs are propagated by the urge to follow someone else who might be better informed; thus high confidence is no better, and no worse, founded than low confidence. Schumpeter, by contrast, believes that high confidence among entrepreneurs is always well founded, for it will emerge only when supported by the evidence of a well coordinated economy; high confidence will always be restored if only we are patient. People are not clever enough to derive their own equilibrium plans directly from the data, but they will get there in the end, provided that governments do not intervene and thereby generate false signals. In this respect, Schumpeter's analysis resembles that of Hayek in *Prices and Production* (1931): equilibrium may be disrupted by new combinations (which are soundly based on genuine improvements in Schumpeter's story, but unsoundly based on excess credit in Hayek's), but, given time, economic activities will become efficiently coordinated once more. When the storm has passed, the sea will be calm again. Keynes did not share this belief in the self-regulating properties of the economic system, and Hayek came to emphasize the need for a proper examination of these properties, which requires something more substantial than fictions of rationality.

The Origin of New Combinations

Before we turn to Hayek's agenda it will be helpful to consider the "special process" by which entrepreneurs acquire their new ideas. Schumpeter does not tell us much about this, but what he does say is significant. First, there is no reason to fear a shortage of ideas: Schumpeter (1943, pp. 111–20) dismisses the suggestion that investment opportunities are diminishing. Second, the new ideas are new combinations; entrepreneurs do not invent (though some inventors may also be entrepreneurs), but rather envisage uses for what has already been invented. Third, the flow of invention requires no more explanation than does the tendency to equilibrium. This may lead us to question whether Schumpeter (1934, p. 63) is really explaining "only such changes in economic life as are not forced upon it from without but arise by its own initiative, from within." Though the innovations that drive his theory of development are the result of entrepreneurial initiative, they are made possible by inventions, which may not be outside economic life, but are certainly outside Schumpeter's (1934) economic model. In his later account, he claims that invention, and even innovation, "is being reduced to routine" (Schumpeter 1943, p. 132), but does not examine the new relationship between routine and discontinuity; that is left to Nelson and Winter (1982), though one might argue that something conceptually similar had been worked out by Marshall (1920) in his examination of the forms of organization that aid the growth of knowledge (Loasby 1990a).

   Of what, precisely, does this entrepreneurial initiative consist? Schumpeter (1934, p. 85) avoids telling us by asserting that "the new is only the figment of our imagination"—and therefore, presumably, beyond analysis—and, at greater length, that "the success of everything depends upon intuition, the capacity of seeing things in a way which afterwards proves to be true, even though it cannot be established at the moment, and of grasping the essential fact, discarding the unessential, even though one can give no account of the principles by which this is done." This warning not to enquire further has been conscientiously observed within conventional economics, and even among evolutionary economists far more attention has been paid to selection than to the generation of the variety on which selection processes work. But if economic development is to depend on the ability of entrepreneurs to correctly prophesyze—and we should remember that Schumpeter takes no account of the damage that may be caused by entrepreneurs getting things wrong, as Hayek (1931) feared they would if led astray by false signals—then are we not entitled to at least a sketch of a plausible argument?

Such a sketch might run as follows (I make no claim that this is what Schumpeter "really meant"). In conventional models we start with a full specification of the data (including contingencies) and work out the implications. If the data, and their implications, are continually changing, then there may be a special function for those who recognize and respond to the change, like Walras's entrepreneurs. We may then adopt Kirzner's (1973) argument that the economy is continually adjusted in the direction of a continually changing equilibrium by the profit-seeking actions of a great many people, each of whom is alert to some particular change in the data. Now Kirzner's model is of a general equilibrium that is approached through local convergence on local equilibria, and it relies on the assumption that movement toward a local equilibrium, which involves trading nonequilibrium quantities at nonequilibrium prices and therefore generates income effects, will not disturb other markets sufficiently to drive any of them away from equilibrium. It is this danger that has prompted theoretical recourse to such fictions as the auctioneer and provisional contracts, and to standard assumptions of gross substitutability.

But both Hayek (1931) and Keynes (1936) have shown how intermarket effects can frustrate equilibrium where complementarities are important; and Lachmann (1986) has urged us to recognize that the implementation of any new plan necessarily frustrates the full implementation of some previously successful plan. Even Kirzner's entrepreneur, in arbitraging price differentials, changes the opportunity sets of some transactors who were previously in a local equilibrium; and so we need a more extended argument than Kirzner has yet provided to dismiss the possibility that even small-scale entrepreneurship may be destructive. Chaos theory may have made us more sensitive to this possibility.

If Kirzner's equilibrating entrepreneur may sometimes turn out to be rather like Schumpeter's disrupter of equilibrium, we may also suspect that the imagination of new combinations by Schumpeter's entrepreneur is not so very different from Kirznerian alertness. The formal distinction is in the degree of complexity: Kirzner's entrepreneur makes local adjustments, while Schumpeter's operates on a wider scale. But from the perspective of the neoclassical definition of the economic problem, both are alert to the implications of new data, and the profit opportunities from innovation are no less implicit in the data than are the opportunities for arbitrage. The ten-dollar bill lying in one's hand is just a little harder for Schumpeter's entrepreneur to see; but working out the implications of the data is a purely logical process, and time will hammer logic into men. In this interpretation, Schumpeter's entrepreneurs, like Kirzner's, are simply more perceptive than other people: they are the first to develop the rational expectations that are implicit in the new data. There is thus no inexplicable principle involved in grasping the essential fact, no need for intuition or imagination; rational choice will do all that is required—especially if all that is required is an instrument for prediction. Indeed, an efficient market for information will eliminate the need for entrepreneurship—or perhaps one should say that a theory of the market for information will eliminate the need for a theory of entrepreneurship. This is precisely what has happened in mainstream economics.

Our sketch of a plausible argument for the correctness of entrepreneurial vision has had the unfortunate effect of removing the distinctive features of Schumpeter's model. The simplest way of putting Schumpeter back into business, and incidentally distinguishing his theory from Kirzner's, is to invoke bounded rationality. We may, for the present, keep our fully specified world, but if the specification includes more data than anyone can handle, working out the implications exceeds the capacity of human logic. Each person's knowledge may be correct, but it is not complete. This appears to be the idea that underlies Casson's (1982, p. 147) conception of the entrepreneur as a synthesizer of information: "the entrepreneur does not necessarily possess any single item of information that no one else does. His advantage lies in the fact that some items of information are complementary, and that his combination of complementary items of information is different from anyone else's."

Schumpeter's description of the circular flow may be better interpreted not as a fiction of substantive rationality, but as a system of procedural rationalities, in which information is synthesized in ways appropriate to established requirements. This is an important aspect of the division of knowledge, to which Hayek (1937, p. 49) called attention, and which has been developed by Nelson and Winter (1982). Kirznerian arbitrage and the operating routines of a firm can both assimilate new data within such procedures, but if changes require new procedures and new forms of synthesis, how are boundedly rational humans to know what they should now start thinking about? New combinations imply the construction of new complementary structures—a concept with which Schumpeter would have been familiar from Austrian capital theory—and potential complementaries are often far from obvious. In particular, the efficient management of what exists by concentrating on closely focused routines may easily become a formidable obstacle to the recognition of such new possibilities; this is the formal justification for Schumpeter's (1943, p. 83) claim that "a system . . . that at *every* given point of time fully utilises its possibilities to the best advantage may yet in the long-run be inferior to a system that does so at *no* given point of time."

Schumpeter was thinking of standard claims for the allocative efficiency of perfect competition, but his proposition can also be applied to a single firm. Long-run performance may require a form of organization and a style of management that are receptive to signals that indicate the desirability of revising, or indeed abandoning, current procedures; and these characteristics impose their opportunity costs on current activities. Schumpeter's original emphasis on the role of new firms in the innovation process may thus be supported by the argument that new combinations imply new ways of structuring knowledge and new ways of organizing business activities, which are often easier to develop from a fresh start than by trying to convert an organization that has been operating within a very different form of procedural rationality. If large organizations do become major sources of innovation, as Schumpeter (1943) later asserts, this may be because they use the profits from earlier innovation to develop search routines, as in Nelson and Winter's (1982) analysis: managerial discretion, which in conventional analysis is a consequence of market failure, may be a necessary, though not sufficient, condition for innovation. But before considering search routines, it will be helpful to go beyond bounded rationality.

Conjectures

The advocates of bounded rationality as a foundation for theory sometimes define complexity as "more information than we can handle"; but we may also think of complexity as "more interconnections than we know about." Both definitions may be valid; it is possible to simultaneously have more information than we can handle and less information than we need. Moreover, the term *information* is liable to imply that our knowledge, though incomplete, is not erroneous: we do not know the whole truth, but what we know is nothing but the truth. Such a concept of "justified knowledge" appears to have been held by Schumpeter (Shionoya 1992): it is characteristic of logical positivism and seems to underlie modern theories of rational choice. However, there is no way of proving the truth of any general empirical proposition, however much evidence we produce, and however extensive our ability to manipulate the data. Further, we can never produce the evidence that is essential for rational decision making: evidence from the future. Our knowledge consists of only hypotheses or conjectures.

This immediately provides a definition of an entrepreneur as someone who makes, and acts on, a novel conjecture. A conjecture is, in Schumpeter's terms, "a figment of the imagination"; but relatively few such figments prove to be true, even for a time. The circular flow is also necessarily based on conjectures, but these are familiar, well corroborated, and assumed (perhaps unconsciously) to be true, even though they are eventually falsified by innovation. The falsification of the conjectures that support apparently rational procedures is the proximate cause of Schumpeterian depression, as of Kuhn's paradigm crisis: the logic hammered into men by repeated experience eventually betrays them, and no alternative logic is readily available. Why, then, should we assume, within the same model, that entrepreneurial intuition is reliable? By confining his attention to figments of the imagination that afterward prove to be true, Schumpeter excludes everything in the process of innovation except the entrepreneur's struggle to overcome opposition. Nor does the real-world counterpart of Kirzner's entrepreneur simply find the ten-dollar bill already lying in his hand; even a simple arbitrage opportunity may turn out to be a false conjecture, for the difference in price that the entrepreneur perceives may reflect, for example, a difference in the bundles of characteristics, or simply the cost of arranging a transaction between two markets. Neither theory deals adequately with entrepreneurial error, or the ways in which the possibility of error may be reduced.

There remains, however, an important difference between the Kirznerian and Schumpeterian "ideal types." Each Kirznerian entrepreneur has a rational procedure that he applies to new data and that indeed may guide the search for new data; if different people have different rational procedures, then they may be expected to be alert to different opportunities, even, as Kirzner (1985, p. 28) points out, when walking together along a city street. A new combination, by contrast, implies a new rational procedure, a new way of organizing data; this is a conjecture not about the applicability of a familiar pattern to a new situation, but about the appropriateness of a new pattern. Patterns are conjectures that are imposed on phenomena; what we call event regularities are classifications that we invent, borrow, or have been trained to use, or that are part of our genetic inheritance. Now these ideal types shade into one another, as one considers modifications to existing patterns. Even apparently revolutionary ways of thinking—whether about business opportunities or about academic disciplines—will normally be found to contain familiar elements; it is the combination, as Schumpeter claimed, that is new. But this distinction is as useful as that between the short and the long run—which is indeed a distinction of a similar kind. We shall henceforth concentrate our attention on the Schumpeterian ideal type.

Conjectures may be either conscious or unconscious. The moment-by-moment conjectures that determine our actions are the brain's responses to what are received as stimuli, and these responses seem to be determined by connections that are built up over time. Our brains have the capacity to store vast amounts of data, much of it instantly accessible, but they cannot access many items at any one time, and cannot process very much very quickly. So we rely on simple models and short chains of unconscious reasoning—what may be conveniently defined as routines. These routines are subject to selection; responses that seem to work are more likely to be evoked in what are deemed to be similar circumstances, and responses that fail are less likely to be used if there are alternatives that are accessible within our particular neural network. But creating a radically different pattern is not easy, either for our self-organizing brains or by conscious thought (for a summary exposition in terms of evolutionary psychology, see Cosmides and Tooby 1994).

The process of origination of new combinations is necessarily something of a mystery, but there do seem to be some general principles at work. One is the reinterpretation of familiar ideas: within economic theory, outstanding examples are the redefinition of the concept of a good to include location, date, and state of the world, and the extension of the division of labor to include the division of knowledge. In cosmology, the relabeling of the body around which the planets revolve from "earth" to "sun" is a simple, though momentous, redefinition. Another general principle is the attempt to apply patterns that are already established in another context, as, for example, economists have copied both celestial mechanics and Darwinian evolution. Early American automobiles were conceived of as horseless carriages, whereas the French thought of them, more effectively, as road locomotives; aeronautical pioneers were led astray by concentrating on the flapping of birds' wings rather than on their stabilizing function. A third principle is the deliberate questioning of assumptions, which is easier for someone new to the system, who may, however, introduce change simply by applying the different assumptions that underlie practice in the environment from which they come.

The Assessment of Conjectures

Once Schumpeter's entrepreneur has conceived of a new combination, all that is required is the determination to proceed and a stable pattern of activity that permits the calculation that it is worthwhile to proceed. We have systemic innovation in an orderly world. This is an inadequate conception of the innovative process, as many empirical studies have demonstrated. By contrast, George Shackle, who became a professional economist in the 1930s, was first impressed by the coordination failures that afflicted all industrial countries, and then by Keynes's theory of unemployment, which, in chapter 12 of the *General Theory* and his *Quarterly Journal of Economics* article of 1937, was firmly based on the unknowability of the future. It is therefore not surprising that Schumpeter's model had no appeal for him; what he sought to provide was a theory of reasoned decision making in a disorderly world, for that was the world in which decisions had to be made. People could not simply wait until order was restored.

Shackle's (1949) own theory of decision making under uncertainty nevertheless shares two characteristics with Schumpeter's: the decision maker's ideas spring from the decision maker's imagination, and the sources of these ideas are not explained. Shackle does not, however, accept the givens of the Schumpeterian system; much more is involved than working out the implications of established technologies and preferences. Nor is he content with an instrumentalist model; he wishes to understand how people actually decide what to do. Thus, instead of calculations based on what *will* happen, such as are required to launch Schumpeterian ventures, Shackle's decision makers try to decide what *can* happen: in place of the imagined, deemed profitable, of Schumpeter's entrepreneurs, we have "the Imagined, deemed Possible" (Shackle 1979, p. 26).

Shackle has no time for the allocation of numerical probabilities to lists of contingencies that are known to be complete. Instead, he turns to Keynes's (1921) theory of probability, which is based on nondemonstrative logic. Keynes's question is. how can we assess the likelihood that a particular proposition is true, given the evidence currently available to the individual who is making the assessment? The concept of probability is thus applied to propositions, not to events (though of course some propositions may be about the occurrence of particular events). It is a concept that admits numerical measures, but only as a special, and relatively uncommon, category. Instead of applying Keynes's theory directly, Shackle inverts it, as Popper inverted the problem of verification, and focuses on the nondemonstrative logic of disbelief: How strong are the arguments for ruling out a possible future event, or a possible consequence of a contemplated action? What can prevent it, and are these obstacles in place, or likely to appear? Imagination is therefore constrained by logic and evidence, but free to explore whatever possible futures are reasonably credible. The outstanding example of this method in practice is the development of multiple scenarios by Royal Dutch-Shell (Loasby 1990b).

The Process of Research and Development

It is not my purpose to rehearse Shackle's (1949) argument, in which the range of consequences that survive this subjective test are first divided into favorable and unfavorable categories and then summarized into a focal gain and focal loss, the balance between which is the basis of the decision maker's choice of action. I shall bypass this model because, if applied to entrepreneurial ventures, it shares a major deficiency with Schumpeter's theory—the assumption that what is chosen is a complete action plan. Despite Shackle's enthusiasm for the sequence analysis developed in Sweden in the 1930s, he does not explore decision sequences in which estimates of consequences and their likelihood are revised, and actions taken that are designed to assist in that revision. These are the sequences that characterize innovative processes.

An entrepreneurial venture is based on a conjecture. Success is not guaranteed by calculations conducted in a stable environment, or by anything else (except perhaps by selling the idea for cash), and failure after a full commitment is likely to be very costly for the innovator, and perhaps for many other people. Now although, in the end, plans must be tested in the market, it is possible to develop many kinds of surrogate tests that, in Keynes's (1921) terminology, may change the assessment of possible outcomes, and will certainly increase the weight of evidence behind that assessment and therefore the confidence to accept, reject, or modify a plan. The development and application of such tests is a major part of the activity of a research-and-development department, and it is in the organization of such tests in an effective sequence that large firms are most likely to possess a comparative advantage within the process of innovation.

Popper's (1959) logic of scientific discovery is a logic of testing. He has little to say about the origin of new ideas; indeed, his fundamental argument for the open society is that no one can say where new ideas will arise, and that therefore we should seek to avoid any barriers to entry into the business of idea generation. But once a conjecture has been put forward then there is ample scope for logical analysis of its implications and prerequisites, and the investigation of these implications and prerequisites is an effective way of testing that conjecture. Shackle's formulation, in which the decision maker examines a range of imagined futures in order to see which can be excluded, which are perfectly possible, and which can be realized only if specific obstacles do not appear or can be circumvented, is directly applicable to the management of research, but with an important addition: a research department can investigate potential obstacles before the conjecture becomes a commitment. Indeed, the remit of a development project may be interpreted as the investigation, by experiment, modeling, market research, or any other available means, of every aspect of what is necessarily a complex conjecture, in an attempt to anticipate the results of market testing—and therefore to avoid exposing to the market those products that would fail that test. The neglect of this process is a major weakness in rational choice models of research and development.

There is no way of ensuring that this remit can be fulfilled, and the evidence of innovative failure demonstrates that it often is not; but outsiders are unlikely to know of the much greater number of occasions when it is fulfilled and when false conjectures are thereby rejected at much lower cost than would be incurred by exposure to the market. The management of development projects is characterized by a great deal of procedural rationality, in the form of both scientific principles (which are themselves conjectures about patterns and causal connections) and organized experience. This rationality, like the procedural rationality of the circular flow, often serves to prevent departures from established practice; much that is imagined is deemed impossible and quietly discarded. Entrepreneurs and entrepreneurial firms who follow these procedures may therefore appear to possess the capacity of seeing things in a way that afterward proves to be true.

It is important to recognize that the falsification of part of an entrepreneurial conjecture does not necessarily mean the abandonment of the project; it is often possible to amend the conjecture to overcome a particular obstacle and try again. The variety of skills and specialist knowledge available in a large firm may allow innovative ideas to be shaped toward success in ways that are simply not available to the small firm or individual entrepreneur. Thus the common story of an original idea that is brought to successful fruition by someone other than the originator may be a story of complementary skills producing comparative advantage at different stages of the process. There appear to be relatively few examples of innovations in which the original conception was precisely realized, and even fewer in which the original conception turned out to be the most important aspect of the innovation. What proves to be true is often not what was originally seen, and the capacity to imagine new combinations is not necessarily associated with the capacity to redesign an imagined combination into a successful form.

The potential disadvantage of large organizations is that logical procedures will drive out imagination. This disadvantage is exemplified in the unhappy history of strategic planning, which has recently been examined by Henry Mintzberg (1994): attempts to develop a formal procedure for generating business strategies have impeded the process of strategy formation, which requires someone to offer novel conjectures. Logical procedures can be very effective in examining and testing ideas, but they rest on the assumption of established patterns and therefore suppress, rather than encourage, thoughts of new combinations. The great Danish physicist, Niels Bohr, "never trusted a purely formal or mathematical argument. 'No, no' he would say. 'You are not thinking. You are merely being logical'" (Frisch 1979, p. 95). Entrepreneurship cannot be reduced to logic. But neither is it merely imagination plus the calculation of profitability. An entrepreneurial idea is the imagined, deemed possible, and what is deemed possible is susceptible to procedural rationality. Innovation is a process, not an event; it is a discovery procedure for which the entrepreneur's new combination provides an organizing framework. Schumpeter's own theory provides such a framework, and leads us toward an analysis that, like so many innovations, differs in some important respects from what he had in mind. Schumpeter's instinct, to combine imagination and routine in a theory of entrepreneurship, was sound, even if his particular model, like many entrepreneurial conjectures, requires some modification.

REFERENCES

Casson, Mark. 1982. *The Entrepreneur: An Economic Theory.* Oxford: Martin Robertson.

Cosmides, Leda, and John Tooby. 1994. Better than Rational. *American Economic Review, Papers and Proceedings* 84 (2):327–32.

Frisch, Otto. 1979. *What Little I Remember.* Cambridge: Cambridge University Press.

Hayek, Friedrich A. 1931. *Prices and Production.* London: Routledge.

Hayek, Friedrich A. 1937. Economics and Knowledge. *Economica* n.s., 4:33–54.

Jaffé, William, ed. 1965. *Correspondence of Léon Walras and Related Papers.* 3 vols. Amsterdam: North-Holland.

Keynes, J. Maynard. 1921. *A Treatise on Probability.* London: Macmillan.

Keynes, J. Maynard. 1936. *The General Theory of Employment, Interest and Money.* London: Macmillan.

Keynes, J. Maynard. 1937. The General Theory of Employment. *Quarterly Journal of Economics* 51:209–23.

Kirzner, Israel M. 1973. *Competition and Entrepreneurship.* Chicago: University of Chicago Press.

Kirzner, Israel M. 1985. *Discovery and the Capitalist Process.* Chicago and London: University of Chicago Press.

Kuhn, Thomas S. 1962, 1970. *The Structure of Scientific Revolutions.* Chicago: University of Chicago Press.

Lachmann, Ludwig M. 1986. *The Market as an Economic Process.* London: Basil Blackwell.

Loasby, Brian J. 1990a. Firms, Markets, and the Principle of Continuity. In J. K. Whitaker, ed., *Centenary Assays on Alfred Marshall,* 108–26. Cambridge: Cambridge University Press.

Loasby, Brian J. 1990b. The Use of Scenarios in Business Planning. In S. F. Frowen, ed., *Unknowledge and Choice in Economics,* 46–63. London: Macmillan.

Marshall, Alfred. 1920. *Principles of Economics.* 8th ed. London: Macmillan.

Mintzberg, Henry. 1994. *The Rise and Fall of Strategic Planning.* London: Prentice Hall.

Nelson, Richard R., and Sidney G. Winter. 1982. *An Evolutionary Theory of Economic Change.* Cambridge, Mass.: Harvard University Press.

Popper, Karl. 1959. *The Logic of Scientific Discovery.* London: Hutchinson.

Richardson, George B. 1960, 1990. *Information and Investment.* 1st and 2d eds. Oxford: Oxford University Press.

Schumpeter, Joseph A. 1934. *The Theory of Economic Development.* Cambridge, Mass.: Harvard University Press.

Schumpeter, Joseph A. 1943. *Capitalism, Socialism and Democracy.* London: Allen and Unwin.

Shackle, George L. S. 1949. *Expectation in Economics.* Cambridge: Cambridge University Press.

Shackle, George L. S. 1979. *Imagination and the Nature of Choice.* Edinburgh: Edinburgh University Press.

Shionoya, Yuichi. 1992. Taking Schumpeter's Methodology Seriously. In F. M. Scherer and M. Perlman, eds., *Entrepreneurship Technological Innovation, and Economic Growth*, 343–62. Ann Arbor: University of Michigan Press.

Walras, Leon. 1877. *Eléments d'Economie Politique Pure ou Théorie de la Richesse Sociale*. 2d part. Lausanne: Imprimerie L. Corbaz et Cie; Paris; Guillaumin et Cie; Bâle: H. Georg.

Bounded Rationality, Social Learning, and Viable Moral Conduct in a Prisoner's Dilemma

Ulrich Witt

Conditions under which the clash of rationality and morality, as epitomized by the prisoner's dilemma, can be overcome are explored within an evolutionary approach. Starting from a reinterpretation of bounded rationality, the role of social learning processes is discussed. Interactions are assumed to take place in a local neighborhood structure. Provided moral behavior is associated with aggressive response to defection, imitation can be shown to lead to morality, that is, cooperative behavior, to be a viable strategy in a prisoner's dilemma in certain settings.

Introduction

The clash between individual rationality and the standards of moral conduct is epitomized, in game-theoretic terms, in the prisoner's dilemma. Following the lead of biologists in explaining the emergence of "reciprocal altruism" among animals (Trivers 1971), an increasing number of attempts have been made in recent years to apply evolutionary game theory to the question of how the dilemma might be overcome in the economic domain (Güth and Yaari 1992; Hansson and Stuart 1992). Conditions have been derived in this literature under which, in a suitably defined human population, agents who share genetically fixed "altruistic" preferences have a selective advantage because they behave cooperatively, that is, morally, even where, with self-interested preferences, rationality forbids such behavior as in the prisoner's dilemma. However, economic behavior is able to adapt far more quickly than genetic endowments would allow. Culturally conditioned, collective learning processes systematically modify and reshape genetic influences (Witt 1991), and there is little reason to believe that those learning processes should follow exactly the dynamics of selective genetic replication.

The author is grateful to Burkhard Flieth, Douglas Heckathorn, Jack Hirshleifer, and Georg von Wangenheim for helpful comments on earlier drafts.

For these reasons, the present chapter sets out to explore, in a broader view of what "evolution" means to economics, the conditions under which the clash between rationality and morality, epitomized by the prisoner's dilemma, can be overcome. In doing so the notion of bounded rationality or, more precisely, cognitive limitations in perceiving choice alternatives, will be given a key role. As has rarely been acknowledged, these limitations give rise to socially shaped, and thus collectively shared, cognitive commonalities—features characterized by "social models" of behaving—that bear on the way in which the agents within an interacting population choose among strategies. The chapter proceeds to discuss the implications on the basis of a prisoner's dilemma game with neighborhood interactions. As will be shown, structured interactions as defined by a neighborhood are crucial for the emergence and persistence of cooperative, that is, moral, behavior within a population. A condition of whether or not certain social models can invade, and propagate in, (sub-) populations will be introduced in that context. The condition resembles the concept of an evolutionary stable strategy, yet it is explicitly derived from boundedly rational choice calculus and imitation behavior. Some final remarks on the evolutionary nature of the analysis that has been conducted conclude the paper.

The Essence of Bounded Rationality: Limitations in Perceiving Alternatives

Bounded rationality, it has been claimed since the seminal paper by Simon in 1955, is due to the fact that man's capacity to process and memorize information is limited. The limitations basically result from a severely constrained human short-term, or working, memory that is incapable of processing all of the sensory information offered to the nervous system (see Anderson 1990, chap. 3). Recording and processing information are therefore necessarily selective. In conceiving of the choices that can be made, the individual cannot grasp the actual multitude of existing alternatives and their consequences. What is being considered in every moment of time is only a fraction of what could, in principle, be imagined to be possible series of choices that unfold into the future. As a consequence, individual choice behavior is likely to be biased by selective perceptions. Moreover, because of the very same limitations, learning takes place selectively and cannot provide more than partial and often provisional experience of what is relevant for evaluating alternatives.

In general, selective attention processes determine which particular information is processed, which thought is pursued, and what can be learned. Selective attention processes, in turn, depend on three factors: sensory strength and frequency of signals; recognition of already-known patterns that have been stored in the memory and must be activated by appropriate cues on an associative basis; and association with a significant preference or aversion, that is, recognition of earlier rewarding or aversive experience with the stimulus. The cues employed in classificatory and associative activities, that is, in memorizing patterns and identifying new information, are usually formed into larger and more complex systems called frames. These allow knowledge to be represented in a meaningful way (Anderson 1990, chap. 5), often in a symbolically encoded form. (Once a symbolic representation is achieved, knowledge can be stored externally to the individual memory and can be acquired by others through symbolic experience.) The huge associative capacity of human long-term memory is able to create, from a limited number of probably genetically coded cues, longer and longer associative chains with increasingly more complex sets of frames. This cognitive development starts in the very core of individual socialization, of the learning of language, and of the identification of meaning. Mental attitudes of sometimes fairly rigid nature thus emerge and "frame" information with already existing interpretation patterns (knowledge representations). The level of deliberate reasoning and decision making so central to economics is no exception.

Social Contingencies in the Perception of Choice Situations

The cognitive development just described is molded in social processes of communication with other agents (Bandura 1986, chap. 2). These processes tend to induce certain similarities in the otherwise subjective individual interpretation patterns and frames. The "agenda-setting" effect is a prominent example: the frequency with which particular information is (at the expense of potentially rivaling information) exchanged and attracts attention systematically changes through communication. In addition, people involved in certain communication circles are usually exposed to the same symbolic representation of knowledge. This often suggests similar mental attitudes and agreement on what are rewarding or aversive experiences. In spite of all the subjective diversity that results from each individual's unique cognitive history, these common features mean that a tacit, collectively shared bias can be expected to occur in communicating populations with respect to what are selectively perceived, and are disregarded, as alternatives for action. The scientific community is a significant example, as the reader may confirm.[1]

---

1. As far as the static model of economic behavior is concerned, a tacitly shared, cognitive bias could be expressed as a constraint of a special kind. It shapes the actually perceived choice set, separating it from a hypothetically imaginable set. Common beliefs and interpretations emerge tacitly and similarly for the agents in the population. This means that the agents do not

The socially shared cognitive commonalities can be expected to result in behavioral similarities that, as long as the cognitive frames cohere, should not be challenged by individual learning from experience. In fact, in the form of observational learning, the process of learning from behavioral feedback itself has a social dimension that reinforces and creates further cognitive commonalities (cf. Bandura 1986, chap. 2). Information on actions of other agents and their consequences is usually available to an agent in a communicating population. Knowledge about actions and consequences can thus be expanded even without the risks and costs of experimenting being borne by oneself. If the actions of others qualify as models of behavior, that is, when they occur in a sufficiently stereotypical and persistent manner, then inferences with respect to success or failure of certain actions may be particularly meaningful.

Models of behavior displayed by some agent(s) can assume a vicarious character. In that case, their own consequences are likely to attract significant attention of other agents and may thus become an important part of collectively shared knowledge. They develop into "social models" that, as commonplace patterns of behavior, are abstracted from the particular historical contingencies of their emergence. In a given population, observational learning focuses on many of the same social models and, therefore, tends to produce correlated results. New and old members of a population—and even the scientific observer—can identify the behavioral regularity of a social model and its contingencies and consequences more easily than the underlying cognitive commonalities in the subjective sphere. For this reason, generalizations tend to be made on the phenomenological level. The more frequently some social model occurs in a population, the more convincingly it may be inferred to represent a "rule of conduct." (By inverse conclusion, distinct populations that do not communicate, or do so only very loosely, should not be expected to show a comparable degree of similarity in their rules of conduct.) Once a model is perceived as a rule, people may feel confirmed in the biased, selective views that have led to the emergence of the social model. Serving as a basis for deliberate instruction and learning within the population, rules of conduct thus reinforce, in their easily grasped form, the cognitive commonalities from which they have originated.

Sources of Perceptional Variety within Populations of Agents

While in the previous section cognitive commonalities were emphasized as a population feature, the actual variance of subjective knowledge, interpreta-

---

normally recognize the fact that, due to their selective information processing, potential choices go unnoticed, because the cognitive system that processes some information cannot at the same time reflect on how that information is processed.

tions, and, correspondingly, behavior has a no less important role to play in an evolutionary perspective. The particularities of the individual learning histories, ambiguities in associating meaning with one and the same information, or simple misconceptions generate and maintain variety. Moreover, by reflection and inventive thinking, as well as by accidental discovery of choices not perceived earlier, individuals are able to create novel choices and actions and to widen their knowledge experimentally. For the individual it is thus possible to gradually shift cognitive constraints and to deviate from earlier patterns of behavior. The result on the level of the population is a tendency to increasing cognitive variety: when new ideas are put to a test, variety of behavior within the population increases.

New ways of behaving created by someone are likely to be noticed by others as a deviation from the prevailing social models and rules of conduct. The attention that this event arouses is likely to focus on the consequences experienced by the innovator. The observed vicarious success or failure on the part of the innovator allows the other agents to assess their current behavior in the light of the new opportunities without themselves having to experiment. As long as the members of the population at least roughly agree in their appraisal of which outcomes are more or less preferable, the innovator's vicarious reward or loss tends to, respectively, induce or inhibit corresponding behavior adjustments by imitation (Bandura 1986, chap. 7). Where the variety of behavior leads to differences in rewards, there is therefore an inherent tendency for variance in behavior to erode through observational learning and imitation.

Both tendencies, that of increasing and of decreasing behavioral variety, taken together can well stabilize the actual degree of variance within narrow bounds. At the same time, cognitive commonalities as well as behavioral regularities within the population—the rules of conduct—may be subject to continuing change. Social learning thus strengthens or weakens the tacit constraints in perceiving the choice set, depending on whether behavior deviating from the social models implied by those constraints is observed to lead to rewarding or to penalizing consequences. However, since the members of the populations usually determine these consequences in their mutual interactions, the vicarious outcomes themselves depend on what the presently pursued social models suggest as a response to deviating behavior—a situation of mutual dependency inviting a game-theoretic analysis.

Modeling Neighborhood Interactions within Populations

Before the impact of the cognitive constraints and social learning processes can be investigated within a game-theoretic setting, it is necessary to briefly consider the conditions under which the members of a population interact and communicate. Imagine a population of k agents, indexed $i = 1, \ldots, n$. As time elapses, let the population members be involved in pairwise interactions with other members, where interactions are structured by neighborhood relationships. In order to express the idea that neighborhood matters, the n agents can be imagined as being distributed in space along a one-dimensional lattice with n nodes arranged on a closed circle. Each of the equidistant nodes on the circle symbolizes an agent i. The more or less close neighbors to the left and to the right are indicated by the number of nodes between any two agents on the lattice.

Agent i's interaction network may thus be characterized by denoting all agents, $j \neq i$, (s)he is connected with in a range of nodes on each side and the likelihood of an interaction within that range. For convenience, let the range of contacts, c_d, $d = r,l$ for right and left direction respectively, be identical for all i, where $(n - 1)/2 \geq c_d \geq 1$. The smaller the variable c_d, the more directly the members of the whole population interact. Now consider the likelihood of an interaction. If bilateral interactions are all equally likely and if, moreover, $c_d = (n - 1)/2$, then the limiting case of an entirely unstructured population results, where everyone is connected with everyone else. In reality such undifferentiated patterns of interaction do not appear relevant. Therefore, the likelihood of agent i interacting with some particular agent j within i's range will be assumed here to decrease with the distance between i and j. Lacking more specific information, interaction possibilities can reasonably be supposed to be symmetric so that an interaction has an equal chance of $1/2$ of occurring on either side. Under this assumption, the probability, p_{ij}, of an interaction between agent i and agent j on *one* side depends on c_d as follows:

$$p_{ij}(c_d) = (c_d - j + 1)/c_d(c_d + 1), \ 1 \leq j \leq c_d. \tag{1}$$

For any given c_d, $\Sigma_j \, p_{ij}(c_d) = 1/2$. In the limiting case $c_d = 1$, interaction with the immediate neighbors has equal probability $1/2$ on both sides and interaction with other agents has probability 0. Let us define a neighborhood N adjacent to agent i on one side, say the right-hand side, by a segment (or closed set) of k nodes on the circle. By summing over equation (1), it follows that

$$\Phi_k = \sum_{j=1}^{k} p_{ij} = 2c_d k - k^2 + k/[2c_d(c_d + 1)] \quad \text{for } 1 \leq k \leq c_d, \tag{2}$$

where $0 < \Phi_k < 1/2$ for $1 \leq k < c_d$ and $\Phi_k = 1/2$ for $k = c_d$.

With respect to the information transmission within the population, let us assume that a piece of information originating somewhere may spread out through the entire population independent of whether or not each single population member interacts with all other members. More specifically, assume that information about actions and outcomes created in any local interaction is immediately communicated and available throughout the population. This means that observational learning can build on information about all kinds of behavior present in the population and their consequences.

Strategies and "Social Models" in a Two-Stage Prisoner's Dilemma Game

After clarifying the local interaction conditions in a given population, we are now prepared to turn to a discussion of the actual game to be investigated on this basis. As is well known, prisoner's dilemma games can be tailored to cover diverse interaction schemes ranging from a pure one-shot interaction to an infinitely repeated game. For the present purpose a variant that combines aspects of both extremes will be discussed. The encounter between two agents is interpreted as a one-shot prisoner's dilemma with elementary strategies cooperation (co) and defection (df). After completing this stage and after realizing the payoffs there is, however, a retaliation option assumed available. In that second stage of the game each of the two agents makes a unilateral choice between accepting the first stage results at zero costs (ac) or seeking costly vengeance (sv).[2]

The payoffs or their components will be denoted mnemo-technically by capital letters: R (reward), S (sucker's payoff), T (temptation), P (punishment), V (vengeance). Since sv is assumed to incur a cost V on the retaliator, but also a cost V on the addressee, an order relation

$$T > R > P > S > R - V \text{ and } P > T - V. \qquad (3)$$

can be derived for the payoffs of the game. According to order relation (3), vengeance is only effective insofar as a defecting agent does not get away with the tempting payoff T. However, the agent who affects this by seeking vengeance is thereby made even worse off. Since sv does not make sense after mutual cooperation or mutual defection in the first stage, mutual cooperation/defection is supposed to be followed by ac in all cases.

The remaining combinations of stage one and two choices can be summarized in three compound strategies:

---

2. This setup is meant to capture the notion of "moral aggression" in a possible strategy of the game. Moral aggression has been claimed to arise from a genetic disposition (Trivers 1971). This fact, if true, not withstanding, cultural influences may transform or even suppress an action impulse emanating from the genetic disposition. See Witt 1991.

  – an "aggressive moralist" (AM), who chooses co in the first stage and, contingent on the observation of her/his opponent's strategy, sv in the second stage when observing df, or ac when observing co;
  – a "passive moralist" (PM), who always chooses co in the first stage and ac in the second stage;
  – a "defectionist" (D), who always chooses df in the first stage and ac in the second stage.

Since human intelligence certainly allows more complex contingencies to be recognized and more complex choices to be made, a strategy using the available information in a more sophisticated way should be considered in addition to the three just mentioned:

  – an "opportunist" (OP), who chooses co conditional on interacting with AM and df otherwise in the first stage and always chooses ac in the second stage.

Thus, OP always chooses the best reply, a pattern that, given the common knowledge assumption made previously, may be identified with "rational" behavior (once again conflicting with notions of moral conduct). On the basis of the compound strategies, the extended game can be characterized in normal form for any two agents i and j as in figure 1.

Let us now turn to the impact of collectively shared cognitive constraints and of social learning. How do these concepts fit into the setup of a game? What interpretation of choosing strategies and of payoffs suits a situation where the agents are neither genetically programmed in their behavior (as in evolutionary game theory) nor entirely nonselective and thus free from collective biases in their information processing (as in rational game theory)? What information about strategies and payoffs can reasonably be assumed to be available to the players? Collectively shared cognitive constraints limit attention to, and observational learning operates on, behavioral regularities, or social models. However, they do so only *as far as they are present in the population*. Social models associate certain general contingencies with a certain stereotype of behavior, an association that can be stated as a rule of conduct. If the general contingency is established by the structure of interactions as described by some game, a social model may thus be represented by a pure or a mixed strategy of that game and the respective payoffs will be common knowledge within the population. In the present extended prisoner's dilemma game the compound strategies AM, PM, D, and OP are the obvious, but certainly not the only candidates for social models. Even if only one social model prevails in a population at a time, the occurrence of a variation or innovation can never be excluded. In that case, people observe the payoff

		agent j plays compound strategy	
		AM	PM	D
AM		R R	R R	T-V S-V
agent i plays compound strategy **PM**		R R	R R	T S
D		S-V T-V	S T	P P

Fig. 1. Extended prisoner's dilemma game

obtained by the deviating strategy and, depending on its relative size, tend to adopt or reject the newly introduced alternative social strategy as a social model.[3]

Social Models Resisting Innovations

We are now ready to address the clash of individual rationality on the one hand and rules of moral conduct on the other, as epitomized in the special variant of the social dilemma outlined in the previous section. Is there a possibility for moral behavior (i.e., the pursuit of the cooperative strategy) to be a viable choice if the agents are boundedly rational in the sense previously defined? In the simple setting outlined so far the question has to be analyzed in

---

3. There is thus a difference between this interpretation and the one implied by evolutionary game theory. Individuals involved in the game are supposed to be able to change strategies through imitation, a property implying a Lamarckian character for the resulting process of evolutionary change. There is also an obvious difference between the present approach and rational game theory. In the presence of cognitive constraints and social learning, rational choices can be made at any time only among a subset of the strategies that characterize a game.

a stylized, exemplary way. Nonetheless, the impact of social learning and collectively shared cognitive constraints on the social evolution of behavior in a dilemma situation should become apparent. Assume, as a limiting case to start with, that initially one and only one of the compound strategies discussed in the previous section prevails in the population for whatever reasons, genetic or cultural. Let this be challenged as a social model by a single innovator who introduces a new, not yet pursued strategy out of those compound strategies characterizing the extended prisoner's dilemma game of the previous section. According to the assumptions made with respect to the communication processes, information about the new strategy immediately disseminates throughout the population, although interactions with the new strategy are in the beginning only local. The vicarious payoff that the innovator realizes is the basis of observational learning by other population members and induces or inhibits imitation of the new strategy. However, the situation is complicated by the fact that with the dissemination of the new strategy, the expected payoffs of all strategies change. The effect differs depending on whether a member of the population is or is not a neighbor of the innovator.

Two different assumptions are thus necessary. For members of the population who do not directly interact with the innovator (nonneighbors) imitation of an observed success may be the motive to change.

ASSUMPTION 1. *Nonneighbors have a probability of adopting the new strategy that increases from zero, if the difference between the innovator's observed average payoff and the nonneighbors' presently realized own payoff increases from zero; the greater the positive difference, the shorter the expected waiting time until a switch is made.*

The gradually increasing adoption probability (rather than a zero-one jump) accounts for subjective factors, above all the delaying influence of an "internalization" of the prevailing rule of conduct by the agents. Such an internalization may be considered a result of social learning processes, yet it presupposes rewarding experiences and may be "unlearned" if experiences turn nonrewarding (Bandura 1986, chap. 8).

A similar reasoning can be applied to the members of the population in the range of the innovator, although these neighbors have a different motive to change, given the fact that they face changed payoffs in their local interactions with the new strategy.

ASSUMPTION 2. *Neighbors have a probability of adopting the new strategy that increases from zero, if the difference between the expected payoff of playing the prevailing strategy and the expected payoff of playing the new strategy increases from zero; the greater the positive difference, the shorter the expected waiting time until a switch is made.*

Finally, the (relative) payoffs that the innovator experiences while playing a new strategy may induce her/him to change behavior.

ASSUMPTION 3. *An innovator continues to play a newly introduced strategy, provided it yields a higher payoff than the previously played strategy. Otherwise (s)he switches back to the former strategy after playing the innovative strategy for a limited number of periods (persistence interval).*

Given the assumptions introduced so far, the following can be shown to hold:

PROPOSITION 1. *If prevailing in the population*

—the compound strategy D

(a) *cannot be invaded by AM and*
(b) *cannot be invaded by PM;*
(c) *can be invaded by OP, but the latter cannot propagate endogenously;*

—the compound strategy PM

(d) *can be invaded by AM, but the latter cannot propagate endogenously;*
(e) *will be invaded by D and OP with probability 1;*

—the compound strategy AM

(f) *can be invaded by PM and OP, but the latter cannot propagate endogenously;*
(g) *is not proof against invasion by D.*

A sketch of the proof can be found in the appendix. Except for assertion (g), proposition 1 seems intuitively appealing. Assertion (g) implies that a population of aggressive moralists does not necessarily have to fall victim to the occurrence of a defecting strategy. Cooperation, that is, moral conduct, can be a rational choice and a stable feature, if protected by "moral aggression" against defecting. The decisive variables for this to hold are the relative size of the payoffs, the range of contacts, the length of the innovator's persistence interval, and the shape of the neighbors' probability functions (see the appendix). The larger the range of contacts of each agent is, the more evenly distributed are the costs of seeking vengeance when hitting on a defecting innovator. The inclination to switch to strategy D as a neighbor is then lower.[4]

Furthermore, the following can be shown to hold (for a sketch of the proof see the appendix).

PROPOSITION 2. *If prevailing in the population, the compound strategy OP*

(a) can be invaded by D and
(b) PM, but both compound strategies cannot propagate endogenously;
(c) is not proof against invasion by AM.

Thus, ironically enough, opportunists are conducive to the dissemination of moral conduct (provided it is accompanied by moral aggression) in an environment that is locked into a defective mode of interacting, the scent of moral decay that is commonly associated with opportunism not withstanding.

Can Moral Conduct Become a Social Model?

While according to proposition 2 aggressive moralism may have a real chance to emerge within a population with initially opportunistic attitudes, proposition 1 seems to show that cooperative, that is, moral, behavior cannot gain a foothold in an all-immoral population. Given the assumption that interactions on the lattice are equally probable on either side of the lattice, there is indeed little to argue. By this assumption moralists cannot systematically discriminate against immoral members by orienting themselves in their interactions toward the moralists' side. However, even under this fairly unfavorable condition there is a chance for cooperation to emerge from a prisoner's dilemma, provided it is possible for innovators to appear in clusters rather than as single individuals in their neighborhood. This is, of course, a special though not unrealistic assumptions on how interactions take place. Once a sufficiently large cluster, or neighborhood N, of innovators exists in the population, the following can be shown to hold—this time without distinguishing a difference between aggressive moralists and passive moralists.

PROPOSITION 3. *If, in an all D population, AM occurs as an innovation that occupies all n nodes of a closed segment N on the one-dimensional lattice, a range of contacts c_d always exists for sufficiently large k so that the*

---

4. It is worth noting how much, in the present setting, the social model "passive moralist" contrasts with its aggressive counterpart, that is, how important "moral aggression" is. Indeed, PM is the only compound strategy that is not proof against innovations in all specifications. Even if it were assumed to prevail initially, both imitation and the immediate neighborhood effects contribute to a spectacular downfall.

innovation has a chance to invade the entire population. (For a sketch of the proof see the appendix.)

Innovators who appear in clusters are, of course, hardly applicable as a random phenomenon, even less so if they practice a moral conduct in an otherwise immoral environment. A systematic reason for such an event to occur seems necessary and may be given, for example, by referring to the case of a homogeneous group of agents migrating into the population from outside. Another, and with respect to morality perhaps more significant, explanation may point to the role that religious founders, prophets, preachers, and moral philosophers have played in history (Witt 1992a). The model discussed here allows us to understand how the agitation of such "change agents" can lead to the emergence of clusters of interacting agents who, committed to behaving morally, initially differ in their behavior from the rest of the population. As time elapses, the clusters may grow and moral conduct may eventually become the prevailing social model.

Conclusions

A core issue of an evolutionary approach in economics is the reappraisal of individual behavior in the perspective of "population thinking" (see Witt 1992b). This means, on the one hand, that the variety of individual behavior within a given population is explicitly acknowledged and considered a major fact on which those forces driving economic evolution operate. On the other hand, population thinking suggests reflecting on the role of commonalities by which a population can be identified. Both aspects have been assigned a crucial role in the discussion in this chapter of how populations may be able to overcome the prisoner's dilemma. Some empirical hypotheses have been suggested to characterize individual behavior as it occurs in, and is influenced by, communicating populations. It has been argued that tacit, collectively shared, cognitive limitations and the attention-shaping communication processes bring about certain commonalities among the population members in their perception and framing of alternatives of action.

These collectively shared constraints in the selective representation of reality do not mean that people are prevented from choosing the most preferred alternative among those they do recognize. What is implied, of course, is a deviation from the choices the rationality postulate would lead to, if information processing were perfect, that is, selective and therefore unbiased. Unless the particular cognitive constraints of the respective communicating population are specified, the concept of rationality is therefore insufficient to actually determine what behavior should be expected. Within a communicating population, rules of moral conduct may well acquire the status of collectively shared cognitive features or "social models." In order to relate these concepts to a game-theoretic setting an extended prisoner's dilemma game has been designed and analyzed. As the derived results show, a social model of cooperative, that is, moral, behavior has a good chance to persist or to emerge where it is absent. For this chance to be used it is important, at least within the framework analyzed here, that immoral behavior is faced with moral aggression, that is, discouraging consequences—a fact that may explain the commonly upheld attitude of "setting a warning example" even if this is costly.

APPENDIX

Sketch of the proof of proposition 1:

(*a*) In an all D population a single AM innovator i realizes a payoff $S - V$ $< P$. Hence no switching will be induced under assumption 1. With respect to a switching according to assumption 2, consider the immediate neighbor j. If anyone is likely to switch it will be j, given eq. (1). j's expected payoff in case of not switching is

$$E(\pi_D) = {}^1\!/_2 P + \Phi_1(T - V) + ({}^1\!/_2 - \Phi_1)P.$$

When a switch is made

$$E(\pi_{AM}) = {}^1\!/_2(S - V) + \Phi_1 R + ({}^1\!/_2 - \Phi_1)(S - V).$$

By assumption 2 there is a positive probability of switching if $E(\pi_{AM}) - E(\pi_D) > 0$. Equating both expected values and solving yields

$$\Phi_1^* = [S - P - V]/[S - P - V + T - R - V] > {}^1\!/_2$$

because of order relation (3). Hence, there is no value of Φ_1 in the admissible interval $(0, {}^1\!/_2]$ such that a switch may occur according to assumption 2. Moreover, the innovator is to return to playing the previous strategy after a finite series of trials according to assumption 3.

(*b*) Likewise, in all D population a single PM innovator realizes a payoff $S < P$. Hence no switching will be induced under assumption 1. Under assumption 2, by the same procedure as in part (*a*) of the proof, a value

$$\Phi_1^* = [S - P]/[S - P + T - R]$$

can be derived. If $|S - P| \geq |T - R|$, then $\Phi_1^* > {}^1\!/_2$; otherwise $\Phi_1^* < 0$. Once again, no $\Phi_1^* \in (0, {}^1\!/_2]$ exists. No switch can occur under any of the assumptions. Again, the innovator is to return to playing the previous strategy after a finite series of trials according to assumption 3.

(*c*) Behaving like a "defectionist" in all D population, OP cannot be distinguished from the prevailing pattern. Hence no switching is induced. Any innovator invading the population for exogenously given reasons may, on the other hand, maintain her/his new strategy forever—without any practical relevance.

(*d*) For the members of an all PM population it is impossible to distinguish an AM innovation. Hence the same holds as for part (*c*) of the proof.

(*e*) When playing against PM, an OP innovator cannot be distinguished from a D innovator. We thus confine ourselves to the case of the D innovator. In an all PM population a single D innovator realizes a payoff $T > R$. Hence there is a finite waiting time for switching to occur under assumption 1. With the increase of the fraction of D strategies in the population the payoff realized by defection converges to P while at the same time the payoff from cooperating converges to $S < P$. Thus no reverse switching will be induced. Moreover, neighbors will be switching under assumption 2, so that the entire population is going to adopt D in finite time.

(*f*) When playing against AM, an OP innovator behaves cooperatively in the first stage so that OP cannot be distinguished from AM as well as PM in that combination. We can confine ourselves to the case of the PM innovator and part (*d*) of the proof holds analogously.

(*g*) In an all AM population a single D innovator realizes a payoff $T - V$ $< R$. Hence no switching will be induced under assumption 1. Under assumption 2, by the same procedure as in part (*a*) of the proof, a value

$$\Phi_1^{**} = [T - R - V]/[T - R - V + S - P - V] < 1/2$$

obtains. Hence for values $\Phi_1 \in (\Phi_1^{**}, 1/2]$ there is a finite waiting time for switching to occur according to assumption 2. If the D innovator maintains her/his new strategy for a long enough time, incurring the respective loss $R - (T - V)$, the expected payoff may improve through switching of the neighbors into P in the best case. P is better than $T - V$ but still inferior to R so that the innovator may eventually be inclined to return to playing the old strategy according to assumption 3. However, if a neighbor has already switched, such a move would amount to just changing places with the neighbor. Thus, even in the most favorable case, $\Phi_1 = 1/2$, a dissemination of the new D strategy cannot be excluded, but it may be a matter of extended cyclical convergence (probably even infinite cycling). In case $0 < \Phi_1 \leq \Phi_1^{**}$, by contrast, that is, for large enough c_d, switching according to assumption 2 can definitely be excluded so that at least for these parameter values the strategy AM cannot be invaded by a D innovation.

Sketch of proof of proposition 2:

(*a*) By assumption, everyone defects against everyone else in an all OP population. Therefore a single D innovator cannot be distinguished from the prevailing strategy and no switching is induced. Any innovator invading the population for exogeneously given reasons may, on the other hand, maintain her/his new strategy forever without any practical relevance.

(*b*) Playing df in the first stage, an all OP population creates the same conditions for a single PM innovator as an all D population. Hence, the proof of proposition 1(*b*) holds by analogy.

(*c*) Since by definition OP plays co in the first stage when interacting with AM, a single AM innovator and later any aggressive moralist realize a payoff $R > P$. Hence, there is a finite waiting time for switching to occur somewhere in the population according to assumption 1. Moreover, OP neighbors of an AM agent can always do better by adopting AM themselves. Hence, the waiting time for switches corresponding to assumption 2 is also finite. Provided the innovator's persistence interval defined in assumption 3 is sufficiently long, both effects together will convert the population into an all AM population in finite time.

Sketch of proof of proposition 3:

For a sufficiently large closed segment N of AM innovators on a lattice otherwise occupied by D individuals, $c_d < n/2$ can be chosen such that a critical number of inner members of N realize the payoff R by exclusively interacting within their neighborhood. (Border members of N, by contrast, obtain R with probability $1/2$ and $S - V < P$ with probability $1/2$. The critical number of inner members is that value where, despite the inferior expected payoff of the border member of the neighborhood, the innovators' observed average payoff exceeds the presently realized payoff of the D strategy playing against itself. In that case there is a finite waiting time for switching to occur somewhere outside N under assumption 1. However, this switching can only be expected not to be reversed immediately if it occurs itself in closed segments or adjacent to N. If the waiting time for such events to occur is short enough relative to the time a border member of N tolerates experiencing a loss from keeping to AM rather than switching to D, the innovation has a chance to disseminate throughout the population.

REFERENCES

Anderson, J. R. 1990. *Cognitive Psychology and Its Implications.* 3d ed. New York: Freeman.

Bandura, A. 1986. *Social Foundations of Thought and Action—A Social Cognitive Theory.* Englewood Cliffs, N.J.: Prentice-Hall.

Güth, W., and M. E. Yaari. 1992. "Explaining Reciprocal Behavior in Simple Strategic Games: An Evolutionary Approach." In U. Witt, ed., *Explaining Process and Change—Approaches to Evolutionary Economics,* 23–34. Ann Arbor: University of Michigan Press.

Hansson, I., and C. Stuart. 1992. "Socialization and Altruism." *Journal of Evolutionary Economics* 2:301–12.

Simon, H. A. 1955. "A Behavioral Model of Rational Choice." *Quarterly Journal of Economics* 69:99–118.

Trivers, R. L. 1971. "The Evolution of Reciprocal Altruisms." *Quarterly Review of Biology* 46:35–57.

Witt, U. 1991. "Economics, Sociobiology, and Behavioral Psychology on Preferences." *Journal of Economic Psychology* 12:557–73.

———. 1992a. "The Endogenous Public Choice Theorist." *Public Choice* 73.117–29.

———. 1992b. "Evolutionary Concepts in Economics." *Eastern Economic Journal* 18:405–19.

Schumpeterian Competition and Social Welfare

T. Y. Shen

Social welfare consequences of entrepreneurial activities hinge on the trade-off between dynamic efficiency and income distribution. Simulation shows that, starting from a stationary state, economy-wide social welfare first rises and then declines as entrepreneurs exploit the newly arisen innovation opportunities in the manufacturing sector of the economy.

Schumpeter taught us that entrepreneurial pursuit of quasi rent leads to innovation. One implication of this proposition, that entrepreneurs are catalysts of technological progress, is now a mainstay in economics. Another implication, that quasi rents disturb income distribution, is rather neglected. Yet it too boasts a distinguished lineage hearkening back to Ricardo's celebrated "machinery chapter" and Marx's foreboding analysis of the changing "organic composition" of capital.[1] Perhaps this concern has faded because we are too ready to believe that innovations are mere eddies in a smoothly flowing stream, quickly dissipated by some invisible hand. But if technological change does not subside in a dynamic economy, doesn't the turbulence become pervasive? If continued technological progress leads to persistent income inequality, is this still unqualifyingly desirable? Can we rely on competition among entrepreneurs, the Schumpeterian competition, to keep the inequality in check? And if not, what are the forces that shape the balance between progress and equality?

An entrepreneurial act fosters technological progress in some sector and in some region. Since adjustments by the other participants in the product and

---

I would like to thank Richard Day, Gunnar Eliasson, B. J. Loasby, Stan Metcalfe, and Richard Musgrave for their helpful comments.

1. Innovations have two impacts on income distribution, both of which were touched on by Ricardo and Marx. The first is a change in the relative factor share, the result of factor saving bias. This impact has (of course) been thoroughly studied. However, it has little to do with entrepreneurship or Schumpeterian competition, and will not concern us in this chapter. The second is the generation of quasi rent. This was a central theme in Schumpeter's work and is our main topic.

the factor markets take time, specific factor owners (including the entrepreneurs) may reap quasi rents that "worsen" the previous income distribution. The consequence can be momentous.[2] A good example is contemporary China, where unleashed entrepreneurship has sharply aggravated income disparity and undermined the cherished socialist egalitarianism. Income inequality from entrepreneurship in the capitalist economies has also troubled policy makers. Progressive income taxation is sometimes suspended lest it dim entrepreneurial spirits (Eliasson 1988).[3]

The relationship between technological progress ("dynamic efficiency") and income distribution hinges not only on market conditions, but also on the activity sequence of entrepreneurs. This sequencing distinguishes Schumpeterian competition from market competition. Entrepreneurial activities can broaden or deepen technological progress. With broadening, an innovation is inaugurated in *terra nova,* a previously nonexistent industry or an industry in long-run equilibrium. If successful, it generates dynamic efficiency and quasi rent. By itself the isolated innovation engenders a negative trade-off between dynamic efficiency and distributional equality in a previously stationary economy. But if broadening activities extend to a wide front of industries, at some point *both* dynamic efficiency and distributional equality may increase in the context of the economy, as quasi rents accrue to a majority of the constituents.

With deepening, further entrepreneurial activities are carried out in the industry already impacted by an initial innovation. One class of deepening is creative destruction, under which the favorable position of an earlier innovator is superseded by a later innovator. A second class of deepening is imitation. In addition, both creative destruction and imitation are aided by the circulation of entrepreneurs in search of locales where they have the highest probabilities of success. This self-selection is undoubtedly an important component of entrepreneurial activities. If entrepreneurs perceive correctly their own endowments, better-endowed entrepreneurs tend to congregate in industries offering superior opportunities. The circulation of entrepreneurs levels the relative entrepreneurial endowments in each of the industries and quickens the flow of innovations and imitations in industries with the highest potential. All three of these entrepreneurial activities—creative destruction, imitation,

---

2. An indication of the significance of quasi rent is given by the fact that before its dissipation due to Schumpeterian competition, its magnitude is in the same order as the increase in real incomes from the innovations. Monopoly pricing would further increase the profits reaped by the innovators, an extension into which we will not go.

3. Some writers have questioned this. Keynes, for example, has asserted that "it is not necessary for the stimulation of these [entrepreneurial] activities . . . that the game should be played for such high stakes as at present. Much lower stakes will serve the purpose equally well as soon as the players are accustomed to them" (quoted by Wiles 1963, p. 74).

and circulation—not only extend technological progress in an industry, but also curtail the streams of quasi rents. They *may* increase dynamic efficiency and distributional equality simultaneously.

The present chapter aims to shed some light on the circumstances under which entrepreneurial activities improve social welfare. Social welfare increases with dynamic efficiency. It also increases with distributional equality under the usual assumptions on the concavity of the individual utility function and the dependence of social welfare on the sum of individual utilities. If dynamic efficiency and distributional equality are both increased, social welfare is higher. If they move in opposite directions, an appraisal of their net impact on social welfare requires us to state both of them in utility or income terms. To do this I resort to Atkinson's notion of "equally distributed equivalent level of incomes" (Atkinson 1970) to calculate the impact of the different entrepreneurial activities on social welfare.

The approach adopted here is simulation. It is not my intention to generate time paths that mimic the observed time series. The latter inevitably reflect the multifaceted complexity of the real world. The power of simulation is that it enables us to abstract from the complications that are irrelevant to the problem at hand, and to probe different hypothetical scenarios that have not (yet) been observed. As such, simulation is akin to analytics. True, it does not have the generality of an analytical model, a shortcoming that can be partially remedied by repetitions blueprinted on different specifications. In compensation, it allows greater freedom. Applied to a complex, dynamic, and stochastic problem, it need not be inhibited by the simplifying assumptions that have to be made to keep an analytical model tractable.

The organization of this chapter is straightforward. In the first section I discuss some basic notions: technological change, supply of entrepreneurship, and market operation in a dynamic environment. In the second section I model Schumpeterian competition. Starting from a stationary economy, entrepreneurs enter the stage. They then circulate, innovate, and imitate, driving the dynamic process to generate changes from t to $t + 1$. These hypothetical entrepreneurial activities promote dynamic efficiency and generate quasi rents. They create feedbacks that ignite new entrepreneurial activities. In the third section I present the simulation results based on the model. I calculate the paths of the social welfare index. It turns out that, at a moderate level of tolerance for distributional inequality, social welfare will rise and then decline as innovation opportunities, confined to the manufacturing sector, appear and then expand at a constant rate. The extent of social welfare improvement in a regime of Schumpeterian competition depends principally on the breadth and the direction of the expansion of innovation opportunities. This conclusion is briefly discussed in the final section of this chapter.

In this section I prepare the ground in the three major areas of the simulation model, leaving the detailed specifications to the next section. First I quantify process and product technology. The focus is on the manufacturing sector, divided into industries and populated by firms. Each firm operates a production activity to produce a single (composite) product. An activity is characterized by (T,u), respectively the "technology index," T, monotonically and inversely related to variable costs of production, and the "product quality index," u, monotonically and directly related to the price the consumers are willing to pay for the product.

Incorporating learning, the technology index T at time t is obtained from an activity-specific logistic function:

$$T_{ijt} = \frac{\hat{T}_j}{1 + m_j * e^{-b_{ij}(t-\tau)}} \tag{1}$$

where subscript i refers to the firm and j to the activity.[4] $\hat{T}$ is the "ceiling technology," the maximum T attainable with the activity. τ is the year an activity was launched and t the current year. $1/(1 + m_j)$ represents the fraction of $\hat{T}$ attained at the time when the activity j is launched by the firm, $t = \tau$. b is the speed of learning. The product quality index u is a scalar.

Five ways by which a change in (T,u) may take place are distinguished. The first, major innovation, is defined by the replacement of an existing activity by another activity drawn from an "innovation opportunity set" generated by knowledge. A (major) process innovation summons forth a new logistic function (with the resetting of τ). It raises $\hat{T}$, so that after learning it increases T, saves labor, but leaves the capital output ratio untouched. A product innovation increases u. Changes in T and u are independent of each other.

The second is major imitation, the adoption of an activity operated by another firm. The next two categories of technological change are incremental modifications of an ongoing activity. A minor innovation raises $\hat{T}$ (while leaving τ untouched) or u moderately. A minor imitation moderately reduces the gap between the highest values of $\hat{T}$ or u in the industry and the $\hat{T}$ or u of the firm (while leaving τ untouched). The final category of technological change is learning, represented by a traverse along the logistic function over time.

Next I quantify the supply of entrepreneurship. Probabilities of technological changes undertaken by a firm are assumed to be proportional to "entre-

---

4. To simplify notations we omit a separate industry designation in the equation and use j to represent both activity and industry, even though the activity index is a subset of the industry index. Wherever confusion may arise we will specify in the text whether we are referring to an activity or an industry.

preneurial endowments" possessed by its members. Five types of firm entrepreneurial endowments, $e_1, \ldots, e_5$ are distinguished, corresponding to the five types of technological change.[5] Of these e_1 is the most important. It is normally embodied in the top executives, or peak entrepreneurs (PEs), who preside over firm organization and personnel decisions, and thus have a hand in determining the entrepreneurial endowments of other firm members.

PEs also circulate. Their movements are modeled by means of an entrepreneurial pool. In each time period PEs who (voluntarily or otherwise) depart from existing firms enter the pool and are joined by a new cohort entering from the "outside." A PE in the pool takes over the helm of a firm if he (or she) succeeds in the pursuit of one of three options. He may fill a post left vacant by a departing PE of an ongoing firm. He may replace an incumbent PE of an ongoing firm if his e_1 is superior. Or he may start a new firm. The occurrence is simulated by stochastically determined "encounters" that match a PE from the pool with an ongoing firm or a potential entrant. A PE who fails in these pursuits disappears from the scene.

Technological change engineered by entrepreneurship finds its fruition in the market. High endowment of e_1 of a firm directly generates more major innovations and indirectly generates (through e_2, e_3, e_4, and e_5) other types of technological change. Improved technology translates into lower production costs and higher product quality. The firm gains market share and reaps greater profit. This increases research and development expenditures and the probability for further technological change. The firm, however, competes in the market and the outcome depends critically on market operation.

I confine my attention to quasi-rent earnings by different firms in the product markets, dismissing the factor markets by ignoring intrafirm income distribution. The model is driven by a uniform pricing rule followed by all firms. The rule is dictated by the consideration that PEs cannot foresee the future turns of technology. Profit maximization, by comparing the alternative discounted net income streams, is infeasible. A more realistic decision rule is to aim for the greatest market share so as to widen the base of future quasi rents. A useful model that incorporates this objective has been proposed by Metcalfe (1989). It has the additional virtue of allowing for product differentiation, another critical feature of technological change. In his model, a firm balances supply growth with the (expected) demand growth. Supply growth is given by the Rule of Accumulation:

$$g_{ij} = f(p_{ij} - h_{ij}) \tag{2}$$

---

5. One consequence of the broad participation in entrepreneurship is that many members of the firm may have a legitimate claim to the quasi rent. However, because practically it is difficult to ascertain their precise contributions, in our analysis of the implication of entrepreneurship on income distribution we will not attempt to disentangle their separate claims.

It states that the output growth rate of the ith firm in the jth industry, g_{ij}, is determined by the available surplus (output price p_{ij} over the unit cost, h_{ij}) and by f, the reciprocal of the (incremental) capital output ratio, adjusted for retention ratio and debt financing.

Expected demand growth follows the Rule of Customer Selection:

$$s_{ij} = g_{ij} - G_j = n\,[(P_j - p_{ij}) - m(U_j - u_{ij})] \tag{3}$$

where s_{ij} is the rate of change of market share for its products, G_j is the industry sales growth rate, u_{ij} is the quality of the firm's product, and P_j and U_j are the (perceived) average price and average product quality for the industry. The parameters n and m reflect consumer sensitivity to price and quality differentials. According to the equation, a gain in market share is expected if the firm sets its product price below the industry average, or if its product quality is above the industry average. Consistency in firm planning requires that supply growth given by equation (2) be equal to demand growth given by equation (3). Noting that (from equation (2)) $p_{ij} = (g_{ij} + f * h_{ij})/f$ and $P_j = (G_j + f * H_j)/f$, this yields the equilibrium growth rate for the firm:

$$s_{ij} = [nf/(n + f)] * [(H_j - h_{ij}) - m(U_j - u_{ij})] \tag{4}$$

where H_j is the average cost of production for the industry. Since h is determined by T, equation (4) shows how firm growth is determined by the technologies (T, u) of the firm and of its competitors. It captures the essence of Schumpeterian competition, in which entrepreneurs increase their market shares by creative destruction and by imitation. As for the other half of the demand-supply growth equilibrium, the price must be set at

$$p_{ij} = P_j - [s_{ij}/n] - [m(U_j - u_{ij})] \tag{5}$$

As diffusion takes place, raising U_j, the firm has to lower its prices and the benefits of product improvements are passed on to consumers.

Building on the main concepts just discussed, in this section a simulation model of Schumpeterian competition is presented. To track the story in full, I start with a stationary state at t_0. Schumpeterian competition begins with the introduction of technological change at t_1.

At t_0 there are 64 ongoing firms, divided equally among eight industries. Eight additional vacant firm slots are reserved in each industry for future entries. The industries are ordered around a circle (Dosi 1988). At one point on the circle, Industry 1 is characterized by a high rate of advance in the underlying knowledge, offering abundant opportunities for innovations. Arching away from it the innovation opportunities diminish. In one direction, Industries 2, 3, and 4 consist of larger firms operating vertically integrated complex processes. Process innovations are relatively more important and economies of scale are significant. Industry 5, at the apogee to Industry 1, is the "traditional industry," where innovations are rare. Proceeding back toward Industry 1, Industries 6, 7, and 8 consist of smaller firms producing specialized equipment. Product innovations predominate and entry rates are higher. Industry 1 and its neighboring industries will be referred to as "high tech industries."

For each firm in t_0 the values of the following key variables are specified.

1. Entrepreneurial endowments: values of e_1 and e_5 are drawn from lognormal distributions. Values of e_2, e_3, and e_4 are drawn from normal distributions with e_1 as their means.
2. Firm size. value of capital assets is drawn from industry-specific lognormal distributions, with means directly correlated with the e_1 endowment. Output is computed on the basis of an industry-specific (constant) capital output ratio. Asset age is drawn from an industry-specific uniform distribution, with a wider range for the more traditional industries.
3. Costs are divided into fixed costs and variable costs. Fixed costs are proportional to capital and subject to industry-specific economies of scale. Variable costs are determined by T.
4. Funding for initial capital is assumed to be divided equally between debt and equity.
5. Technology: the initial stationary state is arrived at after the full diffusion of a best practice technology in each industry. By normalization, each firm—regardless of its industry affiliation—operates an activity with the same $(\hat{T}, u)$. Each activity in use is assumed to have been known for a very long time, so that all minor innovations, minor imitations, and learning have been exhausted. Consequently, for all firms the initial T is equal to $\hat{T}$, despite the differences in the age of their assets. It then follows that at t_0 all firms in each industry (except for the minor effect of economies of scale) have the same costs, set the same price, and have constant market shares over time. There is no Schumpeterian competition.

The events taking place from t to $t + 1$ may be summarized with reference to figure 1.

1. Technological change: Schumpeterian competition starts at t_1 with the introduction of opportunities for new innovations. Under the assumed initial conditions, firms are differently poised for action. They differ in size, so that the resources available to them for pursuing innovations as well as the benefits

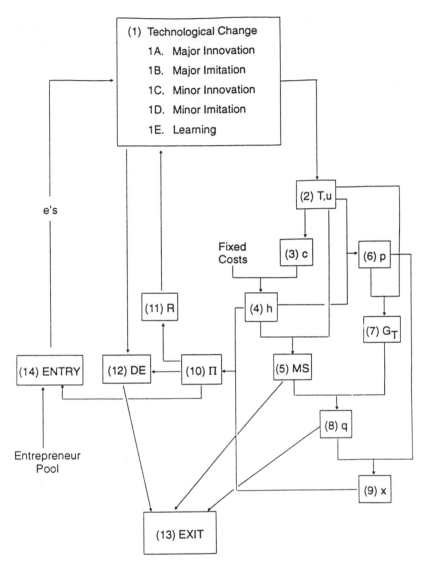

Fig. 1. *t* to *t* + 1 changes

from successful innovations are different. Their different entrepreneurial endowments lead to different probabilities of achieving success.

Specifically, the actual technological changes are generated by multistage random drawings, building on the Nelson-Winter (1982) evolutionary model. For major innovations, as an example, three draws are made to determine whether a major innovation takes place, whether it is a process or a product innovation,[6] and, finally, the magnitude of the innovation. The probability of success is higher for firms in the high-tech industries, firms spending more on research, or firms possessing a superior e_1. In the case of a product innovation, a new u is drawn from a lognormal distribution whose mean increases with time at an industry-specific rate.[7] In contrast, process innovations are assumed to build upon existing processes. First the highest $\hat{T}$ among the ongoing activities in an industry is identified. The firm undertaking a process innovation draws a new $\hat{T}$ from the upper half of a normal distribution whose mean is equal to the best practice $\hat{T}$.[8]

Rate of learning is represented by the speed in traversing the logistic function, as given by b_{ij} in equation (1). I assume $b_{ij} = b_i * b_j * {}_ib_j$, where b_i is a firm-specific learning rate based on e_5, b_j is an industry-specific constant, and ${}_ib_j$ the firm-industry interaction term, increases with $(t - \tau)$.[9]

2. All five categories of technological changes (between t and $t + 1$) are then superimposed on (T, u) at t to yield (T, u) at $t + 1$.

3. The variable unit cost of production, c, is determined by T:

$$c_{ijt} = \alpha_0 / [T_{ijt}\alpha_1] \tag{6}$$

4. The total unit cost of a firm, h, is obtained by adding together c, fixed cost, and research costs (see following). Fixed cost is the sum of depreciation

---

6. Overall, we assume that 80 percent of the major innovations are product innovations (Brouwer 1991).

7. The assumption that the underlying opportunity set for product innovation expands exogenously with time is based on the psychologists' finding that stimulus level reaches an optimum at some intermediate departure from the current adapted level—the so-called Wundt Curve (Berlyne 1972). New products based on new knowledge will be better accepted if the Wundt Curve approaches that optimal level. Consumer response must therefore be a function of time, which enters into the determination of the rate of adaptation-level change.

8. Since a new activity involves learning, its adoption may entail a lower T. Hence a payback period test is imposed: the acceptance of a new process innovation is conditional on the new activity yielding a T higher than that of the existing technology within three years. We also allow a possible decline in u in the case of product innovation to reflect uncertainty in consumer acceptance of new products.

9. The classical example of learning is the Horndal Iron Works in Sweden, where without any new investment for a period of 15 years the productivity (as measured by output per man-hour) rose by an average of 2 percent per year (Elster 1983, p. 151). In our simulation we assume ${}_ib_j$ to increase by 1 percent per year.

charges and imputed interest for the existing value of physical capital, after adjustment for capacity changes. It is then modified by an economies-of-scale parameter ζ:

$$\zeta_{ijt} = \{\{[1/\ln (q_{ijt})]^\rho - 1\} * v_j\} + 1 \tag{7}$$

where ρ is set at 0.1 and v is an industry-specific constant.

5. Market share at $t + 1$ is determined by firm growth and new firms entering between t and $t + 1$. Sales change from t to $t + 1$ for each ongoing firm is calculated, using equation (3), from the prices (p and P) and the product qualities (u and U) at t.

6. Price: new prices at $t + 1$ are calculated by equation (5). Each firm uses the average price and the average product quality of the industry at t as the expected P_j and U_j at $t + 1$. New P_j is then calculated.

7. Industry demand: an industry price elasticity, $\ni_1 < 0$, and an industry product quality elasticity, $\ni_2 > 0$, are assumed. Industry demand (= industry output), Q_j, is given by:

$$Q_{j,t+1} = Q_{j,t} * [(P_{j,t+1}/P_{j,t})^{\ni_1}] * [(U_{j,t+1}/U_{j,t})^{\ni_2}] \tag{8}$$

8. Firm output (q_{ij}) is the product of market share and industry output:[10]

$$q_{ij} = ms_{ij} * Q_j \tag{9}$$

9. Firm revenue (x_{ij}) is the product of price and output:

$$x_{ij} = p_{ij} * q_{ij} \tag{10}$$

10. Firm profit (Π_{ij}) is the difference between revenue and costs:

$$\Pi_{ij} = x_{ij} - h_{ij} * q_{ij} \tag{11}$$

Adjustments are made for royalty receipts and payments.

11. Research expenditure is a fraction of Π. The fraction size depends on e_1 and e_2 endowments, the technology gap between the firm in question and the best-practice firm, and the industry affiliation of the firm.

12. Debt-equity structure: since I am abstracting from intrafirm earning differences, I assume each firm member has the same wage and owns an equal share of the firm. Quasi rents increase the net worth of the firm and accrue equally to all firm members. They are retained to reduce debt and increase the shareholders' equity. Losses and capital expenditures are added to the debt. A

---

10. Since all variables are in the same time period, the time subscript is omitted.

new debt-equity ratio is calculated each year and serves to constrain innovation or expansion.

13. Firm exit: a firm exits if (a) its debt-equity ratio rises above 2.5; (b) its market share falls by more than 30 percent in one year; (c) its output falls below a minimum threshold; or (d) the price it must charge to maintain its growth equilibrium (as given by equation (5)) is negative. A newly established firm is exempt from these exit criteria for five years.

14. Firm entry and entrepreneur circulation: Firm entry is driven by entrepreneur circulation. At each t a new cohort of ten PEs with e_1's is drawn from a lognormal distribution and enters an entrepreneurial pool. They are joined by entrepreneurs departing from ongoing firms. Each of the PEs in the pool has the opportunity to start a new firm if he/she encounters a "vacancy." Some of these vacancies are created by firm exit or PE exit. Others are vacant slots reserved for entry. In addition, PEs from the pool may also encounter ongoing firms and replace their incumbent PEs.

Specifically, the process begins with a two-stage draw by all vacant and ongoing firms. The first draw determines whether they are entitled to encounters, and the second draw generates the identity of the PEs from the pool with whom an encounter takes place.[11] The PEs from the pool are assumed to go through a (stochastic) filtering process. More of the better-endowed PEs attempt to enter the more profitable industries. Because of this self-selection, firms in these industries have a higher probability of drawing a better-endowed PE (z_5) from the pool.

When a vacant firm is filled by a PE as the result of an encounter, a new firm is started. New firms are smaller, but otherwise the choice of their technology obeys the rules of major innovation and major imitation discussed earlier. On the other hand, if the new PE takes over an existing firm, its existing technology is assumed to be undisturbed. The new PE and his team leave their mark on future technological changes.

In this section the simulation results are presented. First, I demonstrate how the model specifications discussed in the last section, along with one set of assigned "plausible" parameter values, have yielded realistic values for some of the key industry variables. For this base case the inequality and the welfare indices are calculated. Then I show how these indices vary with postulated changes in the values of 12 selected parameters (the z's). All the simulations

---

11. As a result of the drawings, several firms may have encounters with the same PE candidate. In this case another random draw determines which of the winners will in fact have the claim on the PE. Conversely, a firm may have encounters with several candidate PEs. The candidate PE with the highest e_1 endowment wins—which may involve the ouster of an incumbent PE.

TABLE 1.   Simulation Results for Industries

	Industries								Manufacturing
	1	2	3	4	5	6	7	8	
1. Values at $t = 40$									
Firm no.:	8	5	5	12	12	9	13	9	73
T	112	34	15	16	16	29	30	139	59
U	5.0	3.5	2.6	1.8	1.5	2.5	3.4	4.2	3.2
π	2.7	1.7	1.1	1.1	1.3	1.9	2.4	2.7	2.2
2. Frequencies from $t = 1$ to $t = 40$									
A	5	5	3	4	4	2	7	8	38
B	5	8	6	0	0	1	2	7	29
C	34	55	39	39	36	38	40	51	332
D	26	3	0	1	3	5	3	25	66
E	94	41	19	10	7	3	16	66	256

Notes: A: Firm entries; B: firm exits; C: (peak) entrepreneur turnovers; D: major process innovations; E: Major product innovations.

are run for at least 40 years, allowing Schumpeterian competition to reach full swing after the appearance of innovation opportunities.

Part 1 of table 1 summarizes the simulated results for selected industry and sectorial variables in year 40. The number of firms in the manufacturing sector has grown from 64 to 73. Industries 2 and 3 have fewer firms and Industries 4–8 have more, reflecting their different economies of scale. Underlying the change is a higher rate of turnover. As part 2 of the table shows, there are 38 entries and 29 exits of firms over the 40 years, rates quite similar to those in the real world.[12] Turnovers are more frequent in the high-tech industries, particularly where significant economies of scale are absent (Industries 6, 7, and 8).

Schumpeterian competition surfaces elsewhere. The number of major process and product innovations varies widely among industries.[13] The initially identical values of industry T and U become disparate at the end. Quasi rents per unit of output, Π, are greater in the high-tech industries. There are 332 turnovers—voluntary departures or severance due to poor performance—

---

12. Audretsch and Acs (1992, p. 305) reported that the number of establishments in the United States rose by slightly more than 1 percent annually between 1900 and 1986. In contrast, between 1980 and 1986 the "gross" entry rate was 45.8 percent and the exit rate was 38.6 percent. The high rates reflect their inclusion of frequent turnovers of small firms. The same results were also reported by Dunne, Roberts, and Samuelson 1988.

13. Comparable differences among real-world industries have often been noted. See, for example, Acs and Audretsch 1988.

of PEs, implying an average tenure of about 8.5 years, again matching that in the real world.[14]

I have calculated inequality and social welfare indices based on Atkinson's (1970) notion of the "equally distributed equivalent level of income," that is, the income level $\hat{w}$ that, if received by all N individuals in the population, would yield the same level of utility as that from their actual incomes (w_i):

$$U(\hat{w}) = 1/N \sum U(w_i) \tag{12}$$

$\hat{w}$ hinges on the underlying utility function U, assumed to be identical for all individuals. The utility function proposed by Atkinson is

$$U(\hat{w}) = c_1 + c_2 \{[x^{(1-\epsilon)}]/(1 - \epsilon)\}, \quad \epsilon \neq 1$$

$$\qquad\quad = \ln x, \qquad\qquad\qquad \epsilon = 1 \tag{13}$$

where c_1 and c_2 are constants. The parameter ϵ reflects the society's tolerance for inequality. A higher value of ϵ signifies less tolerance. Atkinson's inequality index, A, is equal to one minus the ratio of $\hat{w}$ (as calculated from equation (12)) to the actual mean income $\bar{w}$. With given ϵ, a higher value of the index reflects greater inequality. For a given population, the social welfare index, SW, depends on mean income and A:

$$SW = N \, U \, [\bar{w}(1 - A)] \tag{14}$$

To calculate A and SW, I begin with the simulated incomes received by workers in the manufacturing sector. These incomes have three components. Since I confine myself to the interfirm distributional consequences of entrepreneurship, I assume each worker receives a wage and a capital income that are both identical and constant for all firms and in all years. The third component is quasi rent. I assume each manufacturing worker receives an identical share of the quasi rent earned by his or her firm. The nonmanufacturing workers receive the same wage and the same capital income, but in the absence of entrepreneurial activities they do not receive quasi rent.

Next I calculate the number of workers receiving the different incomes. In each manufacturing sector firm, employment varies directly with output and in inverse proportion to the variable unit cost, c. In the nonmanufacturing

---

14. According to *Forbes* (Dec. 1993) in the first nine months of 1993 there were 64 new CEOs in 361 Fortune 500 firms, of whom 19 came from outside of the firm, implying annual turnover rates of 24 and 7 percent, respectively. Assuming that the e_1 endowment of most of the "inside" CEO succession does not change because the successor belongs to the same executive team, the 12 percent PE turnover generated by our simulation appears reasonable.

sector, with uniform income, only total employment needs to be calculated. It is assumed that the total labor force in the economy is constant. At t_0, 35 percent of the total labor force is assumed to be in the manufacturing sector (World Bank 1987). In the subsequent years any worker in the manufacturing sector made superfluous by technological progress is assumed to find employment in the nonmanufacturing sector. Based on these employment figures and the previously calculated per capita incomes, I calculate the income shares of the differently employed workers.

The real income received by the workers depends on product quality improvements in the manufacturing sector. The latter are not adequately reflected in the simulated price changes. Under the Metcalfe Model, the price increase associated with a product improvement is held back by seller competition for market share. To estimate welfare increase it is necessary to peel back to the consumer response to product quality. Accordingly, I return to the output of each firm in each year and adjust it by the change in *um,* where *u* is the quality index and *m* the consumer sensitivity parameter. As the argument in the bracket of equation (3) shows, *um* is the price equivalent of the consumer response to a superior (or inferior) product. After this adjustment to nominal products, the summed "real" product (equal to the real income) is distributed to all workers in accordance with their income shares.

From individual incomes the inequality index is calculated, using equations (12) and (13) and setting $\epsilon = 0.5$, 1, 2, and 3. As shown in table 2, for the manufacturing sector, inequality increases (at a decelerating rate) from zero as technological change intrudes into the stationary state.[15] This is caused by the uneven rate of technological change, driven by the different entrepreneurial endowments and innovation opportunity sets. The continued increase in inequality, despite Schumpeterian competition, precludes technological progress as an unqualified source of Pareto-optimal improvement. The question then is whether, under some level of tolerance for inequality, the trade-off between dynamic efficiency and income distribution results in a net gain in social welfare.

In the manufacturing sector all welfare indices rise, regardless of ϵ. The higher incomes from quasi rents and the greater consumer satisfaction from product improvements outweigh the rising income inequality. In contrast, the direction of economy-wide welfare change depends on the tolerance level for equality. *SW* increases continuously if $\epsilon = 0.5$. With $\epsilon = 1$ or 2, *SW* rises initially, levels off, and then declines. What happens is that, in addition to the inequality between the manufacturing and the nonmanufacturing sectors, welfare is negatively influenced by two other factors. First, there is shrinkage of

15. Jeffrey Williamson (1985) calculated the index for the British nonagricultural sector. It rose from .189 in 1827 to .259 in 1851 for $\epsilon = 1.5$ and from .243 to .308 for $\epsilon = 2.5$. One reason why our result is different is our disregard of intrafirm inequality.

TABLE 2. Inequality and Social Welfare Indices

Year	Inequality Index (mfg.)				Welfare Index (mfg.)				No. of Firms
	$\varepsilon = 0.5$	$\varepsilon = 1$	$\varepsilon = 2$	$\varepsilon = 3$	$\varepsilon = 0.5$	$\varepsilon = 1$	$\varepsilon = 2$	$\varepsilon = 3$	
1	.005	.010	.020	.032	0.318	0.547	.415	.650	64
10	.014	.028	.052	.072	0.419	0.686	.484	.722	70
20	.032	.061	.108	.143	0.541	0.834	.543	.774	72
30	.045	.081	.133	.167	0.671	0.988	.605	.831	75
40	.049	.091	.154	.197	0.789	1.118	.649	.863	73
50	.062	.112	.185	.230	0.850	1.175	.663	.873	62
60	.060	.110	.184	.232	0.996	1.328	.711	.906	60
70	.071	.132	.221	.277	1.095	1.412	.728	.914	65
80	.078	.145	.245	.308	1.175	1.478	.741	.921	56

t	Welfare Index (Economy)			
	$\varepsilon = 0.5$	$\varepsilon = 1$	$\varepsilon = 2$	$\varepsilon = 3$
1	.309	.275	.224	.688
10	.353	.300	.230	.685
20	.398	.323	.234	.684
30	.452	.352	.242	.686
40	.480	.361	.237	.678
50	.486	.357	.230	.672
60	.491	.346	.211	.653
70	.500	.340	.199	.643
80	.501	.333	.190	.635

employment in the high-income manufacturing sector as a result of process innovations. Second, with a concave utility function, increase in real income yields diminishing marginal utility. Indeed, with $\epsilon = 3$, the negative factors dominate and *SW* falls from the beginning.

What happens to the *SW* under alternative scenarios? Evidently the economy-wide *SW* will be greater if innovation opportunities are extended to the nonmanufacturing sector. If innovations blossom across all fronts of the economy, then the *SW* increase will extend from the manufacturing sector to the whole economy. The economy-wide *SW* will rise even at a high intolerance level for inequality, so long as consumer demand does not falter and give rise to unemployment. Any widening of entrepreneurial activities pushes the economy toward this end.

It is more difficult to foretell the consequences of a deepening of entrepreneurial activities within the innovating—in our case, the manufacturing—sector. Deepening derives from creative destruction, imitation, and entrepreneur circulation. In the model these are represented by a number of parameters. Selecting some of these, I run the simulation again, changing their values

TABLE 3.   Role of Parameters (at t = 40)

Parameter	Inequality Index		Welfare Index				Firm No.	Π	T	U
			Mfg.		Economy					
	$\varepsilon = 1$	$\varepsilon = 2$	$\varepsilon = 1$	$\varepsilon = 2$	$\varepsilon = 1$	$\varepsilon = 2$				
Base	.091	.154	1.12	.649	.361	.237	73	2.24	58.9	3.21
z_1	.157	.249	1.48	.745	.496	.302	40	3.28	60.5	7.29
z_2	.102	.172	1.21	.677	.323	.204	81	1.94	80.7	3.18
z_3	.089	.151	1.09	.638	.364	.243	79	1.77	52.0	3.11
z_4	.091	.153	1.13	.652	.362	.237	72	1.87	55.9	3.25
z_5	.098	.164	1.12	.646	.354	.233	70	1.81	66.5	3.16
z_6	.088	.149	1.14	.656	.352	.230	71	1.86	62.9	3.17
z_7	.096	.161	1.13	.651	.355	.232	69	1.87	69.7	3.21
z_8	.095	.156	1.14	.657	.355	.231	78	1.92	61.6	3.27
z_9	.084	.141	1.12	.650	.360	.237	75	1.85	54.8	3.15
z_{10}	.082	.136	1.16	.666	.366	.263	70	1.75	52.3	2.98
z_{11}	.108	.181	1.01	.604	.374	.209	79	1.94	64.4	3.41
z_{12}	.051	.090	0.95	.595	.454	.337	73	0.94	57.8	3.21
z_{12a}	.041	.074	0.91	.585	.461	.344	74	0.91	43.8	3.13

(one at a time) from the base case. The results (at t = 40), along with the base case results, are presented in table 3.

1. Parameters on the intensity of creative destruction.

a. z_1: the expected rate of improvement in u from (major) product innovations. Tripling this rate relative to the base case, as the results along the z_1 row show, leads to major increases in inequality and SW. Higher U benefits all individuals in the economy.

b. z_2: frequency of major innovations in industries. Tripling the probability of successfully drawing a major (product or process) innovation by all firms leads to a sharp increase in T but little change in U. This is attributable to my assumption that the opportunity set underlying the changes in T builds from prior process innovations, while the opportunity set underlying the changes in U expands as a function time. As the pace of process innovations quickens, manufacturing employment shrinks. There are fewer recipients of the benefits from technological change, inducing a decline in SW. The result is further aggravated by the lower Π, attributable to the more intense competition.

2. Parameters on imitation.

a. z_3: frequency of major imitation by existing firms. A 60 percent increase in this frequency from the base case leads to a decline in inequality. Π is lower and welfare in the manufacturing sector declines. On the other hand, there is less sectorial employment shift and economy-wide welfare is higher.

b. z_4: in the base case the first-comer advantage is reflected by a 20 percent discount on u when the best-practice activity is copied by an imitator. The removal of this discount has little impact on *SW*, as the different forces it generates offset each other. Inequality, as expected, declines slightly, as does Π. The increase in U helps the imitators but hurts both the innovators and the firms that do not innovate or imitate. The shifting market share weights of firms with different technology standings result in a mixed bag of minor changes in *T, U,* and *SW*.

The results shown in the preceding highlight the sharp difference in the welfare impacts of product and process innovations. Entrepreneurial activities that culminate in better products benefit all consumers and therefore contribute positively and significantly to economy-wide social welfare. On the other hand, labor-saving process innovations may lead to a shrinkage of employment in the progressive sector. With fewer individuals partaking in the quasi rent, a more intensive advance in process technology lowers *SW*.

3. Parameters on the supply of entrepreneurship.

a. z_5: self-selection of entrepreneurs. In the new simulation both the exit and the entry conditions for *PE*'s are changed. In the base case the *PE*'s competing to enter the relatively more profitable industries have higher e_1 endowments. To increase the responsiveness in the supply of entrepreneurs, the elasticity of their e_1 with respect to the relative profit of target industries is raised by 50 percent. In addition, the PE exit rate from less successful firms is also raised. For a firm whose Π is one half of the industry average, for instance, the probability of exit by its PE is raised from 8 to 22 percent. These modifications dramatically increase the disparity of e_1 between industries and reduce the disparity of e_1 among firms within an industry. The result from the more intense Schumpeterian competition within an industry is quite similar to that of z_2. *T* is higher, *U* is lower, and *SW* declines.

b. z_6: quality of entrepreneurial endowment. In the base case the e_1 of each *PE* is drawn from a lognormal distribution with mean 0 and standard deviation .5. The mean is now changed to .5, so that the *PE*'s are both better and more evenly endowed. This lowers inequality and Π. The greater innovativeness increases *T* and again the declining employment in manufacturing lowers *SW*.

c. z_7: dispersion of entrepreneurial endowment. The standard deviation of the e_1 distribution is changed from .5 to .75, increasing its skewness. This heightens inequality, increases *T* and welfare in the manufacturing sector, and reduces economy-wide welfare.

d. z_8: entrepreneurial learning. In the base case the e_1 endowment of a *PE* rises by 3 percent with each major product innovation. This is raised to 20 percent, increasing the chance that the already successful PE's will make further innovations. The result is an increase in inequality and T. Despite the moderate increase in U, economy-wide SW declines.

e. z_9: research and development effectiveness of large firms. These firms are sometimes alleged to be ineffective innovators, and may even hold back innovations to avoid "spoiling" the market. To mirror this, R & D effectiveness is made to vary inversely with market share. A dollar of research expenditure by a firm with a 70 percent market share, for example, is made half as effective as that by a firm with a 10 percent market share. This modification results in a lower inequality, Π, T, and U. Their countervailing impacts leave SW unchanged.

4. Parameters related to consumer demand.

Interfirm demand: A change in consumer sensitivity to price and quality differences in the products of the different firms within an industry is equivalent to a change in the rate of advance of the innovation opportunity set. A higher sensitivity to product quality, for example, is the same as a faster rate of change in product quality. No separate simulation is required: if consumers are willing to pay more than before for a superior product, the effect is the same as that of a greater product quality improvement. The impact on SW is the same as described under z_1.

Interindustry demand:

(a) z_{10}: price elasticity. Consumer substitution between products of different industries is described in the model by the two demand elasticities in equation (8). To simulate a change in consumer response to a change in the average industry price, the price elasticity, $\ni_1$, is raised from -1 in the base case to -2. As shown in the z_{10} row of table 3, this reduces the overall inequality, T, U, and Π for manufacturing industries. Under the Metcalfe pricing rule, the average price of products in an industry rises when their qualities improve. A higher price elasticity reduces the sales of the more progressive industries and increases the sales of the less progressive industries. With the passage of time, the latter becomes more labor intensive than the former. Accordingly, there is less employment loss by the manufacturing sector as a whole, and economy-wide SW improves.

b. z_{11}: product-quality elasticity. To reflect the greater responsiveness of consumers to a change in the average product quality of an industry, the product quality elasticity, $\ni_2$, is raised from 0.5 to 1. As shown in the z_{11} row of table 3, inequality increases as consumers shift their spending from the products of the less progressive industries to those of the more progressive industries. There is an overall employment loss in the manufacturing sector, sufficient to diminish the economy-wide *SW*.

5. Taxation.

z_{12}: tax on quasi rents. Inequality due to entrepreneurial activities may be lessened directly by a tax on quasi rents. How does it affect *SW*? In my base case simulation, no tax is assumed. Imposing a 50 percent tax, as in z_{12}, results in lower R & D and a slowdown in the rate of technological change. However, the slowdown is more than offset by the greater distributional equality. With the tax revenue redistributed economy-wide in proportion to their income shares, the sharp decline of inequality is sufficient to raise the economy-wide *SW* even at the moderate level of intolerance for inequality ($\epsilon = 1$). This result is further magnified if an additional incentive effect is introduced, as in $z_{12}a$, where I assume a lower mean of the entrepreneurial endowment distribution to reflect the curtailed entrepreneurship.

It is commonly believed that entrepreneurial activities are important to the performance of an economy, but they tend to worsen distributional equality. What is their net effect on social welfare? The trade-off between dynamic efficiency and distributional equality, as we have just seen, is embroiled by the crosscurrents in Schumpeterian competition. On balance, my simulation results suggest that entrepreneurial activities confined to a single sector may not promote economy-wide welfare at a high level of intolerance for inequality. At a moderate level of intolerance, welfare rises at the start of technological progress and then declines after some point. This result is not significantly altered by more intense Schumpeterian competition.[16]

The decisive factor that shapes the trade-off and determines social welfare improvement is the advancement of (commercially usable) knowledge. If the opportunities found in the manufacturing sector in my simulation are extended to all sectors of the economy, the economy-wide *SW* will rise continually in the same fashion as that I have simulated for the manufacturing sector. An increase in *SW* is also achieved if knowledge advance culminates largely in product improvements desired by consumers.

The conditions for unambiguous welfare increase from entrepreneurial activities are more likely to be realized in developing economies, where large technology gaps exist in many sectors and consumer desire is fanned by demonstration effect. In developed economies the innovation opportunities are often limited to refinements concentrated in a few industries and con-

---

16. The simulation results also raise doubts as to whether some of the frequently discussed topics in Schumpeterian competition, such as first-comer advantage (z_4) and innovation ineffectiveness of large firms (z_9), are significant from the welfare point of view.

sumers are already awash in conveniences. Entrepreneurial activities may have limited—or even a negative—impact on social welfare.

REFERENCES

Acs, Zoltan, and David Audretsch. 1988. Innovation in Large and Small Firms: An Empirical Analysis. *American Economic Review* 78:678–90.

Atkinson, A. B. 1970. On the Measurement of Inequality. *Journal of Economic Theory* 2:244–63.

Audretsch, David, and Zoltan Acs. 1992. Technological Regimes, Learning and Industry Turbulences. In *Entrepreneurship, Technological Innovation and Economic Growth,* ed. Frederic Scherer and Mark Perlman. Ann Arbor: University of Michigan Press.

Berlyne, D. E. 1972. The Vicissitudes of Aplopathematic and Thelamatoscopic Pneumatology. In *Pleasure, Reward, Preference,* ed. D. E. Berlyne and K. B. Madsen. New York: Academic Press.

Brouwer, Maria. 1991. *Schumpeterian Puzzles: Technological Competition and Economic Revolution.* New York: Harvester.

Dosi, Giovanni. 1988. Sources, Procedures, and Microeconomic Effects of Innovation. *Journal of Economic Literature* 26:1120–71.

Dunne, Timothy, Mark Roberts, and Larry Samuelson. 1988. Patterns of Firm Entry and Exit in the U.S. Manufacturing Industries. *Rand Journal of Economics* 19:495–515.

Eliasson, Gunnar. 1988. Schumpeterian Innovation, Market Structure, and the Stability of Industrial Development. In *Evolutionary Economics: Application of Schumpeter's Ideas,* ed. H. Hanusch. Cambridge: Cambridge University Press.

Elster, Jon. 1983. *Explaining Technological Change.* New York: Cambridge University Press.

Metcalfe, Stan. 1989. "Evolution and Economic Change. In *Technology and Economic Progress,* ed. Aubrey Silberston. London: Macmillan.

Nelson, Richard, and Sidney Winter. 1982. *An Evolutionary Theory of Economic Change.* Cambridge: Harvard University Press.

Wiles, J. D. 1963. *Prices, Cost and Output.* New York: Praeger.

Williamson, Jeffrey. 1985. *Did British Capitalism Breed Inequality?* Boston: Allen & Unwin.

World Bank. 1987. *World Development Report.* New York: Oxford University Press.

On Technological Systems and Technological Paradigms: Some Recent Developments in the Understanding of Technological Change

Nicola De Liso and J. Stanley Metcalfe

Introduction

For scholars who have been involved in the development of an evolutionary perspective on economic change, the study of technological development has been a powerful stimulus to their thinking. A comparison of Schumpeter's *Theory of Economic Development* (1912) with Nelson and Winter's *Evolutionary Theory of Economic Change* (1982) provides ample confirmation of the rich network of connections between technology and evolution. In this chapter we are not concerned with the formal modeling of the technology economy relationship, rather we pose the following question: "What kind of framework for the study of technological change is most appropriate for advancing the evolutionary perspective on economic and social change?" This is no small task as in all scientific fields it is necessary to find conceptual guidelines in order to analyze and interpret the phenomena under investigation. This is especially so when the phenomena are complex and difficult to define. The study of technology is such a case and it is, at a minimum, necessary to distinguish technology as knowledge, skill, and artifact if a full characterization of technical change is to be obtained. Our method in this chapter is to draw together recent work on the nature of technological change, using the concepts of technological paradigm and technological system. In so doing we draw upon and attempt an effective synthesis between two principal literatures: that concerned with the historiography of technological change and that concerned with the evolutionary economics of technological change.

The concept of "technological paradigm" has been repeatedly appealed to during the 1980s, particularly among the less orthodox economists. We

A preliminary version of this chapter was presented in a seminar at IDSE-CNR. The authors are grateful to the participants. Comments by Gilberto Antonelli, Riccardo Leoncini, and Moshe Syrquin are acknowledged, the usual caveats applying.

71

shall argue that the paradigm-like nature of a technology can be more fruitfully applied to economics when complemented by two other distinct notions, namely *technological systems* and *technology support systems*. By a technological system we mean the set of principles and entities that interact and define a particular group of related artifacts. In this sense a fountain pen is a system, as is a drug and as is a modern airplane. By a technology support system we mean the set of institutions that individually and jointly support the operation and development of a technology. It is a matter of some interest as to whether the boundaries of a technology support system are coterminous with the boundaries of a nation-state, on which we comment further in the following.

The reason we believe that systems concepts should be explicitly brought into the study of technological change arises from a number of studies concerned with the evolution of, and the interaction between, technology, organizational development, and the institutional division of labor in the development of technology. Many of these studies have been carried out in parallel with theoretical investigation of the evolutionary economic analysis of technological change. We shall argue that technologies have emergent properties and exhibit strong features of self-organization. In short, no technology develops free from systemic restrictions, which are reflected in an appropriate division of labor in design, construction, and utilization.

The approach we have chosen takes into account the evolution of technology in history and its possible path-dependent nature. There are two justifications behind such a historical emphasis. First of all, in the creative process that attaches to a technological system there exists a historical element associated with the related phenomena of path dependency and inertia. Second, historical analysis enriches the gains from using evolutionary approaches to technological change. In this context evolution means unfolding and development from within the economic system. In turn, the development process is characterized by variety generation and selection in the presence of variety.

The literature on technology is immense. To supply a definition of technology can be one of the simplest as well as one of the most difficult tasks. The debate on the intrinsic nature of technology has concerned, in particular, the relationships between science and technology and the knowledge content of technology itself. A list of definitions of technology can easily be traced, and indeed we can trace the origins of the debate back to the disputes concerning the liberal and mechanical arts (Rossi 1976). Perhaps, the best way to begin a description of technology is not through a description of actual techniques, because time simply renders any such definition outdated, but rather through a search for general principles to characterize technology. For example, as long ago as 1588, Agostino Ramelli, in the *Prefatione* of his book, drew an analogy between technology and a river that grows bigger and bigger as it goes away from the spring and cumulatively receives the water of confluent streams. Clearly this general characterization incorporates the idea of cumulative development of technology and the idea of creodic development (Waddington 1957) of technology, in the sense that technologies cut their own particular pathways. These general characterizations emerge in the works of many of the authors that have dealt with technology, so that they speak of technical system (Gille 1978) or technical complex (Mumford 1946), or stress the imbalances engendered by technological creation, as in the case of reverse salients (Hughes 1983) or structural tensions and development blocks (Dahmén 1989). It is worthwhile emphasizing that in each of these concepts there does *not* exist a simple definition of what technology is.

We shall provide an overview of recent thinking on the creative process that generates new technologies and defines technological opportunities. If we draw the distinction between creativity in technological development and efficiency in the use of the technology, then our concern is to give the former priority over the latter. Although our concern is with technological opportunities, we do recognize a wider "hidden" agenda that has to do with incentives and the resources allocated to technological development. Technological opportunity is only one foundation for a theory of innovation, but we believe it is fundamental and intrinsically more difficult to deal with than questions of incentive mechanisms and resource availability, important though these are. In conditions of modern capitalism, the development of technology is primarily carried out in firms, but these firms operate in a wider institutional matrix in which we observe the existence of a technological community and a set of institutions and mechanisms that define a particular technology support system and its traditions of practice. Different institutions generate different kinds of knowledge, which, in turn, imply different accumulation mechanisms. What, thus, fits all together? Coordination through the market is not sufficient for our purpose, and other kinds of coordination between institutions are of paramount importance.

Our argument is divided into four sections: the first is devoted to a brief synopsis of evolutionary ideas; the second discusses paradigms; the third covers systems, and the fourth is devoted to the notion of a technology support system. A final section contains the conclusions.

Elements of Evolution

We must begin by saying a little about the meaning of the word *evolution* as used in our discussion. In its literal sense, evolution means unfolding as captured by the development of a particular entity over time (ontogeny). Life cycle models of technological development with their stages from youth to maturity are typical examples of this ontogenetic-like approach. Models of this kind have received widespread application in relation to the notion of cumulativeness in technological development and to industry life-cycle approaches to economic change, and can be traced back to the work of Kuznets, Burns, and others in the 1930s. This approach has a natural affinity with the paradigm literature outlined in the following. The central analytical problem here is how a change from one life-cycle phase to another is to be explained, absent a theory of technological aging (Utterback and Suarez 1993; Klepper and Grady 1990).

Quite different in scope and content are the "natural selection" based theories of evolution in which technological change is the outcome of competition between different varieties of technology. The central analytical problem here is to explain the stimuli to and the limits upon the generation of technological variety. In all these models, variety is confronted with a selection process that leads to changes over time in the relative importance and frequency of competing alternatives. Crucial to this approach is the requirement to state clearly the units of selection, the relevant dimensions of variety, and the properties of the selection environment. In many cases, where the unit of selection is a technological artifact, variety and selection are dealt with in the context of industrial competition. In other cases, when a body of knowledge is a unit of selection, these issues are posed in terms of the dynamics of a community of technological practitioners.

Of course, the life-cycle and the variety-selection models of evolution are mutually reinforcing. Life-cycle considerations help explain differences in performance between competing alternatives and contribute to the variety that drives selective change. Equally, the process of selective change creates important feedback experiences that shape the life-cycle evolution of any particular technology. Several of our historical examples provide evidence for this twin-pillar view of evolutionary change.

In the simplest models of evolution, the degree of technological variety is given and is subject to ex post selection in the market place. This provides only one of the levels of selection relevant to understanding technological change. Equally important are the ex ante selection processes within organizations that shape the emergence of technology. We shall argue in the following that these ex ante processes can be understood in terms of the twin themes of technological paradigms and technological systems. It is clear from the historical record that ex ante and ex post selection interact in a number of complex ways and that their interaction is related to the growth of organizational and institutional structures surrounding a technology and its application (Nelson 1994).

One final point needs to be made here. In biology, mechanisms of random mutation play a central role in the generation of variety. In an economic and social context this clearly cannot be the whole story. Any evolutionary approach to technological change has to confront the possibility of guided, intentional variation in which experience and anticipation play central roles in shaping behavior. Far from weakening the evolutionary theme, these elements of intentional behavior greatly strengthen the basis for an evolutionary argument based upon the inherent diversity of human behavior. The development of technology must be guided by the expectations of practicing technologists and users of technology, whatever their institutional location, and it is within this rich set of imagined worlds that the paradigmatic nature of technological knowledge plays a crucial role.

Several issues follow for the evolutionary perspective. The first is the Lamarckian drift of technological development: experience from the prior development and application of technology naturally shapes the expectations of the technological community as to what is likely to constitute a viable future development. Thus, past selection shapes future technological change. On the one hand, this helps us understand how small historical events become embedded in future outcomes and are not averaged away. On the other hand, this also helps us to understand the conservative nature of the forces that shape technological development. This leads us to the distinction made by Mokyr (1990) between micro- and macrotechnological mutations, that is, between continuity and saltation. Our framework of paradigms and systems precisely helps us to distinguish and understand the different forces that generate minor and major technological events and to understand the level at which these events are being defined. Necessarily, of course, expectations rest in the minds of individuals who work in technological communities sharing a common tradition of practice and work within a diverse set of institutions.

We come, finally, to the requirements for a theory of evolutionary technology; they appear to be three in number. First, grounds for explaining the generation of technological diversity in terms of different solutions to common problems and the addition of solutions to new problems. Second, arguments to explain the factors that limit the generation of diversity and focus the development of a technology around a small number of options. Third, arguments to provide an understanding of the rate and direction in which individual design configurations develop and the limits to the development of those configurations. Naturally, all this is to be understood in a context in which technologies and their economic environments jointly evolve.

Before we turn to matters of technology directly, it is necessary to say a little about the potential optimality of the process of technology generation. There are plenty of models of optimal induced invention and innovation to make this a serious question. Any question of the technologist as rational

optimizer naturally raises more general questions about decision-making behavior. At one extreme is the Olympian model of fully informed instantaneous
and comprehensive calculation, but, as is now widely recognized, when taken
beyond all but simple problems this view hides more than it enlightens. Limits
on perception of opportunities, limits on awareness of means-ends relationships, and limits in the speed of computation have each encouraged a procedural rather than a substantive view of rationality (Simon 1981). It is not
that agents intentionally seek to do other than the best, but rather what is the
best is imperfectly understood and does not necessarily correlate closely with
the best ex post outcome (Langlois and Robertson 1990). Thus decision
makers may optimize within the relevant constraints, but their optimizations
are necessarily local. As Shackle always insisted, optimization itself is mechanical; what matters is the perception of the set of options with respect to
which calculation takes place, and there is every reason to expect that organizations differ in their perceived option set. Wilson (1990) has presented these
questions in an interesting fashion in terms of a distinction between behaviors
based upon models of reality and behaviors based on adaptive imaginary
representations. The former are theories, a rational basis for conducting mental experiments that are valued in relation to their closeness to reality, while
the latter are fictional worlds, sets of instructions that greatly simplify reality
and that are judged by their selective values or adaptiveness, not their truth.
Indeed, in a changing world there may be no tendency for fiction to converge
to truth. Each organization operates with rules that filter certain information
from the outside world, its representation of reality, which is always a subset
of what is available, as any cognitive map must be. No doubt, the smaller the
subset of what is perceived, the lower the chances of survival (Jacob 1982).
What is perceived is not the only issue; rather it is what is interpreted that is at
the core of the variety-generating process. Even if different organizations
perceive the same reality, they will generally interpret it in different ways.
While Wilson sees bounded rationality as a feeble model of reality, it is rather
obvious that Simon's concept straddles the model-artificial representation distinction. As Arthur has emphasized, once problems pass a certain level of
complexity, deductive, theory-based behavior is replaced by inductive,
analogy-dependent behavior, which is exactly what links Wilson's fictional
worlds with cognitive and computational limitations. In passing, we should
also note that evolutionary processes are not compatible with random development of technology either. Such a notion ignores the "hereditability" requirements of any evolutionary argument, namely that behavioral characteristics
must be correlated over time. This is one reason why concepts of inertia play
an important role in the analysis of evolutionary processes, for the behavior of
organizations must change more slowly than the rate at which selection is
taking place, a topic to which we will return.

Scientific and Technological Paradigms

Scientific Paradigms and Normal Configuration

In languages like Latin, the paradigm of a verb supplies those few fundamental roots from which all the tenses of the verb itself can be derived. We stress the term *derived,* as distinct from *formed,* because the paradigm gives us the minimum information, and not all that would otherwise be necessary to form the different tenses by simple aggregation. The parallel cannot be pushed very far because the main function of the paradigm of a verb, as Kuhn himself points out, is to allow for systematic replication, while any scientific paradigm is rarely an object for replication (Kuhn 1970, p. 23). The main analogy thus consists of the existence of a given set of rules to define problems and suggest workable solutions.

Paradigms are closely related to *normal science,* by which Kuhn (p. 10) means a pattern of research based on past scientific achievements; these achievements, to become a paradigm, have to be characterized by two features: they must be sufficiently unprecedented to attract an enduring group of adherents who are rival with competing modes of scientific activity, and they have to be sufficiently open-ended to leave problems for the redefined group of practitioners to resolve (ibid.).[1]

Thus the creation of a new paradigm represents an agenda for the growth of knowledge. Such a device serves to delimit the field, setting the initial conditions and boundaries for new research and providing a conceptual scheme within which theoretical speculation is bounded. Thus a paradigm defines an unexplored opportunity, an opportunity that has self-defining limits on the possible patterns of discovery. Had we no instrument of analysis to glue our thoughts together, we would simply be gathering unrelated facts.

In the postscript added to the second edition of his book, Kuhn outlined various misunderstandings arising from the use of the term *paradigm,* of which Masterman (1970, pp. 61–65) points out no less than 21 different senses, and drew a distinction between a *paradigm* and a *disciplinary matrix.* To draw such a distinction he isolates a scientific community and asks: What do the members of this community share? While at first his answer was a paradigm or a set of paradigms, he then later changed this to a disciplinary matrix (as distinct from a theory or set of theories): " 'disciplinary' because it

---

1. An example in economics is the emergence of the *marginalist paradigm* during the 1870s, which determined a shift of economic analysis from themes related to accumulation and dynamics (Classical tradition) to themes related to exchange, optimum resource allocation and equilibrium. This example fits well in Kuhn's words where he says that paradigms, as *accepted* examples of research, provide models from which spring particular coherent traditions of scientific research (Pheby 1988, Blaug 1980).

refers to the common possession of the practitioners of a particular discipline; 'matrix' because it is composed of ordered elements of various sorts, each requiring further specification" (Kuhn 1970, p. 182).

The main components of a disciplinary matrix are symbolic generalizations, metaphysical parts of paradigms, values, and the shared commitments of a scientific group. It is this latter component that has the paradigmatic qualities that Kuhn redefines as shared *exemplars*. We can see immediately that a disciplinary matrix is a system comprising the elements and the way in which they are configured. Hence, disciplinary change is of two kinds: adding or deleting elements and changing the configuration of elements. Here we see immediately the rich texture of the paradigm notion, for, as Masterman suggests, it relates together three broad categories of science: metaphysical (an organizational principle governing perception itself), sociological, and artifactual.

The concept of a shared exemplar deserves a further comment because it characterizes the paradigm and because it allows us to draw an immediate parallel with technological knowledge. By *shared exemplar* Kuhn means not only the "concrete problem-solutions that students encounter from the start of their scientific education," but also the "technical problem-solutions found in the periodical literature that scientists encounter during their post-educational research careers" (p. 187). The translation from this concept to that of a *normal design configuration* as developed in the technological field is, mutatis mutandis, relatively easy, as we explore in the following.

The central question is how and why changes in paradigms occur. In the case of science no paradigm can subsume all the phenomena it intends to explain. As a paradigm develops, anomalies begin to appear. The first reaction is to develop ad hoc modifications of the original paradigm in such a way that it can still "explain" an otherwise inexplicable phenomenon. The paradigm experiences a crisis properly defined when complexity increases faster than accuracy (p. 68) so that a common awareness that something has gone wrong develops (p. 181). The effect of growing complexity, of an increasing number of anomalies, and of the failure of the existing rules to provide understanding is not purely destructive: in fact, in any developed science the rejection of a paradigm implies the acceptance of another.[2] As a rule, the new paradigm emerges as "a reconstruction of the field from new fundamentals, a reconstruction that changes some of the field's most elementary theoretical generalizations as well as many of its paradigm methods and applications" (p. 85).

When we turn to technology we find similar processes, but the parallels

---

2. We remind the reader here of the Schumpeterian process of creative destruction implied in the capitalistic dynamics of technological change.

are not exact. In technology, in fact, much progress builds on past achievements, cumulative effects are at work, and development from within engenders a process of small changes that give rise to incremental advances in technology. Equally, we observe more drastic changes in technology where new design principles and new knowledge bases establish a new technological paradigm. In many cases, however, the new does not overthrow the old in an epistemological sense: the different technological accounts continue to coexist as viable alternatives and it is only their relative degree of economic and social application that measures the degree to which a revolution has occurred.

Technological Paradigms, Design Configurations, and Categories of Knowledge

Though the first explicit mention of the Kuhnian paradigm with respect to technical change in the economic field is due to Freeman (1979, p. 211), it was Dosi who made the concept of technological paradigm his grand theme (Dosi 1982).[3] In his pathbreaking article, in fact, Dosi proposes an interpretation of the process of technological development within the context of a technological paradigm. He supplies first of all a definition of technology, seen as a set of pieces of knowledge that includes both the practical and the theoretical side.

Thus, along the logical sequence of science-technology-production, he defines

> "a 'technological paradigm' as 'model' and a 'pattern' of solution of *selected* technological problems, based on *selected* principles derived from natural sciences and on *selected* material technologies. We will define a *technological trajectory* as the pattern of 'normal' problem solving activity (i.e., of 'progress') on the ground of a technological paradigm. [A] technological paradigm (or research programme) embodies strong prescriptions on the *directions* of technical change to pursue and those to neglect." (Dosi 1982, p. 152)

Given this definition, a technological paradigm, characterized by a certain theoretical and technical knowledge, tends to set the rate and direction of technological change in both positive and negative terms; that is, the paradigm influences the positive steps in certain technological directions, while avoiding steps toward other uncharted waters. It is a focusing device that raises productivity in the search for technical improvement precisely because it limits the questions that are asked. The associated trajectories have an ex

---

3. The reader is advised to refer to the original text by Dosi, of which we supply a résumé.

post existence as a realized pattern of technical development, and an ex ante existence in terms of the expectations and intentions that shape the day-to-day activities of technologists.

The general thrust of this paradigmatic perspective is cognitive. To paraphrase Vincenti (1990), what do technologists know and how do they come to know it. Such a paradigm indicates fruitful directions for technological change, defines concepts of progress, establishes tests to judge performance, and has a powerful exclusion effect on the collective thinking of engineers, technologists, and the organizations they represent. A technological paradigm builds cumulatively by suggesting a sequence of puzzles sometimes guided by theory but often solved entirely empirically. A progressive technology generates many performance-enhancing puzzles and in this routine aspect it is akin to normal science. However, technological design and development is more concerned with puzzle solving than with hypothesis testing, more concerned with verifying what works than with theoretical falsification. A technological puzzle is solved when the performance standards of an artifact are improved or become more predictable, not when a puzzle solution yields a better understanding of a natural phenomena (Vincenti 1990). Moreover, technologies involve practice as well as knowledge, and this is why it is necessary to investigate the development of a technology in three dimensions: the growth of codified knowledge, the acquisition of tacit skills, and the development and application of product and process artifacts (Layton 1974). It is because of these different dimensions of technology that it is so difficult to distinguish satisfactorily between radical and incremental forms of innovation. What is radical in terms of a change in knowledge may yet be trivial in terms of the performance of technological artifacts, and conversely. Advances in scientific knowledge may result in the development of a new design configuration based on previously unknown principles and requiring a new community of practitioners to articulate a new paradigm. Technological change is always a mix of the familiar and the new, in proportions that vary along the knowledge artifact spectrum.

What Dosi has meant, in more general terms, by a technological paradigm applies also to our more focused concept of a normal design configuration. Indeed, a paradigm will normally have within it a range of design configurations for specific groups of closely related artifacts. The paradigm is a broad, aggregative concept, for some purposes too broad to effectively explain exactly what technologists focus upon in their day-to-day activities. We therefore prefer the narrower concept of a design configuration that relates to a specific group of artifacts and their production process. These lower levels of technology define more precisely the frameworks within which engineers and technologists think. They share the general feature of the paradigm, but differ significantly in important details. For example, within the paradigm of electricity generation, there were two competing design configurations, one based upon direct current and the other on alternating current. They were sufficiently similar, yet sufficiently different. Similarly, diesel and gas engines are different design configurations within the internal combustion engine paradigm, and water-jet and air-jet looms are different design configurations within a paradigm for weaving cloth. We note also that Nelson and Winter (1982) have employed the phrase *technological regime* as an equivalent to technological paradigm, comprising a collection of design configurations each one defining a specific realization of the technology.

By a normal design configuration, as applied to engineering technology, we mean the set of fundamental design concepts, that is, "the general shape and arrangement that are commonly agreed to best embody the operational principle," which in turn implies the understanding of how a device works, and how the parts of which a device is made concur in achieving a wanted purpose (Vincenti 1990, pp. 208–9).[4] Design configurations relate to specific transformation processes. The development of normal design configuration, in advanced technologies, depends on both scientific and technological knowledge interacting symbiotically and is reached through a series of dynamic processes in which normality, that is, the standard against which development is measured and assessed, emerges and evolves (Wojick 1979). Thus, a normal design configuration is a shared mental framework by means of which the relevant community of practitioners addresses the question of how to advance the performance of the technology. That technology applies science in many cases is well understood, but it is not reducible to applied science and, as is well known, technology often precedes scientific understanding (Wise 1985; Vincenti 1990).

The airfoil case recounted by Vincenti constitutes a good example. The performance problem was clear: how to obtain the desired lift while minimizing the induced and profile drag, that is, the "price" that is paid for lift. By the mid-1930s a series of different airfoil shapes were available that were considered to be the exemplars to be followed. These shapes had been obtained through experience and the trial-and-error accumulation of knowledge, through mathematical models, and through wind tunnel experiments, and taken together were considered to be the normal design configuration for a while. Thus the technologists had a clear set of procedures for solving their problem.

As is well known in technology, design principles and their associated artifacts do not always evolve in proportion to the development effort devoted to them, and sometimes they remain unchanged for long periods. Some de-

4. To further clarify, by operational principle is meant how the characteristic parts of a device fulfill their special function in combining to achieve the purpose of the device itself (Vincenti [quoting Polanyi] 1990, p. 208).

sign configurations are more fruitful than others, and each configuration can be depicted in terms of a life cycle of development in which an initial phase of rapid progress becomes limited as the technology approaches maturity. To break free from this constraint some change in the configuration is required, and with it a change in the underlying knowledge base. In the airfoil case, to achieve higher performances a new mathematical method had to be developed, because empirical testing, whatever its other virtues, could succeed only by luck (Vincenti 1990, p. 39). Hence a normal configuration consists of an interrelated set of design principles or concepts according to which artifacts must be built, together with rules for resting, comparing, and operating those artifacts.

The point to emphasize here is the role of the normal design configuration in focusing the activities of a technological community. It is a device to avoid the dangers of combinatorial explosion. If a technology always consists of more than one design concept and there are N possible design concepts, then the total number of possible technologies is approximately 2^{N-1}, an impossibly large number for any realistic estimate of the number of available design principles. The design configuration indicates where to search and still produce workable artifacts fit for their purpose. Paradoxical though it might seem, to make progress it is necessary to limit progress. In this regard, paradigms and configurations can also serve to insulate particular technologies from immediate commercial or other ex post selective pressures. Schatzberg (1994) has analyzed the development of the metal airplane in the 1920s at a time when the advantages of wooden construction were paramount. He suggests that the demise of wooden construction is not to be found in the relative performance of metal and wood as construction materials, but rather in the ideology and mental framework of the aeronautical engineering community. In short, the demise of wooden airplane construction was based on a belief that metal represented the outcome of progress and that the adoption of metal construction was based on scientific rather than craft principles. In his analysis, it is important to note that ideology is not presented as a set of false beliefs, but rather as an interpretive system embodied in a community of practitioners, which rationally blinded them to the advantages of wood. In the process they kept metal design alive when commercial pressures might have rationally locked into the wooden technology.

One further implication of the trial-and-error notion of technological development and the imperfect dependence on scientific knowledge is that the limits of any technology are often only poorly understood. When the operation of the artifacts strays beyond the bounds of normal operation, the consequence is often disastrous and we have, in Constant's (1980) words, a functional failure.

As soon as we recognize that any one broad paradigm normally contains within it a number of competing design configurations, we can see more clearly some of the principles and features of technological evolution. One clear example is provided by the historical development of tabulating machines between 1900 and 1940, as explored by Norberg (1990). As he explains, the development of punched card machinery followed a long sequence of improvements within two competing design configurations, each championed by a different company, one configuration based on electrical design principles, the other on mechanical design principles. Both technologies competed vigorously, although gradually the electrical configuration drew ahead in terms of performance and market share and, most significantly, when the invention of the electronic computer opened up a new configuration in the industry it was the electrical-based company that was best positioned to capitalize on the new technological opportunities. That company became IBM. A second example is provided by the case of technological rivalry between competing propulsion systems for turbine-driven ships (McBride 1992). This was not a solution to a commercial problem, but rather a problem in naval strategy in which the U.S. navy required efficient ships able to patrol the Pacific for lengthy periods of time without refuelling. Three alternatives presented themselves: direct drive, reduction gearing, and electric drive. It is the latter that is the focal point of McBride's study. Developed by the General Electric Company, electric turbine drives enjoyed a 20-year period in which they were fitted to major warships, until this particular design configuration was overtaken by developments in reduction gearing. Improvements in metallurgy and in machining techniques finally produced compact lightweight reduction gears that proved to be superior to electric drive. What is significant about this study is the nature of the selection environment in which strategic, not economic, considerations dominated. Notice that what we have in each of these cases is a process of competition between rival design configurations, each based on different principles and championed by specific business units that develop specialized competencies to underpin their articulation of the technology. Although competition is in the first instance in terms of artifacts, it ultimately reflects the potential contained in the different competing configurations.

The closer we get to the firm, the more specific the technology is; the articulation process, though drawing substance from the same body of knowledge, leads to differentiated artifacts. There is no contradiction between the notion of normal configuration on the one hand and artifact differentiation on the other. In fact, normal configuration, as we have seen, represents the result of a research process embodying scientific and technological principles as well as experience. Such a process generally leads to the creation of a set of artifacts characterized by differences that, in the continuous process of articulation, can evolve along different paths. Kuhnian scientific paradigms overlap with the concept of technological paradigms. Insights drawn from a given scientific paradigm may underpin development in a number of technological paradigms. Conversely, the development of technological paradigms poses puzzles for the underlying science so that as a general proposition, science both stimulates and is stimulated by technology; it is a two-way street (Rosenberg 1990).

Systems and Technological Systems

Some Definitions of *System*

As a prelude to our discussion of technological systems, it will be helpful to make a few remarks concerning system concepts. The system concept is an old one: it was Condillac (1749) who argued that our reality is made of systems that are there to be discovered, while more recently Bertalanffy suggested that in all fields of knowledge, "in one way or another, we are forced to deal with complexities, with 'wholes' or 'systems'" (Bertalanffy 1971, p. 3). In all cases systems are defined by component parts and the interrelationships between these parts, and in some systems the characteristics of the parts cannot be defined independently of the system. In this sense, the most difficult analytical question concerns where the boundary is to be drawn, so that the system in question may be considered identified. Any boundary contains an element of arbitrariness and is as much a matter of analytical convenience as anything else. From this follow two major features of any system: first, there must exist unifying elements to provide the holistic features so that the whole has properties not reducible to the individual elements alone; and second, there must exist dynamic features that characterize the ongoing development of the system and its relationship with its external environment. This is an issue that Simon (1981) has clarified by suggesting that complex systems evolve to exhibit the property of near decomposability with the dynamic evolution of the system driven by links between, rather than within, different subsystems.

From this perspective it is apparent that system concepts can be applied to technologies in at least three ways: (1) system with respect to artifacts, which is the most common idea; (2) system with respect to technological competence of an organization, defined in terms of the knowledge and skills of individual members that are brought together to define a collective capability; or (3) system as a community of practitioners and institutions jointly practicing a division of labor and collectively defining a technology support system.

Technological Systems

One of the most well known attempts to define a system as a whole characterized by a set of techniques, which in turn are shaped by natural resources, energy, and human resources, was carried out by Mumford. In his book on technics and civilization he divides the history of the development of machinery and the machine civilization into three different phases: eotechnic, paleotechnic, and neotechnic. This divide is used as an explanatory device, as the phases are overlapping and interpenetrating (Mumford 1946, p. 109). Each phase is characterized by the fact that it forms a *technological complex:*

> Each phase . . . has its origin in certain definite regions and tends to employ certain special resources and raw materials. Each phase has its specific means of utilizing and generating energy, and its special forms of production. Finally, each phase brings into existence particular types of workers, trains them in particular ways, develops certain aptitudes and discourages others, and draws upon and further develops certain aspects of the social heritage. (Mumford 1946, pp. 109–10)

A more technical view is found in Gille, who elaborates the notion of the technical system in the prolegomena to his history of techniques (Gille [1978] 1986, pp. 1–96). The essence of Gille's approach is to provide a hierarchical set of definitions to break down the technical system concept. The route to the definition of what a technical system is, in fact, begins with an elementary level called *technical combination.* Such a combination entails at least the coupling of matter and energy combined by some intelligent technical act (Gille [1978] 1986, pp. 10–11). The second step is that of the *technical ensemble,* which implies the existence not of a unitary technique, but of the confluence of more techniques whose combination defines a particular production process. As an example Gille ([1978] 1986, p. 14) makes use of cast iron. The third step is that of the *technical concatenation (filière,* in French). Here we visualize a final product that results from a number of stages of production. The concatenation is then the combination of the necessary technical ensembles. The example used by Gille is that of the textile industry.

Connected with the notion of *filière,* and partly anticipating the notion of the technological system, are two further notions due to the Swedish economist Erik Dahmén (1989), namely, *structural tension* and *development block.* The latter phrase indicates that advances in technology in some areas of the economic system often cannot be fully exploited or profitably utilized unless a series of other connected tributary developments occur. As Dahmén put it:

> The concept *development block* refers to a set of factors in industrial development which are closely interconnected and interdependent. Some of them are reflected in price and cost signals in markets which are noted by firms and may give rise to new techniques and new products. Some of them come about by firms creating new markets for their products via entrepreneurial activities in other industries. (Dahmén 1989, p. 136)

This mirrors Gerschenkron's analysis ([1957] 1991, p. 104), which points out that there are technological and economic complementarities that require coordination and cooperation between a large number of entities often spread over a number of industrial branches. Furthermore, "if progress in one field is not 'timed' in relation to progress in another, one may speak about 'structural tensions' within the frame of incomplete blocks of development" (Dahmén [1957] 1991, p. 63). Thus, when a new development block appears it is largely incomplete. There exist potentialities and opportunities that will not necessarily be transformed into actuality. Moreover, the existence of blocks can be perceived ex ante, that is, entrepreneurs visualize the block itself in advance and behave consequently, but the majority of the cases are ex post perceptions, that is, entrepreneurs work in the direction of gap filling.

From a different perspective, Laudan (1984) defines technology at three levels, in a manner not dissimilar from Gille. At the lowest level are technologies proper, artifacts designed for specific purposes. Systems of multiple artifacts arranged for a productive purpose define the second level, technological complexes, which at the top level are systems, sets of related complexes. Each of these sets of definitions appeals to the decomposability of systems into subsystems and, indeed, it is decomposability that ultimately permits change to take place.

The general thrust of these contributions is to define technological systems as combinations of subsystems and the relationships and interfaces between these subsystems. Subsystem compatibility emerges as the major consideration in defining a system and as a requirement that places additional constraints on the design process. In general, each subsystem will have its own particular design configuration so that any system constitutes a set of interlinked design configurations with its knowledge base and set of skills, so that every system reflects a division of labor in the development of technology.

On Imbalances, Linkages, and Constraints:
A Systemic View
As we have pointed out, the difficulty in analyzing phenomena related to technological change lies in that whenever one element varies, a series of connected and often unforeseen events occur. From this we can identify a number of consequences flowing from the system perspective. First, the interface problem implies the creation of standards to achieve compatibility between subsystems, and necessarily any chosen standard sets limits on the design process and constrains future development. Second, the concept of imbalances that focus the development of a system becomes a central theme in understanding the pattern of development. Several authors have drawn atten-

tion to this phenomenon as a guide to learning effects: thus Rosenberg (1990) writes of imbalances and focusing devices, Sahal (1981) of technological guideposts, and Hughes (1983) of reverse salients. Each of these concepts is based on a systemic view of technology and the opportunities and pressures that shape innovative activity. It is to be expected that different design configurations will progress at different rates and that developments in a subsystem will only be integrated into the system as a whole when any necessary complementary changes in other subsystems have been achieved. Compton (1982) provides an interesting example of these systematic constraints in his discussion of the development of the automobile engine. To improve the engine's (system) performance it was necessary not only to attend to matters of mechanical design, but also to improve the fuel. The principal problem to be solved was the development of antiknocking agents, a solution that depended on design configurations in chemistry and drew upon different knowledge bases and traditions of practice from those involved in engineering design. In America in 1919, Thomas Midgely was successful in a way that Compton describes as follows. "Guided sometimes by wrong hypotheses, proceeding sometimes by pure trial and error, Midgely found that several chemical compounds, when added in small quantities to gasoline, have higher usable compression rates and significant improvements in power and fuel economy. Finally, one compound, tetraethyl lead, was found to have the optimum combination of properties" (1982, p. 30). It is this pattern of interaction between different design configurations which Nathan Rosenberg (1976) has aptly described in terms of imbalances and focusing devices, reflecting the fact that improvements in our subsystem may be of limited value unless there are improvements in other subsystems. Of course there is no guarantee that improvements in a constraining subsystem can be achieved, and this may trigger the search for a more radical solution in terms of the creation of a new subsystem based on different knowledge base and design principles. Very similar ideas have been expressed by Hughes (1983) with the notion of reverse salients, a device to capture the idea of different subsystems developing out of step.

A salient is a protrusion in a geometric figure, a line of battle, or an expanding weather front. As technological systems expand, reverse salients develop. Reverse salients are components in the system that have fallen behind or are out of phase with the others. Because it suggests uneven and complex change, this metaphor is more appropriate for systems than the rigid visual concept of a bottleneck. Reverse salients emerge, often unexpectedly; the defining and solving of critical problems is a voluntary action. When a reverse salient cannot be corrected within the context of an existing system, the problem becomes a radical one, the solution of which may bring a new and competing system. (Hughes 1989, pp. 73–75)

We shall note here that as systems shape opportunities to learn, they also place interrelatedness constraints on what might be achieved. An improvement in one subsystem can be adopted only if the costs of engineering compatibility with the rest of the system keep the overall portfolio of changes economically feasible.

Because different subsystems are typically developed by different organizations, the problem of imbalances is closely related to questions of incentive structures and externalities in technological development. The gains from improving one subsystem accrue to other subsystems while the failure of other subsystems to develop can limit incentives elsewhere. This problem is a familiar one for historians of technological change and it is seen at its sharpest in large-scale system technologies such as railways and electricity generation. Indeed, Paul David has proposed the idea of gateway technologies to focus upon developments that serve to define interface standards between previously incompatible subsystems (David 1992).

Imbalances in the system may arise for a number of reasons, including changes in the economic and social environment, functional failure, and what Constant has defined as presumptive anomaly: "Presumptive anomaly occurs in technology, not when the conventional system fails in any absolute or objective sense, but when assumptions derived from science indicate either that under some future conditions the conventional system will fail . . . or that a radically different system will do a much better job. No functional failure exists . . ." (Constant 1980, p. 15).

The example Constant makes use of relates to the transition from the propeller-piston engine to the turbojet as the technology to make aircrafts fly. During the second half of the 1920s aerodynamics made clear that aircraft speed could double from 200 mph to 400 mph by proper streamlining, that the laws of aerodynamics itself underwent violent change as the velocity approached the speed of sound, and, finally, that the propeller would not function at near-sonic speed.[5] It is not difficult to see that it is not possible to develop all of the components of the aircraft, engine and body, at the same rate; so a new engine could not be exploited because the fuselage could not cope with the speed and pressure.

The recent work of Henderson and Clark (1990) has clarified the systems perspective on technological change by distinguishing the components as subsystems from their interconnection or arrangement within the whole and

---

5. The traditional technology, however, given the real state of things, had not failed by any means (cf. Constant 1980, pp. 15–16).

thus distinguishing component innovation from architectural innovation. Component knowledge defines core design concepts, while architectural knowledge defines the configuration of the system as a whole. Moreover, it is the architecture that becomes stabilized in a dominant design and that greatly limits the freedom to develop the technology in other than limited directions.

Technology Support Systems

Thus far, we have suggested that technologies are articulated from systems of interlocking design configurations and are embodied in artifacts, traditions of skill and competence, and cognitive frameworks that shape expectations as to the future development of the technology. We now suggest that the systemic and paradigmatic dimensions of this perspective are reflected in an institutional division of labor between organizations that respond to different incentives and that are effective in developing technology only to the extent that they are connected or bridged together. By such a set of institutions we mean a *technology support system* (TSS). The first point to be clear upon is that this is not the same as a national innovation system as defined by Freeman (1988) and others, in terms of that distinct set of institutions that contribute to the development and diffusion of new technologies. Of course, there is a national policy dimension and a framework of law and regulation in which every TSS must operate. However, a TSS has a narrower focus in relation to a particular set of system based paradigms, while, on the other hand, its domain need not be coterminous with, and generally is not coterminous with, national boundaries. The concept has been eloquently presented by Carlsson and Stankiewicz (1991, pp. 111–12), although where they speak of a technological system that corresponds to our TSS. As they put it, technological systems have many dimensions, such as subject area (it is technology-specific), number and characteristics of actors and their interdependence, institutional infrastructure, and so on. This is one way in which they differ from national systems of innovation. Technological systems, they argue, are not necessarily bounded by national borders, although they are certainly influenced by cultural, linguistic, and other circumstances that facilitate or impede contacts. Finally, technological systems place more emphasis on diffusion and utilization of technology (as distinct from creation of new technology) and therefore take microeconomic and entrepreneurial aspects into account.

The unity of the TSS arises from the shared background and training of practitioners in promoting a particular technological area, and while the TSS may have formal aspects to its organization (for example, standards-setting authorities), it will also depend to a great extent on informal interactions as defined through networks of scientists and technologists in firms, universities, and other research laboratories. Nonetheless, the operating incentives of the different institutions may cut across the sense of shared purpose and prevent effective bridging. The structure of each TSS will reflect a particular division of labor in the accumulation of knowledge and provide, in G. Tassey's (1991) terms, a technological infrastructure. As an infrastructure, the primary purpose of the TSS is to promote dialogue between its component institutions. It is thus a device for managing the exchange of externalities in the generation and application of new technological knowledge. We use this notion particularly to bridge the gap between the firm and the external technological environment in which the firm itself operates. The environment is composed of cooperative knowledge-sharing mechanisms as well as competitive market mechanisms. By cooperative mechanisms we thus mean the different forms of cooperation that can be established between firms and between firms and the public sector, and the various kinds of incentives that can be activated to promote innovation as well as research and development activities. At the basis of this notion is the idea that while on the one hand science and technology are partly characterized by self-organizing forces, due to forms of unity, autonomy, and self-referentiality, on the other hand there exists the need for coordination and regulation to reach higher performances for both.

This having been said, a point we want to emphasize is that intentional science is different from intentional technology, and they operate in terms of different incentives and mechanisms for advancement. Technology must pass practical, economic, and social tests rather than tests of its truth or immunity to refutation alone. In this it is quite distinct from science: both are problem-solving activities, but carried out to quite different rules. It is precisely because they differ in these ways that it is efficient to locate them in different institutional contexts, so raising Adam Smith's question of how their different activities are to be coordinated. One of the aims of the TSS is to reconcile the needs of both. The TSS takes into account both the knowledge and the institutional dimensions, broadly considered in such a way as to also encompass the links and the mechanisms through which the relationship between the firm and what is outside the firm becomes structured. It considers the way in which the microworld of the firm interacts with, and is supported by, the macroworld external to the firm itself.

Constituent parts of the TSS are institutions that supply different kinds of knowledge, codified and tacit, procedural and conceptual. In all the developed countries there exist a series of research bodies (universities, research councils, research departments of ministries) whose main scope is to produce and diffuse knowledge. The interdependence between science and technology can be strengthened through the TSS to generate more effective understanding of reality that can then often be translated into useful applications.

The concept of a TSS raises many interesting questions for the conduct and formulation of science and technology policy. If policy is to be effective it must work through the appropriate support system, and therefore policy makers must be able to identify the appropriate sources of technological development and the related sets of design configurations. Research programs to boost specific areas that require cooperation between business- and state-financed research have been promoted for many years as support-enhancing devices. Examples are the *Framework Programmes* of the European Union, within which some key technological sectors are recognized as being important but insufficiently covered. Funding is made available so that the gap can be filled. More recently, the exchange of knowledge, including tacit forms, between institutions and countries has become an explicit aim of many organizations and governments. While publications have always played an important role, now a new emphasis is laid on human capital mobility. Here mobility concerns both scientists and technologists, and the exchange activity can occur in different ways, like mutual visits, one-way exchanges, or even consultancy. Demonstrator programs have been explicitly formulated to bridge industry with the academic community. Within the TSS we also have to consider the incentives offered in support of particular technologies, from public purchasing programs for the acquisition of specific devices to tax allowances for R & D.

From our previous discussion it is clear that the identification of a TSS depends upon the existence of some general technological principles (paradigms and design configurations) accepted by a specific technological community, because exchange and interrelatedness depend upon mutual understanding and a shared body of knowledge. This also implies that there exist some generic elements of a technology capable of integrating the intentional actions of a wide range of practitioners and policy makers, in which the latter play a regulatory and normative role. The more general paradigm concept thus underpins an alignment of objectives that makes it possible to focus on specific directions, strengthening each member of the system, as well as the structure as a whole. There thus develop a series of links that grow within the TSS. Links evolve and can become different from what they were at the beginning, and it is important to realize that once a system is started, its history matters, that is, it "biases" the technological direction undertaken.

In this context the relationships developed between knowledge and institutions, skill and institutions, and artifacts and firms can be assessed. Also, the notion of TSS, besides encompassing supernational cooperation plans,[6] seems to be able to subsume the notion of a national system of innovation, where the former gives an account of the availability of different mechanisms

---

6. We have already mentioned the European *Framework Programmes,* but we have to think of other supernational organizations dealing with different technological problems, from NATO to FAO, all characterized by the need for mutual understanding between member countries, institutions, researchers, and so forth.

through which technology can be supported, while the latter tells us how the national systems have developed. Diffusion phenomena need to be emphasized too, not least because of the Lamarckian feedback that is implied by application and learning.

Conclusions

In concluding this overview of some recent thinking on the evolution of technology, it remains only to remind ourselves that theories of evolution are explanations of how and why the world changes. We have suggested that the internal development of technologies and their process of selective attention can best be understood by drawing together the twin themes—technological paradigms and technological systems—within the overarching concept of a technology support system. While the analysis of technical change in terms of systems of artifacts has enjoyed a long tradition, the analysis of technological knowledge systems is less developed. It is this which brings together the idea of technologies as systems of interlocking design configurations, often with quite different knowledge bases and therefore quite different dynamics of development. The more broadly the system is defined, the greater the likely disparity in contributing design configurations and the more complex the pattern of development that ensues. Thus, paradigms and systems combined explain both the generation of diversity and its limitation.

REFERENCES

Basalla, G. 1988. *The Evolution of Technology.* Cambridge: Cambridge University Press.
Bertalanffy, L. von. 1971. *General System Theory.* London: Penguin Press.
Blaug, M. 1980. *The Methodology of Economics.* Cambridge: Cambridge University Press.
Campbell, D. T. 1987. Blind Variation and Selection Retention in Creative Thoughts as in Other Knowledge Processes. In *Evolutionary Epistemology, Theory of Rationality and the Sociology of Knowledge,* ed. G. Radnitzky and W. Bartley. New York: Open Court.
Carlsson, B. 1994. Technological Systems and Economic Development Potential: Four Swedish Case Studies. In *Innovation in Technology, Industries and Institutions,* ed. Y. Shionoya and M. Perlman. Ann Arbor: University of Michigan Press.
Carlsson, B., and R. Stankiewicz. 1991. On the Nature, Function, and Composition of Technological Systems. *Journal of Evolutionary Economics* 1:93–118.
Clark, N., and C. Juma. 1987. *Long-Run Economics. An Evolutionary Approach to Economic Change.* London: Pinter.
Compton, D. 1982. Internal-combustion Engines and Their Fuel: A Preliminary Exploration of Technological Interplay. *History of Technology* 7:23–36.

Condillac, É. B. de. 1749. *Traité des Systemes*. Reprinted in Oeuvres Philosophiques de Condillac, Volume 1, 121–217. Paris: Presses Universitaires de France, 1947.

Constant, E. W. 1980. *The Origins of the Turbojet Revolution*. Baltimore, Md.: Johns Hopkins University Press.

Dahmén, E. 1989. Development Blocks in Industrial Transformation. In *Development Blocks and Industrial Transformation: The Dahménian Approach to Economic Development*, ed. B. Carlsson and G. H. Henriksson. Stockholm: Almqvist and Wicksell.

David, P. 1992. Heroes, Herds and Hysteresis in Technological History: Thomas Edison and the Battle of the Systems Reconsidered. *Industrial and Corporate Change* 1:129–80.

Dosi, G. 1982. Technological Paradigms and Technological Trajectories. *Research Policy* 11:147–62.

Freeman, C. 1979. The Determinants of Innovation. *Futures* 11(June): 206–15.

Freeman, C. 1988. Japan: A New System of Innovation. In *Technological Change and Economic Theory*, ed. G. Dosi, C. Freeman, R. Nelson, G. Silverberg, and L. Soete. London: Francis Pinter.

Georghiou, L. et al. 1986. *Post-Innovation Performance*. London: Macmillan.

Gerschenkron, A. 1957. A Schumpeterian Analysis of Economic Development. *Review of Economics and Statistics* 39 (November): 471–76, reprinted in B. Carlsson and G. H. Henriksson 1991, 103–11.

Gille, B. [1978] 1986. *The History of Techniques—Volume 1 Techniques and Civilization*. New York: Gordon and Breach.

Henderson, R. M., and K. B. Clark. 1990. Architectural Innovation: The Reconfiguration of Existing Product Technologies and the Failure of Established Firms. *Administrative Quarterly Journal* 35, no. 1 (March): 9–30.

Hughes, T. P. 1983. *Networks of Power: Electrification in Western Society, 1880–1930*. Baltimore, Md.: Johns Hopkins University Press.

Jacob, F. 1982. *The Possible and the Actual*. Seattle: University of Washington Press.

Klepper, S., and E. Grady. 1990. The Evolution of New Industries and the Determinants of Market Structure. *Rand Journal of Economics* 21:27–44.

Kuhn, T. S. [1962] 1970. *The Structure of Scientific Revolutions*. Chicago: University of Chicago Press.

Langlois, R. N., and P. L. Robertson. 1990. Networks and Innovation in a Modular System: Lessons from the Microcomputer and Stereo Component Industries. *Economics and Management*, Working Paper no. 3 (July), University of New South Wales, Australia.

Laudan, R., ed. 1984. *The Nature of Technological Knowledge: Are Models of Scientific Change Relevant?* Dordrecht: Reiter.

Layton, E. T. 1974. Technology as Knowledge. *Technology and Culture* 15, no. 1 (January): 31–41.

Lundvall, B-A. 1988. Innovation as an Interactive Process: From User-Supplier Interaction to the National System of Innovation. In *Technical Change and Economic Theory*, ed. G. Dosi, C. Freeman, R. Nelson, G. Silverberg, L. Soete. London: Francis Pinter.

Lundvall, B-A. 1992. *National Systems of Innovation*. London: Pinter.

McBride, W. M. 1992. Strategic Determinism in Technology Selection: The Electric Battleship and U.S. Naval-Industrial Relations. *Technology and Culture* 33, no. 2 (April): 248–77.

McKenzie, D. 1992. Economic and Sociological Explanation of Technical Change. In R. Coombs, P. Saviotti, and V. Walsh, *Technological Change and Company Strategies*. London: Academic Press.

Masterman, M. 1970. The Nature of a Paradigm. In *Criticism and the Growth of Knowledge,* ed. I. Lakatos and A. Musgrave, 59–89. Cambridge: Cambridge University Press.

Mokyr, J. 1990. *The Lever of Riches: Technological Creativity and Economic Progress*. New York: Oxford University Press.

Mumford, L. 1946. *Technics and Civilization*. London: Routledge.

Nelson, R. 1993. *National Innovation Systems*. New York: Oxford University Press.

Nelson, R. 1994. The Co-evolution of Technologies and Institutions. *Industrial and Corporate Change* 3:47–64.

Nelson, R. R., and S. Winter. 1982. *An Evolutionary Theory of Economic Change*. Cambridge, Mass.: Harvard University Press.

Norberg, A. L. 1990. High-Technology Calculation in the Early 20th Century: Punched Card Machinery in Business and Government. *Technology and Culture* 31, no. 4 (October): 753–79.

Pheby, J. 1988. *Methodology and Economics*. London: Macmillan.

Ramelli, A. 1588. *Le Diverse et Artificiose Machine*. Paris.

Reuleaux, F. 1871. *Teoria Generale delle Macchine*. Milan: Hoepli. English translation: *The Kinematics of Machinery*. London: Macmillan, 1876.

Rosenberg, N. 1976. *Perspectives on Technology*. Cambridge: Cambridge University Press.

Rosenberg, N. 1990. Why Do Firms Do Basic Research (with Their Own Money)? *Research Policy* 19, no. 2 (April): 165–74.

Rossi, P. 1976. *I Filosofi e le Macchine*. Milano: Feltrinelli.

Sahal, D. 1981. *Patterns of Technological Innovation*. London: Addison-Wesley.

Schatzberg, E. 1994. Ideology and Technical Choice: The Decline of the Wooden Airplane in the United States, 1920–1945. *Technology and Culture* 35:34–69.

Schumpeter, J. A. [1912] 1961. *The Theory of Economic Development*. New York: Oxford University Press. (First English translation 1934.)

Simon, H. A. 1981. *The Sciences of the Artificial*. Cambridge, Mass.: MIT Press.

Süsskind, C. 1981. The Invention of Computed Tomography. *History of Technology* 6:39–80.

Utterback, J., and F. Suarez. 1993. Innovation, Competition and Industry Structure. *Research Policy* 22:1–21.

Tassey, G. 1991. The Functions of Technology Infrastructure in a Competitive Economy. *Research Policy* 20:345–61.

Vincenti, W. G. 1990. *What Engineers Know and How They Know It*. Baltimore, Md.: Johns Hopkins University Press.

Waddington, C. H. 1957. *The Strategy of the Genes*. London: Allen and Unwin.

Wilson, D. S. 1990. Species of Thought: A Comment on Evolutionary Epistemology. *Biology and Philosophy* 5:37–62.

Wise, G. 1985. Science and Technology. *Osiris* 1:229–46.

Wojick, D. 1979. The Structure of Technological Revolutions. In *The History and Philosophy of Technology,* ed. G. Bugliarello and D. Doner. Urbana: University of Illinois Press.

The Evolution of Economic Complexity: A Division-of-Coordination-of-Labor Approach

Esben Sloth Andersen

This chapter suggests ways in which evolutionary economics can cope with economic complexity through a combination of Smithian-Marshallian and Schumpeterian approaches. The proposed solution emphasizes the innovation-driven evolution of vertical disintegration, the standardization of the interfaces between firms, and the emergence of highly complex products through evolutionary design trajectories.

Introduction

The purpose of the present chapter[1] is to suggest ways in which evolutionary economics can cope with economic complexity in a more complex and less stylized way than appears to be the result of the studies in relation to Artificial Life and Adaptive Economic Agents (Holland and Miller 1991; Arthur 1993; cf. Waldrop 1992). The chapter approaches this task through a combination of aspects of Smithian-Marshallian and Schumpeterian approaches to economic evolution, which are treated by means of some tools of modern evolutionary economics.

This combination of approaches is introduced in the first section while the second section suggests the outlines of a model in relation to Adam Smith's ideas of the division of labor as an element in the analysis of economic evolution and growth. The section focuses on the emergence of inter-firm, vertical specialization, which is seen as driven by Schumpeterian discrete innovations. The outcome of repeated attempts to obtain innovative profits through vertical specialization is a complex interindustrial system,

---

1. The chapter presents a theoretical framework that has partly been developed in relation to a research project on "New Credence Goods" within the Programme on Market-Based Process and Product Innovation in the Food Sector (MAPP). An extended version of parts of the framework that more explicitly deal with the problems of quality specification, quality control, and quality management is described in Andersen 1994b. Henry W. Chesbrough, Nicolai Juul Foss, and Bengt-Åke Lundvall have made useful comments on an earlier version of the chapter.

which serves as a starting point for the following sections. The third section deals with the need to standardize the qualities of products delivered between the different firms and industries in a highly complex system of interindustrial relationships. While standardization appears to be a necessary consequence of the attempts of economic agents to exploit economies of scale and to avoid dealing with impossible amounts of information, this may also lead to difficulties for innovative activities. To be more specific, there is a trade-off between two principles of the evolutionary "design" of complex interindustrial systems, the principle of interface abstraction and the principle of innovative linkages. In the fourth section we turn to the emergence of highly complex products that apparently contradict the tendency toward standardization. However, the contradiction is shown to disappear to the extent that minimum quality characteristics are allowed to be added to one another. Each quality dimension of a specific product of an industry may undergo a quality-characteristic life cycle in which a key success factor for firm competitiveness emerges and disappears after it (perhaps) is turned into a minimum standard. A series of such subsequent cycles constitutes a trajectory in a largely unknown and complex space of possible product specifications. The concluding section summarizes the type of complexity studies presented in the rather dense chapter.

Combining Smithian-Marshallian and Schumpeterian Approaches

Old Evolutionary Economics (i.e., analysis of economic evolution unguided by an explicit population dynamics approach) is marked by an unfortunate split between a Smithian-Marshallian approach and a Schumpeterian approach, a split that has not yet been fully overcome by the modeling-oriented New Evolutionary Economics.[2] The background for this split is partly that the Schumpeterian theory of evolution was developed as an explicit alternative rather than as a complement to the dominant Smithian-Marshallian theory of evolution.[3] In a certain sense, the latter theory considers economic evolution as "organic growth" (Marshall 1898, 42 f.), in analogy with "the gradual organic growth of a tree" (Schumpeter 1934, 216). Schumpeter (1939, 203) considered this "picture of a steady march of progress to be misleading," since

---

2. On the split between old and new evolutionary economics and some of the main modeling approaches of the latter, see Andersen 1994a.

3. Schumpeter concentrates on "the Marshallian theory of evolution" (1954, 1165), which he considers to be an important development of Adam Smith's suggestions. Among Schumpeter's explicit discussions of this model one should note the treatment of the concepts of internal and external economies (Schumpeter 1939, 90–93). The evolutionary part of the Marshallian tradition is characterized by names like Young, Kaldor, Penrose, Richardson, and Loasby.

"evolution is lopsided, discontinuous, disharmonious by nature" (1939, 102). To emphasize his own evolutionary vision, Schumpeter developed a theory that removed gradualist and adaptive aspects from the focus of attention and made the incommensurability between old and new a core characteristic of his concept of innovation (like Kuhn later with respect to scientific evolution). At the same time Marshall's "manager" was transformed into a routine-following agent while the creative tasks were left to the Schumpeterian entrepreneur.

The split between the Smithian-Marshallian approach and the Schumpeterian approach appears to the modern researcher as a need to choose between different hypotheses all of which seem to reflect aspects of the real process of economic evolution. One example is that Schumpeterian consumers have to be persuaded of the advantages of a product innovation by the Schumpeterian entrepreneurs, while Smithian-Marshallian decision makers are normally able to judge the quality of a modified product or a modified process. In the Smithian-Marshallian approach there is no need for a concept of innovation, since economic evolution can be studied in terms of gradual quality improvements (called "incremental innovations" by neo-Schumpeterian researchers[4]), while the Schumpeterian approach focuses on significant innovations and leaves the realm of quality improvements to the routine-based behavior of Schumpeterian managers.

To overcome the split between the Smithian-Marshallian approach and the Schumpeterian approach, we need to find some common ground. This is not easy since the two approaches have very different concepts of production, consumption, and economic change. The Smithian-Marshallian notions of intra- and interfirm division of labor and the related internal and external increasing returns to scale presuppose an interest in the details of the organization of the process of production (and consumption). The original Schumpeterian model emphasizes exchange, while production (and consumption) is treated as a black box that can be characterized fully in terms of a production function (or a consumption function); innovations are defined in this context.[5] The fundamental character of the split may be seen by recognizing that the exchange-oriented model is inspired by the overall neoclassical approach (which is most clearly expressed by Walras) while the production-process-oriented model has deep roots in classical economics. We should, however, note that some neoclassical economists who relate to the classical tradition (like Marshall, Menger, and Böhm-Bawerk) emphasize the structure of production in their treatment of economic evolution. Furthermore, neo-Schum-

---

4. The emphasis on this kind of change might suggest that some of the present-day "neo-Schumpeterians" could more adequately be called "evolutionary neo-Marshallians."

5. See Schumpeter 1939, 87 ff.

peterians like Nelson and Winter (1982) have tried to put production at the center of their evolutionary theory of economic change.

The present chapter suggests an integration of parts of the Schumpeterian approach into the classical conception of the changing organization and knowledge of the process of production—as a way of introducing problems of the emergence and innovative functioning of complex interindustrial systems and of complex product specifications.[6] This integration is helped by some tools of modern evolutionary-economic modeling (especially from the Nelson and Winter tradition).

Outlines of a Smithian-Schumpeterian Model of the Evolution of Interfirm Complexity

For economists who know Adam Smith's theory of economic evolution primarily from his vivid example of the productivity effects arising from an increased intrafirm division of labor in pin manufacturing (Smith 1976, 14 f.), the gulf vis-à-vis Schumpeter may appear to be unbridgeable. But a closer look at Smith's arguments demonstrates that his "very trifling" (p. 14) pin-making example relates to an overall theory of evolution that also includes the "separation of different trades and employments from one another" (p. 15). Especially in the area of vertical "separation of trades" (i.e., market creation), there are plenty of possibilities for introducing Schumpeterian innovation and entrepreneurship, although Smith saw the emergence of interfirm division of labor as a more or less automatic process. To emphasize this part of the evolutionary process, it is convenient to develop the pin-making example for a stylized presentation of a model rather than as a precise historical account.

As a first approximation we deal with the evolution of the production techniques of the industry, M, which produces a homogeneous M-product (pins). The industry has, in a certain period of time t, m firms $(1, \ldots, j, \ldots, m)$. Output is made by means of labor and "primary" materials, and it is restricted by the accumulated organizational capacity of the firm. During period t, the jth firm has labor costs per unit of output, L_{jt}, which is divided between n different tasks $(1, \ldots, i, \ldots, n)$. For instance, the tasks of pin making may include pointing of pieces of wire, making of the head, and putting the head on (Smith, like the French *Encyclopédie*, mentions eighteen distinct tasks of pin making). The overall labor cost per unit of output is the sum of the labor costs applied to each of the individual tasks.

---

6. An alternative strategy of integration is to develop the notion of (more or less classical) natural trajectories within techno-economic paradigms and (Schumpeterian) shift between paradigms; see the development from Nelson and Winter (1982, 258–62) to Dosi (1982; 1988). As indicated in the following, I consider it problematic to delimit the Schumpeterian concept of innovation to rare radical innovations.

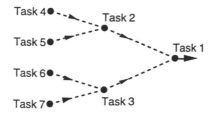

Fig. 1. The interconnections between seven production tasks. (Flows of labor services and primary materials are not included.)

In order to analyze the emergence of interfirm division of labor with respect to the different tasks, it is important to collect information about the structure of the process of production. This structure can be depicted by a directed graph; its nodes depict the necessary tasks and its arrows depict the way the outputs of the individual tasks are combined to create intermediary, as well as final, output. Figure 1 depicts the following top-down structure of tasks related to the production of the final output by a simplified M-form:

Task 1. Make an M product (e.g., a pin) by combining the results of tasks 2 and 3.

Task 2. Make a task-2 product (a pin head) by combining the results of tasks 4 and 5.

Task 3. Make a task-3 product (a pin body) by combining the results of tasks 4 and 5.

Task 4. Make a task-4 product (a pin-head tool).

Task 5. Make a task-5 product (materials prepared for pin-head making).

Task 6. Make a task-6 product (a pin-body tool).

Task 7. Make a task-7 product (materials prepared for pin-body making).

The production graph depicts a vertical dimension of production that is present even in a Robinson Crusoe economy. But the all-around activities of Robinson lead to large costs of switching tasks and little time for task-specific learning. In the present context with many firms, it is convenient to assume a minimum size of firms that exploits static economics of scale and an exploitation of simple learning effects within each period of time. Instead, we shall, like Schumpeter, emphasize the role of innovation in terms of novel methods of production that are introduced in discrete steps. The search for novelties and decision making about them may, in the neo-Schumpeterian tradition, be described in terms of the well-known procedures of *innovation, imitation,* and *techno-choice,* which we find in, for example, the Nelson and Winter model (cf. the reconstruction in Andersen 1994a, chap. 4), together with a novel procedure for *specialization.*[7] These procedures specify how M-firms find and select new production techniques during each period as the result of the stochastic outcomes of a costly (re)search within n different spaces of possible production routines (defined in terms of labor coefficients). Most basic is the *innovation* procedure, which implies that in period t the firm j may find a new method with respect to task i that can be applied in period $t + 1$, so that $L_{ij,t+1} < L_{ijt}$ and thus $L_{j,t+1} < L_{jt}$. For instance, one of the pin firms may find a new and more productive way of putting pin heads on pin bodies.

The *techno-choice* and *specialization* procedures are used to decide whether and how the results of innovative (and imitative) search with respect to task j in period t are to be applied. The procedures must take into account that an innovative possibility can be applied by the successful firm in two ways. First, the firm can apply the innovative possibility within its own production and thus, given unchanged prices, obtain a profit in period $t + 1$. During the next periods, the innovating firm will use its profits to expand its organizational capacity. At the same time the profits will gradually be eroded by a fall in the price due to an increased aggregate output by the innovative firm and by other firms that have successfully applied the *imitation* procedure.

Second, the successful firm can apply the *specialization* procedure that specifies decisions about vertical disintegration. The purpose of the innovating firm is to sell the output from the innovated task (e.g., pin heads) to other firms within the M-industry.[8] Its decision thus presupposes that other firms make a complementary specialization by means of an *adoption* procedure. In this way the innovative firm can obtain a part of the profits that are gained by other firms that adopt the new product rather than by performing the related task themselves. In the simplest case, the innovating firm may assume that all M-firms have exactly the same complex structure of internal tasks (e.g., like fig. 1) and that in period t they have equal labor costs with respect to task j. The innovating firm's choice of specialization rather than internal application of the novel possibility will partly be determined by its perception of the

---

7. The unconventional talk of "procedures" and the masking of them by italics are partly applied in the chapter because this makes cross-references easy. However, this is also related to an algorithmic approach to evolutionary-economic modeling (Andersen 1994a, chap. 4 and app.). This approach applies, to a large extent, the top-down method of the specification of algorithms—a method that allows us to focus on the core elements of an algorithm and on their interconnections before any programming is made. The present chapter is only related to these "top-level" parts of the top-down approach. The present author considers them important, even for researchers who do not intend to make any programming.

8. Once more, it should be noted that the interfirm division of labor in relation to the "pin industry" should not be considered as being part of a realistic account for the evolution of pin making. The issue of interfirm and interindustry specialization could be more realistically related to Smith's comments on the textile and clothing industries—but then the account would be too complicated for the present context.

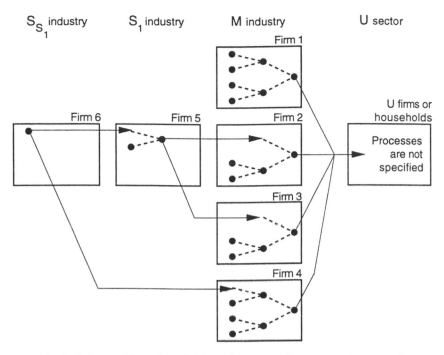

Fig. 2. Intra- and interfirm division of seven tasks at a certain stage of evolution.

willingness and ability of other firms to specialize, of its own capacity to cover the whole market for the new intermediate product, and of the inability of other firms to imitate.

The repeated application of the *specialization* procedure creates a complex industrial system that is illustrated by figure 2. In this highly simplified case[9] we initially have six M-firms with identical task structures (see fig. 1). In the situation depicted by figure 2, one of the M-firms (firm 1) has kept all the original tasks within its own boundaries. The other firms have changed their structure of production. The first structure-changing innovation was made by firm 5, which exploited the innovation by specializing in tasks 2, 4, and 5 (making of pin heads) and thus became the first member of the S_1 industry. The complementary specialisation was made by firms 2 and 3, which adopted the product from the S_1 firm and became specialists in pin-body production and pin assembly. The second structure-changing innovation was made by firm 6, which specialized because of an increased productivity with

---

9. Figure 2 is constructed to illustrate different types of specialization rather than to be realistic. Thus, no attempts have been made to supply it with realistic labor coefficients.

respect to task 4 (production of tools for pin-head production). The complementary specialization was made by firms 4 and 5, which belonged to different levels in the hierarchy of specialization. The classification in figure 2 (firm 6 belongs to the S_{S1} industry) reflects the fact that firm 6 first joined the S_1 industry and subsequently specialized in order to supply the other firm (firm 5) of the S_1 industry. However, even a firm in the M industry (firm 4) chose to adopt the product from firm 6. Thus, the classification reflects the dynamics of the process of specialization rather than the static structure of an input-output system.

The original specification of the structure of tasks (like in fig. 1) defines clear limits to the possible complexity in the resulting industrial system. It is, therefore, important to note that the task structure of even relatively simple firms are immensely complex and cannot be known completely at any point in time. First, a task can often be divided into subtasks. The increasing use of mechanical, electronic, and chemical processes in production often reveals old aspects of the task structure and creates novel ones. Second, the tasks of quality control, adaptation to new customer demands, and other "management" tasks were not explicitly included in the Smithian account. But they were strongly emphasized by Marshall (1949, book 4, chap. 12), who thought that the subdivision of the tasks of "business management" represented "the central problem of the modern organisation of industry" (p. 236). These tasks are very complex and allow the evolution of many specializations. Third, we should recognize that the neo-Schumpeterian model of the process of specialization should also cover innovative activities, just like Smith's (1976, 21 f.) inventive "philosophers and men of speculation" engage in division of labor. We may assume these innovative activities are initially characterized by an intrafirm division of labor. The *innovation* procedure presupposes a certain probabilistic productivity of these activities. An interfirm and interinstitution specialization may serve to enhance the productivity of certain tasks among the innovative activities (according to a *meta-innovation* procedure). Fourth, we have not yet discussed new specialization possibilities between the M industry and the sector that uses its products (the U sector). In particular, we should recognize that the process of household production can be modeled in more or less the same terms as the process of interfirm production. Thus much of Adam Smith's (1976, 31) thinking started from the farmer in the Highlands of Scotland who "must be butcher, baker and brewer for his own family." The existence of the four new areas of specialization emphasizes that we should not be too hasty in assuming an exhaustion of the possibilities of specialization. If we add occasional technological revolutions, we may easily imagine an ever-changing structure of an economic system with a long-term increase in its level of complexity.

If we apply the present Smithian-Schumpeterian approach to macrolevel issues, it seems clear that the *specialization* procedure serves as a mechanism for the diffusion of the results of a productivity-enhancing innovation from one firm to other firms. In this respect it has the same function as the *imitation* procedure—but specialization[10] is normally a more powerful mechanism than imitation. In this connection we may (by paraphrasing Smith) formulate the hypothesis that the spread of innovation is limited by the extent of the vertical division of labor. In other words, an economic system that hinders the vertical division of labor will delimit the possibilities of exploiting innovation.[11] However, the increase in interfirm specialization leads to coordination problems (partly comparable to the intracorporation coordination problems modeled by Marengo 1992). The most obvious one is the simple coordination problem that arises if the using firm has to order and buy the intermediate products in the period before they are used, while it can organize all the steps of the intrafirm process of production during a single period. This time lag makes the higher levels of specialization very unstable. There are, however, many other coordination problems. We shall analyze some of them in the next sections.

Quality Standardization versus Incremental Product Innovation in Complex Economic Systems

In the previous section, in a simplistic way, we introduced Schumpeter's discrete innovations into a classical, production-process-oriented model of economic evolution. The combination of the two approaches meant that the decision making of firms that perform innovations entered into the focus of attention, while the pure classical approach dealt with the more or less automatic change of firms in general. The ease with which the combination of the two approaches was made depended, however, on the narrow version of the concept of innovation that was applied: that is, labor-saving innovations with respect to specific production tasks that can be introduced without changing the qualitative characteristics of the output of these tasks. Thus, we might have talked of a "*process-innovation* procedure" rather than of the more general "*innovation* procedure." Although this limited type of process innovation is included in the Schumpeterian concept of innovation, Schumpeter (1939, 78) emphasizes that his concept "covers the case of a new commodity, as well as that of a new form of organization such as a merger, of the opening

---

10. Specialization transforms a process innovation into an innovation with respect to the market—the first commercialization of an intermediate good.

11. If we take into account that an innovative, specialized supplier may serve several industries, we have an important reason why internal economies of scale are transformed into external economies of scale rather than being exploited by firms of increasing size. We thus relate to Stigler 1951.

up of new markets, and so on." To deal with these other types of innovation we need to consider novelties in the economic system that, by necessity, directly involve more than one firm. We have already dealt with one type of new markets: the creation of a new market through the vertical *specialization* procedure. We may also imagine an *integration* procedure that deals with liquidation of markets. Finally, we may, in a *product-innovation* procedure, describe "discrete product innovation," which is probably the most typical of the Schumpeterian types of innovation. Such procedures, which involve the creation of novel "interfaces" between the firms and industries, are important for the understanding of the emergence and restructuring of complex economic systems.

We start with a question: why and to what extent should we consider the introduction of vertical disintegration of the process of production to be a Schumpeterian innovation? Or, to be more concrete: why and to what extent should the establishment of a pin-head making S_1 industry be considered an innovation, provided that pin-head making is already a task performed within the M industry? Such questions appear to be foreign to the classical-neoclassical approach to evolution. Adam Smith has no explicit treatment of the difference between inter- and intrafirm division of labor, and Marshall (and Coase 1937) suggests that the shift between intra- and interfirm execution of tasks can be made in an incremental manner. But the questions appear to be perfectly compatible with Schumpeter's (1939, 78 ff.) definition of innovation as "new production functions" considered as the future norm or standard of performance used by decision makers in the economic system. As long as pin heads are made as one of many production tasks within the different M firms, there is no economy-wide standard of how to perform the task of pin-head making. Thus a certain degree of heterogeneity with respect to the specification of pin heads and to the cost of producing them is allowed to exist between the firms. The specialization that leads to an S_1 industry will disclose much of this heterogeneity that is present in the *M* industry, and this disclosure is followed by market processes that promote the emergence of standards of quality specification (of S_1 products) and norms of performance in terms of (labor) costs (in the S_1 industry as well as in the part of the M industry that upholds its pin-head-making activities). This means that a realistic version of the *specialization* procedure thus has several features in common with the *product-innovation* procedure.

In Schumpeter's (1939, 103 ff.) simplified model, a product innovation is made in a single step because the innovative entrepreneur is by definition successful while actions taken before the time of successful innovation are ignored or treated in terms of inventive activities. We may accordingly specify the *product-innovation* procedure in a way in which the product of the innovating firm becomes the standard for the imitators as well as for the firms that adopt the new product. However, this picture is too unrealistic (and too far from the present-day neo-Schumpeterian studies of incremental innovation). What is lacking is an explicit treatment of the process that leads from the initial, unfinished version of the new product (or process) to a specification that can be applied as a general rule. Just like in the classical literature on the evolution of the institution of money (Smith 1976, 38–44; Menger 1892) and in the recent literature on the industry-level product life cycle (e.g., Abernathy and Utterback 1978; Abernathy and Clark 1985), we need a kind of evolutionary process (or at least a two-step approach) that includes a period with alternative proposals and incremental innovations as well as the emergence of a standardized solution (or a dominant design).

In relation to the pin-making example we can recognize the need for such a process even in relation to a process of specialization, provided that the M firms are not producing exactly equal intermediate products. Before the development of interfirm specialization of labor, each firm is free to choose its own way of fitting the results of the different tasks (of fig. 1) together. For instance, the necessary restriction for a feasible production process is mainly that pin heads and pin bodies fit together, rather than that they have individually specified sizes. Thus each M firm may have its own specification of pin heads. This fact does not create difficulties in the case where an innovating firm becomes specialized to supply only a single purchaser. The pin-head producer of figure 2 (firm 5) will probably apply the specifications of pin heads previously used by the first purchaser (firm 2). But as soon as the pin-head producing firm 5 starts to deliver to the next customer (firm 3), a problem emerges. Assuming that the pin-head specifications of firms 2 and 3 differ, the pin-head producer has to decide whether to produce pin heads in two batches or to persuade firm 3 to follow standardized specifications of pin heads. Similarly, the pin-head tool maker (firm 6) may initially have developed its tools for small-scale production of pin heads (in firm 4). When a specialized pin-head maker (firm 5) enters as a customer, the question is whether or not the tools shall be adapted for the larger-scale production.

The discussion in relation to the simplified situation of figure 2 does not allow us to decide how the second customer of a new industry will be treated (much less about the next customers). However, if we assume that the M industry consists of hundreds of firms that are supplied by many different industries, each of which consist of several firms, then it is not difficult to recognize that a tendency to standardize many of the products will prevail. There are at least two major explanations for this propensity to standardize the interfaces between industries in complex economic systems.[12] The first explanation is supply-side oriented and made in terms of economies of scale, and it

---

12. There are many aspects of the phenomenon of standardization (including technical compatibility) that are presently much discussed but that shall not be dealt with in the present context. David (1987) represents an attempt to promote conceptual clarification that includes a taxonomy.

follows more or less directly from the classical approach to economic evolution. It is especially Marshall (1919) who has studied the tendency to standardize as a core theme in both his comparison between the industrial history of the major industrial countries (UK, France, USA, and Germany) and his description of major problem areas with respect to industrial organization and technical change. His explanation emphasizes (1) internal economies of scale obtained by a firm by standardizing its output rather than delivering tailor-made products (and by shifting from order production to inventory production) and (2) external economies of scale obtained at the industry level through the intensified evolution of suppliers to an industry that, because of an industrial standard, has a large output as well as equalized problems. Even intermediate products can be commercialized if they are strictly standardized—because this means that repair work of complex products becomes a question of buying a new part rather than of buying a tailor-made solution by a skilled artisan. The second explanation of standardization (broadly conceived) is made in terms of boundedly rational, partly standardized economic behavior that is considered as a dominant feature when highly complex, information-rich, and conflict-ridden economic systems are confronted with the relatively limited capabilities of the economic agents with respect to information gathering and computation. The approach has a background in the Austrian and Schumpeterian treatment of the difficulties of economic decision making, but it is mainly developed by modern behavioral, cognitive, and informational economies.[13] The problems of information and conflict are seen as partly solved by the standardization of most of the interfaces between firms, industries, and sectors of the economic system. This fundamental way of coping with complexity (cf. Simon 1981, chap. 7) may appear ex post as an application of the principle of commodity abstraction (Andersen 1991), but the standardized interfaces are normally the outcome of an evolutionary process, rather than of rational systematic design.

Whether we choose the Marshallian or the more or less Schumpeterian approach to standardization, it is not difficult to see that only one or a few different specifications of the interfirm output from a certain production task (e.g., task 2 in fig. 1) can coexist. If the S_1 industry supplies pin heads according to one or a few standards, then the consequence is (1) an increase in the extent of the market and the related internal and external economies of scale and (2) a decrease in the requirements for the individual M firm with

---

13. The modern view is found in, for example, Simon 1982 and Heiner 1989, but the approach was also more or less clearly present in Schumpeter's (1934, 9, 6) account of the widespread tendency to "cling as tightly as possible to habitual economic methods," partly because of the limited cognitive abilities of normal economic man, and partly because past history has "entangled him in a net of social and economic connections which he cannot easily shake off."

respect to information and coordination with S_1 firms. Through the decrease in production costs of the S_1 firms, as well as in transaction costs of the M firms, the quality standard(s) defines the more or less final form of the S_1 product and allows its spread throughout the economic system. However, the conditions for (incremental) product innovations with respect to the core product have, at the same time, deteriorated radically.[14] One of the major basic problems can be described in terms of the principle of innovative linkages or interactive learning in product innovation (Lundvall 1992).

In a complex economic system that has evolved in a way such that the principle of commodity abstraction has become predominant, very difficult conditions exist for (incremental) product innovation. The reason is that innovations will not take the finished and information-poor form from the time when they are first introduced on the market. The way out of the resulting evolutionary stasis (the Schumpeterian "circular flow") appears to be the evolutionary jumps promoted by Schumpeterian entrepreneurs. However, from a closer look, such jumps are never made in a single step and it is important to make an explicit analysis of the unfinished character of the new product (or process)—even if it means an end to a realized "circular flow" in any formal sense. Instead, we have a constant conflict between the principles of commodity abstraction and of innovative linkages. But the conflict is seldomly unbridgeable, since a given *M* firm may organize most of its interfaces to customers and to supplying industries and firms in an information-poor form, while a few interfaces are organized in the innovation-promoting, information-rich form. The latter may be called innovative linkages (developed in Andersen and Lundvall 1994).

Two stylized facts underlie the idea of innovative linkages. First, the interfirm division of labor has been developed to a point where two or more relatively independent parties often have to interact in order to produce a successful innovation. Second, an innovation is not normally a unique event, but rather a part of a sequence of innovations; the next innovation in this sequence can often (but not always) be found by means of the same pattern of interaction as the previous one. This gives motivation for investments in (and imitation of) promising patterns of interrelated activities. At the firm level we

---

14. The most fascinating and controversial example of lock-in is the "fable of the keys," the story of the continued success of the QWERTY keyboard (Arthur 1983; David 1985; Liebowitz and Margolis 1990), which may be interpreted within the present framework of intra- and interfirm specialization, innovation, and standardization. For instance, we note that during the period in which writing work in offices became massively influenced by typewriters, a large number of specializations took place. Books on typewriting were written, firms specializing in producing typing courses emerged, a market for skilled typists was created. These specializations could relate to any keyboard design, but a dominant design had a clear advantage. Through a mix of a random walk and conscious promotion, the peculiar QWERTY keyboard design emerged as a winner, although it soon appeared to be suboptimal.

may illustrate the reasons for establishing and maintaining such linkages in relation to an innovation that takes place in a production chain from the S_1 industry via an M firm to the U sector (see fig. 2). Assume that the M firm has innovative ideas about new types of pins for the U sector, which it is not able to implement because the ideas presuppose new inputs from the S_1 industry. If the involved M firm has an information-rich interface with an innovation-oriented S_1 firm, then it has a higher probability of succeeding in innovative activities than M firms without such access. The innovative linkage is, however, also potentially profitable for the involved S_1 firm, provided that the M firm shows a supernormal innovative activity. The new product delivered for the M firm may later be generalized and sold to other M firms. Thus the S_1 firm will have a higher probability of succeeding in innovative activities than S_1 firms with weaker or absent innovative linkages.

The fact that innovations often occur in sequences may be modeled in several ways. For instance, the innovative M firms may create a list of new products that are not feasible in the present period because of input constraints. The existence of such lists radically changes the search conditions of the S_1 firms (and thus their *innovation* procedure). Suppliers with privileged access to such lists will have a higher probability of succeeding in the innovative activities than S_1 firms without such access. But the lists of different M firms are not equally relevant to an S_1 firm. If the S_1 firm has privileged access to the problem list of an M firm that is behind the productivity frontier of industry M, then some of the items on the list may represent trivial problems whose solution will not contribute much to the competitive position of the S_1 firm. Lead users are much more interesting collaboration partners for an innovation-oriented S_1 firm (Hippel 1988; Lundvall 1985, 1992).

The coexistence of the principles of commodity abstraction and innovative linkages may explain some of the controversy over the relative importance of users and producers in innovation. The modern version of the gradualist approach to innovation has studied the emergence of product innovations in close interaction between producers, and here the initiative is often taken by buyers/users. This has become, to some extent, the dominant approach (see the review by Mowery and Rosenberg 1982). But during the transformation of the initial product innovation(s) into more and more standardized products, the roles change. Now the producer is the king "who as a rule initiates economic change, and consumers who are educated by him if necessary; they are, as it were, taught to want new things, or things which differ in some respect from those which they have been in the habit of using" (Schumpeter 1934, 65). This viewpoint clearly presupposes "debugged" and otherwise full-fledged commodities, since we would else have to consider feedback from the consumers. A product innovation might in some cases take this form from the very beginning (simple goods, often for consumer's markets), but the modern analysis of innovation and evolution has shown that this is the exception rather than the rule.

The Evolution of Complex Product Designs

The introduction of semipermanent quality standards allows the economic system to grow to a larger degree of interindustrial complexity than could exist without such standards. But if the interfaces of the economic system get locked in, they may also hinder quality changes that are, in the long run, preconditions for the transformation and increased complexity of the system. This is a real problem, but the way quality standards were specified in the last section may have created a wrong impression about the character of the limits to complexity. It is, for instance, difficult to understand the evolution of highly complex product specifications within the simplified picture of quality standardization. The task of the present section is to suggest a way of treating the evolution of this aspect of the complexity of the economic system.

The multidimensionality of product quality can, in principle, be discussed in relation to the pin-making example. The n tasks involved in the production of a pin (fig. 1) defines an n-dimensional space of qualities within which the different supplies can be evaluated. In this way we relate to the characteristics approach to demand theory (see, e.g., Lancaster 1979), which identifies products or goods by quality characteristics, that is, product properties that are important for the actual choices of buyers. Thus each product is represented by an n-dimensional vector $(c_1, \ldots, c_i, \ldots, c_n)$. The designs that we have discussed hitherto were, however, highly simplified. For instance, we may characterize the S_1 product that substitutes task 2 (and thus tasks 4 and 5) by either $(0,1,0,0,0,0,0)$ or $(0,1,0,1,1,0,0)$. But if we allow product innovations in supplying firms (e.g., S_1 firms), then the vectors of characteristics become much more complicated. For instance, we may try to depict the situation where the supply of a pin head from the S_1 industry is not only substituting the old pin-head production but also making it easier to put on the body of the pin within the M industry. This information is relevant to the supplying firm, which will try evaluate a potential product innovation within the characteristics space of the buyer in order to find out whether it may obtain a price premium.

There is, however, an obvious alternative to the application of a well-defined space of characteristics. That is to consider the introduction of a new quality dimension as an innovation. In other words, we may consider the number of dimensions as a variable, n_r. This idea may be discussed in relation to the interface between the M industry and the U sector (fig. 2). Since the characteristics space of the U sector has been left unspecified until now, we are free to make up still more characteristics. For instance, the first firm to introduce a new quality dimension may explicitly emphasize that its pin heads will never fall off, the second that its pins are "handy," the third that its pins are stainless. With respect to certain characteristics, we may see the emergence of a horizontal specialization. Thus firms may emphasize that their pins are fit for specific materials, for special purposes (toy pins, hat pins), and so on. This open-ended evolution of the dimensionality of the characteristics space is a typical aspect of economic evolution. It should be included in the analysis of the evolution of economic complexity.

The multidimensionality and the increasing complexity of the characteristics suggest ways of introducing the Schumpeterian idea of the incommensurability between the new and the old products, and the related problem of the persuasion of the customer by the entrepreneur. Such problems simply do not arise as long as the product from the innovating firm can be evaluated one-dimensionally and precisely because it represents a simple substitute for an intrafirm performance of the task. The problems emerge, however, if we recognize that practically all products or goods are complex systems used for complex applications. In principle, they can be described by a vector of characteristics that has a very large number of elements. However, even if all of these potential characteristics are easily discernible by the buyer (which they are not!), the testing of them all is practically impossible. Therefore, they cannot all be "characteristics," that is, properties that are important for the buyer's actual choices. A possible alternative is that the seller integrates k important properties of a good or brand j into a single characteristic (e.g., "basically satisfactory" or "according to present-day standards"). This can be done by defining k minimum standards and then formulating a composite characteristic of the product, namely the conjunctive proposition or metastandard that it satisfies all the individual standards.

This composite characteristic is clearly a "credence characteristic" (Darby and Karni 1973), since it is very costly and probably impossible for any buyer to know all the standards, much less to check whether a specimen of the product is satisfactory with respect to them all. If the buyer has no trust in the seller of a product with many minimum standards, he or she will normally find a more credible seller rather than try to cope with the individual elements of the conjunctive statement.

The fight against complexity by establishing a composite credence characteristic has developed in a piecemeal fashion. The hypothesis that the properties of a product are adequately reflected in one (or a few) abstracted notion(s), is based on earlier trials and errors of the buyer or his or her references. But this process will only lead to relatively stable and usable knowledge provided there is a high degree of credibility concerning the stability of the output of the seller. This credibility is dependent on the credible commitment (and the persuasive efforts) of the seller, but the standards are sometimes enforced by government, by sellers' organizations, and by many interorganizational customs and institutions. This institutional framework has been established partly to cope with earlier violations of the above-mentioned principle of commodity abstraction. The need for establishing the preconditions for making conjunctive statements is probably among the most important factors that have led to the development of a complex set of standards.

The idea of minimum standards suggests why an important characteristic may disappear from the buyers' focus of interest: it is simply transformed from a decision-making parameter to a part of the conjunction of minimum standards, which is normally taken for granted. Actually, this disappearance is part of the typical life cycle of most quality characteristics, and it explains why "key success factors" in a certain industry are changing through time. The quality characteristic life cycle is clearly a market-level phenomenon that presupposes a relatively complex analysis. But a simplified analysis will help to clarify several issues with respect to credence characteristics: In period t a pin is considered as a simple "search good" (Nelson 1970), while period $t + 1$ shows a sudden burst of consumer awareness about, for example, corrosion. The initiative to create this awareness may come from the consumers themselves, but it is more likely that it comes from a seller who has developed a method to make corrosion-resistant pins. We may talk of a subcase of the *innovation* procedure, namely the *dimensional-innovation* procedure. This new situation creates a market process that may end up in different ways: (1) corrosion may disappear from the interest of the buyers (and thus from the characteristics space); (2) a few firms may create a market niche for corrosion-resistant pins; or (3) corrosion resistance may be transformed into a minimum standard that characterizes all types of the product. In the latter case, the interest in standard characteristics and minor price differentials may reemerge as totally dominant issues. However, at a later point of time a new quality characteristic (e.g., handiness and design) may enter into the attention of sellers and buyers, and in this way another quality characteristic life cycle may be started.

This sketch of the quality characteristic life cycle suggests that products have no fixed place in the taxonomic system of information economics (search goods, experience goods, credence goods). The attention of buyers may shift from complex quality characteristics to price differentials in combination with simple search and experience characteristics. But as more and more search and experience characteristics can be taken for granted through a process of standardization, the attention of buyers may then turn to new types of credence qualities. The attention of sellers is also shifting. Characteristics that once were at the center of attention of their quality control systems may later be turned into simple minimum standards, while increasing parts of their resources for quality control and quality improvement may be used in relation to what now appear as key success factors.

The shifts in attention are easy to understand from the viewpoint of Simon's (1982) bounded-rationality approach. In this context the buyer cannot simply add more and more useful characteristics to the specification of the product that he or she wants. Instead, we have to introduce time and complexity in an evolutionary way. Our main problem is to give an account of the apparent contradiction between (1) the limited and more or less constant cognitive capabilities of the individual buyer, and (2) the increasing complexity of many product designs. A simplified solution to this problem is to say that the number of characteristics, n_t, dealt with by the buyer at any point of time, t, is more or less constant over time and, especially, that it is smaller than some cognitive maximum, n^{max}. While the decision-making parameters may be exchanged by others in a later period, the combined minimum standards may (in the present simplified case) be seen to develop in an orderly way: new minimum standards are simply added to the already existing minimum standards. Thus, the number of minimum standards, k_t, increases with time and the conjunctive statement becomes more complex with time. This puts a heavy pressure on the standard-setting and quality control system, which has to cope with a hitherto unrecognized quality property that emerges as an important part of the competitive process and that may end up as a part of the set of minimum standards. The reason why the characteristic was originally latent may, for example, be that the buyers had been unaware that it was not included in the set of minimum standards to a satisfactory degree, or that no seller had succeeded in developing a product that was superior with respect to this characteristic and that was recognized as such by buyers.

As defined here, the k_t-dimensional standard part of the product design gives an ex post description of an evolutionary design trajectory that has successively explored some of the potential characteristics. The sequence by which the potential characteristics are explored reflects a mixture of random events, technological possibilities, and buyers' preference orderings. Typical design trajectories reflect important issues for evolutionary-economic research. Such an evolutionary design trajectory can be related to what Lancaster (1979, 26–29) calls vertical and horizontal differentiation between product designs. A design can be said to be vertically differentiated from (better than) another design if they are identical with respect to all but one standard, and if only one of the designs has a satisfactory performance with respect to the last standard (or is better with respect to a graded quality characteristic). Horizontal differentiation means that the two designs differ in a nonproportionate way with respect to several dimensions; for this reason comparisons are difficult. If each of the two horizontally differentiated designs gives rise to an evolutionary trajectory, we have a simple evolutionary design tree with a single bifurcation. Since each evolutionary design trajectory may be split into two or more branches, a complex evolutionary tree may emerge.

The aggregate-level design trajectories reflect an incremental and cumulative trial-and-error process that explores an immensely complex space of possibilities. The sellers generate new varieties that differ to only a limited extent from their immediate predecessors; the buyers perform the testing of and the selection between the varieties. Such a process may degenerate if all aspects of the preliminary solution are questioned in each period. Therefore, evolutionary design trajectories (and evolutionary design trees) are based on a process of partial standardization. In other words, the partial standardization of the interface between sellers and buyers stabilizes the preliminary results. The emergence of standards of product design allows the seller to exploit economies of scale in production and trade, while the buyer can decrease his or her costs of information about and utilization of the product. But the application of such standards is not unproblematic. Actually, they suggest two connected problems: On the one hand, some of the strongly defended standardized characteristics may hinder the introduction of new dimensions of characteristics. Thus, the evolutionary design trajectory may end up in a lock-in (Arthur 1983, 1993). On the other hand, free riders may be able to exploit the fact that buyers take the standardized part of the design trajectory for granted. The free riders may succeed in selling a product design as equal to the standard quality even if it does not satisfy some of the standardized characteristics. In this way they obtain lower costs than the honorable competitors, but in the long run they undermine the existence of a complex standard. These problems may help to bring Schumpeterian perspectives back into the analysis of the evolution of complex product designs, which in the above argument has tended to become too gradualist.

Summary and Conclusions

The present chapter has suggested several ways in which New Evolutionary Economics may cope with the high level of complexity that characterizes the economic system as a whole, as well as many of its constituent parts. Our method was to make a combination of aspects of Smithian-Marshallian and Schumpeterian approaches to economic evolution—supported by some of the tools of modern evolutionary-economic analysis.

The first task was to make sense of Adam Smith's analysis of the division of labor in relation to the problem of interfirm, vertical specialization by applying a notion of discontinuous innovation. In a neo-Schumpeterian model, specialization and innovation were shown to be closely connected. At the microlevel, vertical specialization appeared to be a way in which a previously unspecialized firm could often increase the returns from its innovation. At a more aggregate level, specialization was shown to be a way of increasing the diffusion of the innovation. But the most interesting result of the (repeated) process of specialization was the emergence of a complex interindustrial system that may serve as a starting point for the discussion of many problems of coordination.

The second task was to deal with the functioning of a highly complex system of interindustrial relationships with respect to innovative performance—which appears to be one of Schumpeter's initial research questions. From the microlevel viewpoint of the individual economic agents, such a system represents an impossible amount of information and an impossibly complex set of alternatives. One partial solution to this problem appears to be the standardization of the quality characteristics of the products delivered between firms. At the same time, this solution helps producers to exploit economies of scale. However, from the microlevel viewpoint of innovative agents, as well as from the macrolevel viewpoint of the development of overall complexity, this solution seems to be more dubious. The problem is that it may undermine the possibilities of relatively easy innovative activities through a close interaction between pairs of firms that have created "broadband" information channels between themselves. The contradiction between the principles of commodity abstraction and innovative linkages appears to be a real one that should be explored further.

The third task was to explore the question of how the emergence of highly complex products can coexist with the tendency to standardize the qualities of the interfirm and interindustrial deliveries of products. That is, we studied the evolution of a single interface between two industries or between an industry and the household sector. The solution was to sketch a model of the evolution of complex product designs, a model with two major constituents. First, the model deals with what may be called the quality characteristic life cycle of a product. If an innovative firm succeeds in drawing attention to an important new quality dimension of a product produced by several firms, then a competitive process starts that often ends because a minimum standard has been established. Second, the model deals with the possible sequence of such minimum standards, which in evolutionary retrospect may be considered the result of a design trajectory in the largely unknown and immensely complex space of possibilities of product specifications. The discussion of the model ends by suggesting evolutionary design trajectories as an area for theoretical and empirical investigation. A research question is, for example, which degree of semipermanent fixing of minimum standards is most supportive for the emergence of complexly adapted products.

The sketches of solutions to the three tasks suggest several kinds of modeling. But the main question is whether such work will help the New

Evolutionary Economics to deal with empirically and politically relevant issues. Indirectly, the paper has answered this question positively, although there is no possibility in the present context of arguing for the different solutions. But the overall tendency in the proposed solutions is clear: they argue for approaching the question of how and to what degree real-life economic evolution has been able to solve major problems about the quality aspects of economic complexity. In this way the chapter suggests that it is time to try to apply the tools of the New Evolutionary Economics (including "population thinking") to problems that show apparent analogies with the problems of evolutionary ecology within biology. Like the biologists of the forties and later, we should develop a "modern evolutionary synthesis" that combines formal and algorithmic analyses of the evolutionary microlevel with theories dealing with macroevolutionary phenomena (Mayr and Provine 1980). Here we need a whole new set of concepts that have some similarities to the concepts of the neo-Darwinian synthesis of evolutionary theory, genetics, and taxonomy—like "isolating mechanisms," "sympatric and allopatric speciation," "founder principle," "gene flow," "isolation," "stabilizing selection," "taxon," and so on.

REFERENCES

Abernathy, William J., and Kim B. Clark. 1985. Innovation: Mapping the Winds of Creative Destruction. *Research Policy* 14:3–22.

———, and James M. Utterback. 1978. Patterns of Industrial Innovation. *Technology Review* 50:2–9.

Andersen, Esben S. 1991. Techno-Economic Paradigms as Typical Interfaces between Producers and Users. *Journal of Evolutionary Economics* 1:119–44.

———. 1994a. *Evolutionary Economics: Post-Schumpeterian Contributions.* London and New York: Pinter.

———. 1994b. The Evolution of Credence Goods: A Transaction Approach to Product Specification and Quality Control. Programme on Market-based Process and Product Innovation in the Food Sector, Aarhus, Aarhus School of Business.

———, and Bengt-Åke Lundvall. 1994. Innovation Systems and Economic Evolution: A Division-of-Labour Approach. Paper presented at the Conference on Evolutionary Economics and Technological Change, Strasbourg, October 6–8, 1994. Department of Business Studies, Aalborg University.

Arthur, W. Brian. 1983. Competing Technologies and Lock In by Historical Events. International Institute for Applied Systems Analysis, Laxenburg.

———. 1993. On Designing Economic Agents that Behave Like Human Agents. *Journal of Evolutionary Economics* 3:1–22.

Coase, Ronald H. 1937. The Nature of the Firm. *Economica* 4:386–405.

Darby, Michael R., and Edi Karni. 1973. Free Competition and the Optimal Amount of Fraud. *Journal of Law and Economics* 16:67–88.

David, Paul A. 1985. Clio and the Economics of QWERTY. *American Economic Review. Papers and Proceedings* 75:332–37.

————. 1987. Some New Standards for the Economics of Standardization in the Information Age. In *Economic Policy and Technological Performance,* ed. P. Dasgupta, and P. Stoneman, 206–39. Cambridge: Cambridge University Press.

Dosi, Giovanni. 1982. Technological Paradigms and Technological Trajectories: A Suggested Interpretation of the Determinants and Directions of Technical Change. *Research Policy* 11:147–62.

————. 1988. Sources, Procedures and Microeconomic Effects of Innovation. *Journal of Economic Literature* 26:1120–71.

Heiner, Ronald A. 1989. The Origin of Predictable Dynamic Behavior. *Journal of Economic Behavior and Organization* 12:233–57.

Hippel, Eric von. 1988. *The Sources of Innovation.* New York and Oxford: Oxford University Press.

Holland, John H., and John H. Miller. 1991. Artificial Adaptive Agents in Economic Theory. *American Economic Review. Papers and Proceedings* 81:365–70.

Lancaster, Kelvin. 1979. *Variety, Equity, and Efficiency: Product Variety in an Industrial Society.* Oxford: Blackwell.

Liebowitz, S. J., and Stephen E. Margolis. 1990. The Fable of the Keys. *Journal of Law and Economics* 33:1–25.

Lundvall, Bengt-Åke. 1985. *Product Innovation and User-Producer Interaction.* Aalborg: Aalborg University Press.

————. 1992. *National Systems of Innovation: Towards a Theory of Innovation and Interactive Learning.* London: Pinter.

Marengo, Luigi. 1992. Coordination and Organizational Learning in the Firm. *Journal of Evolutionary Economics* 2:313–26.

Marshall, Alfred. 1898. Distribution and Exchange. *Economic Journal* 8:37–59.

————. 1919. *Industry and Trade: A Study of Industrial Technique and Business Organization; and their Influences on the Conditions of Various Classes and Nations.* London: Macmillan.

————. 1949. *Principles of Economics: An Introductory Volume.* Basingstoke and London: Macmillan.

Mayr, Ernst, and Wiliam B. Provine, eds. 1980. *The Evolutionary Synthesis: Perspectives on the Unification of Biology.* Cambridge, Mass. and London: Harvard University Press.

Menger, Carl. 1892. On the Origins of Money. *Economic Journal* 2:239–55.

Mowery, David, and Nathan Rosenberg. 1982. The Influence of Market Demand upon Innovation: A Critical Review of some Recent Empirical Studies. In N. Rosenberg, *Inside the Black Box: Technology and Economics,* 193–241. Cambridge: Cambridge University Press.

Nelson, Phillip. 1970. Information and Consumer Behavior. *Journal of Political Economy* 78:311–29.

Nelson, Richard R., and Sidney G. Winter. 1982. *An Evolutionary Theory of Economic Change.* Cambridge, Mass. and London: Belknap Press.

Schumpeter, Joseph A. 1934. *The Theory of Economic Development: An Inquiry into*

Profits, Capital, Credit, Interest and the Business Cycle. London: Oxford University Press.

———. 1939. *Business Cycles: A Theoretical, Historical, and Statistical Analysis of the Capitalist Process*. New York and London: McGraw-Hill.

———. 1954. *History of Economic Analysis*. London: George Allen & Unwin.

Simon, Herbert A. 1981. *The Sciences of the Artificial*. Cambridge, Mass. and London: MIT Press.

———. 1982. *Models of Bounded Rationality*. Vol. 2. Cambridge, Mass. and London: MIT Press.

Smith, Adam. 1976. *An Inquiry into the Nature and Causes of the Wealth of Nations*. Oxford: Clarendon.

Stigler, George J. 1951. The Division of Labour is Limited by the Extent of the Market. *Journal of Political Economy* 59:185–93.

Waldrop, M. Mitchell. 1992. *Complexity: The Emerging Science at the Edge of Order and Chaos*. Harmondsworth: Penguin.

The Quest for Ecological Tax Reform: A Schumpeterian Approach to Public Finance

Jürgen Backhaus

Recent quests for ecological tax reform are difficult to evaluate from an economic point of view, as they typically are based on an interdisciplinary argument drawing on contributions from biology, systems theory, and economics. In order to create a framework for reference and analysis, this chapter sets out Henry George's theory with respect to the natural environment. The environment is shown to be the very broad and potentially productive tax base for George's Single Tax constitution. The tax constitution is shown to be a self-enforcing one, checking public sector growth by linking it to material progress in the economy. Also, the Georgist tax constitution is shown to provide incentives for optimal use of environmental resources in the interest of both present and future generations.

Disregarding the controversial case for a Single Tax for the moment, the remainder of Henry George's framework can very well serve to evaluate ecological taxes in terms of their main objective, that is, to ensure sustainable economic development. The chapter argues that a more convincing case for ecological taxes can be made if that case is based on Georgist precepts.

Introduction

Ecological tax reform is on the political agenda of most Western European countries today. Even the European Community is seeking to introduce ecological charges. Although purely fiscal, that is, revenue seeking, motives certainly explain part of the political impetus, ecological taxes present a specific class of revenue instruments that present political, but, for the purpose of this paper more importantly, also analytical issues different from

---

Paper prepared for presentation at the Fifth Conference of the International J. A. Schumpeter Society on *Economic Dynamism: Analysis and Policy,* Münster, Germany, August 17–20, 1994.

The author should like to thank Nicolaus Tideman for helpful comments.

standard taxes as discussed in public finance textbooks. The differences relate to three issues or dimensions, the combination of which renders ecological taxes as typically proposed an extremely complex and potentially harmful instrument, which may not easily fit into the general tax structure of known fiscal regimes. Under these circumstances, it is sensible to evaluate ecological taxes from the point of view of a simple benchmark alternative, which nevertheless is not inconsistent with the basic purpose of the proposed ecological taxes. Since ecological taxes have a particular purpose, that is, the prudent use of the natural environment in general, and certain energy sources in particular, and since, unlike Pigouvian charges, they are not necessarily supposed to be fiscally infertile (that is, they may very well generate a substantial revenue), the benchmark case can be neither the classical tax raised for purely fiscal purposes nor the Pigouvian charge raised in order to correct for market failure. Rather, a third benchmark needs to be chosen. This is where Henry George comes in. Henry George has many admirers, but only a few scholarly economists would regard him as one of their own. In this chapter, I argue not only that Henry George made a sound contribution to political economy; I also claim that his analysis is eminently significant for environmental economics today, and in particular for an evaluation of current proposals for ecological charges. This evaluation is meant to be critical and constructive.

The subtitle of this essay perhaps requires a word of explanation. Schumpeter is less well known for his public finance contributions (but see Backhaus 1994), his contributions almost never being mentioned in modern public finance textbooks.[1] The strength of Schumpeter's approach to public finance lies in his ability to analyze entire economic systems as they are confronted by complete structures of taxation and public spending. He pioneered what is today called constitutional public finance, and his approach is therefore particularly apt for an analysis of suggested new tax institutions such as ecological taxes.

The chapter starts with a short characterization of the typical case of ecological charges. It highlights the three characteristics mentioned previously. The chapter then proceeds with a short presentation of George's biography and offers a brief characterization of his approach to economic analysis. The next three sections are, in turn, devoted to the focus of his analysis, viz. natural resources, the tax constitution envisaged, and the implications of this tax constitution for environmental policy. The final section offers a few general conclusions on the importance of Georgist thought for environmental economics and more specific conclusions with respect to the case for ecological taxes.

---

1. The only exception to my knowledge is Wagner 1983, 245–47.

The most eloquent case for ecological tax reform has perhaps been made by Ernst Ulrich von Weizsäcker, in various publications (e.g., von Weizsäcker and Jesinghaus 1992). The case is obviously made by natural scientists, and it is made in terms of a natural science argument, not in terms of an economic argument or an argument in the tradition of public finance analysis. CO_2 emissions are contrasted with population growth, and the extreme (sometimes exponential) growth of both of these magnitudes lies at the heart of the case for containing CO_2 emissions in order to achieve a (biologically) sustainable economic growth. The chief variable, then, is also biologically defined, although at first glance it looks like an economic variable.

> CO_2 productivity may (and here we are disregarding the fact that GNP is a measure of turnover, not prosperity) be broadly defined as one unit of GNP per unit of CO_2. (von Weizsäcker and Jesinghaus 1992, p. 10)

The purpose of ecological taxes is then to increase CO_2 productivity, as defined in the preceding.

Although the most important increases in future CO_2 emissions have to be expected outside the highly developed Western and East-Asian countries, the case is still made for employing ecological taxes in those very countries, as they are supposed to be much better equipped to technologically respond to the imposition of such taxes. This is an important assumption about the adaptability of these economies consequent to imposing ecological taxes that will not further be questioned.

Three characteristics of this approach stand out in contrast to the mainstream of received tax theory. The first and most stunning characteristic is the peculiar purpose of ecological taxes. While they are also expected to generate revenues, their most important focus is to reduce the use of particular parts of the natural endowment (in energy sources) with a view to employing them most productively. However, the notion of productivity is not defined as it would have to be in order to make an economic case for the ecological taxes. CO_2 productivity is defined in terms of relating physical inputs to market-valued outputs, that is, the measure is defined in terms of two different dimensions. We then have two purposes with two different dimensions: the achievement of natural resource productivity, as measured by a composite of physical and market-based values. This discongruence results in a third characteristic of ecological tax reform proposals that is inherent in the methodology but troublesome from the public finance point of view. In public finance, a case for a particular tax can be made when the benefit from taxation (typically measured in social welfare terms) exceeds the direct resource cost of the tax plus the excess burden imposed on the economy by raising the tax. All three characteristics are measured in market-based terms, and are therefore easily comparable. Ecological taxes are different in that they cannot easily be subjected to a test in terms of their welfare implications. By necessity, the welfare cost of their imposition in terms of both the welfare foregone as a consequence of reducing natural resource use and the cost imposed as a consequence of administering the tax have to be neglected, as they cannot be measured. The neglect of the welfare costs of environmental taxation that has been built into the interdisciplinary methodology can have serious consequences for their practical applicability. The welfare losses will, of course be experienced by people who, in turn, will express this experience in the political process and thereby conceivably derail the entire ecological program. It is in this sense that the interdisciplinary methodology may result in a utopian program, even though the aspired goals might be utterly realistic. Although the purpose of the ecological tax seems to be very much in congruence with Henry George's objective of obtaining the most prudent use of natural resources, George does not add the additional problem of incongruous dimensions, which somehow makes the case for ecological tax reform difficult to maintain in economic terms. Let us therefore take a look at Henry George's approach in order to determine whether it could yield a more defensible case for ecological tax reform.

Henry George (1839–97) was a self-taught American economist and political writer whose name is commonly associated with the notion of a Single Tax on land. George had worked as a sailor, printer, and newspaperman when he became fascinated with the rapid and uneven development of California and began to probe the economic causes determining the price of land. He undertook this investigation in order to solve "the great enigma of our times," which he held to be "the association of poverty with progress" (1979, p. 10). He systematically developed his insights in his *Progress and Poverty,* first published in 1879.[2] The book began to receive wider attention in Britain in

---

2. *Progress and Poverty* was first published by D. Appleton & Co. in New York in January, 1880. However, in his preface, George refers to the November 1890 edition as already the fourth. His account of the editorial history is as follows:

> This work was written between August, 1877, and March, 1879, and the plates finished by September of that year. Since that time, new illustrations have been given of the correctness of the views herein indicated. . . . But there has been nothing in the criticisms they have received to induce the change or modification of these views—in fact, I have yet to see an objection not answered in advance in the book itself. And except that some verbal errors have been corrected and a preface added, this edition is the same as previous ones. (1979: p. xxx)

A twenty-fifth anniversary edition with a preface by Henry George, Jr. was published in

connection with the Irish question and later made George famous in his own country, too. He spent the last part of his life as a public speaker at home and abroad, and it was George himself who made the Single Tax proposal a political issue in his (unsuccessful) bids for the mayoralty of New York, first in 1886 and then again in 1897.

His place in the history of economic analysis is aptly sketched by Joseph Alois Schumpeter, who writes:

> The points about him that are relevant for a history of analysis are these. He was a self-taught economist, but he was an economist. He acquired most of the knowledge and of the ability to handle an economic argument that he could have acquired by academic training as it then was. In that he differed to his advantage from most men who proffered panaceas. Barring his panacea (the Single Tax) and the phraseology connected with it, he was a very orthodox economist and extremely conservative as to methods. They were those of the English "classics," A. Smith being his particular favorite. . . . Even the panacea—nationalization not of land but of the rent of land by a confiscatory tax—benefitted by his competence as an economist, for he was careful to frame his "remedy" in such a manner as to cause the minimum injury to the efficiency of the private-enterprise economy. . . . The proposal itself . . . is not *economically* unsound, except in that it involves an unwarranted optimism concerning the yield of such a tax. In any case, it should not be put down as nonsense. If Ricardo's vision of economic development had been correct, it would even have been obvious wisdom. (1954, p. 865)

Schumpeter was correct in characterizing George's economic methods as conventional. Yet *Progress and Poverty* is not mainly a work of economic analysis, but a decidedly unorthodox and nonconservative social reformer's treatise. The book was written in order to provide the answer to a practical question of economic policy: How can we design an institutional order in which economic progress goes hand in hand with a reduction of poverty? Schumpeter, like many other critics of George, probably was incorrect in casually dismissing George's assertion about the practical possibilities of George's tax constitution from the standpoint of revenue yield. George may

---

1905. The son explains that the publisher had insisted on George bearing the cost of making the plates, which George did in the shop of a friend in San Francisco. There, "an 'Author's Proof Edition' of five hundred copies was struck off" (1979, p. xxiii). A centenary edition prefaced by his grandaughter, Agnes George de Mille, appeared in 1979 in New York, published by the Robert Schalkenbach Foundation. This 1979 edition contains the aforementioned prefaces, as well as an extensive index and a glossary of terms.

In conclusion, the first edition was San Francisco 1879, the first published edition New York 1880, and the final authorized edition with any changes New York 1890.

very well have been justified in his optimistic estimate of the yield of his Single Tax. This tax is a far cry from the real estate taxes a superficial reader may associate with the term *tax on land*. Rather, as I try to explain on the following pages, George presents us with a comprehensive package of an environmental tax reform that, politically, has teeth. The program is, in fact, a tax constitution so comprehensive and far-reaching that no attribute could be more misleading than the term *conservative*.

As this author reads *Progress and Poverty,* George comes across as a scholar in the best tradition of political economy. His analysis is motivated by a clearly defined social policy problem. George analyzes a problem in order to solve it. He succeeds in designing a solution—his "remedy"—that relies on an institutional reform. That is, George understood the interdependence between economic processes and the institutional order in which they take place. Finally, George went about his analysis in what today would be described as an interdisciplinary approach; that is, the questions he would consider were forced upon him by the subject matter under consideration and not by disciplinary boundaries as they might have developed over time. When, for example, he looks at the effects of his "remedy," he takes them up in this order: effects on (1) production, (2) distribution, (3) individuals and classes, and (4) social organization and social life (George 1979, IX).

The shortest book in *Progress and Poverty,* and at the same time the most important, is book VI, in which George spells out his program. The central chapter, entitled "The True Remedy," barely covers two printed pages, and the solution itself is stated in just one sentence: "We must make land common property" (1979, p. 328).

The explosive potential of his program is wrapped into this rather innocuous sentence. The true extent of the proposal can be discerned by looking at the implementation rule and his concept of land. The implementation rule is stated in equally concise terms: "It is not necessary to confiscate land, it is only necessary to confiscate rent" (1979, p. 405). Finally, there is an underlying principle also worth reporting: "What is necessary for the use of land is not its private ownership, but the security of improvements" (1979, p. 398). This quote also points to Henry George's differentiation between improved and unimproved natural resources and the idea of the unearned improvement. The unearned improvement today turns out to be a hindrance to improvements tomorrow, since the possibility of gaining unearned improvements diverts energies from the very process of improving upon natural resources. In contemporary language, one might say that George tried to prevent wasteful rent-seeking activities by insisting on the principle that the benefits from improvements should accrue to whoever made the improvements, whereas unclaimable externalities should belong to the common domain.

The purpose of the entire reform program, according to this principle, is to encourage the use of land by designing a structure of property rights that allows individuals to reap the benefits of their labor, viz., the improvements, without barring the use of common property resources by others. His definition of land, as spelled out in a chapter appropriately entitled "The Meaning of the Terms" (1979, bk. I chap. 2), is not confined to the surface of the earth. His is an analytical definition based on the concept of factors of production. There are, in George's model, two original factors of production, called *labor* and *land. Capital* is a secondary or derived factor of production, comprising only things "which have resulted from the union of these two original factors of production" (1979, p. 39). Since labor is defined in a more standard way as "all human exertion," including, by the way, *human capital,* because "human powers, whether natural or acquired can never be classed as capital" (1979, p. 39), this leaves land as the all-encompassing category of those original means of production that are not labor. In short, *land* stands for the endowment of natural resources.

Characteristically, George defines land both analytically and by giving a sequence of examples illustrating the basic, comprehensive concept:

> The term land necessarily includes, not merely the surface of the earth as distinguished from the water and the air, but the whole material universe outside of man himself, for it is only by having access to land, from which his very body is drawn, that man can come in contact with or use nature. The term land embraces, in short, all natural materials, forces, and opportunities, and, therefore, nothing that is freely supplied by nature can be properly classed as capital. A fertile field, a rich vein of ore, a falling stream which supplies power, may give to the possessor advantages equivalent to the possession of capital, but to class such things as capital would be to put an end to the distinction between land and capital, and, so far as they relate to each other, to make the two terms meaningless. (1979, p. 38)

It is obvious that, commensurate with technical progress, the window of opportunities granted by nature is pushed ever more open, and in this way the Georgian term *land* assumes an ever more encompassing meaning. Simultaneously, the tax base of the state entrusted with the power of the Single Tax on the rent of natural resources is also broadening in pace with technical progress. While George defines *land* in exactly the same way as we define natural resources today, George differs from most present-day proponents of environmental tax reform by wishing to encourage the prudent use of natural resources, whereas the standard approach today is to design schemes seeking restriction of such use.

Henry George's definition of land clearly also includes natural resources beyond land, and certainly also includes energy resources. The application of the term even goes beyond this, however, in that it can also include collectively used natural resources, such as the oceans, the air, and even the climate. This aspect points to a wider applicability of George's approach than is usually suggested. It is here that the potential for applying George's approach to the issue of ecological taxes comes in.

The twin objective of open access to the use of all opportunities provided by the natural environment while, at the same time, granting full security of all improvements made upon the resource as found in the state of nature requires a partitioning of property rights along this distinction. This partitioning[3] must have struck many of George's contemporaries as unusual or artificial. But, as he tries to show in his long survey of "Property in Land Historically Considered" (1979, bk. VII chap. 4), the partitioning should not be considered that unusual after all. You don't saw a ship in half if it is owned by two men, is his common sense comment.[4]

The partitioning of property rights is effected through the instruments provided by the modern tax state. Owners retain their property titles, but these titles are reinterpreted as designating the accumulated improvements, while the entire land rent remains the common property of the state. The tax state, in this way, becomes a partner in the development of the land, a residual claimant of all the *external benefits* not appropriated by the individual owners. Since this point is very important for understanding the dynamics of the Georgian scheme, let us look at his own statement:

> Every productive enterprise, besides its return to those who undertake it, yields collateral advantages to others. If a man plant[s] a fruit tree, his gain is that he gathers the fruit in its time and season. But in addition to his gain, there is a gain to the whole community. Others than the owner are benefitted by the increased supply of fruit; the birds which it shelters by far and wide; the rain which it helps to attract falls not alone on his field; and, even to the eye which rests upon it from a distance, it brings a sense of beauty. (1979, p. 435)

Assigning the unappropriable positive externalities of production to the state implies that George's concept of common property in natural resources

---

3. For a modern statement, see Eirik G. Furubotn 1979.

4. An anonymous referee has pointed to the difficulty of measuring what part of the "unearned" increment is due to nature, what part to society, and what part to entrepreneurship or effort. Dr. Krabbe and I have dealt with this issue elsewhere and at length. (See Backhaus and Krabbe 1991/1992.)

actually goes even beyond the original state of nature. It likewise includes the accumulated externalities or, put in more accessible terms, the cultural heritage of a country, its vegetation, climate, architecture, landscape, and so on. And, by virtue of the tax scheme, this cultural heritage also forms the tax base that the state is expected to foster.

"Nature laughs at a miser" (1979, p. 436), Henry George tells us in characteristic prose, and he certainly also laughs at too parsimonious a use of the natural endowment. Not only is his tax scheme designed to minimize disincentives (1979, bk. IX chap. 1); stronger still, it coerces people into either making productive use of the resources they possess or else relinquishing them: "If land were taxed to anything near its rental value, no one could afford to hold land that he was not using" (1979, p. 413). As Von Weizsäcker and Jesinghaus (1992) suggest, the purpose of making the most productive use of an environmentally based energy source is completely consistent with Henry George's approach. However, productivity in George's terms is measured in such a way that the economist can make use of it. As a consequence of the tax levied on natural resources, irrespective of whether they are used or not, the user has to make the most productive use of the natural resource made available to him or her, and this use has to be made in such a way that the source is not depleted.

This growth-oriented fiscal constitution, however, has a clever check on public-sector growth built into it. It is here where the seemingly ideological and often misunderstood insistence on the *Single* Tax assumes importance. This feature of the Georgian proposal has always bewildered many commentators, including the public finance expert,[5] Schumpeter. The explanation lies in the systematic unity of George's proposal. George suggested a tax constitution that defines incentives faced by the tax-collecting authorities. George wanted to foster progress by using the power to tax in a very specific way, but he was also suspicious of government bureaucracies (1979, bk. VIII chap. 3). By designating a broad tax base but limiting the power to tax to just one tax— the tax of up to 100 percent on the rent of natural resources—he hoped to find the proper balance. On the one hand, the Georgian tax constitution creates incentives for those in public office to support equitable economic development, which flushes ever-increasing tax revenues into public coffers. The state can grow, unimpeded by any preconceived restrictions, as long as this public-sector growth is financed from the increasing rental value of natural resources. On the other hand, as soon as the value of these rents stagnates or even declines, the state has to curtail its own expenditures. By virtue of the Single

---

5. The welfare theoretic aspects of the Single Tax have been dealt with in a separate paper. See J. Backhaus, "Henry George and the Environment." *Journal of the History of Economic Thought* Vol. 13, no. 1 (Spring 1991): 90–98.

Tax constitution,[6] the state is harnessed into prudent, long-term natural resource use, just as the private sector is coerced into attaining the production possibility frontier. Built into George's reform is a "tax constitution for Leviathan," to use Buchanan's term, a public choice approach *avant-la-lettre*. In one respect, however, George's tax constitution is different from the typical Leviathan tax constitutions that we owe to the modern public-choice school. The limits on the size of the state budget are not predetermined, but determined according to the tasks the state may face. For instance, as natural resource use creates negative externalities, to the same extent it increases the claim of the state on financial resources to mitigate these effects. On the other hand, if nature is left in a pristine state, the state's claim on financial resources is very limited indeed; but so are the state's tasks in such an economy.

Even more surprisingly, this growth-oriented tax constitution clearly deserves the label *environmental* due to its built-in dynamic structure. By an environmental or ecological tax scheme one understands a fiscal constitution that induces economic agents to make optimal use of the environmental resources, neither squandering nor oversparing them. This is precisely what the Georgian system is designed to accomplish. The clue to the conservational feature of the Georgian tax constitution, again, lies in the partitioning of property into (internalizable) improvements (private ownership) and the rent of the resource as such (public ownership). The size of this rent is a positive function of the state of economic development of the surrounding economy and a negative function of the exhaustion of the natural resource. Obviously,[7] the rent on resource use is paid exclusively for the use of the natural endowment and not for its abuse. Depletion of a natural resource requires an additional compensation owed to the community that, in the Georgian model, is represented by the tax state. The state is thereby entitled to two streams of revenues, viz., the rent collected from the use of its natural resources and, more generally, the environment and the compensation for the abuse of those resources. Clearly, George was not a strict conservationist in the sense of sparing nature from any form of depletion. He wanted the ore to be mined and not to be left in the

---

6. This modern language should not lead the reader to suspect that the single tax might be without problems. It is conceivable that the single tax might not be Pareto optimal, notably because of effects on the timing of development. But one should keep in mind that George was making a contribution to economic policy, and not to the theory of optimal taxation. Even in the case of suboptimality just mentioned, one has to keep in mind that these cases require a resort to second-best analysis, and that it is by no means inconceivable that the least distorting tax regime in the world of second-best remains the single tax.

7. The following paragraphs are not literally grounded in Henry George's *Progress and Poverty;* they follow directly from his definition of land as including all natural resources and his definition of improvements. But he did not himself spell out these implications, nor did he spell out details of the requisite implementation rule.

ground (1979, p. 38). Yet, at the same time, he wanted the community to extract a fair compensation for this impairment. While the guarantee of improvements is the core of the state guarantee of private property rights, impairments of common property resources require a compensation. The state can thereby plan the intertemporal use of the natural resource endowment in the interest of overall fiscal concerns.

The operational coherence and conclusivity of the abuse-correction mechanism, of course, needs to be spelled out in institutional detail. Much will depend on the particular tax administration a country has set up. Such an administration will have to be backed by a system of tax courts in such matters when judgment is required as to whether or not an action constitutes an abuse.[8]

This intertemporal dimension embedded in Henry George's tax constitution assumes additional importance when we consider the change or reversal of uses environmental resources may be put to. Keeping the door to change and, notably, changes in resource use wide open is vital for preventing the rise and persistence of monopolies. The Georgian scheme, of course, requires that every resource be put to its most productive use. Again, the dynamic adjustment process is carefully conceived. The most productive use determines the rent of the resource, irrespective of whether the owner operates at the production possibility frontier or not. The automatic adjustment of rents, as a consequence of technical progress, constantly pushes economic agents to make the most judicious use of environmental resources. This implies that the Georgian system actually encourages the reversal and change of production methods involving natural resources. Unlike the present system of private property in land (1979, bk. VII chap. 5), the scheme does not favor the first user at all, since a more valuable use makes it too expensive to continue the first use. The opportunity costs of natural resource use, by virtue of the land rent tax, thus enter into the present user's cost function.

Reversal of use can be a more vexing problem if natural resources are irretrievably devoted to some production (or consumption) process. The safeguard provided by the Georgian system is not a perfect one, since George opposed the conservation of natural resources for their own sake. Yet George provided for two checks. The irreversible use of an environmental resource is checked on the one hand by the compensation payment required for abuse. The amount of this payment, in turn, will increase with the introduction of competing, more valuable uses as a consequence of technical progress. The

---

8. For the United States, one can start thinking about such procedures by looking at the reclamation of land used for surface strip mining. See the U.S. Surface Mining Control and Reclamation Act of 1977, (P.L. 95-87). This law calls for bonding and specifies landscape contours, vegetation, and so on. For Germany, a course of action has been described in Jürgen Backhaus 1988.

second check lies in the communal nature of environmental resources. Since the environment is in the common property, that is, the state domain, a political decision can override private commercial concerns. The political decision will be informed, above all, by the revenue consequences for the Single Tax state, a state that George has placed in the position of guardian of the environment in order to ensure its own fiscal survival.

This chapter sets out Henry George's theory with respect to the natural environment. The environment is shown to be the very broad and potentially productive tax base for George's Single Tax constitution. The tax constitution is shown to be a self-enforcing one, checking public sector growth by linking it to material progress in the economy. Finally, the Georgian tax constitution is shown to provide incentives for an optimal use of environmental resources in the interest of both present and future generations.

In terms of evaluating Henry George's contribution from today's point of view, what stands up is the overall focus on designing a self-enforcing tax constitution on natural resources that is clearly embedded in an otherwise wildly flowering prose that is quite apt to sidetrack the modern reader. As the reader can gauge from the earlier footnote, George was very eager to see his book in print, not because of professional vanity—he was not a professional economist—but because of his feeling that the proposed "remedy" was the cornerstone of an attractive political program. As a politician, Henry George has largely been proven wrong so far. The basic differences, then, between Henry George's approach to ecological taxation and the current proposals for ecological taxes are two: On the one hand, by making use of every type of natural resource taxable, but completely exempting the improvements, Henry George puts forth the most ecologically minded tax system conceivable. Second, by also taxing any type of impairment, Henry George builds in a differential incentive discriminating against energy use that is either nonsustainable or involves the creation of negative externalities.

REFERENCES

Backhaus, J. 1988. Justiziable Bedarfsprüfung im Genehmigungsverfahren: ein Lüneburger Vorschlag. In *Recht und Risiko,* ed. Jörg Finsinger and Jürgen Simon, 94–112. Munich: VVF.
Backhaus, J. 1994. The Concept of the Tax State in Modern Public Finance Analysis. In *Schumpeter in the History of Ideas,* eds. Mark Perlman and Y. Shionoya. Ann Arbor: University of Michigan Press 1994.
Backhaus, J., and J. Krabbe. 1991/1992. Henry George's Contribution to Modern Environmental Policy. *American Journal of Economics and Sociology* 50 (4): 485–501; 51 (1): 1–18.

Furubotn, E. 1979. Codetermination and the Efficient Partitioning of Ownership Rights in the Firm. *Journal of Institutional and Theoretical Economics* 135 (2): 207–15.

George, H. 1979. *Progress and Poverty: An Inquiry into the Causes of Industrial Depressions and of Increase of Want with Increase of Wealth: The Remedy.* New York: Robert Schalkenbach.

Schumpeter, J. 1954. *History of Economic Analysis.* New York: Oxford University Press.

Wagner, R. E. 1983. *Public Finance: Revenues and Expenditures in a Democratic Society.* Boston: Little, Brown and Company.

Weizsäcker, E., von, and J. Jesinghaus. 1992. *Ecological Tax Reform: A Policy Proposal for Sustainable Development.* London: Zed Books.

Part 2. Empirical Studies: Innovation, Growth, and Technological Progress

Part 3. Empirical Studies

Creative Destruction: Turbulence and Economic Growth in Germany

David B. Audretsch and Michael Fritsch

The link between market turbulence and economic growth posited by Joseph S. Schumpeter in 1911 is examined. We address a question of considerable concern to policy makers: Does a relatively stable industry or a turbulent industry structure over time tend to promote or hinder economic growth? While some evidence for the United States provides support for the Schumpeterian Thesis, we find no evidence that economic growth is associated with a turbulent environment in Germany, at least during the late 1980s.

Introduction

In his 1911 classic treatise, *Theorie der wirtschaftlichen Entwicklung*, Joseph A. Schumpeter proposed a theory of *creative destruction*, where new firms with entrepreneurial spirit displace the tired old incumbents, ultimately leading to a higher degree of economic growth. Even in his 1942 classic, *Capitalism, Socialism and Democracy,* Schumpeter still argued that entrenched large corporations tend to resist change, forcing entrepreneurs to start new firms in order to pursue innovative activity:

> The function of entrepreneurs is to reform or revolutionize the pattern of production by exploiting an invention, or more generally, an untried technological possibility for producing a new commodity or producing an old one in a new way. . . . To undertake such new things is difficult and constitutes a distinct economic function, first because they lie outside of the routine tasks which everybody understands, and secondly, because the environment resists in many ways. (1942, 13)

Perhaps it was Schumpeter's earlier work which motivated Alfred Marshall in 1920 to link the degree of turbulence in a market to economic growth.

Revised version of a paper presented at the biannual meetings of the International Joseph Schumpeter Meetings, Münster, Germany, August 1994.

137

Marshall (1920) described the process of industrial evolution where one can observe, ". . . the young trees of the forest as they struggle upwards through the benumbing shade of their older rivals."[1]

Thus, while the public consciousness is generally alarmed by the news of firm closings, Brown et al. (1990, p. 271) warn that

> The concern for policy makers and economic observers should be the rates of birth and long-term job growth and the types of firms experiencing decline and failure. What we may be observing is the regeneration of the economic forest. In manufacturing, the losses are likely the result of large, older firms losing their competitiveness in the world economy. In some instances these firms may be simply going out of business or dramatically reducing their activity. These declining firms are being replaced by a large number of new, small firms. Over the past decade, these new firms have shown a higher rate of employment growth that has led to net long-term job creation. This is the process one hopes to find in a mature forest with a number of large, older trees.

The purpose of this chapter is to shed at least some light on the link between market turbulence and economic growth, as posited by Schumpeter in 1911. We hope to provide insight into a question of considerable concern to policy makers: Does a relatively stable market structure over time tend to promote or hinder economic growth more than one characterized by a high degree of turbulence? By relating turbulence rates to subsequent growth rates across 75 regions in West Germany, we test the hypothesis that economic growth is promoted by a turbulent economic environment. The findings suggest that, despite Schumpeter's theory of *creative destruction,* there does not appear to be any evidence supporting the link between market turbulence and subsequent economic growth for Germany in the 1980s.

The Link between Turbulence and Economic Growth

We define industry turbulence as the simultaneous movement of firms into and out of a market. Based on this definition, a general framework linking turbulence to subsequent economic growth can be developed. Such a framework is based on three hypotheses and sets of observations regarding the nature of

---

1. Building upon Marshall's analogy, Charles Brown et al. (1990, p. 270) observe that, "The health of a forest fluctuates from year to year, depending upon rainfall, temperature, etc. and their effect on the rates of birth, death, growth, and decline. In the long run, the forest will get larger or smaller and more or less dense depending upon how these rates react to the ecological environment, the richness of the soil, disease, management practices, and so forth. And, over extended periods, a forest may (will) need to develop new varieties of trees or new strains of existing vegetation in order to adapt to changing circumstances."

industrial turbulence and its relationship to economic growth. The first of these is drawn from the literature on the product and firm life cycle. Klepper (1992) points out that among the most heavily studied aspects of the life cycle is the evolution of the number of firms. These studies typically find that the entry of new firms is greatest during the formation stage of a new industry, and then levels off and begins to decline, even before the industry has attained the mature phase. What Klepper terms as the shakeout phase, where the greatest number of exits from the industry occur, typically takes place well after the number of new entrants into the industry has declined. The combination of the drop in new entrants along with the high number of exiting firms during the stakeout phase leads to a decline in the total number of firms during the mature and declining stage of the life cycle.

According to the model of the life cycle, the extent of industry turbulence becomes the greatest where the combined numbers of new firms and firms exiting, relative to the existing stock of firms, are the greatest. That is, the degree of turbulence is relatively high in the early stages of the life cycle because the number of new entrants relative to the total stock of firms is high. At the same time, the number of exits tends to be relatively low. As the rate of increase of new firms into the industry starts to fall, the number of firms exiting continues to rise. At some point before the industry reaches maturity—that is, during the growth phase—the combined amount of entry and exit relative to the existing stock of firms, or the extent of turbulence, is highest. During the declining phase the number of exits will tend to be relatively high, but the number of new firms entering the industry will be relatively low.

A second view suggests that the industrial organization of virtually every manufacturing industry can be represented by a conical revolving door, where the top part—which represents the largest enterprise in the industry—revolves much more slowly than the lower part—which represents the small firms in the industry. This evolutionary view comes from a series of studies[2] finding that (1) the likelihood of survival is positively related to firm size and age, and (2) firm growth tends to be negatively related to firm size. According to this view, which is consistent with the most recent empirical evidence, firms are not deterred from entering an industry where scale economies and capital intensity play an important role. Firms may begin at a small and even suboptimal scale of output and then, if merited by subsequent performance, expand. Those firms that are successful grow, while those that are not successful remain small and may be forced to exit from the industry if they remain at

---

2. These studies include Mansfield 1962; Dunne, Roberts, and Samuelson 1988 and 1989; Evans 1987; Phillips and Kirchhoff 1989; Audretsch 1991 and 1995b; Hall 1987; Mata 1994; and Wagner 1992 and 1994.

a suboptimal scale of output.[3] Audretsch (1995b), Audretsch and Mahmood (1995), and Mahmood (1992) find that firms entering industries characterized by a high degree of innovative activity face a greater prospect of growth, but they are burdened with a lower likelihood of survival. In industries where the probability of innovation is greater, more entrepreneurs take a chance that they will succeed by growing into a viably sized enterprise. In such industries, entry may actually tend to be higher while the likelihood of survival is lower. Thus, Audretsch (1995b) finds that the extent of turbulence is actually greater in industries where small firms tend to have the innovative advantage.

The evolutionary view suggests that the greater the degree of technological change and the extent of scale economies in the industry, the faster this conical door will revolve. That is, as the literature suggests, new firms will continue to enter the industry, but the barriers to survival will determine the speed of the door, at least at the small end of the firm-size distribution. This view is consistent with Schumpeter's (1911) theory of creative destruction. According to the theory of creative destruction, firms will enter a market not to equilibrate it by increasing the amount of output, but rather to disequilibrate it by doing something different from the incumbent firms. By doing something different—and presumably better, at least in some cases—new firms will ultimately displace the incumbent enterprises. Thus, turbulence is generated by the entry of new firms and the exit of incumbent ones.

These two theories differ considerably in their emphasis on the source of turbulence, and therefore also in their prediction of whether turbulence promotes or impedes subsequent economic growth. If turbulence, T, is defined as $B + D$, where B represents the number of new firms entering an industry and D represents the combined number of exits from new firms, ENF, and from incumbent firms, EI, then

$$D = ENF + EI \tag{1}$$

In order to compare the extent of turbulence across different-sized units of observations (geographic regions in our case), the degree of turbulence is measured relative to the existing stock of enterprises, which yields the turbulence rate,

$$T = [B + (ENF + EI)]/(B + I) \tag{2}$$

or

$$T = (B + D)/B + I, \tag{3}$$

where I represents the number of incumbent enterprises.

3. See, for example, Siegfried and Evans 1992; Austin and Rosenbaum 1990; and the country studies contained in Geroski and Schwalbach 1991.

According to the life-cycle view of industry evolution, the combined amounts of births and deaths, that is, $B + D$, relative to the stock of firms, $B + I$, will be the greatest at some point of time prior to the growth stage of the industry, where both B and D are large relative to the stock of firms. Notice that in the introductory phase of the life cycle, B tends to be the largest, relative to the existing stock of firms, which is to say the birth rate, $B/(B + I)$, tends to be the highest, while the death rate, $D/(B + I)$ is increasing. However, once the growth stage is attained, the number of entrants begins to drop off. It should be emphasized that this relationship is not exactly one of causality; rather, both phenomena reflect the phase of the underlying technological change in the market, resulting in the simultaneous occurrence of a high net entry rate, $(B - D)/(B + I)$, and industry growth. During the mature and declining stages of the product life cycle, the entry rate drops off sharply while the exit rate rises, leading to a lower net entry rate.

According to the evolutionary view, referred to above as the Schumpeterian view of the market process as an inverted conical door, the turbulence rate will tend to be greatest when the market can be characterized by what Nelson and Winter (1974) termed as an *evolutionary regime*. According to Winter (1984, p. 297), "An entrepreneurial regime is one that is favorable to innovative entry and unfavorable to innovative activity by established firms; a routinized regime is one in which the conditions are the other way around." Under these technological conditions the entry rate of new firms will be relatively high, but as Audretsch (1991 and 1995a) and Audretsch and Mahmood (1995) found, so will be their propensity to exit, rendering high rates of both B and *ENF* relative to $(B + I)$. According to Schumpeter's 1911 theory, creative destruction should lead to subsequent economic growth through an injection of innovative activity, leading to superior products and methods of production.

The link between market turbulence and subsequent economic growth has remained virtually unexplored. One reason for such a paucity of studies is undoubtedly the lack of longitudinal data sets, hindering the requisite measurement for examining aspects of industry evolution. In one of the few empirical studies linking industry turbulence to economic growth, Reynolds and Maki (1991) found that employment growth in U.S. regions tends to be greater where the degree of turbulence is higher. Their study was among the first to provide at least some support for the Schumpeterian thesis of creative destruction.

Measurement

The database identifying the principle components of industry turbulence, new business start-ups, and exits was compiled from the social insurance statistics in the Federal Republic of Germany. These social insurance statistics are collected for individuals. Each record in the database identifies the establishment at which an individual is employed.[4] The start-up of a new firm is recorded when a new establishment identification appears in the database, which generally indicates the birth of a new enterprise.

Results

There are three main components of market dynamics—new-firm start-ups, exit, and turbulence (start-ups plus exits). Because the 75 regions vary in terms of size, comparing the absolute number of, say, new-firm start-ups across regions is misleading, since larger regions would be expected to have more start-up activity than smaller regions. As we show in our 1994 paper, there are two main methods for standardization. Under the ecological approach, the birth rate is measured as the number of new establishments divided by the total number of establishments in existence. Under the labor market approach the entry rate is measured as the number of new establishments divided by the number of workers in the region. While the ecological approach is particularly prevalent in the industrial organization literature, where empirical studies have attempted to explain why the degree of entry varies so much across product markets, the labor market approach has a particular theoretical appeal, in that it is based on the theory of entrepreneurial choice proposed by Frank Knight (1921). That is, each new firm is started by someone. The labor market approach implicitly assumes that the entrepreneur starting a new business is in the same labor market within which that new firm operates. It should be pointed out that the labor market approach does not assume away the phenomenon of cross-market worker mobility. This approach recognizes that labor is mobile, in terms of both spatial and product markets. However, it is assumed that some experience as an employee in the market has been gained before starting a new business.[5]

Between 1986 and 1989 there were between 125,000 and 130,000 new establishments registered annually, which represents a birth rate of between 8 and 10 percent. The birth rate in the service sector of between 9 and 11 per-

---

4. It should be noted that neither the name of the individual nor the name of the establishment can be identified. For more details describing the database, see Fritsch 1992; Fritsch, König, and Weißhuhn 1993.

5. In the product market dimension, this assumption is probably more accurate in manufacturing industries and less valid in nonmanufacturing sectors, whereas in regional markets it is more likely to hold for nonmanufacturing than for manufacturing. Of course, the validity of this assumption clearly depends upon the degree to which markets, along either a product or a spatial dimension, are delineated. Clearly, the more aggregated the market, the more likely such an assumption is to hold. In any case, the labor market approach has the attractive property that there is a clear lower bound of 0.00 and a clear upper bound of 1.00, which would represent the extreme (and absurd) case where every worker within a labor market has started his/her own firm.

cent was considerably higher than that in manufacturing, which was between 5 and 6 percent.[6] The exit rates tend to be highly correlated with the birth rates. One reason for this high correlation may be the high propensity for new start-ups to exit from the industry within a short period subsequent to being established. A different reason may be that those new businesses that are able to survive ultimately end up displacing less efficient incumbent businesses. In any case, those regions that experienced a particularly high birth rate in one year also experienced a high start-up rate in subsequent years. That is, variations in the birth and exit rates seem to be more associated with region-specific characteristics than with time-specific characteristics.

In order to identify why the birth rates vary so greatly across regions, we estimate a regression model where the dependent variable is the birth rate in a region between 1986 and 1989, using the ecological method to measure the birth rate, or the number of new establishments divided by the total number of establishments existing in the region in 1987. As Krugman (1991) argues, positive externalities may exist among businesses within a specific region. That is, the demand and supply factors may spill over from one business to another within a region, increasing the attractiveness of starting a new business in the region where such spillovers are the greatest.

One of the central supply factors may be the existence of unemployed workers (Storey 1991). That unemployed workers constitute an important source of entrepreneurs and also a source of labor inputs for entrepreneurs derives from Knight's (1921, p. 273) theory of entrepreneurial choice:

> The laborer asks what he thinks the entrepreneur will be able to pay, and in any case will not accept less than he can get from some other entrepreneur, or by turning entrepreneur himself. In the same way the entrepreneur offers to any laborer what he thinks he must in order to secure his services, and in any case not more than he thinks the laborer will actually be worth to him, keeping in mind what he can get by turning laborer himself.

That is, there are two reasons to hypothesize that as unemployment rates increase, the expected value of employment decreases. First, the likelihood of being employed decreases. And second, the actual wage, even if employment is attained or maintained, generally decreases along with increases in the unemployment rate. At the same time, the cost of hiring labor inputs will generally decrease as unemployment rises. Thus, the expected return from starting a new business relative to that from employment would be expected to rise along with unemployment.

---

6. Well over half of all new establishments were registered in densely populated regions and only one-seventh of the new establishments were registered in a peripheral region.

A high level of human capital and skilled labor in the labor force increases the potential supply of entrepreneurs for two reasons. First, skilled workers with high levels of human capital are more likely to possess the competencies that facilitate shifting from being employed by a firm to starting a new firm. Second, a large pool of skilled workers may provide a key source of inputs needed to work in new firms.

Economic growth within the region is an important factor influencing the start-up of new businesses. The profit opportunities for entrepreneurs are created largely, although not exclusively, from increases in economic growth. Thus, start-up activity should be positively associated with regions experiencing high economic growth. Finally, start-up activity would be expected to be greater in highly populated areas than in areas with a low population density. One reason for this is that the infrastructure of services and inputs is more developed in regions that are more densely populated. As Krugman (1991, 484) argues,

> The concentration of several firms in a single location offers a pooled labor market for workers with industry-specific skills, ensuring both a lower probability of unemployment and a lower probability of labor shortage. Second, localized industries can support the production of nontradable specialized inputs. Third, informational spillovers can give clustered firms a better production function than isolated producers.

A slightly different interpretation of Krugman's theory is that the transactions cost of starting and dissolving a business are lower in more densely populated areas. These are referred to as localization and urbanization economies in the regional economics literature.

Table 1 shows the regression results explaining the birth rates over the period 1986–89. Both the 1985 unemployment rate and the change in the unemployment rate between 1984 and 1986 have a positive influence on birth rates. Similarly, both the 1985 population density (measured as a square root) and the population growth between 1980 and 1985 have a positive impact on birth rates. This is certainty consistent with the theory linking agglomerations to higher start-up rates.

The 1985 share of the labor force accounted for by unskilled (and semi-skilled) workers has a negative coefficient, suggesting that new firms have a higher propensity for locating in regions where workers tend to be highly skilled than in those regions comprised mainly of unskilled workers. This is also consistent with the theory that the externalities associated with labor market pooling and information spillovers are more likely to play an important role for highly skilled workers than for unskilled workers.

Similarly, birth rates tend to be higher in regions where the 1985 gross

TABLE 1. Regressions Explaining Birth Rates 1986–89

	All Sectors	Manufacturing Industry	Services
Unemployment rate 1985	0.261*	0.325	0.073**
	(2.61)	(2.80)	(0.58)
Change in number of unemployed 1984–86 (%)	0.364	0.259*	0.307*
	(3.33)	(2.04)	(2.23)
Share of unskilled and semiskilled workers 1985	−0.163**	−0.223*	−0.171**
	(1.95)	(2.31)	(1.63)
Average firm size 1985	0.213**	0.196**	0.481
	(1.84)	(1.46)	(3.30)
Population density 1985 (squared)	0.344	0.298*	0.227**
	(3.40)	(2.54)	(1.79)
Gross value added per inhabitant 1985	0.213*	0.128**	0.052**
	(2.25)	(1.16)	(0.44)
Population development 1980–85	0.259	0.183**	0.435
	(2.94)	(1.78)	(3.91)
R^{2adj}	0.669	0.552	0.473
F value	22.32	14.03	10.48

Note: Standardized regression coefficients are given (t-values in parentheses).
*Statistically nonsignificant at the 1% level.
**Statistically nonsignificant at the 5% level.
All other coefficients are significant at the 1% level.

value added per person is greater. This is consistent with the notion that new economic activity tends to locate in those regions where production convexities yield the greatest returns to that activity.

Inclusion of the mean establishment size controls for the bias inherent in the ecological measure of birth rates. The greater the mean establishment size, the fewer the number of establishments for any given workforce size. Thus, the calculated birth rates tend to be systematically higher for those regions where mean establishment size is relatively high than the other explanatory variables included in the regression equations would predict.

It should be noted that there are considerable variations across sectors. For example, the unemployment rate apparently exerts no significant effect on birth rates in services, while a positive relationship emerges for manufacturing, as it does for all sectors taken together. Similarly, the impact of population growth is apparently greater in the service sector than in manufacturing.[7]

---

7. Two major differences emerge when the labor market approach for measuring the birth rates is substituted for the ecological approach. Probably the most striking difference is that the coefficients of the unemployment rate are negative, suggesting that higher unemployment is associated with lower, not higher, birth rates (although the coefficient for the regression using all sectors of the economy cannot be considered statistically significant). The second major differ-

TABLE 2.   Regressions Explaining Exit Rates of Incumbent Establishments in 1986

	All Sectors		Manufacturing Industry		Services	
	(1)	(2)	(3)	(4)	(5)	(6)
Unemployment rate 1985	0.402 (4.33)	0.508 (6.28)	0.434 (4.10)	0.502 (5.57)	0.387 (3.72)	0.440 (4.93)
Change in number of unemployed 1984–86 (%)	0.273 (2.88)	—	0.202** (1.88)	—	0.122** (1.15)	—
Share of unskilled and semiskilled workers 1985	—	−0.179* (2.20)	—	−0.178** (1.96)	—	−0.061** (0.68)
Population density 1985 (squared)	0.426 (5.41)	0.465 (5.92)	0.327 (3.65)	0.353 (4.04)	0.489 (5.55)	0.508 (5.88)
R^{2adj}	0.567	0.547	0.437	0.450	0.458	0.451
F^{value}	33.29	30.79	20.17	20.37	21.81	21.26

Note: Standardized regression coefficients are given (*t*-values in parentheses).
*Statistically nonsignificant at the 1% level.
**Statistically nonsignificant at the 5% level.
All other coefficients are significant at the 1% level.

The regression results for the 1986 exit rates of incumbent establish-ments are shown in table 2. The propensity of incumbent businesses to exit out of the market is clearly higher in those regions experiencing a higher level of unemployment, as well as in those experiencing greater increases in the unemployment rate. Exit rates also tend to be systematically greater in densely populated regions than in peripheral regions.

What impact do the various components of market dynamics have on subsequent economic growth? Does a greater degree of market turbulence lead to higher or lower growth rates? To shed some light on the relationship between the components of market dynamics comprising industry turbulence

---

ence is that the sign of the coefficient for mean establishment size is negative for the labor market approach, but positive for the ecological approach. This discrepancy can be reconciled by the evidence suggesting that the propensity to start a business is greater for workers with experience in a smaller firm than for those with experience in a large firm. However, the bias inherent under the ecological approach leads to an understatement of start-up activity in regions where the mean establishment size is relatively low, and to an overstatement in regions where it is relatively high. This bias more than offsets the differential in the propensity for a worker to become an entrepre-neur between large and small establishments.

TABLE 3. Correlation Coefficients for the Relationship between Components of Market Dynamics in 1986 and Employment Growth (all sectors)

	Employment Growth				
	1986–87	1987–88	1988–89	1989–90	1986–90
Births	−0.204	−0.044	−0.112	−0.285	−0.224
	(0.079)	(0.707)	(0.339)	(0.013)	(0.053)
	−0.335	−0.186	−0.219	−0.364	−0.401
	(0.003)	(0.110)	(0.059)	(0.001)	(0.000)
Exits (total)	−0.261	−0.069	−0.067	−0.257	−0.228
	(0.024)	(0.554)	(0.567)	(0.026)	(0.049)
	−0.429	−0.307	−0.382	−0.460	−0.530
	(0.000)	(0.007)	(0.001)	(0.000)	(0.000)
Exits of incumbent firms	−0.347	−0.229	−0.212	−0.348	−0.387
	(0.002)	(0.048)	(0.068)	(0.002)	(0.001)
	−0.464	−0.419	−0.435	−0.446	−0.571
	(0.000)	(0.000)	(0.000)	(0.000)	(0.000)
Exits of new firms	−0.166	0.046	0.038	−0.160	−0.091
	(0.154)	(0.697)	(0.746)	(0.169)	(0.439)
	−0.345	−0.189	−0.293	−0.403	−0.428
	(0.002)	(0.105)	(0.011)	(0.000)	(0.000)
Turbulence	−0.250	−0.062	−0.092	−0.286	−0.240
	(0.031)	(0.598)	(0.432)	(0.013)	(0.038)
	−0.411	−0.269	−0.329	−0.443	−0.502
	(0.000)	(0.020)	(0.004)	(0.000)	(0.000)
Net market entry	0.158	0.055	−0.033	0.052	0.082
	(0.176)	(0.641)	(0.777)	(0.658)	(0.486)
	0.261	0.253	0.331	0.273	0.340
	(0.024)	(0.028)	(0.004)	(0.018)	(0.003)

Note: Upper rows refer to all firms; lower rows refer to firms with fewer than 1,000 employees in 1986. Numbers in parentheses give error ratio.

and economic growth, table 3 lists the simple correlation coefficients between these various components of market dynamics measured in 1986 and employment growth over subsequent periods. The results suggest that greater birth rates as well as greater death rates tends to be associated with lower growth rates in the subsequent years. In particular, the exit rate of incumbent business tends to be especially negatively related to subsequent growth. By contrast, the link between the exit rate of new businesses and subsequent growth is considerably weaker. Perhaps most striking is the negative and, in certain cases highly significant, correlation between the turbulence rate and subsequent economic growth. This provides clear evidence that higher growth rates in Germany are associated with less and not more turbulence.

Conclusions

Does creative destruction, as captured by the extent of market turbulence, lead to higher growth, as posited by Joseph Schumpeter in 1911? While some preliminary evidence for the United States does, in fact, provide support for the Schumpeterian thesis, we find no evidence that economic growth is associated with a turbulent environment, at least for the case of West Germany during the late 1980s. In fact, in both the manufacturing and the service sectors, a high rate of turbulence in a region tends to lead to a lower and not a higher rate of growth. This negative relationship is attributable to the fact that the underlying components—the birth and death rates—are both negatively related to subsequent economic growth. That is, those areas with higher birth rates tend to experience lower growth rates in subsequent years. Most strikingly, the same is true for the death rates. That is, the regions experiencing higher death rates also tend to experience lower growth rates in subsequent years.

One possible explanation for the disparity in results between the United States and Germany may lie in the role that innovative activity, and therefore the ability of new firms to ultimately displace the incumbent enterprises, plays in new-firm start-ups. In the 1990 study by Acs and Audretsch, a central finding was that small firms, in fact, have the innovative advantage in a number of manufacturing industries, particularly in high-technology industries. This may be responsible for the increased degree of turbulence characterizing American industry. For example, midway through this century, it took two decades—the 1950s and 1960s—for one-third of the Fortune 500 firms to be replaced by new firms. In the 1970s it took eleven years. And in the 1980s one-third of the Fortune 500 were replaced by new firms within just five years (Audretsch 1995b). It may be that innovative activity does not play the same role in the German *Mittelstand* as it does for small firms in the United States. To the degree that this is true, it may be that the Schumpeterian thesis implicit in his theory of *creative destruction* holds only when entrepreneurial activity is channeled into small firms. Given the stubborn persistence of high unemployment Germany and public debate about *Standort Deutschland,* if this was not the case in the 1980s, it had better become the case in the 1990s.

REFERENCES

Acs, Zoltan J., and David B. Audretsch. 1990. *Innovation and Small Firms.* Cambridge, MA: MIT Press.
Audretsch, David B. 1991. New-Firm Survival and the Technological Regime. *Review of Economics and Statistics* 73, no. 3: 441–50.

Audretsch, David B. 1995a. Innovation, Survival and Growth. *International Journal of Industrial Organization* 13: 440–57.

Audretsch, David B. 1995b. *Innovation and Industry Evolution.* Cambridge, MA: MIT Press.

Audretsch, David B., and Michael Fritsch. 1994. The Geography of Firm Births in Germany. *Regional Studies* 28, no. 4 (June): 359–65.

Audretsch, David B., and Talat Mahmood. 1995. New Firm Survival: New Results Using a Hazard Function. *Review of Economics and Statistics* 77, no. 1 (February): 97–103.

Austin, John S., and David I. Rosenbaum. 1990. The Determinants of Entry and Exit Rates into U.S. Manufacturing Industries. *Review of Industrial Organization* 5, no. 2 (Summer): 211–23.

Brown, Charles, Judith Connor, Steven Heeringa, and John Jackson. 1990. Studying Small Businesses with the Michigan Employment Security Commission Longitudinal Data Base. *Small Business Economics* 2, no. 4: 261–78.

Dunne, Timothy, Mark J. Roberts, and Larry Samuelson. 1988. Patterns of Firm Entry and Exit in U.S. Manufacturing Industries. *Rand Journal of Economics* 19, no. 4: 495–515.

Dunne, Timothy, Mark J. Roberts, and Larry Samuelson. 1989. The Growth and Failure of U.S. Manufacturing Plants. *Quarterly Journal of Economics* 104, no. 4: 671–98.

Evans, David S. 1987. Tests of Alternative Theories of Firm Growth. *Journal of Political Economy* 95, no. 4: 6657–74.

Fritsch, Michael. 1992. Regional Differences in New Firm Foundation: Evidence from West Germany. *Regional Studies* 26, no. 3: 233–41.

Fritsch, Michael, A. König, and G. Weißhuhn. 1993. Die Beschäftigtenstatistik als Betriebspanel-Ansatz, Probleme und Analysepotentiale. In *Firmenpanelstudien in Deutschland—Konzeptionelle Überlegungen und empirische Analysen,* ed. U. Hochmuth and J. Wagner. Tübingen: Tübinger Volkswirtschaftliche Schriften, Francke.

Geroski, Paul A., and Joachim Schwalbach, eds. 1991. *Entry and Market Contestability: An International Comparison.* Oxford: Basil Blackwell.

Gort, Michael, and Steven Klepper. 1982. Time Paths in the Diffusion of Product Innovations. *Economic Journal* 92, no. 3: 630–53.

Hall, Bronwyn H. 1987. The Relationship between Firm Size and Firm Growth in the U.S. Manufacturing Sector. *Journal of Industrial Economics* 35:583–605.

Klepper, Steven. 1992. Entry, Exit, Growth, and Innovation over the Product Life Cycle. Presented at the Conference on Market Processes and Corporate Networks, Wissenschaftszentrum für Sozialforschung, Berlin, November 1992.

Klepper, Steven, and Elizabeth Graddy. 1990. The Evolution of New Industries and the Determinants of Market Structure. *Rand Journal of Economics* 21, no. 1: 27–44.

Knight, F. H. 1921. *Risk, Uncertainty and Profit.* New York: Houghton Mifflin.

Krugman, Paul. 1991. *Geography and Trade.* Cambridge, MA: MIT Press.

Mahmood, Talat. 1992. Does the Hazard Rate of New Plants Very Between High- and Low-Tech Industries? *Small Business Economics* 4, no. 3 (September): 201–10.

Mansfield, Edwin. 1962. Entry, Gibrat's Law, Innovation, and the Growth of Firms. *American Economic Review* 52, no. 5: 1023–51.

Marshall, Alfred. 1920. *Principles of Economics.* 8th ed. London: Macmillan.

Mata, José. 1994. Firm Growth during Infancy. *Small Business Economics* 5, no. 1: 27–40.

Nelson, Richard R., and Sidney G. Winter. 1974. Neoclassical vs. Evolutionary Theories of Economic Growth: Critique and Prospectus. *Economic Journal* 84(December): 886–905.

Nelson, Richard R., and Sidney G. Winter. 1982. *An Evolutionary Theory of Economic Change.* Cambridge, MA: Harvard University Press.

Phillips, Bruce D., and Bruce A. Kirchhoff. 1989. Formation, Growth and Survival: Small Firm Dynamics in the U.S. Economy. *Small Business Economics* 1, no. 1: 65–74.

Reynolds, Paul D., and Wilbur Maki. 1991. Regional Characteristics Affecting Business Growth: Assessing Strategies for Promoting Regional Economic Well-Being. Project report submitted to the Rural Poverty and Resource Program, The Ford Foundation, Grant 900-013.

Schumpeter, Joseph A. 1911. *Theorie der wirtschaftlichen Entwicklung, Eine Untersuchung über Unternehmergewinn, Kapital, Kredit, Zins and den Konjunkturzyklus.* Berlin: Duncker and Humblot.

Schumpeter, Joseph A. 1934. *The Theory of Economic Development.* Cambridge, MA: Harvard University Press.

Schumpeter, Joseph A. 1942. *Capitalism, Socialism and Democracy.* New York: Harper and Row.

Siegfried, John J., and Laurie Beth Evans. 1992. Entry and Exit in United States Manufacturing Industries from 1977 to 1982. In *Empirical Studies in Industrial Organization: Essays in Honor of Leonard W. Weiss,* ed. David B. Audretsch and John J. Siegfried, 253–74. Boston: Kluwer Academic Publishers.

Storey, David J. 1991. The Birth of New Firms—Does Unemployment Matter?: A Review of the Evidence. *Small Business Economics* 3, no. 3 (September): 167–78.

Wagner, Joachim. 1992. Firm Size, Firm Growth, and Persistence of Chance: Testing Gibrat's Law with Establishment Data from Lower Saxony, 1978–1989. *Small Business Economics* 4, no. 2 (June): 125–31.

Wagner, Joachim. 1994. Small-Firm Entry in Manufacturing Industries. *Small Business Economics* 6, no. 3: 211–24.

Williamson, Oliver E. 1975. *Markets and Hierarchies: Antitrust Analysis and Implications.* New York: Free Press.

Winter, Sidney G. 1984. Schumpeterian Competition in Alternative Technological Regimes. *Journal of Economic Behavior and Organization* 5 (Sept.–Dec.): 287–320.

Technical Change and Firm Growth: "Creative Destruction" in the Fortune List, 1963–87

Roberto Simonetti

The changes among the top 300 American industrial corporations between 1963 and 1987 are examined by identifying the dynamics at the industry and the firm level. Technological change was a powerful actor of change at both levels, as it created opportunities that only some firms seized, especially in technologically dynamic industries. Mergers were also an important cause of turbulence, especially in declining industries.

Capitalism as a Process of Creative Destruction

In this chapter, the changes that occurred between 1963 and 1987 among the top 300 firms in the American manufacturing sector are analyzed, adopting a Schumpeterian theoretical framework. Already in 1943 Schumpeter wrote that

> Capitalism . . . is by nature a form or method of economic change and not only never is but never can be stationary . . . [and] . . . the fundamental impulse that sets and keeps the capitalist engine in motion comes from the new consumers' goods, the new methods of production or transportation, the new markets, the new forms of industrial organization that capitalist enterprise creates. . . . The opening up of new markets, foreign or domestic, and the organizational development from the craft shop and factory to such concerns as U.S. Steel illustrates the same process of industrial mutation—if I may use this biological term—that incessantly revolutionizes the economic structure *from within,* incessantly destroying the old one, incessantly creating a new one. This process of Creative Destruction is the essential fact about Capitalism. (Schumpeter 1943, 82–83)

These lines contain three important points that have recently been taken up by evolutionary economists. First, change is seen as the main feature of capitalism, and it is generated endogenously within the system. Second, technological change is the engine that "keeps the capitalist engine in motion." Third, the capitalist enterprise is not an atomistic structure that mechanically allocates resources according to precise criteria, but is rather the major active actor in the process of economic change as it creates new markets through the introduction of innovations and new forms of organization in order to cope with a changing environment.

In the following years, however, scholars in the field of industrial organization largely neglected the three points highlighted by Schumpeter, and concentrated instead on issues concerning the optimal allocation of resources in a static environment, in which change was considered to be exogenous and marginal to the analysis. Since Bain's (1956) seminal work, one of the main issues in industrial organization has been the analysis of the relationship between market structure, usually measured by the degree of sellers' concentration, and profitability. The underlying rationale is that leading firms in concentrated industries collude and set the price above the level that generates normal profits, and therefore enjoy rents that distort the optimal allocation of resources. In this framework changes are only exogenous, and large firms are seen as a potential threat to economic efficiency.

Inspired by the structure-conduct-performance paradigm, most of the previous studies analyzing the turnover and mobility of the top firms in the American manufacturing sector were concerned with the trend in the overall industrial concentration, and, more generally, with the state of competition.[1] The main aim of these studies was to measure whether the overall level of concentration at the top of the manufacturing sector was increasing and large firms were gaining more power, with negative consequences for the degree of competitiveness, and therefore efficiency, in the economy. Most of the studies focused on the changes among the largest firms, either neglecting industry trends and specificities or treating them as a marginal phenomenon. Stigler, however, observed that "the statistical universe of the 100 or 200 largest corporations is inappropriate to studies of monopoly and competition," and that that type of analysis must "be applied on a correct industry basis" (1956, 35).

More recently, the importance of Schumpeter's thought has been widely recognized and two studies have related the changes among the largest industrial corporations to the process of creative destruction. In April 1992, the *Economist* published a leader showing the changes that have occurred in the top 100 places on the *Fortune* list[2] in the last 30 years: only 27 firms have survived in the top positions of the list (Economist 1992). Following an early Schumpeterian approach, the *Economist* highlighted how the new chal-

---

1. See Kaplan 1954; Friedland 1957; Collins and Preston 1961; and Edwards 1975.

2. Every year *Fortune* publishes a list of the 500 largest U.S. industrial corporations, ranked by sales.

lengers, such as Microsoft, engage in new technologically advanced activities, while some old giants, such as General Motors, find it hard to still be profitable. Before the *Economist*, Kirchoff (1990) analyzed the turnover among the 500 largest industrial firms included in the COMPUSTAT database, adopting a Schumpeterian framework.[3]

The analysis carried out in this chapter will differ from the previous ones in two respects. First, the theoretical framework adopted will be, instead of the structure-conduct-performance paradigm, a Schumpeterian approach that stresses the importance of technical and institutional change in the long-run performance of the firms. Second, interindustry trends will not be treated as a factor to control in order to measure the trend in the overall concentration with more precision. Differences between industries will be a major focus of the analysis.

The next section will outline the theoretical background of the empirical analysis. In the third section, the overall turnover in the top 300 places of the Fortune list from 1963 to 1987 will be analyzed in detail, identifying the reasons why some firms disappeared and the origins of the new firms. The overall growth of the surviving firms will also be split into two components: industry trends and changes in market shares. In the fourth section, the analysis of the mobility and turnover will be repeated for each industry, in order to highlight industrial specificities. Intraindustry trends will be studied in the fifth section, stressing the influence of technical change on the firms within their industries.

The Theoretical Background

Schumpeter Mark I and II

Solow's (1957) seminal article revealed the importance of technical change in the process of economic growth. Since then, many scholars have studied in greater detail the relationship between technology and economics, and the work of Joseph Schumpeter (1934, 1942) has been reevaluated. Schumpeter found it hard to reconcile the concept of equilibrium, central in the orthodox economic theory, with the changes observed in the real world. In his early work, often referred to as Schumpeter mark I, he emphasized the role of small firms as sources of innovation and, therefore, of economic dynamism. The flexible structure of small firms, coupled with the presence of an entrepreneur, was seen as an advantage against bureaucratic large firms in the adaptation to a changing environment, the introduction of new products and processes, and the exploitation of new markets. The position taken by the *Economist* can be

---

3. Scherer and Ross (1990) also emphasize the emergence of new technologies as an important factor for the changes among the largest manufacturing firms.

defined as early Schumpeterian. Emphasis is placed on the emergence of new firms that exploit radical new technologies, while old giants, such as General Motors and even IBM, seem doomed to an unavoidable decline.

In his late work, however, Schumpeter recognized that large firms are a very important source of innovation in the economy (Schumpeter mark II). Through their institutionalized R&D laboratories, large firms exploit economies of scale in the innovation process, and are "the most powerful engine of progress" (Schumpeter 1942). Precisely because of the importance of large companies in the introduction of innovation, Schumpeter even argued that a concentrated market structure would be more efficient than perfect competition in the long run.

The work of Chandler shares common features with the position of the late Schumpeter. In his recent work (Chandler 1990) he found consistent stability among the top 200 firms in the USA, Britain, and Germany throughout this century. Chandler argued that firms that invest sufficiently and early in new fast-growing radical technologies gain dynamic advantages, arising from economies of scale and scope, that give them the possibility of leading their industries for a long time. Through their innovative activities, in addition, many large firms are able to diversify into new promising markets and maintain an above-average performance over time.

Firm Size and Innovation in Different Technological Regimes

Many empirical studies have tested the "Schumpeterian hypothesis," that is, whether a concentrated market structure and large firm size are more conducive to innovation. The results vary according to the technological indicator used, and it appears that, on the one hand, large firms are a substantial source of innovation through their R&D activities, while, on the other hand, small firms have often been pioneers in the introduction of radical new technologies.[4] Thus, the question "do small firms innovate more or less than large firms?" neglects the different nature of innovative activity across industries and firm sizes. Research in the last decade has taken into account the fact that technical change is heterogeneous, and important advances in the understanding of the nature of technology have been achieved. The notion of technological regime, introduced by Nelson and Winter (1982), has offered an important theoretical tool for understanding the sources of innovation and the effects of technological change on the evolution of industries. The concept of technological regime, further elaborated on by Winter in 1984, has also been used in recent empirical studies (see Acs and Audretsch 1990).

---

4. For a review, see Scherer and Ross 1990, chap. 17.

Winter identifies two technological regimes, entrepreneurial and routinized, that he associates with the thought of the early (mark I) and the late (mark II) Schumpeter. In routinized technological regimes, where technological progress is cumulative in nature, the capabilities accumulated over time by established firms through learning-by-doing provide them with a competitive advantage against new entrants (Pavitt 1991). Chandler has shown that in many cases large firms have exploited the capabilities accumulated in production, technology, marketing, and management in order to enter new markets successfully, as IBM and Burroughs did at the dawn of the computer industry. However, in entrepreneurial technological regimes, where some important sources of innovation lie outside the boundaries of the firms, some new firms are able to successfully exploit the introduction of radical innovations in fast-growing markets, and enjoy formidable growth rates, as the recent examples of Microsoft, Intel, and Compaq testify. Industries with entrepreneurial regimes show higher rates of growth associated with fast technical change, higher mobility of market shares, and higher rates of entry (Winter 1984; Acs and Audretsch 1990; Jovanovich 1982; and Malerba and Orsenigo 1993).

The *Economist*'s finding that almost three companies out of four have been displaced at the top of the Fortune list, and Kirchoff's (1990) results that nearly 17 percent of the top 500 industrial firms have been displaced between 1960 and 1980 seem to question whether Chandler's results are applicable to the events of recent years. Chandler, however, talks about industry dominance, and it is possible that the changes that occurred among the largest corporations are attributable to a great extent to technological change acting at the industry level, while within each industry the turbulence has been less pronounced, with the top firms retaining their leadership. This should be especially true in more mature industries, in which the advantages accumulated by the market leaders are harder to threaten than in dynamic ones, in which new firms can exploit radical innovations in order to successfully enter and grow.

A Change of Technoeconomic Paradigm

Besides causing the birth of new industries and the decline of others, the emergence of new technologies also affects the structure of existing industries. The overall effect of technical change on the economy is more widespread when innovation takes place in capital goods industries, and its benefits are transferred to users in different sectors through interindustry flows of technology (Scherer 1982). Rosenberg (1976) has shown the importance of innovation in the machine tools sector for the development of the American economy in the last century. More recently, many authors have highlighted the pervasiveness of technical change occurring in the electronics capital goods industry (Piore and Sabel 1984; Freeman 1982, 1993). Piore and Sabel have described how the application of electronics has made possible the appearance of a model of production, named *flexible specialization,* opposed to the traditional *mass production* paradigm mainly based on the exploitation of static economies of scale. The application of flexible specialization to manufacturing processes has created the emergence of clusters of small firms that have been able to compete successfully against large globalized corporations. Freeman has stressed the importance of the changes caused by the development of microelectronics technology even further, writing that:

> even more important than the growth of new industries and services is the effect of information and communication technologies (ICT) on all other industries and services. ICT affects every function within the firm as well as affecting every industry. Since it facilitates much greater integration of research, design, development, production and marketing it leads to a new style of management and a new pattern of organization within and between firms. This change is so fundamental that it amounts to a change of techno-economic paradigm. (Freeman 1993, 2)

A consequence of these radical changes is that large firms that fail to adequately master the new technologies are bound to experience a decline in their market shares. First-movers that successfully invest in new technologies, on the other hand, can gain market shares at the expense of competitors that are technologically less active within the same industry.

Mergers, Acquisitions, Financial Innovations, and the Market for Corporate Control

Another important source of changes in the Fortune list is the disappearance of firms because of mergers and acquisitions. Two merger waves occurred in the American economy during the period covered in this study. The first wave, which peaked in 1968, was characterized by the growth of conglomerate mergers. Many firms diversified geographically and in related fields in order to exploit synergies in production or distribution, and others expanded in completely unrelated business lines. Another novelty of the 1960s merger wave was that, thanks to financial innovations, very large corporations could also be targets of takeover attempts (Ravenscraft and Scherer 1987; Fortune 1969).

This feature became even more pronounced in the 1980s, when the use of "junk bonds" and the presence of powerful institutional investors made possible a high number of hostile takeovers (Fortune 1984; Scherer and Ross 1990). This, in turn, prompted the managers of a number of companies to defend their independence by going private. Fortune reported in 1984 that the number of companies going private increased threefold from 1980 to 1983. Some firms started to buy other companies simply to protect themselves from takeover attempts (Lazonick 1990). Some scholars welcome the increase in takeover activity, as they argue that it reduces the incentives that managers have to undertake wasteful investment and it accelerates restructuring in declining industries by reducing excess capacity (Jensen 1988). However, there is evidence that a significant percentage of the mergers have not been successful (Ravenscraft and Scherer 1987; Scherer and Ross 1990), and some authors even argue that a fierce competition in the market for corporate control is detrimental for American competitiveness in the long run, as it pushes managers to seize short-term objectives in order to keep share valuation high enough to discourage possible raiders (Lazonick 1990).

Mergers are likely to influence the following empirical analysis in two ways. First, pronounced takeover activity will cause more exits of firms as legal entities, and therefore will increase the turnover in the Fortune list for reasons other than technological change. In addition, firms that merge with other large companies simply by pooling of interests (i.e., exchanging shares) automatically experience a high growth rate that is not directly related to their efficiency.

Other Phenomena Influencing the Mobility and Turnover of the Largest Firms

The growing process of globalization of the world economy also influences the structure of American industry. Foreign firms have been able to reply to the American postwar foreign direct investment (FDI), and now some big American companies are owned by foreign multinationals. As Cantwell (1989) has shown, European and Japanese FDI in the United States of America has taken place mainly in the industries where these countries had relative technological advantages over their American counterparts, such as the chemical and food industries, for European firms, and the electronics industry, for the Japanese.

Another phenomenon that influences the structure of the Fortune list is the relative decline of the manufacturing sector in the whole economy. As Chandler (1990) points out, large firms enjoy economies of scale and scope in their distribution services. Given the expansion of the nonmanufacturing sector, some industrial companies have exploited the competencies built in wholesaling, retailing, and finance, and have diversified in nonmanufacturing activities to such an extent that they are not considered industrial companies anymore.

The Issues Examined

The next several sections will show how all of the factors previously mentioned have contributed to the changes observed among the largest 300 industrial corporations in the United States. More specifically, the following statements will be analyzed empirically:

1. Mergers and acquisitions were one of the major sources of turbulence in the list, but when takeover activity is controlled for, many industries show remarkable stability over time.
2. Catching-up from European and Japanese companies was reflected in an increase of the number of foreign-owned companies in the top 300, particularly in industries in which Japanese and European companies are technologically strong vis-à-vis American firms.
3. Technological change is one of the major forces behind the changes in the list, and it has three main effects:

      a. Industries with high innovation intensity grow faster, and broad industry trends account for a large part of the growth observed at the firm level (i.e., belonging to an innovative industry significantly increased the growth of the firms in the period considered).

      b. The nature of competition is different across sectors. In mature industries, the mobility is lower, and it arises mainly from mergers and acquisitions. In dynamic industries, technological opportunities favor entry of new firms and cause greater mobility of market shares. In these industries, innovative activities are crucial for firm success.

      c. The emergence of new fast-growing technologies, such as microelectronics, creates opportunities for the expansion of companies within their industries. Firms that innovate in fast-growing technological areas are able to expand their market shares against their rivals.

"Creative Destruction" in the Fortune List: 1963–87

Life and Death among the top 300 Firms
of the Fortune List

This section will look into the changes that have taken place among the top 300 industrial firms in the U.S. economy from 1963 to 1987, identifying the main reasons for these changes. For this purpose, each firm included in the top 300 in 1963 has been classified according to its status in 1987, and vice versa.[5]

The top 300 in 1963 have been classified into four main groups, which, in turn, have been divided in nine subgroups. *Survivors* are the firms still in

---

5. Note that the lists of the largest companies in 1963 and 1987 are from *Fortune* (1964, 1988).

the list in 1987. Some of them are still independent (*US Survivors*), while others are now controlled by foreign multinationals (*International Survivors*). Some companies (*Acquired*) have disappeared because they have been acquired by other American firms (*US Acquired*) or by foreign multinationals (*International Acquired*), or because they are not public anymore (*Private*), and therefore their data is not published.[6] Other corporations have been excluded by the list because their main activities lie outside the manufacturing sector (*Not industrial in 1987*). Of the remaining firms displaced by the top 300, some are still among the top 500 (*Displaced in the 500*), others have been liquidated (*Liquidated*), while the rest have simply declined too much to be included in the Fortune list (*Declined*).

The top 300 in 1987 have been split into four main groups and seven subgroups. *US Survivors* and *International Survivors* are exactly the same firms as above. *Spin-offs* are divisions or subsidiaries of companies already listed among the top 300 that have been divested in the period considered. *Not industrial in 1963* are companies that already existed in 1963, but were not included in the list because less than 50 percent of their revenues was coming from nonmanufacturing activities. New American entrants have been divided between *Entrants from the 500*, when the companies were already listed in the bottom 200 places of the Fortune list relative to 1963, and *Entrants*, if they were not included in the Fortune list. *New International* are new entrants owned by foreign multinationals. The results are shown in tables 1 and 2. In table 1 the top 300 firms in 1963 have been classified according to their status in 1987, while table 2 presents the top 300 firms of the 1987 list according to their status in 1963.

The answer to the question "are the changes significant?" is a matter of opinion. On one hand, it is noticeable that at least 100 firms have disappeared from the list; thus large corporations are not immortal. Some of these disappearing firms have declined, but the majority have been acquired. On the other hand, one could argue that the list is rather stable over the time period examined. More than half of the firms (59 percent) are still there in good shape in 1987; large firms are likely to survive for a long time. The majority of these (57.3 percent U.S.-based and 1.7 percent foreign-owned) have not undergone major ownership changes, while others have been bought by American firms (26 percent) or foreign multinationals (3.7 percent). Others have disappeared from the list not because of poor performance, but only because they are no longer classified as industrial (3.7 percent),[7] or their

---

6. The difference between *International Survivors* and *International Acquired* is that the former have not been consolidated in the financial statements, and thus their figures are available to the public.

7. A firm is classified as industrial when at least 50 percent of its sales come from industrial operations.

TABLE 1. Status in 1987 of the Top 300 U.S. Industrial Firms in 1963

Status	Number of Firms		Total Sales (1963)	
	No.	%	No.	%
Survivors	177	59.0	606,936	74.8
U.S. survivors	172	57.3	593,930	73.2
International survivors	5	1.7	13,006	1.6
Acquired	89	29.7	152,442	18.8
U.S. acquired	78	26.0	136,825	16.9
International acquired	11	3.7	15,617	1.9
Private	6	2.0	4,971	0.6
Not industrial in 1987	11	3.7	27,132	3.3
Displaced	17	5.7	19,502	2.4
Liquidated	3	1.0	4,395	0.5
Declined	2	0.7	1,897	0.2
Displaced in the 500	12	4.0	13,210	1.6
Total	300	100	810,984	100

Source: Elaborations on USLIF Database.

Note: The USLIF Database has been built by the author using data from various editions of Fortune, the Statistical Abstract of the U.S., and Moody's Industrial Manuals, annual reports of companies, the SPRU-OTAF database of U.S. patents, and the NSF.

results are no longer made public (2 percent). A further 4 percent are still in the Fortune list, although not in the first 300 places. Only 5 out of 300 firms have left the list of the top 500 because of poor performance (decline or liquidation).

It is apparent, looking at table 1, that takeovers are a major source of change in the list. The implications of this phenomenon, however, are difficult to interpret. Acquisition can occur for different reasons, in different circumstances, and with different effects. Some firms are completely absorbed and disappear in the process (such as Chemetron), while others can pass virtually unchanged through various parent companies (see the case of Hertz described by Nelson 1991). According to some surveys (Fortune 1969, 1984), almost nobody is safe from takeovers, even companies like IBM. Treating acquisitions as failures, thus, could be misleading. Some of the firms have been bought by foreign companies merely to have a foothold in the U.S. market, especially in the chemical industry. This reflects the phenomenon of catching-up, especially by European and Japanese firms, that can also be seen in table 2. Some firms, in addition, have been bought by financial companies as investments, and they could be still in the list if their data were public. In this case, it is clear that the acquisition does not mean that the company is not in good shape.

Table 2 shows the same picture from a different perspective. Besides the

TABLE 2. Status in 1963 of the Top 300 U.S. Industrial Firms in 1987

	Number of Firms		Total Sales (1987)	
Status	No.	%	No.	%
Survivors	177	59.0	1,437,106	82.8
U.S. survivors	172	57.3	1,391,911	80.2
International survivors	5	1.7	45,195	2.6
Spin-offs	7	2.3	11,661	0.7
Not industrial in 1963	5	1.7	34,851	2.0
Entrants	111	37.0	251,977	14.5
Entrants from the 500	31	10.3	68,806.7	4.0
Entrants:	68	22.7	155,150	8.9
New firms	11	3.7	28,628	1.6
New international	12	4.0	28,020	1.6
Total	300	100	1,735,595	100

Source: Fortune 1963, 1987, and other editions.

growing importance of international production, the additional information provided by table 2 is the existence of some new firms generated as spin-offs from firms already in the list (2.3 percent of the firms).

Summing up, four main patterns emerge from the data analyzed:

(*a*) The major cause of turnover in the list is the frenetic activity in the market for corporate control. During the period examined, two waves of mergers and acquisitions occurred in the American economy. Although this phenomenon is very important, the analysis of its implications goes beyond the scope of this chapter.

(*b*) The high number of takeovers had two main effects. First, many of the companies that have disappeared have been acquired by others in the list, so that the overall weight of the surviving firms in the list has increased from 74.8 to 82.8 percent. Second, the disappearance of some firms has created room for a significant number of new entrants.

(*c*) Excluding mergers and acquisitions, it is possible to say that large companies were remarkably stable. Only 17 firms out of 300 have been displaced because of poor rates of growth, and 12 of them still rank among the top 500 industrial companies. Moreover, although a good share of firms did not survive (41 percent), they were less important than the survivors in terms of sales (25.2 percent). Of the 99 new American industrial entrants, in addition, 31 already ranked among the top 500 in 1963. A good part of the turnover, thus, was originated by movement around the cutoff line and did not involve the top of the list.[8]

(*d*) The number of foreign-owned firms in the top 300 grew from 5 in 1963 to 17 in 1987, with an increase of more than 200 percent. In addition, during the period considered, 11 more U.S. companies have been consolidated in overseas multinationals, disappearing from the list because the data is not available separately anymore. If they had stayed among the top 300 in 1987, the number of foreign-owned large firms would have increased from 5 to 28.

Industry Trends and Firm-Specific Turbulence

Analysis of Variance on the Overall Growth of the Firm
In the previous section, table 2 showed that a number of new firms have entered the list. Many of the *Survivors* have also substantially altered their ranks. One possible cause for the changes is the fast growth of new industries. Firms in fast-growing industries can experience high rates of growth simply because the demand for their goods is expanding, while the intraindustry position of the firms could remain relatively stable.

An analysis of variance (ANOVA) on LNFIRMCH, the logarithm of the overall growth of the firm, has been performed to see if, within the sample, belonging to an industry significantly affected the growth of the surviving firms. The analysis was carried out on the subsample composed of 215 *stable* firms (i.e., *Survivors, Displaced in the 500,* and *Entrants from the 500,* less five firms that were too diversified to be included in any industry group).

The results, presented in table 3, reveal that interindustry differences are clearly very important. The highly significant *F*-ratio shows that the variability of the average rates of growth between industry groups is more than five times higher than the variability of firms' growth rates within industry groups.[9] This means that, for the sample of the surviving firms, the growth experienced by each firm was related to a large extent to some factors that acted at the industry level, that is, that were common to all of the surviving firms in each industry.

The average growth of the survivors in each industry, however, is not the same as the growth of the sales in the industry, as this also depends upon the changes in their market shares within industries. If the survivors in a declining

---

8. Edwards (1975) came to the same conclusions after reviewing all of the previous studies of turnover and mobility relative to the American industrial sector.

9. The outcome of the ANOVA does not change if transportation equipment, which includes only two firms, is excluded (*F*-ratio = 4.64), or if the plain rate of growth of the firms is used as the dependent variable instead of its logarithm (*F*-ratio = 3.47).

TABLE 3. Analysis of Variance on the Overall Growth of the Firms by Industry Groups (Dependent variable: *LNFIRMCH* by variable *INDUSTRY*)

Source	Degrees of Freedom	Sum of Squares	Mean Squares	*F*-ratio	*F* Prob
Between groups	19	34.8386	1.8336	5.1563	0
Within groups	195	69.3432	0.3556		
Total	214	104.182			

industry acquire a large number of competitors, thus increasing the concentration in the industry, the average growth of their group can be high while industry sales decline. Similarly, the average sales of the firms in a fast-growing industry can be lower than the industry rate of growth if new entrants are catching up with them. In order to measure how industry trends have affected the overall growth of the firm, it is necessary to distinguish between the growth arising from demand factors (i.e., industry growth) and that stemming from firm-specific factors.

A Comparison of Industry-Specific
vs. Firm-Specific Turbulence
It is possible to examine the influence of industry trends on the changes in the overall growth of the surviving firms (*LNFIRMCH*) by splitting this into two distinct components, industry-specific (*LNINDCH*) and firm-specific growth (*LNMSCH*):[10]

$$LNFIRMCH_{ij} = LNMSCH_i + LNINDCH_{ij}.$$

The identity simply means that the overall growth of the firm is the sum of two different factors: $LNMSCH_i$, that is, firm-specific growth independent from

---

10. By definition, the total turnover of the ith firm at time $t(SALES_{it})$ is equal to the product of its market share (MS_{it}) multiplied by the total value of the production in its industry (IND_{it}), that is:

$$SALES_{it} = MS_{it} \cdot IND_{it}$$

Dividing each member by itself at time $t - 1$ and taking the logarithms, we have

$$LNFIRMCH_{ij} = LNMSCH_i + LNINDCH_{ij},$$

where the $LNFIRMCH_{ij}$ is the firm's rate of growth plus 1, $LNMSCH_i$ is the change in market share plus 1, and $LNINDCH_{ij}$ is the industry growth plus 1 (all expressed in logarithms). This means that the growth of the ith firm is equal to the growth of its market share plus the growth of its industry.

industry trends (also called change in market share, for ease of presentation),[11] and $LNINDCH_{ij}$, or the growth of the industry in which the firms operate. It is possible to use this identity to discover whether the observed differences in the rates of growth of the surviving firms are mainly explained by differences between industry rates of growth, with little turbulence within each industry, or by large variations of market shares. In order to assess the contribution of each component of firm growth to the overall turbulence among the surviving firms, the variance of each component has been calculated as follows

$$\text{Var }[LNFIRMCH] = \text{Var }[LNMSCH] + \text{Var }[LNINDCH]$$

$$+ \text{Cov }[LNMSCH, LNINDCH].$$

This means that the sum of the variance of each component is not exactly the same as the overall variance in the rates of growth of the firms (from now on TURBFIRM), the difference being the covariance between the two components (from now on COVINDMS). The terms Var $[LNMSCH]$ (from now on TURBMS) and Var $[LNINDCH]$ (from now on TURBIND) are, respectively, indicators of the turbulence at the firm and at the industry level.

Contrary to the outcome of the ANOVA, factors acting at the firm level ($TURBMS = 0.417$) appear to be more important than those at the industry level ($TURBIND = 0.142$) in explaining the overall variability between the rates of growth of the surviving firms ($TURBFIRM = 0.485$). However, the influence of industry trends on the overall variability is probably higher than the results suggest, as the broad definition of industry adopted means that the effect of fast-growing subsectors on firm growth is captured by the firm-specific component. Since some of the firms that have not been classified as conglomerate are also active in other industries the distinction between the two components considered here is blurred. Tyco Laboratories, for instance, has been classified in the metal products industry, but it also produces semiconductors, as it is specialized in advanced materials. The growth that should be attributed to the expansion of the semiconductor industry appears, in this analysis, as growth of Tyco's market share in the metal products industry.[12]

---

11. In fact, the terms $LNMSCH_i$ does not exactly represent the market share, in three respects, as it includes the firm's overseas operations, sales in other industries, and nonmanufacturing activities. The bias arising from the company's diversification into other industries has been limited by adopting a broad definition of industry and eliminating from the analysis firms with a high level of diversification. These have been grouped in a fictitious industry named *Conglomerates*.

12. The effects of diversification in other industries, in fact, also work in the opposite direction, when firms in fast-growing industries diversify into mature industries, but this case is usually more rare.

This could also explain the negative sign of the covariance term (*COVINDMS* = 0.074), which indicates that the survivors in declining industries experience relatively higher firm-specific growth, although increases in concentration are expected in mature industries that have already gone through a phase of shakeout in which entry decreases sharply, exit continues, and excess capacity is reduced by acquisitions (by definition, every time an exit occurs the market shares of the surviving firms automatically increase as industry size decreases, even if they do not increase their sales).

To summarize, both components seem to play an important role in determining the turbulence observed among the surviving firms. In the next section, the turbulence at the industry level will be analyzed, focusing on the role played by technological change as a source of instability. After that, the influence of technological change on firm-specific growth will be studied using a new technological indicator developed at the Science Policy Research Unit (SPRU) of Sussex University.

An Industry-Level Analysis of Turbulence

Interindustry Factors Affecting the Changes among the Top 300 Industrial Firms

In the previous section, it has been shown that a large part of the overall firm growth among the surviving companies is explained by interindustry differences in growth rates. Differences between industries, therefore, are very important in understanding the changes that have occurred among the largest manufacturing firms. Industries, however, do not differ only in their rates of growth. Table 4 shows some statistics at the industry level. The percentage of surviving firms, acquisitions, entry, foreign presence, and technological intensity and the degree of turbulence vary substantially across industries. For instance, it can be noted that FDI is particularly high in sectors like chemicals (where Bayer, BASF, and Hoechst, three German firms, account for a large part of the foreign presence) and food and tobacco (Unilever is responsible for a great deal of the FDI in this industry), where Germany and the United Kingdom have a high degree of technological specialization. Even more striking is the breakdown of newborn firms (i.e., corporations founded from 1957 onward) by industry: eight of eleven engage in information technology (nine, if Teledyne, here classified as a conglomerate, is considered): six in computers and two, Intel and National Semiconductor, in semiconductors.

Industries also differ in the degree of mobility of market shares. In some industries the positions of the top firms tend to remain quite stable over time, while in others followers catch up with the leaders. Intraindustry turbulence manifests itself in two ways. First, turbulent industries will experience relatively high rates of turnover among the top 300, as followers catch up over

TABLE 4. Industry Statistics

Code	Industry	Number of Firms			Industry Shares Change (%)	R&D Intensity Ratio	Newborn Firms in 1987	Survivor Firms in 1987	Acquired Firms in 1987	Foreign Firms in 1987	Displaced Firms in 1987	Not Industrial in 1987	Code
		1963	1987	Rate of Change (%)									
20	Food, Tobacco	48	34	−29	−22	0.4	0	25	19	6	1	3	20
22	Textile, Apparel, Leather	15	8	−47	−38	0.4	0	7	4	0	2	2	22
26	Wood, Furniture, Paper	15	22	47	17	0.8	0	10	5	3	0	0	26
27	Publishing, Printing	3	12	300	43	n.a.	0	3	0	0	0	0	27
28	Chemicals	23	30	30	14	3.5	0	17	5	7	1	0	28
29	Energy	25	22	−12	23	0.8	0	13	12	3	0	0	29
30	Rubber, Plastic products	5	6	20	61	1.9	0	4	1	1	0	0	30
32	Construction materials	11	11	0	−15	1.3	0	9	1	2	1	0	32
33	Metal manufacturing	27	14	−48	−43	0.6	0	11	12	0	3	1	33
34	Metal products	8	12	50	1	1.1	1	3	4	0	0	1	34
36	Electronics	22	24	9	−2	6.2	2	14	6	2	0	2	36
37	Transportation equipment	5	1	−80	9	3.3	0	0	3	0	2	0	37
38	Instruments	4	10	150	198	6.1	0	3	1	0	0	0	38
40	Motor vehicles	17	12	−29	−1	1.4	1	10	4	1	3	0	40
41	Aerospace, Defense	16	13	−19	22	12.3	0	11	5	0	0	0	41
42	Pharmaceuticals	11	14	27	80	6.3	0	10	1	0	0	0	42
43	Soap, Cosmetics	6	7	17	22	1.8	0	6	0	1	0	0	43
44	Office equip., Computers	6	14	133	247	11.7	6	5	1	0	0	0	44
45	Industrial & Farm equip.	20	14	−30	−3	2.1	0	7	10	0	3	0	45
47	Toys, Music	0	1	n.a.	n.a.	n.a.	0	0	0	0	0	0	47
49	Beverages	5	6	20	17	0.4	0	4	1	1	0	0	49
90	Total manufacturing	8	13	63	0	n.a.	1	5	0	1	1	2	90
	Total	300	300	0	0	n.a.	11	177	95	28	17	11	n.a.

Source: USLIF database.
[a]n.a., not available.

time. Second, in these industries the mobility of the market shares of the stable firms will be higher. Previous research has suggested that technological change influences both industry trends and turbulence. The remainder of this section will try to shed light on the role played by innovative activities on growth, entry, and turbulence at the industry level.

Technological Change and Industry Growth

When innovations are introduced, they either create new demand or substitute demand for existing goods in mature industries that therefore experience a decline. As the demand for traditional goods falls their prices also decrease, making the decline of the industry more pronounced in terms of value. Firms that introduce innovative products, on the contrary, can raise the price of the new goods they sell by exploiting a temporary monopoly given by the novelty of their products. A typical example of this process of "creative destruction" that takes place at the industry level is the shift to electronics capital goods from those based on mechanical technology. Industries with a high rate of innovation, therefore, should grow faster as the demand for their goods increases. To test this proposition, the following equation has been estimated to replicate Freeman's (1982) findings that the technological intensity of an industry is highly correlated with its growth

$$\text{Growth}_j = a + b \cdot \text{Tech}_j + u_j.$$

Growth_j is a measure of growth of the jth industry between 1963 and 1987. Two different indicators have been employed: $INDCH_j$, that is, the rate of growth of the value of shipments for the industry (from various Statistical Abstracts of the U.S.), and $LNINDCH_j$, the measure of industry growth from the identity above. Tech_j is a proxy of the industry intensity of technological activities. Two different measures of technological change have been adopted: $RDINT_j$, the traditional measure of industry R&D intensity on sales (data relative to 1978 produced by the National Science Foundation as reported in Freeman 1982), and $FASTPC_j$, namely the percentage of patents in fast-growing classes granted to the firms in the industry.

This indicator was developed at SPRU by Pari Patel and Keith Pavitt, who selected, from nearly 110,000 patent subclasses, the top 1,000 that recorded the biggest increase in the number of patents between the periods 1963–68 and 1985–90. The percentage of patents belonging to these classes versus the overall number of patents granted in the United States increased from 2.3 to 17.7 percent in the period considered. Subsequently, both the overall number of patents and the number of patents granted between 1985 and 1988 in the fastest growing field have been computed for some of the

TABLE 5. Technological Activities and Industry Growth

Dependent Variables Regression Number	LNINDCH (i)	INDCH (ii)	LNINDCH (iii)	INDCH (iv)	INDCH (v)	INDCH (vi)
R square	0.40	0.42	0.55	0.60	0.62	0.49
Adj. R square	0.36	0.39	0.52	0.58	0.57	0.42
F value	10.77	11.45	19.26	24.13	12.29	7.15
Sig. F	(0.005)	(0.004)	(0.001)	(0.000)	(0.000)	(0.007)
N	18	18	18	18	18	18
Intercept	0.37813[a]	42.8555	−0.0324	−72.4992	−38.7283	85.7111[c]
	(3.234)	(1.411)	−(0.191)	−(1.732)	−(0.680)	(2.052)
RDINT	0.07813[a]	20.9214[a]				18.227[a]
	(3.281)	(3.383)				(2.907)
FASTPC			4.00243[a]	1104.28[a]	1014.12[a]	
			(4.389)	(4.912)	(4.084)	
MAF					−3.6674	−6.65398
					−(0.883)	−(1.443)

Note: t-statistics in brackets.
[a]Significance level 1%
[b]Significance level 5%
[c]Significance level 10%

largest American industrial companies. The percentage ratio between the two figures indicates how many patents in the fast-growing classes out of every 100 patents have been granted to each firm in the four years considered. This indicator has been aggregated from the firm to the industry level by dividing $FASTPAT_j$ (the number of patents in fast-growing classes granted to the firms in the jth industry) by $TOTPAT_j$ (the number of patents in all classes granted to the firms in the jth industry).

Although $FASTPC_j$ is correlated with the R&D intensity, it captures a different aspect of technological change. While $RDINT_j$ quantifies the resources devoted to innovative activity, $FASTPC_j$ reflects the direction of technological change; that is, how much of the output of intermediate innovative activity is directed toward very new and growing areas that increase the output of the industry in which they are included by creating new demand.

Table 5 reports the results of the regressions, which confirm the hypothesis previously presented and Freeman's finding. The fit is always highly significant and robust to the type of indicator used. The results are more significant when $FASTPC_j$ is used, consistent with the hypothesis that fast-growing patent classes are a good proxy for new fast-growing markets. R&D is devoted both to product and to process innovation, and the expansion of demand is mainly linked with the former. Thus, the patent-based indicator is better suited than R&D intensity for capturing the growth in demand created by the emergence of new markets.

In regressions v and vi, the variable MAF_j (the number of companies among the top 300 in 1963 that were acquired by industry before 1987) has been added as explanatory variable to test the hypothesis that merger activity is more pronounced in mature industries (Jensen 1988). When demand growth is slow or declining firms' opportunities for growth are more rare, companies expand through takeovers. The results support this hypothesis, as MAF's coefficient is negatively associated with market growth. The presence of multicollinearity between MAF_j and $FASTPC_j$ (with correlation of -0.41, significant at the 5 percent confidence level), in addition, confirms that two different patterns emerge from the regression analysis. Some industries expand at a fast rate thanks to the growth of demand arising from the innovations introduced. In mature industries, on the contrary, merger and acquisition activity is more pronounced and it is an important vehicle of restructuring.

Technological Change and Turnover among the Top 300

The two typologies of industries identified also help to shed light on inter-industry differences in turnover. A measure of gross entry is used to measure industry turbulence, as net entry is also influenced by exit, which can take place for reasons different from those that stimulate entry (Audretsch 1992).

Among the variables that Acs and Audretsch (1989) found influencing the
entry of small firms are the rate of growth of the markets, the share of
innovations accounted for by small firms, average industry profitability, and
small firms' productivity growth. R&D intensity, concentration, and capital
intensity, on the contrary, are usually high in industries with low levels of
entry. R&D intensity is found to be negatively related to small firms' entry, as
their small size does not permit firms to exploit economies of scale and scope
in innovative activities.

Entry among the top firms, however, is a different matter. The firms
included in this sample are all very large, and should not suffer too much from
size-related disadvantages in relation to R&D activity and capital intensity.
R&D intensity (*RDINT*) in this context is more an indicator of the rate of
technological change in the industry, and therefore is more likely to be positively related to entry among the largest firms. Another indicator of innovation activity in industries is the percentage of patents in fast-growing classes
(*FASTPC*). It is reasonable to assume that when technological change is very
fast, and new markets are created, firms that specialize in these new fast-
growing areas can enjoy faster rates of growth and enter the top 300 industrial
firms.

Consistent with Acs and Audretsch (1989), a measure of industry growth
(*INDCH*) is expected to be positively associated with turnover. This measure
is highly collinear with the percentage of patents in fast-growing classes, as
the results presented in table 5 show, and it can be interpreted as another
indicator of the presence of creative destruction brought about by technological change. As the correlation coefficient between this variable and *FASTPC*
is over 0.7, the two are never included together at the right-hand side, to avoid
problems of multicollinearity.[13]

Kirchoff (1990), in his study of the turnover and growth of the largest
500 firms included in the COMPUSTAT database, showed that a significant
share of growth among new entrants arises from acquisitions and mergers.
Since many times the firms acquired have been split and resold in pieces, it
can be assumed that firms oriented toward growth entered the top 300 partly
because they acquired some incumbent firms or parts of them. Thus, a measure of mergers and acquisitions (*MAF*) has been included among the explanatory variables.

It is likely that in industries in which capital requirements are high per
unit of sales production, processes are more complex and knowledge generated inside the firm through learning-by-doing is more important than knowledge existing outside the firms for generating technological change. This
means that a high level of capital intensity (*KAPIN* is the average ratio of total
assets to sales in 1963 by industry of the firms considered) is probably associ-

---

13. Analogous results are achieved when *LNINDCH* is used instead of *INDCH*.

ated with process innovation and the existence of a routinized technological regime (Winter 1984) in which entry and turbulence are less pronounced. A fast rate of technological change and high industry growth, on the other hand, are probably associated with an entrepreneurial regime that favors entry and mobility within industries (Acs and Audretsch 1990; Jovanovich 1982; Gort and Klepper 1982).

Four regressions have been estimated to describe industry characteristics associated with entry. Part a of Table 6 shows that the variables have the expected signs, and their coefficients are all significant, apart from that of capital intensity. These results confirm that fast-growing industries, in which very new markets are emerging, have a higher number of entrants. In mature industries, in which technological change is more routinized, firms enter the list of the top 300 industrial companies mainly through mergers and acquisitions, while industries in which both innovative and merger activity are low have low levels of entry.

An Analysis of Turbulence among the Surviving Firms

Turbulence brought about by technological change and by mergers and acquisitions entails not only a higher number of entrants, but also higher mobility of market shares. Some regressions, descriptive in nature, have been run in order to identify factors that discriminate between industries. *TURBMS* has been used as a measure of the level of mobility of market shares of the stable firms. Fast-growing industries, in which technological change creates opportunities for growth that can be exploited by new entrants, are also likely to show a relatively high degree of variability in the market shares of the stable firms, as only some of the incumbents are able to seize the opportunities offered by technological change, while others experience a relative decline against the more innovative firms. *INDCH* and *FASTPC*, thus, are expected to be positively related to *TURBMS*.

In routinized regimes, however, incumbent companies have advantages against new entrants, given by their larger size and by the knowledge accumulated through learning-by-doing. Turbulence generated by technological change is usually lower in these industries, which, however, experience more acquisitions and mergers, as has been shown in table 5. A high level of merger activity (MAF) can create a great deal of instability when new entrants buy incumbent companies and leading firms absorb their competitors. As was previously suggested, mergers and acquisitions are likely to be more relevant in mature industries in the process of restructuring.

The outcome of the regressions (part b of table 6) tends to support the theory that interindustry differences in mobility among the surviving firms are linked with the industry patterns identified previously, although the significance levels are low. Mobility (*TURBMS*) is higher in industries that grow

TABLE 6. Industry Characteristics, Entry, and Turbulence among the Top 300

Dependent Variables Regression Number	Part (a)					Part (b)	
	ENTRYF (i)	ENTRYF (ii)	ENTRYF (iii)	ENTRYF (iv)	TURBMS (v)	TURBMS (vi)	TURBMS (vii)
R square	0.38	0.43	0.18	0.44	0.24	0.05	0.05
Adj. R square	0.25	0.30	0.00	0.31	0.10	−0.16	−0.16
F value	2.87	3.46	0.99	3.59	1.67	0.22	0.24
Sig. F	(0.074)	(0.045)	(0.424)	(0.041)	(0.213)	(0.879)	(0.869)
N	18	18	18	18	20	18	18
Intercept	−0.59547	0.65401	0.26989	−1.83601	0.45889[b]	0.54309[b]	0.53846
	−(0.239)	(0.289)	(0.091)	−(0.723)	(2.449)	(2.343)	(2.396)
RDINT			0.21388				0.0044
			(1.131)				(0.308)
FASTPC				20.4562[b]		0.14804	
				(2.880)		(0.228)	
MAF	0.34054[b]	0.32734[b]	0.21454	0.30997[b]	0.0197[c]	0.00869	0.00862
	(2.580)	(2.672)	(1.571)	(2.614)	(1.978)	(0.803)	(0.836)
LNSHIPCH	3.69772[b]						
	(2.521)						
SHIPCH		0.01475[b]			0.00098[c]		
		(2.818)			(1.824)		
KAPIN	−0.58662	−1.15927	1.11079	−0.188	−0.09951	−0.03176	−0.01357
	−(0.222)	−(0.450)	(0.362)	−(0.075)	−(0.458)	−(0.139)	−(0.059)

Note: t-statistics in brackets.
[a]Significance level 1%
[b]Significance level 5%
[c]Significance level 10%

faster (*INDCH*), as the opportunities created by the existence of new fast-growing markets (*FASTPC*) are exploited by only some of the existing firms. Although it has the expected positive sign, the coefficient of *FASTPC* is not significantly different from 0. This suggests that technological change influences the mobility of thee market shares of the surviving firms mainly through its effect on the rate of growth of the industries. In mature industries with routinized regimes, the major source of turbulence in market shares is likely to be the merger and acquisition activity (*MAF*).

Interindustry Differences in the Degree of Turbulence: Some Conclusions

In our discussion of creative destruction in the previous section, it was shown that differences between industries are an important determinant of the changes observed in the top 300 places on the Fortune list. In this section, interindustry differences have been examined in more depth, stressing the role played by technological change, and two primary patterns have been identified.

Some industries, in which rapid technological change generates new fast-growing markets, grow very fast. In these industries, some firms appropriate the benefits offered by new technologies, achieve high rates of growth, and enter the top 300 places on the Fortune list. Among the incumbents, only some capture the opportunities brought about by rapid industry growth and increase their market shares against their competitors. This inequality generates mobility in the market shares within these sectors. These industries can be associated with Winter's concept of an entrepreneurial technological regime, in which market growth, gross entry, and turbulence are high.

In mature industries, in which the slow growth or decline of demand generally stifles firms' internal expansion, the number of mergers and acquisitions is higher. Merger activity, which is negatively associated with industry growth and technological intensity, is the main vehicle of growth for the firms in these industries, and affects industry turnover and mobility. If takeovers are excluded, these industries present a relatively high level of stability, which is consistent with the nature of a routinized technological regime, in which the sources of technological change are mainly internal to the firms, making it more difficult for innovating newcomers to enter or gain market share.

Large Firms' Activities in Fast-Growing Technologies and Firms' Intraindustry Performance

Technology, Acquisitions, and Firm-Specific Growth

In this section, the intraindustry component of overall firm growth will be analyzed in more depth by running some regressions with *LNMSCH* as a dependent variable. It has been shown, in the section "Industry Trends and Firm-Specific Turbulence," that a significant part of the overall growth of the surviving firms is due to firm-specific performance, and thus is determined by entrepreneurial factors. Although a broad definition of industry has been adopted, it can be assumed that each industry is fairly homogeneous, as the firms in the sample are very large, and therefore likely either to have the competencies needed in most of the subsectors, or to be able to acquire them through strategic choices in the long time period considered.

Chandler argues that the top firms enjoy dynamic advantages as they are able to diversify, constantly leaving the declining markets and entering more promising expanding ones through either acquisition or innovation. Innovation, partly generated in institutionalized R&D activities, is an important source of firm-specific growth in two ways. Through product innovation firms create new markets to expand their production, and through process innovation they gain efficiency against their rivals, increasing their market shares in existing markets (Schumpeter 1942).

The effect of diversification into high-tech, fast-growing areas on firm growth will be analyzed in this section using the percentage of patents granted to a firm in the fastest-growing patent classes ($FASTPC_i$). This indicator is calculated here at the firm level and is expected to be positively associated with the growth of the market shares. As the dependent variable is expressed by definition as a distance from the industry average, $FASTPC_i$ is also constructed in this way. Thus, $FASTPC_i = LN[1 + (IFASTPC_i - FASTPC_j)/FASTPC_j]$, where $IFASTPC_i$ is the percentage of patents in the fast-growing classes granted to the ith firm and $FASTPC_j$ is the industry percentage.

While some firms pursue an aggressive strategy of innovation, others exploit economies of scope in management, distribution, or capital raising, and diversify in unrelated lines of business. This trend has been particularly visible recently, as the increase in the number of conglomerates testifies. Made easier by financial innovations, conglomerate diversification has become widespread during recent merger waves (Fortune 1969; Ravenscraft and Scherer 1987; Lazonick 1990).

The influence of diversification into unrelated industries on firm growth is not clear. On the one hand, firms that acquire other large companies increase their sales merely because of the merger, although they sometimes divest part of the acquired companies. Conglomerates might also enjoy economies of scale in access to capital, and should be able to allocate resources among businesses more efficiently because they have insider, and therefore better, information about their performance.

On the other hand, conglomerates are expected to grow less, as the growth of a few dynamic business units will affect the overall growth only up to a limited extent, and because managing many very different businesses can lead managers to be detached from each market and to make decisions relying mainly upon short-term financial indicators of performance (Lazonick 1990). This emphasis on short-term achievements is seen by many as a source of long-term inefficiency that will eventually damage the performance of the conglomerates. Ravenscraft and Scherer's (1987) finding that conglomerate diversification in recent years has been unsuccessful is in line with this hypothesis.

The influence of conglomerate diversification on firm-specific growth is represented by the dummy variable *CONGL*, which has a value of 1 for the firms that had intense acquisition and merger activity in the period considered, especially in unrelated industries. The sign of its coefficient is not easy to predict. On the one hand, diversified firms might have increased their market shares simply by merging with other giants and exploiting the advantages mentioned above. On the other hand, their concern with short-term objectives could have generated a negative coefficient.

The logarithm of the market share at the beginning of the period, *LNMSH63*, has been included as an explanatory variable, and it is expected to assume a negative sign, as temporary advantages that leaders enjoyed at the beginning of the period may have been eroded by followers.

Regression Results

The results of the regression, presented in table 7, confirm that, other things being equal, firms that concentrate their technological activities in new, fast-growing areas grow faster than their competitors. Large firms that shift their activities over time, moving out of declining markets and exploiting opportunities for growth in new dynamic markets, are able to prosper over time.

In the last section it was shown that entry and market share turbulence were related to technological change in dynamic industries, and to merger and acquisition activity in more mature ones. The positive coefficient of the variable *CONGL* supports the finding that an alternative strategy of growth followed by large firms in the period considered was diversification through acquisition. This result is also in line with the findings of Kirchoff's results, and is especially true for firms that engaged in an aggressive strategy of acquisition. When the five conglomerates have been included in the analysis (assigning each one of them to one industry), *CONGL*'s coefficient becomes significant, while when they are excluded it is still positive but not significantly different from 0.

The significant coefficient of *LNMSH63* suggests that the advantages of top firms in an industry whose innovative and acquisition activities were below average were eroded over time by followers who engaged in innovation and acquisitions. Only the leaders who successfully diversified through innovation were able to counteract the process of catching-up, to a certain extent.

TABLE 7. Technical Change, Conglomerate Diversification, and Growth of Market Share

Dependent Variables Regression Number	LNMSCH (i)	LNMSCH (ii)	LNMSCH (iii)	LNMSCH (iv)
R square	0.76	0.74	0.83	0.84
Adj. R square	0.72	0.71	0.80	0.80
F value	21.21	18.91	27.62	20.80
Sig. F	(0.000)	(0.000)	(0.000)	(0.000)
LNMSH63	−0.53517[a]	−0.49419[a]	−0.61458[a]	−0.66311[a]
	−(13.46)	−(12.07)	−(11.20)	−(7.66)
LNFASTPC	−0.19909[b]	−0.21759[a]	−0.33394[b]	0.11486
	−(2.430)	−(2.691)	−(2.100)	(1.133)
CONGL	0.31348[c]	0.20386	−0.0246	0.57437[c]
	(1.736)	(0.914)	−(0.070)	(1.749)
I_20	−1.6723[a]	−1.45997[a]		−2.33535[a]
	−(6.292)	−(5.433)		−(5.202)
I_22	−1.59029[a]	−1.36432[a]		−2.29592[a]
	−(4.309)	−(3.719)		−(4.274)
I_26	−1.68418[a]	−1.48885[a]		−2.30686[a]
	−(6.296)	−(5.554)		−(5.372)
I_28	−1.96636[a]	−1.78623[a]		
	−(9.180)	−(8.196)		
I_29	−0.87587[a]	−0.89664[a]		
	−(4.259)	−(4.419)		
I_30	−2.2087[a]	−1.88581[a]	−2.12746[a]	
	−(6.182)	−(4.518)	−(5.059)	
I_32	−1.48291[a]	−1.33126[a]		−1.96385[a]
	−(5.288)	−(4.798)		−(5.306)
I_33	−1.58604[a]	−1.39441[a]		−2.16257[a]
	−(5.751)	−(4.982)		−(5.286)
I_34	−1.66927[a]	−1.43518[a]		−2.39959[a]
	−(4.770)	−(4.111)		−(4.425)
I_36	−1.36201[a]	−1.12841[a]	−1.62519[a]	
	−(5.944)	−(4.744)	−(5.503)	
I_38	−1.74447[a]	−1.57819[a]	−2.01987[a]	
	−(7.163)	−(6.489)	−(7.041)	
I_40	−1.56743[a]	−1.40151[a]		
	−(6.284)	−(5.634)		
I_41	−1.19442[a]	−1.11307[a]	−1.42314[a]	
	−(5.695)	−(5.340)	−(6.154)	
I_42	−0.87484[a]	−0.75512[a]	−1.08667[a]	
	−(4.377)	−(3.805)	−(4.826)	
I_43	−0.70142[b]	−0.60224[b]		
	−(2.257)	−(1.979)		
I_44	−0.63903[a]	−0.48757[b]	−0.85731[a]	
	−(2.676)	−(2.042)	−(3.164)	

(*continued*)

TABLE 7. *(Continued)*

Dependent Variables Regression Number	LNMSCH (i)	LNMSCH (ii)	LNMSCH (iii)	LNMSCH (iv)
L45	−1.92843[a]	−1.69523[a]		−2.55863[a]
	−(7.656)	−(6.532)		−(5.726)
L49	−0.25019	−0.12565		−0.64458[c]
	−(0.691)	−(0.354)		−(1.685)

Note: t-statistics in brackets.
[a]Significance level 1%
[b]Significance level 5%
[c]Significance level 10%.

The regression has also been carried out on two subsamples. The first sample included only industries with an entrepreneurial technological regime (high values of *FASTPC* and *INDCH*), while the second included mature industries with a routinized technological regime.

The explanatory power of the model changes according to the nature of technological regime. In industries with an entrepreneurial technological regime (iii), activity in fast-growing patent classes is very important, but *CONGL*'s coefficient becomes negative, although not significantly different from 0. When a routinized technological regime prevails (iv), on the contrary, *FASTPC*'s coefficient, although still positive, is not significant anymore, while *CONGL*'s coefficient becomes significant even though the five conglomerates are not included. In addition, *LNMSH63*'s coefficient is much lower (i.e., followers have been able to catch up only to a lesser extent in these industries), indicating a lower degree of turbulence in the presence of a routinized technological regime.

Conclusions

The studies of mobility and turnover among the top American industrial firms carried out in the past decades have mainly been concerned with the trend in the overall concentration in the economy, under the assumption that an increasing concentration at the top of the economy would coincide with increasing inefficiency in the allocation of resources. Recently, two studies have analyzed the universe of the largest firms, looking for evidence of "creative destruction" created by technological change and mergers and acquisition activity (Kirchoff 1990; Economist 1992). Neither Kirchoff nor the *Economist*, however, analyzed how interindustry differences influenced the overall picture. Recent research has shown that significant interindustry differences exist not only in the structure of markets, but also in their technological regimes. Entrepreneurial technological regimes are more common in fast-growing industries, in which some innovative start-ups are able to grow, exploiting the rapid expansion of new markets that large firms enter too late. New firms have a comparative advantage in industries in which efficient production is based on knowledge that is generated outside the boundaries of the firm. Large firms absorb part of the knowledge generated outside their boundaries through their R&D activity, but there is still room for innovative entrants to exploit some markets with exponential growth in order to expand and enter the Fortune list. In routinized technological regimes, on the contrary, technological change is driven by knowledge generated through the activity of production inside the firm (learning-by-doing), and incumbent large firms can maintain their leadership more easily.

In this chapter, the overall growth of the firm has been split into two components: industry trends and intraindustry (firm-specific) performance. Both components have been studied, focusing on the role played by technological change. Interindustry differences have been a very important source of the changes occurring among the top 300 industrial firms. First, industries grow at very different rates, significantly influencing firm growth. Second, two types of industries that can be associated with the technological regimes outlined above were identified. In some sectors, the fast pace of technological change creates opportunities for growth that are exploited by some firms that achieve high rates of expansion, as the regressions carried out in the last section show. In these industries, in addition, entry is more common, and even some companies incorporated in the 1970s or later (such as Apple Computer, Intel, and Compaq Computer) have been able to enter the top 300 industrial firms in 1987 mainly by exploiting the growth of the demand for their main products.

Industries characterized by routinized technological regimes, on the contrary, are mature, and their distributions are fairly stable over time, in the absence of mergers and acquisitions. The frenetic takeover activity in the last decades, however, has also created instability in these industries. The introduction of new financial instruments has made possible the acquisition of very large firms, creating a high degree of turbulence in the Fortune list, as is also shown in Kirchoff's work.

Conclusions and policy recommendations are difficult to formulate. Some authors (Lazonick 1990) argue that a high level of competition in the market for corporate control generates inefficiency in the long run as managers are pushed to seize short-term targets, while others praise the discipline imposed by the threats of takeover (Jensen 1988).

A number of studies have concentrated attention on the structural changes that have taken place since the 1970s. In the work of Freeman (1982, 1993) and Piore and Sabel (1984), the emergence of information technology is associated with a radical change that involves not only some new industries, but many ways in which the economy and society function. The importance of information technology is well documented by the data employed in this chapter. Patel and Pavitt (1994), in addition, have shown that most of the new fast-growing patent fields are related to electronics technology.

The way that production and innovation is carried out is also undergoing major changes. Simulation is increasingly common in several disciplines, reducing the cost and speeding up the process of innovation, so that size advantages are becoming less significant in some areas. Some research has recently shown that the importance of small firms in the production of employment has increased (see Acs and Audretsch 1990). Industrial equipment relies more on electronics, shifting from mass production to flexible specialization (Piore and Sabel 1984). The decrease in the number and the importance of the firms in the industrial and farm equipment industry in the Fortune list reflects this phenomenon.

This process of transformation, however, is not only led by small new firms. A very large share of the patents in fast-growing technologies are produced by large established firms that have understood that they have to be flexible in order to cope with a changing environment. Some of the giants, in addition, are better placed than smaller firms to produce and distribute on large-scale markets that are increasingly global. Policies have to acknowledge that both large and small firms are very important for a healthy economy. Entry of small new firms must be promoted and made easy, as large firms find it difficult to exploit the knowledge generated outside their boundaries. The role played by large firms in the performance of a national economy, however, is still very important, as Chandler (1990) and Cantwell (1989) have shown in their own research. Their finding that the growth of a country is linked to the success of its firms in the key technologies has been confirmed here. In particular, European firms have been able to respond to American FDI especially in those sectors in which their large firms had technological strength.

The factors that influence the changes among the largest industrial firms are many, and their interactions are complex. In this study, these changes have been interpreted, drawing from a number of previous contributions within a Schumpeterian framework. Although some patterns (such as the importance of interindustry differences, the disruptive effects of mergers and acquisitions, and the growing importance of information technology) seem to emerge quite clearly and confirm patterns identified in other research, limitations in the data limit the empirical analysis, and further research is needed to shed more light on the deep changes that the industrial structure is undergoing.

REFERENCES

Acs, Z. J., and D. B. Audretsch. 1989. Small-Firm Entry in U.S. Manufacturing. *Economica* 56 (2): 255–65.

Acs, Z. J., and D. B. Audretsch. 1990. *Technological Regimes, Learning, and Industry Turbulence.* In Scherer and Perlman 1990.

Acs, Z. J., and D. B. Audretsch, eds. 1990. *The Economics of Small Firms: A European Challenge.* Dordrecht: Kluwer Academic Publishers.

Audretsch, D. B. 1992. The Technological Regime and Market Evolution: The New Learning. *The Economics of Innovation and New Technology* 2, no. 1: 27–36.

Bain, J. 1956. *Barriers to New Competition.* Cambridge, Mass: Harvard University Press.

Burch, Gilbert. 1969. The Merger Movement Rides High. *Fortune* 79, no. 2 (February): 79–82, 158, 161.

Cantwell, J. 1989. *Technological Innovation and Multinational Corporations.* New York: Basil Blackwell.

Capitalism's Creative Destruction. 1992. *Economist* 323 (April 4–10): 15.

Chandler, A. D. 1990. *Scale and Scope: The Dynamics of Industrial Capitalism.* Cambridge, Mass: Belknap Press.

Collins, N., and L. Preston. 1961. The Size Structure of the Largest Industrial Firms. *American Economic Review* 51, no. 5 (December): 986–1011.

Dosi, G. 1991. Verso Una Teoria Della Coerenza Della Grande Impresa. In Giannetti and Toninelli 1991.

Dosi, G., C. Freeman, R. R. Nelson, L. Soete, and G. Silverberg. 1988. *Technical Change and Economic Theory.* London: Frances Pinter.

Edwards, R. C. 1975. Stages in Corporate Stability and the Risks of Corporate Failure. *Journal of Economic History* 35:428–57.

The Fortune Directory: The 500 Largest U.S. Industrial Corporations. 1964. *Fortune* 70, no. 1 (July): 179–98.

The Fortune International 500. 1988. *Fortune* 118, no. 3 (August): D1–D55.

Fortune. 1984. Oops! My Company is on the Block. *Fortune* (July 23). Fisher, Anne B. vol. 110, no. 2, pp. 16–21.

Freeman, C. 1982. *The Economics of Industrial Innovation.* 2d ed. London: Pinter.

Freeman, C. 1993. *Technical Change and Unemployment: The Links between Macroeconomic Policy and Innovation Policy.* Paper presented at the OECD Conference on Technology, Innovation Policy and Employment, Helsinki, October 7–9.

Friedland, S. 1957. Turnover and Growth of the 50 Largest Industrial Firms, 1906–1950. *Review of Economics and Statistics* (February).

Giannetti, R., and P. A. Toninelli. 1991. *Innovazione, Impresa e Sviluppo Economico.* Bologna: Il Mulino.

Gort, M., and S. Klepper. 1982. Time-paths in the Diffusion of Product Innovation. *Economic Journal* 92:630–53.

Jensen, M. C. 1988. Takeovers: Their Causes and Consequences. *Journal of Economic Perspectives* 2 (1): 21–48.

Jovanovich, B. 1982. Selection and the Evolution of Industry. *Econometrica* 50:649–70.

Kaplan, A. D. H. 1954. *Big Enterprise in a Competitive System.* Washington, D.C.: Brookings Institution.

Kirchoff, B. 1990. *Creative Destruction among Industrial Firms in the United States.* In Acs and Audretsch 1990.

Lazonick, W. 1990. *Controlling the Market for Corporate Control: The Historical Significance of Industrial Capitalism*. In Scherer and Perlman 1990.

Malerba, F., and L. Orsenigo. 1993. Technological Regimes and Firm Behaviour. *Industrial and Corporate Change* 2 (1): 54–71.

Nelson, R. 1991. Il Ruolo Delle Imprese Nel Progresso Tecnico: Il Punto Di Vista Della Teoria Evolutiva. In Giannetti and Toninelli 1991.

Nelson, R. R., and S. G. Winter. 1982. *An Evolutionary Theory of Economic Change*. Cambridge, Mass.: Belknap Press.

Patel, P., and K. Pavitt. 1994. *Technological Competencies in the World's Largest Firms: Characteristics, Constraints and Scope for Managerial Choice*. Brighton: Science Policy Research Unit, University of Sussex, March. Mimeo.

Pavitt, K. 1991. Alcuni Fondamenti Di Una Teoria Della Grande Impresa Innovativa. In Giannetti and Toninelli 1991.

Piore, M. J., and C. F. Sabel. 1984. *The Second Industrial Divide: Possibilities for Prosperity*. New York: Basic Books.

Ravenscraft, D., and F. M. Scherer. 1987. *Mergers, Sell-offs, and Economic Efficiency*. Washington, D.C.: Brookings Institution.

Rosenberg, N. 1976. *Perspectives on Technology*. Cambridge: Cambridge University Press.

Scherer, F. M. 1982. Interindustry Technology Flows in the United States. *Research Policy* 11 (4): 227–45.

Scherer, F. M., and M. Perlman. 1990. *Entrepreneurship, Technological Innovation, and Economic Growth: Studies in the Schumpeterian Tradition*. Ann Arbor: University of Michigan Press.

Scherer, F. M., and D. Ross. 1990. *Industrial Market Structure and Economic Performance*. 3d ed. Boston, Mass.: Houghton Mifflin.

Schumpeter, J. A. 1934. *Theory of Economic Development*. Cambridge, Mass.: Harvard University Press.

Schumpeter, J. A. 1942. *Capitalism, Socialism, and Democracy*. London: Unwin.

Solow, R. 1957. Technical Change and the Aggregate Production Function. *Review of Economics and Statistics* 39:312–20.

Stigler, G. J. 1956. The Statistics of Monopoly and Mergers. *Journal of Political Economy* 64, no. 1 (February): 33–40.

Teece, D. J. 1993. The Dynamics of Industrial Capitalism: Perspectives on Alfred Chandler's Scale and Scope. *Journal of Economic Literature* 31 (March): 199–225.

Winter, S. G. 1984. Schumpeterian Competition in Alternative Technological Regimes. *Journal of Economic Behavior and Organization* 5:287–320.

Production Workers, Metainvestment, and the Pace of Change

Anne P. Carter

Metainvestment comprises all of the management and adjustment costs occasioned by technical change. Much greater than R&D alone, it is lumped with costs of production in standard accounts. Across three-digit sectors, the proportion of nonproduction workers varies with the level of metainvestment. It ranges from less than 20 percent in standard product industries to more than 75 percent in high-tech sectors. A high proportion of nonproduction workers is associated with rapid growth in both output and labor productivity.

Introduction

This chapter grew out of a theme developed in an earlier paper (Carter 1994) concerning the need to distinguish between costs of production per se and the significant costs of generating and adapting to technological change, broadly defined, in today's economy. In his early work on technological change, Schumpeter (1934) treated innovation as exogenous. Only later (Schumpeter 1950) did he begin to recognize innovation as an ongoing endogenous function. The later work became the basis for the extended discussion of the so-called Schumpeter hypothesis concerning the relation between size of firm and innovative performance (Mansfield 1968; Scherer 1984; and many others).

For the most part, the focus of this discussion has been on research and development and the ability of firms to make the necessary investments in and appropriate the gains from research and development. R&D, while essential, comprises only a small percentage of the economy's metainvestment in change. Start-up firms are known to spend months and even years in developing a product and positioning themselves before any appreciable sales are

The author thanks Ron Kutscher and the staff of the Office of Employment Projects of the U.S. Bureau of Labor Statistics for providing data and advice on its interpretation.

made. Established firms survive through metamorphosis. Beyond the search for new products and processes, significant resources are devoted to marketing, sales, process and product engineering on the factory floor, information processing, and managerial activity.

Metainvestments are made by first movers to develop and implement new technology, and also by those who imitate and adapt to changes in the economic environment. Costs of adaptation tend to reverberate throughout many sectors of the economy. In reckoning costs of change economy-wide, these later-round effects should also be taken into account.

Failure to recognize the significance of investment in change is understandable because available data do not readily yield the requisite measures. The balance sheets and income statements that form the core of our financial records are rooted in early history, when technological change was much slower and less purposive than it is today. Thus our fundamental economic measures associate today's costs with output—current or future—rather than with the activities of research and adaptation associated with change itself.

This chapter still does not solve the problem of measuring the costs of change, but it provides some indirect evidence of their nature and magnitude. It surveys the occupational structure of U.S. industry, with particular attention to the distinction between production and nonproduction workers and highlights a striking association between the proportion of nonproduction jobs and the pace of change at the sectoral level. The distinction gives important clues as to the allocation of resources between production per se and other functions, including change. However, three important problems limit the significance of our findings.

First, labor is not the only cost of production, nor the only cost of change. Second, official job titles don't always give an accurate picture of what workers actually do. Thus a machine operator may contribute ideas that lead to significant improvements in the production process or in the product; a secretary may also function as a salesperson or a manager. Third, and most important, economic theory does not specify what levels of managerial, technical, sales, or clerical employment will be necessary in a no-change world.

It is difficult to imagine what functions managers, technical staff, and even sales and clerical employees would perform if all technologies and consumer buying patterns were fixed over a long period. What problems would they solve? Why keep records if they only document the same old patterns? What remains of the sales function when everyone continues to purchase exactly what he did last time? Familiar economic thought seems to rest on an implicit notion of "normal" or moderate change in the firm's economic environment. Perhaps that normal change rationalizes the employment of a significant staff to reorder and expedite the production process. But the amount of change we consider normal appears to grow over time, and with it the resources required for adjustment. Where should we draw the line?

It might be tempting to assume the radical stance that all nonproduction workers are employed in the service of change somewhere in the economic system. But it is not necessary to argue this extreme position just yet. At this point it seems sufficient to show, as we do, that fast- and slow-changing sectors are in fact staffed very differently, and that the differences are much larger than the expenditures on R&D or patents that we usually measure.

The present study is limited to manufacturing, where products are tangible goods. It concentrates on the proportion of total employment of production workers: craftsmen, operators of machinery, laborers, and so on, and their immediate supervisors. The remaining, nonproduction workers, are comprised of managers, professional and technical personnel, sales staff, and clerical workers. Nonproduction workers are responsible for creating and maintaining the environment in which production takes place; their functions include planning, product and process improvement and troubleshooting, product promotion and documentation, and data management.

Nonproduction employment increases significantly with product and process change. Slow-changing sectors employ as little as 20 percent or less of their workforce in nonproduction jobs; change-oriented sectors employ as much as 80 percent or more in that capacity. The breadth of this range cannot be explained solely by static differences in technology among the sectors.

To the extent that nonproduction workers are change agents, their continued employment is a commitment to continued change. Staffing itself has an essential inertia. Industrial change takes place because engineers, salesmen, and managers promote it. Employees who have successfully effected change tend to remain on the payroll and thus tend to effect more change. Experience builds capability. An engineering, a sales, or a managerial capability is an asset that can provide a stream of benefits. While the stream of solutions or ideas may fluctuate, the continuing employment of individuals capable of solving certain kinds of problems shapes the course of change. This may go a long way toward explaining why change-oriented sectors tend to remain dynamic while others remain relatively static over years or even decades.

The second section of this chapter, "The Falling Relative Share of Production Workers," documents the fall over time in the proportion of production workers (and hence the rise in the proportion of nonproduction workers) for manufacturing as a whole. This fall results from a reduction in the proportion of production workers in most sectors, with marked growth in the sectors employing relatively few of them.

The third section, "The Proportion of Production Workers at the Sectoral Level," indicates that the proportion of production workers to total employment varies dramatically among manufacturing sectors. Furthermore, each sector's proportion tends to persist over time. A low proportion of production workers is often characteristic of sectors that are fast growing, with major qualitative change and rapid increases in productivity. Sectors with a low proportion of production workers also tend to have a correspondingly high ratio of gross output to employment at any given time.

The fourth section, "The Structure of Nonproduction Employment," concerns the composition of nonproduction employment. Change-oriented sectors tend to employ a significantly larger proportion of professional and technical personnel, of whom research and development workers are generally a small proportion. They also employ more management, sales, and clerical personnel per dollar of output than other sectors.

The fifth section, "Observations and Speculations on the Relation of Production and Nonproduction Workers to Aggregate Productivity Change," deals with the implications of a rising proportion of nonproduction workers for measured labor productivity. Conclusions are summarized in the sixth section.

The Falling Relative Share of Production Workers in Manufacturing Employment

The Dictionary of Occupational Titles (U.S. Department of Labor 1993a) divides all workers into seven major groups: managerial and administrative; professional, paraprofessional, and technical; sales and related; clerical and administrative support; service; agricultural, forestry, fishing, and related; and production, construction, operating, maintenance, and material handling. In manufacturing, the last category (with name shortened to "production workers") is by far the largest, both in terms of the number of subcategories of workers covered and in terms of total employment. Service workers, a relatively small category in manufacturing, are combined with the production worker category for present purposes.

The trend in the proportion of production workers in manufacturing has been downward since 1958, as shown in Figure 1.[1] Major fluctuations around the downward trend are probably best explained by the fact that production workers tend to be laid off or dismissed more readily than others in times of low utilization of capacity. The proportion of production workers drops particularly rapidly between 1972 and 1982.

Figure 1 is based on two-digit SIC manufacturing employment statistics (U.S. Department of Labor 1993b). The distinction between production and nonproduction workers is not made prior to 1975 for two sectors, electric

---

1. All of the tables and figures in this paper are based on data furnished on diskette by the U.S. Department of Labor, Bureau of Labor Statistics, Office of Employment Projections (1993b).

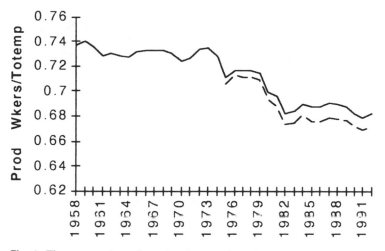

Fig. 1. The proportion of production workers in U.S. manufacturing, 1958–92

and electronic equipment (SIC 36) and instruments (SIC 38). Hence, those sectors are not included in the totals for production worker and total employment underlying the graph for 1958 to 1992. A separate line on the graph that includes these two sectors is given for the period 1975–92. Electronic equipment and instruments are both characterized by rapid change. As will be shown in the following, such sectors tend to have a relatively low and rapidly decreasing ratio of production workers to total employment. A comparison of the two time series for the interval 1975–92 suggests that the 1958–92 comparison overstates the proportion of production workers for manufacturing as a whole and understates its rate of decrease.

The declining proportion of production workers in manufacturing reflects a substantial increase in the relative importance of sectors with a low proportion of production workers, along with a continuing decline in this ratio in most sectors. The proportion of production workers fell most emphatically in sectors where the ratio itself was low. Figures 2 and 3 illustrate this finding. For these graphs, based on 1992 data, three-digit sectors were classified into three groups, those with a low, a medium, and a high proportion of production workers.

Figure 2 shows the proportion of output contributed by the groups characterized by low, medium, and high proportions of production workers. Note that the relative weight of the first group increases substantially over time. While the average proportion of production workers fell in all three groups, the fall for the low-proportion group is clearest. The decline in the high- and

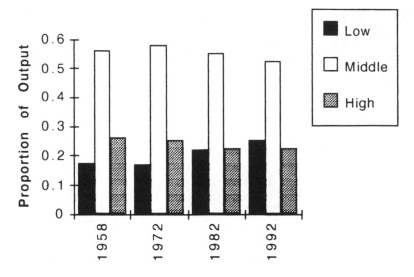

Fig. 2. Proportion of gross manufacturing output contributed by sectors with low, middle, and high proportions of production workers, 1958–92

medium-proportion sectors was modest over the first two intervals and reversed itself between 1982 and 1992 (fig. 3).

The Proportion of Production Workers at the Sectoral Level

Is the Proportion of Production Workers Characteristic of a Sector?

Figure 4 gives sector-by-sector detail of the proportion of production workers in 1975, as compared with 1992. Each dot represents the 1975 and 1992 values for a single three-digit sector. Dots above the line represent sectors that had a larger proportion of production workers in 1975 than in 1992; dots below the line signify an increase in the proportion of production workers between 1975 and 1992. Note that most dots cluster close to the line, indicating a tendency for the proportion of production workers in a given sector to change only gradually over time. While data are missing for some sectors in 1958, the proportion of production workers in 1958 and 1992 (not shown here) is consistent with the findings of the 1975–92 comparison.

Note that virtually all sectors that had low values in 1992 are characterized by dots above the line. This implies that sectors with a low proportion of production workers were all experiencing a decrease in that proportion over

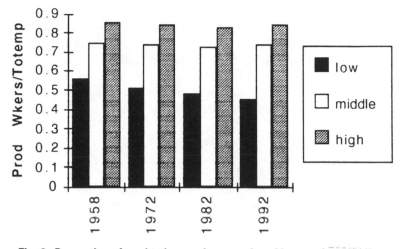

Fig. 3. Proportion of production workers employed in manufacturing by three sectoral groups, 1958–92

the period. By contrast, sectors with a proportion of production workers greater than 0.7 fall on either side: while the proportion of production workers is generally lower in the later year for this group, too, a fair number do have a higher proportion of production workers in 1992 than in 1975.

Across all sectors there is clearly a strong association between the sec-

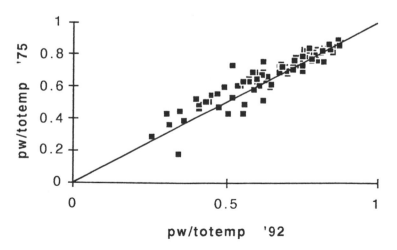

Fig. 4. Proportion of production workers of total employment by three-digit manufacturing sectors, 1975–92

toral proportion in the earlier (1975) and that in the later (1992) year. The proportion of production workers employed is apparently characteristic of a sector rather than a transient or random factor. This evidence confirms the notion that patterns of staffing have considerable inertia. To the extent that nonproduction workers are dedicated to implementing change, it is reasonable to expect that firms with a larger proportion of nonproduction workers will continue to be more dynamic than the rest.

Sectors with Lowest and Highest Proportions
of Production Workers

Table 1 contains a ranked list of the 25 manufacturing sectors with the smallest proportion of production workers in 1992. It comes as no surprise that high-tech sectors like computers, semiconductors, instruments, and drugs dominate the list and that most of the manufacturing sectors reputed to be high-tech are represented here. For these high-tech sectors, it seems appropriate to attribute the relatively large proportion of nonproduction workers to the demands of change itself. These are sectors with rapid succession of products, requiring heavy engineering and technical input, and often strong sales and purchasing networks to reconcile product change with the needs and awareness of potential customers and suppliers.

In addition to the sectors we usually classify as high-tech, the list includes four publishing sectors: miscellaneous publishing (126), newspapers (123), books (125), and greeting card publishing (128). These are essentially information sectors. One might argue that authors, reporters, and design personnel, normally classified as nonproduction workers in manufacturing, are really production workers here because the product is not just a physical object—a book or a newspaper—but rather the information itself. Another approach might focus on the common features of publishing and high-tech activities: a newspaper is similar to a missile or a computer in that the product must be ever-changing in order to be valued. Sales cannot be increased simply by churning out more copies of an old missile or an old newspaper.

Table 2 lists sectors at the other end of the range, with about 80 percent of employees classified as production workers. While there is no fundamental reason why these industries should not become high-tech in the future, they clearly are not so viewed at present. It is significant that five are textile sectors that, along with footwear and boat building, have lost out to heavy competition from abroad. It appears that all of the industries in this group are characterized by vigorous price competition, lacking even the temporary shelter afforded by rapid and radical qualitative change.

Together, these ranked lists confirm the casual impression that proportion of production workers is a fair indicator of the degree to which a sector is

**TABLE 1.   The 25 Sectors with Lowest Proportion
of Production Workers**

Sector	Number and Name	PW/Total Employment
126	Miscellaneous publishing	0.22
70	Office and accounting machines	0.24
69	Computer equipment	0.24
90	Guided missiles and space vehicles	0.24
95	Search and navigation equipment	0.25
133	Drugs	0.34
123	Newspapers	0.34
125	Books	0.36
78	Telephone and telegraph apparatus	0.41
79	Broadcasting and communications equipment	0.41
88	Aircraft and missile engines	0.41
89	Aircraft and missile parts and equipment	0.41
87	Aircraft	0.44
96	Measuring and controlling devices; watches	0.44
100	Photographic equipment and supplies	0.46
135	Paints and allied products	0.48
131	Industrial chemicals	0.49
137	Miscellaneous chemical products	0.51
134	Soap, cleaners, and toilet goods	0.52
128	Greeting card publishing	0.52
80	Semiconductors and related devices	0.53
81	Miscellaneous electronic components	0.53
99	X-ray and other electromedical apparatus	0.53
98	Medical instruments and supplies	0.53
67	Special industry machinery	0.53

change-oriented. Sectors with a low proportion of production workers tend to be those commonly recognized as high-tech, information-intensive industries. Those with a high proportion are more traditional mass producers.

Proportion of Production Workers, Growth, and Productivity Change

As might be expected, change-oriented sectors tend to grow more rapidly and to exhibit more productivity improvement over time than the rest. Table 3, column 3 shows that sectors with the lowest proportion of production workers are the ones that grew the most between 1972 and 1992. Growth rates are simple averages of the sectoral growth rates in output, measured in 1987 dollars, for sectors grouped according to the proportion of production workers to total employment. The 25 sectors with the lowest proportion of production

TABLE 2.   The 25 Sectors with Highest Proportion of Production Workers

Sector	Number and Name	PW/Total Employment
120	Pulp, paper, and paperboard mills	0.77
75	Household appliances	0.77
106	Preserved fruits and vegetables	0.78
35	Mobile homes	0.79
36	Prefabricated wood buildings	0.79
45	Primary nonferrous metals	0.79
55	Automotive stampings	0.79
56	Stampings, except automotive	0.79
54	Forgings	0.79
32	Millwork and structural wood members	0.80
33	Veneer and plywood	0.80
48	Nonferrous foundries	0.80
34	Wood containers and misc. wood	0.80
40	Glass and glass products	0.81
49	Metal cans and shipping containers	0.82
44	Iron and steel foundries	0.82
143	Footwear, except rubber and plastic	0.82
37	Household furniture	0.83
140	Tires and inner tubes	0.83
114	Weaving, finishing, yarn, and thread	0.84
31	Sawmills and planing mills	0.84
118	Apparel	0.85
104	Meat products	0.85
115	Knitting mills	0.86
30	Logging	0.87

workers had an average growth between 1972 and 1992 that was more than four times as large as that of the next group.

Figure 5 is a scatter diagram showing the relation between proportion of production workers and growth in full sectoral detail. The five sectors with most dramatic growth and with the lowest proportion of production workers had to be omitted to preserve a reasonable scale for the graph!

TABLE 3.   Growth of Output and Productivity for Sectoral Groups

(1)	pw/totemp (2)	output 92/72 (3)	emp/out 92/75 (4)	emp/out 92 (5)
Average for				
1st 25	0.46	6.12	0.60	0.0073
2nd 25	0.65	1.44	0.71	0.0083
middle 39	0.74	1.25	0.72	0.0094
last 25	0.82	1.21	0.75	0.0106

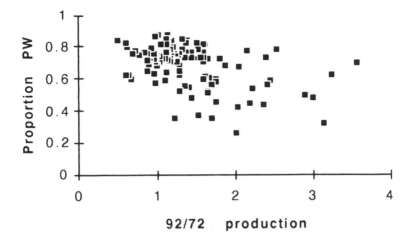

92/72 production

Fig. 5. Variation of proportion of production workers in 1992 with output growth 1992/1972 in manufacturing sectors

Table 3, column 4 shows that the 25 sectors with the lowest proportion of production workers in 1992 also had a relatively large increase in labor productivity between 1972 and 1992. For that first group, employment per constant dollar of output in 1992 was only 60 percent of that in 1972. For the next 25 sectors, ranked by percent of production workers of total employment, 1992 employment per dollar of output was 71 percent of that in 1972. For the rest, productivity gains still vary inversely with the proportion of production workers, but the differences are less dramatic.

In sum, there is a tendency for the proportion of production workers to vary inversely with both growth rates of output and improvement in labor productivity across all sectors. The sectors with the lowest proportion of production workers stand out because they employ such a low proportion of production workers and exhibit such dramatic growth in volume and productivity.

Employment per thousand dollars of gross output (the inverse of productivity) also varies inversely with the proportion of production workers (column 5). Apparently employment per dollar of revenue is lowest where nonproduction workers predominate. Of course, there are many conceptual problems involved in comparing gross revenues across sectors, because sectors differ in the proportion of intermediate goods they purchase and in capital intensity. However, casual evidence suggests that manufacturing sectors with a low proportion of production workers are not capital-intensive and purchase relatively few intermediate inputs. Further research is needed to more clearly understand this association between employment requirements per dollar and the proportion of nonproduction workers.

TABLE 4. Employment Coefficients by Function 1992 (jobs per $10,000 of output)

Group	Management	Profess. & Tech.	Sales	Clerical	Production
1st 25	9.70	16.34	4.12	12.00	30.92
2nd 25	7.90	7.77	3.06	9.89	54.82
middle 39	7.84	4.59	2.72	10.73	67.72
last 25	6.11	2.72	1.93	8.29	86.58

The Structure of Nonproduction Employment

In this section, gross output per employee is elaborated by specifying more detail for nonproduction employment in each of the major job categories (managerial, professional and technical, clerical, and sales). Administrative support is combined with managerial. Table 4 includes the additional detail for each of the four sectoral groupings. A smaller proportion of production workers in the change-oriented sectors is offset primarily, but not entirely, by much larger professional and technical staffing than in less dynamic sectors. Change-oriented sectors also employ a relatively large number of workers per dollar of output in each of the other nonproduction worker categories, including management and sales.

While virtually all of the R&D employment consists of professional and technical employees, only a fraction—less than 8 percent—of professional and technical employment is classed as R&D employment (U.S. Department of Labor 1994). It seems likely that the bulk of professional and technical employment is engaged in problem solving that supports implementation and adaptation to primary change, rather than in the direct search for distinct new products and processes.

Observations and Speculations on the Relation of Production and Nonproduction Workers to Aggregate Productivity Change

Table 5 shows computed average rates of productivity improvement in manufacturing for various periods. Two measures, gross output per employee and gross output per production worker, are given for each period. Gross output is measured in 1987 dollars. The estimates in table 5 are based on information for those two-digit manufacturing sectors where production worker and total employment series cover the entire period, that is, for all sectors except electric and electronic equipment (SIC 36) and instruments (SIC 38).

Output per employee increased at 2.2 percent per year over the interval

TABLE 5. Average Growth Rates of Manufacturing Productivity (percentage change in total employment and production workers)

	1958–92	1958–70	1971–92	1975–92[a]
1. Output/pw	2.5	2.8	2.3	2.4
2. Output/total	2.2	2.7	1.9	2.1
2/1	88.9	96.5	83.1	84.0

[a]1975–92 rates are based on data for all 2-digit sectors. Data for electric and electronic equipment and instruments were incomplete for years before 1975. Those sectors are excluded from estimates for the other intervals.

1958 to 1992. Between 1958 and 1970 the average rate was 2.7 percent; between 1971 and 1992 it was 1.9 percent per year. The rate of improvement in production worker productivity was 2.5 percent, higher than that for all employees, over the full period from 1958 to 1992. Improvement in production worker productivity was very similar to that for all employees between 1958 and 1970, but much higher between 1971 and 1992.

A difference between rates of change in productivity per employee and per production worker is not surprising. To the extent that nonproduction workers create the conditions for increased efficiency of production, their contribution constitutes a kind of metainvestment, that is, investment in change itself. Measured productivity improvements are likely to be slow during a period of heavy metainvestment for two reasons. First, regardless of the time profile of payoffs, metainvestment is charged as an input to current production. The higher the rate of metainvestment being made in the current period, the greater the denominator of the output/employment ratio.

Second, it generally takes time before metainvestment begins to bear fruit. Stephen Roach (1986) cites a similar phenomenon in computerization. He argues that in the mid-eighties, many firms had invested in computers but had not yet realized the major productivity improvements that those computers might eventually deliver. Computerization, he predicted, would effect increased efficiency, but only with a lag. Bear in mind, however, that computers appear in the national accounts in the year they are produced as plant and equipment, a final output, whereas metainvestment is counted as current account labor input.

Metainvestment is treated very differently from plant and equipment in the national accounts. The national accounts view plant and equipment as part of final output at the time it is produced. Whether or not a given item of capital equipment will improve future productivity, that benefit is anticipated when the equipment, really an intermediate good, is counted as final output at the time of its production. Plant and equipment costs as inputs to further production are distributed over time through depreciation accounts. Despite its potential long-range benefits, metainvestment is not counted as a final output, nor is it assigned an explicit economic life beyond the present. Its cost is allocated directly to present, rather than future production.

The current practice of charging the cost of nonproduction employment against current production can distort measures of productivity. A sector's nonproduction employment may be fairly stable over time, but the changes that result from it may come on-line sporadically, or with a lag. Time series of output per employee and per production worker in manufacturing show that the two increase roughly in tandem during some periods, but that they can also diverge. It is not yet clear whether such considerations have significant bearing on the apparent "productivity slowdown" of the seventies.

Conclusions

This chapter has described changes in the detailed structure of manufacturing employment over the period from 1958 to 1972. It presents strong evidence that the proportion of nonproduction employment and the composition of that employment in a sector is related to its pace of change. On average, the more rapidly a sector is growing and changing, the higher its proportion of non-production employment and, in particular, the higher the proportion of professional and technical personnel it employs. Total employment of professional and technical personnel is an order of magnitude larger than R&D employment.

While nonproduction employment is normally recorded in the current account, I have argued that employing nonproduction workers is often an investment in change, or a metainvestment. Payoffs to metainvestment may be short-term, but they also may be longer term and, like any investments, they may not pay off at all. Carrying metainvestment in the current account can distort measures of sectoral or aggregate productivity. Under this practice inputs that do not affect current outputs will nevertheless be charged against them, overstating their costs; costs of later outputs may then be understated.

These findings, however tentative, leave us in an uncomfortable position: questioning our tried-and-true perspectives on the matching of inputs and outputs in the production process and doing so before we're ready to propose a more satisfactory alternative system. Long ago Schumpeter pulled the cork and let the change-genie out of the bottle. Now the genie appears on the regular payroll, along with a sizeable band of genie-helpers, and they all have expense accounts. Should the national accounts treat them like ordinary workers? Like housewives? Like plant and equipment? Or how?

REFERENCES

Carter, A. P. 1994. Change as Economic Activity. Brandeis University, Department of Economics working paper no. 133.

Mansfield, E. 1968. *Industrial Research and Technological Innovation*. New York: Norton.

Roach, S. S. 1986. Macrorealities of the Information Economy. In R. Landau and N. Rosenberg, eds., *The Positive Sum Strategy*, 93–103. Washington, D.C.: National Academy Press.

Scherer, F. M. 1984. *Innovation and Growth*. Cambridge, MA: MIT Press.

Schumpeter, J. A. 1934. *The Theory of Economic Development*. Cambridge, MA: Harvard University Press.

———.1950. *Capitalism, Socialism and Democracy*. 3d ed. New York: Harper.

U.S. Department of Labor. 1993a. *Occupational Employment Statistics. Dictionary of Occupations*. Washington, D.C.: U.S. Government Printing Office. March 1993.

U.S. Department of Labor, Bureau of Labor Statistics, Office of Employment Projections. 1993b. Industry Output and Employment: Historical, 1958–1992; Projected, 1993–2005. On diskette.

U.S. Department of Labor, Bureau of Labor Statistics. 1994. *Occupational Employment Survey*. On diskette.

Embodied and Disembodied Innovative Activities: Evidence from the Italian Manufacturing Industry

Rinaldo Evangelista

Using data from the Italian innovation survey on 8,220 manufacturing firms, this chapter investigates the combination of disembodied innovative activities (measured by R&D and design and engineering expenditure per employee) and technical change embodied in innovative investment in new machinery and equipment, at the firm and sectoral levels.

- *Innovative investment has emerged as a major component of total innovative activities for the manufacturing industry as a whole, and as the most widespread innovative source across both firms and sectors.*
- *A clear* complementarity *emerges in the general distribution of firms between the two forms of innovative activities. At the sectoral level, both a* trade-off relationship *between embodied and disembodied innovative patterns and the presence of important complementarities between R&D and investment can be identified. The clustering of industries clearly emphasizes the predominant importance of R&D and design and engineering for machinery, electrical, and electronic components sectors and the role of investment in the chemicals, food, rubber, and metals industries. Along with these two patterns, the most representative high-technology sectors, such as aerospace, office machinery, telecommunications, and radio-TV apparatus show very high levels of both R&D and investment.*
- *The performance indicator represented by the value added per employee appears positively related across firms and sectors to greater efforts in either aspect of innovative activities, and to more structural aspects of production such as capital intensity and firm size.*

I am grateful to Daniele Archibugi, Mario Pianta, and Uwe Cantner for valuable comments. The usual disclaimer applies.

199

Introduction

The centrality of technological change for the dynamics of growth and competition was rediscovered and reemphasized by Schumpeter (1919, 1939, 1942). In a long-term perspective, discussion of these relationships has been characterized by a shift in the conceptualization of technological change. While the classical economists (Smith, Ricardo, and Marx) regarded technological change as largely embodied and related to accumulation of capital and investment activities of firms, more recent contributions, especially of an empirical nature, have tended (explicitly or implicitly) to conceptualize technological change as largely disembodied and related to the production of new knowledge and innovation. Thus investment in new machinery has progressively lost its centrality in the analysis of technology change while increasing attention has been given to innovative activities aimed at producing new technological knowledge. This shift can be easily recognized when we look at the technological indicators used in empirical studies on these subjects. Innovative performances and technological profiles of countries, sectors, and firms have usually been measured using "disembodied technological indicators." Technological indicators such as R&D, patents, licenses, and innovation counts measure the innovative activities aimed at *producing* new ideas, whereas equally developed indicators of the innovative efforts consisting of the *use* and *diffusion* of these new technologies through investment in new process technologies have not been developed and are not generally emphasized in these studies.

Yet, more recently investment seems to have regained a place in the research agenda (Scott 1988). Investment has been found to play an important role, along with other technological inputs, in the explanation of cross-country differences in growth rates (Dosi, Pavitt, and Soete 1990; Maddison 1991; Amendola, Dosi, and Papagni 1993; Pianta 1995). Basic differences between industrial sectors and firms have also been described in terms of the technological sources, among which the efforts in the improvement of process technologies through R&D and investment have been identified as important, in different degrees for different sectors (Pavitt 1984).

In this new attention to the embodied side of technological change, the quantitative relevance of investment as a distinct technological source in firms' innovative conduct and their relationship with disembodied innovative efforts have not been fully investigated.

In this chapter we will empirically explore the two aspects mentioned using data provided by the Cnr-Istat innovation survey. This survey has provided a unique set of information on the innovative activities carried out by a very large sample of Italian firms. These data will allow us to

- show the quantitative relevance of investment in new technological machinery and equipment with respect to more disembodied forms of innovative activities represented by R&D and design and engineering activities;
- explore whether complementary or substitutive relationships between disembodied and embodied technological activities emerge at the firm and sectoral levels;
- identify the main sectoral innovative patterns based on the disembodied/embodied nature of innovation performed, along with firm size and labor productivity.

Description of the Database and Variables Used in the Study

The empirical work reported in this chapter refers to the case of Italy and uses data provided by the Cnr-Istat (National Research Council of Italy-Italian National Statistical Institute) survey on innovation in the Italian manufacturing industry for 1981–85.[1] This database provides data on total innovation costs sustained by 8,220 innovating Italian firms in undertaking a wide range of technological activities. Total innovation costs include expenditures on research and development (R&D), design and engineering (D&E), innovative investment (INV), and innovative activities in marketing. These data have been matched with 1985 data from the Gross Industrial Product survey in order to have, for a slightly smaller sample of firms (6,839), data on sales, total investment in machinery, and value added.[2]

This disaggregation of the total innovation costs provided by the Cnr-Istat database allows us to distinguish between innovative activities devoted to the *production* (and development) of new knowledge, as measured by R&D and D&E activities, and those devoted to the *use* and *application* of such technology on an industrial scale, measured by the innovative investments. We label the first two components as *disembodied* and the second one as

---

1. The survey was carried out at the level of legally defined enterprises rather than consolidated industrial groups and was designed to provide reliable quantitative evidence on individual firms on a wide range of innovative activities undertaken by a large sample of Italian firms, as well as to give additional information on the main technological sources of innovative activities, their inducement factors, and economic effects (Methodological information on the Cnr-Istat survey are reported in appendix 1. See also Cesaratto, Nangano, and Sirilli 1991).

2. Data on innovation costs incurred by firms between 1981 and 1985 have been divided by five in order to make them comparable with the industrial survey data. The matching of the two databases makes available innovation and economic data for 6,839 firms (which cover more than 50 percent of the Italian manufacturing industry, in terms of sales and employees).

embodied.[3] Thus, quantitative measures of *disembodied innovative intensity* are obtained by dividing R&D and D&E expenditures by the number of employees. *Embodied innovative intensity* will be represented by the innovative investment per employee.

Indicators of the internal *composition of innovative activities* are represented by the shares of R&D, D&E (for the *disembodied* component), and innovative investment (for the *embodied* one) with respect to total innovation costs.

Total investment in machinery per employee (INVMAC) is considered as a proxy for the capital intensity of production process, and value added per employee (VA) as a proxy for labor productivity. Firm size will be measured by sales (SALES).

Table 1 shows the variables used in the statistical analysis of the later sections.

The Relative Importance of Embodied and Disembodied Innovative Activities

Table 2 shows the average values of the economic and innovation variables listed in table 1 for the total manufacturing industry and for 30 industrial sectors. The average values for both composition of innovative activities and innovative intensity show the importance of innovative investment expenditure. The latter represents 53 percent of total innovation costs and approximately one-third of the total investment in machinery. Also interesting is the relatively *small share of R&D activities* in total innovation costs. On average, R&D expenditures count for as little as 17.4% of the total firm innovative efforts. The percentage devoted to D&E activities is also quite low when compared to the embodied component of innovative activities. The innovative efforts related to marketing show the lowest percentage.

Table 2 highlights the large differences across industries in the variables related to the composition and intensity of innovative activities. This in fact indicates that a wide variety of sectoral innovative patterns exist that emerge when all of the different components of innovative activities are taken into account.

Innovative investment (INV) emerges as a very important source of technology in all sectors. Innovative investment per employee is high both in some R&D-intensive sectors, (e.g., office machinery computing, precision instruments, radio/TV and communication components) and in sectors with a low R&D and D&E innovative intensity, such as nonmetals, food, wood and

---

3. In this study the distinction between embodied and disembodied technical change does not refer to the nature of the technological input or output, but rather to the nature of innovative activities, that is, to whether or not they are finalized to the *production* or *use* of technology.

TABLE 1. List of Variables

Industrial	SALES	Sales per firm (billions of Lit)
structural	INVMAC	Investment in machinery per employee
variables	VA	Value added per employee
Innovative	INCOST[a]	Total innovation costs per employee
intensity		
variables	R&D	R&D expenditure per employee
	D&E	Design and Engineering (D&E) expenditure
Disembodied		per employee
	RDDE	R&D + D&E
Embodied	INV	Innovative investment expenditure per employee
	MKT	Innovative expenditure in marketing per employee
Innovative	%R&D	% of R&D innovation cost over total
composition		innovation costs
variables[b]	%D&E	% of D&E innovation costs over total
		innovation costs
	%INV	% of innovative investment over total
		innovation costs
	%MKT	% of innovative expenditure in
		marketing over total innovation costs

[a]R&D + D&E + INV + MKT = INCOST.
[b]%R&D + %D&E + %INV + %MKT = 100.

furniture, textiles, paper and printing, and plastic. The large shares of innovative investment (%INV) for most of the traditional consumer goods sectors show that they rely heavily upon external technological sources even if the effective expenditures per employee are below the average. On the other hand, metals and machinery show a low R&D intensity and a much higher D&E intensity and composition. D&E intensity is also high (over 2 million Lire per employee) in sectors like textile machinery, office machinery computing, radio/TV and communication components, aircraft-aerospace, and rubber.

Table 2 also shows wide sectoral differences in firm size and, to a lesser extent, in capital intensity and labor productivity. Traditional industries (e.g., textiles, leather, footwear and clothing, and wood and furniture) and specialized sectors (e.g., specialized machinery, general mechanical machinery, metal machinery, textile machinery, and precision instruments) are characterized by small and medium firm size and a low capital intensity. Sectors characterized by continuous production processes and where scale factors are relevant, such as energy, metals, synthetic fibers, chemicals, rubber, plastic, and motor vehicles are characterized, on the contrary, by medium-high capital

TABLE 2. Innovation and Industrial Structure Variables by Industrial Sectors (average values)

Industrial Sectors	Firm Size	Capital Intensity	Labor Productivity	Innovative Intensity[b]					Innovative Composition (%)			
	SALES[a]	INVMAC[a]	VA[a]	INCOST	R&D	D&E	INV	MKT	R&D	D&E	INV	MKT
Energy & Gas	1469	25.9	107.2	3.66	0.52	0.46	2.63	0.06	14.2	12.5	71.8	1.5
Metals	124	9.8	40.3	1.79	0.17	0.30	1.22	0.10	9.6	16.9	67.9	5.6
Nonmetals, Minerals	16	6.2	43.7	3.90	0.19	0.34	3.26	0.11	4.9	8.7	83.7	2.7
Chemicals	89	8.9	56.3	2.72	0.64	0.42	1.50	0.17	23.3	15.6	55.0	6.1
Pharmaceutical	65	5.9	66.7	3.57	1.40	0.58	1.15	0.44	39.3	16.2	32.2	12.2
Synthetic fibers	222	11.0	49.0	2.22	0.26	0.22	1.69	0.05	11.6	10.1	76.1	2.1
Metal products	11	4.2	40.6	2.08	0.14	0.34	1.53	0.07	6.6	16.3	73.5	3.6
Gen. mechan. engin.	22	3.5	46.3	2.50	0.41	0.76	1.22	0.11	16.5	30.4	48.7	4.4
Metal machinery	10	3.3	43.1	3.51	0.72	1.36	1.28	0.14	20.6	38.7	36.6	4.1
Textile machinery	16	3.8	39.8	4.74	0.37	2.15	2.06	0.17	7.7	45.2	43.5	3.5
Office mach. comp.	786	17.1	107.2	14.40	4.99	3.85	3.56	2.00	34.7	26.8	24.7	13.9
Electrical comp.	26	3.3	43.5	1.89	0.30	0.47	1.05	0.07	16.0	24.7	55.7	3.6
Electronic eq. & comp.	62	4.2	48.3	6.56	2.13	2.72	1.47	0.24	32.5	41.5	22.4	3.6
Radio/TV & Commun. Comp.	56	8.0	46.2	7.64	1.65	2.35	3.34	0.29	21.7	30.8	43.7	3.8

Electrical appl.	32	2.8	27.4	1.56	0.17	0.34	0.91	0.14	10.7	21.7	58.4	9.1
Motor vehicles comp.	25	4.5	37.6	2.80	0.43	0.68	1.62	0.06	15.5	24.3	58.0	2.2
Motor vehicles	1936	6.4	44.3	6.38	0.98	1.50	3.75	0.12	15.3	23.5	59.4	1.8
Other transport	43	2.0	28.1	1.18	0.18	0.33	0.62	0.05	15.2	27.9	52.3	4.6
Aircraft-aerospace	174	4.6	47.1	13.32	0.31	6.68	6.32	0.01	2.3	50.2	47.4	0.1
Precision instruments	12	4.2	41.2	5.13	1.06	1.39	2.27	0.41	20.7	27.1	44.2	8.0
Food	42	7.3	44.3	2.77	0.10	0.17	2.37	0.13	3.6	6.2	85.5	4.6
Sugar, Drinks	96	6.2	48.9	1.83	0.20	0.24	1.33	0.06	11.0	13.3	72.6	3.2
Textiles	15	4.7	40.5	2.05	0.13	0.15	1.71	0.06	6.4	7.1	83.5	3.0
Leather	11	3.0	38.8	1.55	0.06	0.15	1.28	0.05	3.8	10.0	82.7	3.3
Footwear, Clothing	15	1.6	33.8	0.69	0.04	0.13	0.49	0.05	5.4	18.0	70.0	6.6
Wood, Furnitures	7	3.3	36.1	2.02	0.16	0.24	1.50	0.12	7.7	12.1	74.4	5.8
Paper, Printing	28	5.8	55.0	2.91	0.13	0.13	2.52	0.13	4.4	4.3	86.6	4.6
Plastic	13	5.8	46.9	3.29	0.31	0.56	2.25	0.16	9.5	17.0	68.6	4.9
Rubber	34	5.0	37.3	8.46	3.17	2.42	1.69	1.18	37.5	28.7	19.9	13.9
Other manufacturing	10	3.9	36.0	2.04	0.26	0.32	1.38	0.07	12.9	15.6	67.9	3.6
Intersect. Coeff. of var.	2.43	0.78	0.38	0.83	1.49	1.34	0.60	1.75	0.70	0.55	0.33	0.68
Total	35	5.9	46.8	3.62	0.63	0.87	1.93	0.19	17.4	24.1	53.3	5.2

Source: Elaboration on Cnr-Istat data base.
[a]Billions of Italian lire (1985).
[b]Millions of Italian lire (1985) per employee.

TABLE 3.   Innovation and Industrial Structure Variables by Firm Size (average values)

Firm Size (billions of Lit.)	Capital Intensity	Labor Productivity	Innovative Intensity[b]					Innovative Composition (%)			
	INVMAC[a]	VA[a]	INCOST	R&D	D&E	INV	MKT	%R&D	%D&E	%INV	%MKT
Up to 100	4.6	42.8	2.74	0.33	0.48	1.80	0.13	12.2	17.4	65.6	4.8
100 to 500	5.9	50.2	3.45	0.68	0.83	1.81	0.13	19.9	24.0	52.5	3.7
Over 500	7.8	50.3	5.06	1.04	1.50	2.21	0.31	20.6	29.6	43.6	6.2
Total	5.9	46.8	3.62	0.63	0.87	1.93	0.19	17.4	24.1	53.3	5.2

Source: Elaboration on Cnr-Istat database.
[a]Billions of Italian lire (1985).
[b]Millions of Italian lire (1985) per employee.

intensity and large firms. Among the highly innovative sectors, office machinery shows a surprisingly high level of investment in machinery per employee.

Along with sectors, firm size also represents an important determinant of innovative patterns. Table 3 presents the data broken down by firm size, measured in terms of sales. All the indicators of innovative intensity (both disembodied and embodied) increase with firm size, with R&D and D&E showing higher differences between small and large firms (Archibugi, Evangelista, and Simonetti, 1995). Differences among firm size classes also emerge in the composition of innovative activities. Spending on R&D accounts for 20 percent of total spending for the largest firms and 12 percent for the smallest, providing confirmation of how much this indicator underestimates the innovative efforts of the smaller firms. The D&E indicator shows the same pattern. Conversely, the relative weight of innovative investment displays an inverse relation with firm size, confirming a higher propensity for this category of firms to concentrate most of their innovative efforts in the use of technologies embodied in machinery and equipment. These differences are thus related to the sectoral evidence in table 2.[4]

The Relationship between Embodied and Disembodied Technical Change at the Firm Level

In this section we use the data set to investigate whether *complementary* or *substitutive* relationships between disembodied (R&D and D&E) and embodied (INV) innovative activities emerge, when considering the data at the level of the firm. Table 4 shows the correlation coefficients between the indicator of disembodied innovative intensity (the sum of R&D and D&E—RDDE in the table), innovative investment (INV), firm size (SALES), capital intensity (INVMAC) and labor productivity (VA). All correlation coefficients have been computed using logarithmic values.[5]

The analysis of the correlation matrix shows the presence of a clear *complementarity* between embodied and disembodied innovative activities. R&D and D&E expenditures per employee (RDDE) are positively correlated

---

4. Both tables 2 and 3 point to the danger of relying exclusively on R&D expenditures as the key indicator of innovative activities in manufacturing industry, and confirm the need for a broader view of innovative efforts, including D&E and especially investment activities. More particularly they point out that for economies where a larger number of firms are small rather than big in terms of size variables, relying on R&D expenditures as indicators of innovative activity seriously underestimates innovative activity and overestimates its importance as a source of innovation.

5. This is because of the log-normal distribution of most of the variables considered and the nonlinearity of most of the relationships. The use of logarithmic values has also allowed us to exclude firms that have not performed both the embodied and the disembodied innovative activities.

TABLE 4.   Interfirm Correlation Matrix (log. values)

	LSALES	LINVMAC	LVA	LINCOST	LRDDE	LINV
LSALES	1.000					
	P = .000					
LINVMAC	0.309	1.000				
	P = .000	P = .000				
LVA	0.368	0.387	1.000			
	P = .000	P = .000	P = .000			
LINCOST	0.050	0.342	0.270	1.000		
	P = .001	P = .000	P = .000	P = .000		
LRDDE	0.082	0.203	0.248	0.803	1.000	
	P = .000	P = .000	P = .000	P = .000	P = .000	
LINV	0.006	0.358	0.215	0.891	0.514	1.000
	P = .348	P = .000	P = .000	P = .000	P = .000	P = .000

Notes: The first row shows the correlation coefficients and the second row the statistical significance. The number of cases considered is 3,734.

to innovative investment.[6] The link is much weaker, even if still highly significant, when we use total investment in machinery (INVMAC) as a proxy of embodied innovative activities.

These two results, together with the relatively low correlation between total investment in machinery per employee (INVMAC) and innovative investment (INV), have the following important implication: total investment in machinery is only an imperfect proxy of firms' embodied innovative efforts or, in other words, the technological content of total investment in machinery varies greatly among firms. Total investment in machinery instead reflects the organizational and structural aspects of production activities. These are the capital-intensive nature of production processes, with which are usually associated large-scale productions (SALES) and high levels of labor productivity (VA).

The relatively low values of the correlation coefficients that emerged in table 4 reflect the presence of a high interfirm variance in the data set. This is due to two factors. The first is the large size of the sample, which makes all coefficients statistically significant even when correlation coefficients are rather low. The second is the nonselected nature of the sample, which covers many different industrial sectors and size classes, which, as already shown, are characterized by different technological profiles.

---

6. The correlation coefficient computed on the total sample of firms is slightly lower but remains highly significant.

TABLE 5.   Multiple Regressions with Sectoral Dummy Variables

| Independent Variables | Dependent Variables | | | |
| | LRDDE | | LVA | |
	T	Sig. *T*	*T*	Sig. *T*
Constant	−6.34	0.0000	47.01	0.0000
Sectoral dummies variables				
Energy & gas	−3.96	0.0001	5.77	0.0000
Metals	−6.70	0.0000	1.88	0.0597
Nonmetals, minerals	11.55	0.0000	1.45	0.1466
Chemicals	0.73	0.4632	10.24	0.0000
Synthetic fibers	−0.99	0.3208	0.92	0.3588
Metal products	−8.24	0.0000	−0.24	0.8083
Mechan. engin.	0.56	0.5738	3.69	0.0002
Office mach. comp.	4.06	0.0001	0.68	0.4940
Motor vehicles	−2.67	0.0077	−3.62	0.0003
Precision instr.	1.38	0.1680	−0.23	0.8184
Food	10.24	0.0000	−0.10	0.9219
Sugar, drinks	−5.69	0.0000	3.13	0.0018
Textiles	10.10	0.0000	0.06	0.9560
Leather	−4.44	0.0000	0.18	0.8575
Footwear, clothing	−8.56	0.0000	−4.82	0.0000
Wood, furnitures	−8.60	0.0000	−3.17	0.0015
Paper, printing	−9.36	0.0000	3.32	0.0009
Rubber, plastic	−7.41	0.0000	2.09	0.0370
Other manufacturing	−4.41	0.0000	−1.98	0.0475
LINV	40.13	0.0000	3.24	0.0012
LINVMAC			14.73	0.0000
LSALES			14.84	0.0000
LRDDE			7.05	0.0000
R^2		0.367		0.302
F		107.6		69.8
P		0.0000		0.0000

The Relationship between Embodied and Disembodied Technical Change at the Sectoral Level

We can now analyze the major sectoral innovative patterns based on the disembodied-embodied nature of innovative activities. The existence of fixed sectoral effects on firms' propensity toward embodied or disembodied innovative activities is indicated by the results of regressions with sectoral dummy variables (LSDV). Table 5 shows that the sectoral effects on the intensity of disembodied innovative activities are usually very significant, reflecting marked differences across sectors in the levels of the technological opportunities (in the generation of new knowledge and innovations) independent of the embodied innovative efforts. Fixed sectoral effects, on the contrary, are less important for explaining the level of value added per employee when both innovative and structural variables are taken into account. Value added per employee is significantly linked to firms' innovative efforts, both embodied and disembodied, capital intensity, and firm size, suggesting that all of these factors combine to explain sectoral differences in labor productivity.[7]

Without going through an analysis of the correlation matrix, we can summarily describe the intersectoral links between the different dimensions of innovative activities by looking directly at the results of the factor analysis applied to a larger number of innovation variables (innovative composition variables have also been included), using average values for 104 industrial sectors (three-digit).[8] Table 6 shows the results of the factor analysis. The first two factors explain a large percentage of the total variance (67.9 percent). The rotated factor matrix and the plot of the variables according to the first two factors allow us to interpret the technological and economic meaning of the factors.

- The first factor indicates (1) the *disembodied innovative intensity,* measured by the expenditure in R&D and D&E per employee (RDDE) and (2) the *relevance of disembodied innovative expenditures* with respect to total innovation costs, measured by the shares of innovation costs devoted to R&D and D&E (%R&D and %D&E).
- The second factor reflects the *relevance of embodied innovative activities* and sectoral *industrial structure features* represented by innovative investment (INV), the capital intensity of the sectors (INVMAC), firm size (SALES), and labor productivity (VA). This confirms the conclusions of the previous section, based on the firm-level aggregation of data, that total investment in machinery is associated first of all with the structural and organizational aspects of production such as capital intensity, large scale, and higher labor productivity. Here, the significant difference, however, is that, at sectoral level, the complementarity between embodied and disembodied innovative activities becomes much weaker. The link between innovative investment and total investment in machinery appears much stronger and associated (as at firm level) with firm size and labor productivity.

---

7. However, the rather low levels of the R^2 show the presence of a large intrafirm variance not explained by sectoral specificities. This has also been shown by Cesaratto and Nangano 1993 and discussed in Athreye and Evangelista 1994.

8. Corresponding to a three-digit industrial classification. Four industrial sectors with fewer than three firms have been excluded.

TABLE 6. Intersectoral Factor Analysis (3-digit; 104 sectors)

Final Statistics

Variable	Communality	Factor	Eigenvalue	% of Var.	Cum. %
SALES	.36319	1	3.01522	37.7	37.7
INVMAC	.81718	2	2.41835	30.2	67.9
VA	.65861				
RDDE	.75154				
INV	.49532				
YR&D	.66576				
YD&E	.70966				
YINV	.97231				

	Rotated Factor Matrix	
	Factor 1	Factor 2
(8) %INV	−.98039	.10557
(7) %D&E	.81970	−.19432
(6) %R&D	.81398	.05651
(4) RDDE	.78604	.36563
(2) INVMAC	−.09731	.89873
(3) VA	.13023	.80103
(5) INV	−.23012	.66510
(1) SALES	.14714	.58441

Horizontal Factor 2   Vertical Factor 1

```
                     Factor 1   (Disembodied innovative
                                 intensity and composition)
                        *
            7    6  %R&D
          %D&E   *        4 RDDE
                 *
                 *
                 *
                 *
                 *
                 *
                 *         1     3 VA    Factor 2  (Embodied innovative
                 *       SALES                      intensity and structure)
********************≈********************
                 *
                 *              2 INVMAC
                 *       5 INV
                 *
                 *
                 *
                 *
                 *
                 *  8 %INV
```

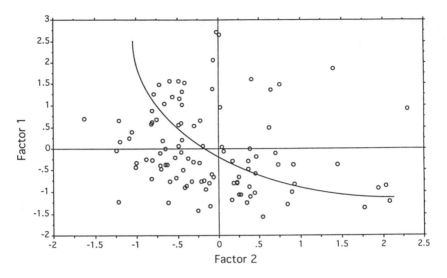

Fig. 1. Scatterplot of the sectors along the two factors (104 sectors)

These results show the *variety of sectoral innovative patterns* in terms of composition and intensity of innovative activities. Figure 1 represents the plot of 104 industrial sectors according to their position with respect to the two factors. This allows us to interpret the relationship between factor 1 (i.e., disembodied sources of innovation) and factor 2 (embodied sources of innovation and size-related factors) by studying the distribution of sectors along these two dimensions. A large number of sectors are positioned along a concave curve that shows an inverse relationship between factor 1 and factor 2.

This suggests that for most of the sectors an increase in embodied innovative intensity (which is associated with size in this data set) is accompanied by a decrease in the disembodied content of innovative activities. However, the clustering of some sectors in the bottom left and upper right quadrants also suggests that there are quite a few exceptions to this rule. These are constituted by a group of very low innovative sectors and a few sectors showing both a high disembodied and a high embodied innovative intensity.

Sectoral Innovative Patterns Based on the Embodied and Disembodied Nature of Technical Change

In order to identify the main sectors and sectoral patterns, as well as to reduce the number of sectors to manageable and meaningful categories, a factor analysis has been performed on a reduced number of sectors (30).[9] The clustering statistical procedure has been stopped at the level of 11 clusters, chosen on the basis of both the statistical and the technological significance of the clusters formed. Figure 2 shows the different clusters according to their approximate position with respect the two technological axes already used (average values of the main innovation and structural variables used in this study are also shown). The different groups of sectors can be labeled and described as follows:

Technology Users and Traditional Sectors

In the bottom left side of figure 2 cluster 4 is found. These are *low innovative sectors* characterized by both a low disembodied and a low embodied innovative intensity and containing a large number of small firms. R&D and D&E expenditure per employee are very low and firms innovate almost exclusively by purchasing and using technologies embodied in new machinery and equipment. In these sectors almost 80 percent of innovative activities rely upon this technological source. These sectors are also characterized by a low level of value added per employee, probably related both to the low technological content of final products and to the low capital intensity of the production processes.

Investment-Intensive Sectors

In this group of sectors, investment activities play an important role, both as a key factor defining the structure and organization of production activities and as a form of innovative activity. The key technological feature of these sectors is that innovative activities are mainly embodied in investment in new machinery and equipment, while R&D and D&E play a marginal role. There are, however, significant intersectoral differences in the intensity and technological content of investment activities, as well as in the relevance of scale factors. Synthetic fibers, nonmetals, food and paper in cluster 3 are more

9. A cluster analysis based on the *complete linkage method* has been used. In the cluster analyses the jointing procedure is based on the distances between the different cases or clusters. There are several clustering methods, depending on how the distances are estimated. The essential aim, however, is to group the original observations into more aggregated groups in order to minimize the internal variance (within each group) and maximize intergroup variance. With *the complete linkage method* the distance between two clusters is calculated as the distance between their two furthest points. The use of other clustering methods (i.e., single linkage and average linkage methods) has given the same result.

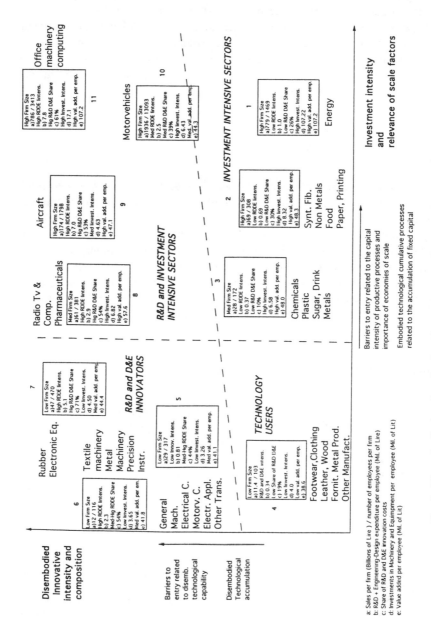

Fig. 2. Disembodied and embodied innovative patterns and industrial structure

capital-intensive and scale-based than the sectors in cluster 2.[10] As far as innovative patterns are concerned, chemicals, plastic, metals, sugar, drink, and tobacco (in cluster 3) along with innovative investment, also carry out some R&D and D&E activities, while the more capital-intensive scale-based sectors in cluster 2 show higher innovative investment per employee.

R&D and D&E Innovators

Clusters 5, 6, and 7 are characterized by the combination of high expenditure on R&D and D&E per employee, small production units, and low levels of investment (both total and innovative) per employee. Cluster 6 includes all of the most innovative mechanical engineering sectors. Firm size and investment intensity are very low. In these sectors the relatively high disembodied innovative intensity is due, first of all, to the relevance of D&E innovative activities. Cluster 7 shares the same structural characteristics with cluster 6, though it presents higher R&D and D&E expenditure per employee. The higher innovative intensity of these sectors might also explain their relatively higher value added per employee. Cluster 5, composed of the electrical and mechanical sectors, is constituted by the less innovative sectors among R&D and D&E innovators. Industrial sectors in this group show R&D and D&E expenditure per employee just over the average and a rather low level of value added per employee associated with both a low capital intensity and an average R&D and D&E expenditure per employee.

R&D and Investment-Intensive Innovators

In clusters 8, 9, 10, and 11, high R&D and D&E expenditure per employee are accompanied by medium or high levels of investment in machinery per employee and medium or large scale of production.

At the top right side of the figure we find cluster 11, consisting of the electronics-office machinery industry. Large firms, high expenditure on R&D and engineering activities, and a surprisingly high investment intensity are the characteristics of this high-tech sector. The value added per employee is also very high, being related to the high technological content of products and processes, as well as to the high capital intensity of these sectors.

A similar pattern, but with less extreme values, is shown by clusters 9 (aircraft) and 8 (radio/TV and telecommunication equipment and phar-

---

10. The combination of a rather small firm size and a medium investment intensity in cluster 2 is the result of the specific characteristics of the production processes in these industries (chemicals, plastics, metals, sugar, drink, and tobacco). Also, in the case of small production units, the "continuous process" nature of production activities often requires relatively capital-intensive structures of production associated with a medium-high labor productivity.

maceuticals), where a high disembodied innovative intensity is associated with a medium and large firm size and capital intensity. In these sectors innovative activities aimed at producing new technological knowledge represent a large part of total innovative activities.

The automobile industry (cluster 10) is an outlier of this group, as far as firm size is concerned. This reflects the fact that the automobile industry is the sector where mass-production systems are more extensively exploited. Investment expenditure in machinery per employee is high, but the relevance of economies of scale is related not only to the amount of fixed capital invested, but also to the organizational complexity of the productive processes. R&D and D&E intensity and their shares of total innovation costs are also average in this sector.

A More Interpretive Analysis of the Sectoral Innovative Patterns

How can these statistical associations based on data at a point of time be interpreted in a more dynamic perspective? A possible dynamic qualification of the patterns identified could be done in terms of (1) technological barriers to entry, and (2) technological states of industries. (1) In figure 2 the vertical and horizontal distances between clusters can be considered as an indicator of technological distances among sectors.[11] These distances can also be seen as barriers to intersectoral movement of the firms and to diversification strategies in technology and production. Moving from one sector to another requires a firm to face structural, technological, and organizational barriers both to entry and to exit (due to the presence of sunk costs both in technology and in production assets) whose nature and importance vary according to the starting point and the direction of movement.[12] The vertical axis reflects the relevance of the barrier to entry related to the cumulative process of disembodied and more tacit technological knowledge, whereas the horizontal axis shows the relevance of the barriers to entry related to the amount of fixed capital and embodied technology accumulated, as well as to the complexity of industrial organization models.

This double nature of the technological barriers to entry might partly explain the nonlinear relationships between innovative intensity and firm size

---

11. The concept of *technological distance* has been developed by Jaffe (1986). Interfirm technological distances have been measured looking at the patenting portfolio of firms. See also Archibugi 1988 and Goto and Suzuki 1989.

12. This point has already been pointed out by Gort and Klepper, who, along with stating that "technical change (innovations) plays a critical role in determining both entry rates and the eventual number of firms in the market," also stress that "the number of firms in product markets technologically adjacent to those of a new product—that is, the number of potential entrants— influence the entry rates" (Gort and Klepper 1982, p. 634).

(and market structure) found by the empirical literature in this field (Cohen and Levin 1989). In some industries (R&D and investment-intensive sectors in fig. 2) the full exploitation of the technological opportunities requires a large amount of investment, the development of complex organizations, and large volumes of production, while in other innovative sectors (R&D and D&E innovators) such combination is not found. Only in the first group of sectors does the joint presence of static and dynamic economies of scale in production and learning economies related to the accumulation of disembodied technological capabilities favor large firms and concentrated market structures. The relationships between firm size (as well as market structure) and innovative intensity seems, therefore, related to the extent to which disembodied and embodied technological activities turn out to be complementary innovative sources.

The different patterns in figure 2 could also be read within the product cycle model. According to product cycle theory (Vernon 1966; Utterback and Abernathy 1975; Abernathy and Utterback 1978; Utterback and Suàrez 1993), in the mature phase of industries, technology is fairly standardized, innovations are aimed at cost reduction and tend to be based on improvements in processes. This appears to be consistent with a rising proportion of embodied to disembodied technology in mature, scale-based, and investment-intensive industries. New industries, conversely, are associated with a lower level of standardization, and could be characterized by a high proportion of disembodied to embodied technological activities. However, the behavior of some sectors is contrary to what one would expect from a reading of the product cycle approach. On the one hand, old innovative industries, like most of the specialized machinery producers, do not seem to have ever passed through a large-scale standardization stage, still being characterized by a large number of small firms due to the high customization of their products and technologies. On the other hand, more recent R&D-intensive sectors like office machinery, telecommunication, and radio/TV have, in a relatively short time, reached a significant level of standardization of products, processes, and technologies, together with concentrated market structures. The set of technological, structural, and market dimensions that characterize the dynamics of industrial sectors has emerged even from our static analysis as highly complex and interactive.

Conclusions

This chapter, based on the empirical findings of the Italian survey, was intended to investigate the relevance of investment as a distinct technological source and its relationship with disembodied innovative activities at the firm and the sectoral level.

It has been shown that there are large differences across sectors and firms in the importance of different sources of technology, confirming a large empirical and theoretical literature (Pavitt 1984; Von Hippel 1988; Malerba and Orsenigo 1990; and Archibugi, Cesaratto, and Sirilli 1991). These differences are not limited to the relative amount of resources devoted to innovative activities aimed at creating or improving technological knowledge (R&D and D&E), but are also related to the amount of investment required for the acquisition and use of these technologies on an industrial scale, that is "embodied technological change." *Innovative production investment has emerged as a major component of innovation* for the manufacturing industry as a whole and as the most important innovative source of innovation across both firms and sectors.

The analysis based on disaggregated data at the firm level has shown a clear complementarity between the two forms of innovative activities. However, the presence of a large interfirm variance in the embodied and disembodied mix of firms' innovative activities was also found. This suggests that sectoral differences are important explanatory factors. The analysis of data at a more aggregated level of industrial sectors has shown the presence of a variety of distinct innovative patterns. Thus, there is both a *trade-off relationship* between embodied and disembodied innovative patterns for a large group of sectors and a *complementarity* relation between R&D and investment for a few very innovative sectors. The clustering of industries clearly emphasizes (1) the predominant importance of R&D and D&E for machinery, electrical, and electric components sectors, and (2) the role of investment in the chemicals, food, rubber, and metals industries. Along with these two opposite patterns, (3) the most representative high-technology sectors such as aerospace, office machinery, telecommunications, and radio/TV apparatus show very high levels of both R&D and investment, with which are associated large-scale organizations. Finally, the performance indicator represented by the value added per employee appears positively related across firms and sectors to greater efforts in either aspect of innovative activities, and to more structural aspects of production such as capital intensity and firm size.

A major limitation of this analysis has been the inability to fully interpret the dynamic causation behind these results. This is because the time dimension along which such causation could be studied is not available for analysis. It is hoped that the forthcoming new survey data (1994) will provide some clues in this regard. Nevertheless, some explanation in terms of the cumulativeness of structural and technical barriers to entry and in terms of the product cycle have been suggested.

The general indication of this chapter is that in the analysis of the technological profiles of firms and industries there is a need to combine the widely used indicators of disembodied technology (such as R&D and patents) with an adequate consideration of innovative investment that is associated with distinct forms of technological capabilities, learning processes, and organizational structures. This suggests that an enlarged framework is also needed in the analysis of the innovative activities and growth performances of firms. Innovation surveys represent a major source of information that give empirical support to such an enlarged perspective on technological change. In this context, the recent standardization of innovation survey proposed by the OSLO manual (OECD 1992) and the ongoing European Community Innovation Survey (EUROSTAT 1994) are extremely important. The latter will make available for the first time an internationally comparable database on the key dimensions of innovation activities investigated in this chapter.

APPENDIX

Between October 1987 and April 1988, the Italian Central Statistical Office (ISTAT), in collaboration with the Institute for Studies on Scientific Research and Documentation of the Italian National Research Council (ISRDS-CNR), carried out a survey of technological innovation in the Italian manufacturing industry. The aim of the survey was to investigate the process of technological innovation and its impact on firms. The period referred to was the five years between 1981 and 1985. A preliminary survey was carried out in 1985 by means of a questionnaire mailed to about 35,000 manufacturing firms with more than 20 employees; 16,701 firms—69.3 percent of the 24,104 firms that answered the questionnaire—declared that they had introduced technological innovations in the period 1981–85. On the basis of the answers to the above-mentioned preliminary survey, these firms were subdivided into two groups. One, comprising 3,200 firms, included those firms that had introduced both product innovations and process innovations based on in-house innovative activities (in particular, R&D and patents held). These firms, deemed the most innovative on the basis of the preliminary survey, were then subjected to a direct interview using a 33-item questionnaire. The second group of firms, numbering about 13,000, were those having declared that they had innovated mainly by purchasing technology from outside the firm through capital goods. This second group was mailed a simplified 21-item questionnaire. Overall, 8,220 firms responded to the questionnaire, 5,519 by post and 2,701 by direct interview. The fall-off in the number of firms actually participating in the survey compared with the total number of 16,701 innovating firms originally identified can be explained both by the comparative complexity of the new questionnaire and by the more rigorous criteria used in the innovation survey to define technological innovation. The 8,220 firms included in the innovation survey represent about 27 percent of the 30,449 manufacturing companies included in industrial survey. They account for an even higher percentage of employees, more than 52 percent. Overall, the average size of Italian innovating firms appears larger as compared to the average size of Italian manufacturing firms.

REFERENCES

Abernathy, W. J., and J. M. Utterback. 1978. Patterns of Industrial Innovation. *Technology Review* 7.
Amendola, G., G. Dosi, and E. Papagni. 1993. The Dynamics of International Competitiveness. *Weltwirtschaftliches* 3.
Archibugi, D. 1988. In Search of a Useful Measure of Technological Innovation. *Technological Forecasting and Social Change* 34.
Archibugi, D., S. Cesaratto, and G. Sirilli. 1991. Sources of Innovative Activities and Industrial Organization in Italy. *Research Policy* 20.
Archibugi, D., R. Evangelista, and R. Simonetti. 1995. Concentration, Firm Size and Innovation. Evidence from Innovation Costs. *Technovation* 15, no. 3: 153–63.
Athreye, S., and R. Evangelista. 1994. *Limiting the Notion of Variety. Consideration for Empirical Research.* Paper presented at the 1994 EAEPE conference, Copenhagen, 27–29 October.
Cesaratto, S., and S. Nangano. 1993. Technological Profiles and Economic Performance in the Italian Manufacturing Sector. *Economics of Innovation and New Technology* 2.
Cesaratto, S., S. Mangano, and G. Sirilli. 1991. The Innovative Behaviour of Italian Firms: A Survey on Technological Innovation and R&D. *Scientometrics* 21, no. 1.
Cohen, W. M., and R. C. Levin. 1989. *Empirical Studies of Innovation and Market Structure.* In R. Schmalensee and R. D. Willig, ed., *Handbook of Industrial Organization,* Vol. 2. Amsterdam: Elsevier Science Publishers B.V.
Dosi, G., K. Pavitt, and L. Soete. 1990. *The Economics of Technical Change and International Trade.* London: Harvester Wheatsheaf.
EUROSTAT. 1994. *The Community Innovation Surveys. Status and Perspectives.* Luxembourg.
Freeman, C. 1982. *The Economics of Industrial Innovation.* London: Frances Pinter.
Gort, M., and S. Klepper. 1982. Time Paths in the Diffusion of Product Innovations. *Economic Journal* 92, no. 367 (September): 630–53.
Goto, A., and K. Suzuki. 1989. R&D Capital, Rate of Return on R&D Investment and Spillovers of R&D in Japanese Manufacturing Industries. *The Review of Economics and Statistics* 71, no. 4.
Jaffe, A. 1986. Technological Opportunity and Spillovers in R&D: Evidence from Firms' Patents, Profits and Market Values. *American Economic Review* 76, no. 5.
Maddison, A. 1991. *Dynamic Forces in Capitalist Development.* Oxford: Oxford University Press.
Malerba, F., and L. Orsenigo. 1990. *Technological Regimes and Patterns of Innovation: A Theoretical and Empirical Investigation of the Italian Case.* In A. Heertje

and M. Perlman, eds., *Evolving Technology and Market Structure*. Ann Arbor: University of Michigan Press.

OECD. 1992. *Oslo Manual. OECD Proposed Guidelines for Collecting and Interpreting Technological Innovation Data*. Paris.

Pavitt, K. 1984. Sectoral Patterns of Technological Change: Toward a Taxonomy and a Theory. *Research Policy* 13.

Pianta, M. 1995. Technology and Growth in OECD Countries, 1970–1990. *Cambridge Journal of Economics* 19, no. 1: 175–87.

Rosenberg, N. 1963. Capital Goods, Technology and Economic Growth. *Oxford Economic Papers* 15.

Schumpeter, J. A. [1919] 1934. *The Theory of Economic Development*. Cambridge, MA: Harvard University Press.

Schumpeter, J. A. 1939. *Business Cycles*. New York: McGraw-Hill.

Schumpeter, J. A. 1942. *Capitalism, Socialism and Democracy*. New York: Harper.

Scott, M. F. G. 1988. *A New View of Economic Growth*. Oxford: Clarendon Press.

Smith, A. [1776] 1976. *An Inquire into the Nature and Causes of the Wealth of Nations*. Oxford: Clarendon Press.

Utterback, J. M., and W. J. Abernathy. 1975. A Dynamic Model of Product and Process Innovation. *Omega* 3.

Utterback, J. M., and F. F. Suàrez. 1993. Innovation, Competition, and Industry Structure. *Research Policy* 22.

Vernon, R. 1966. International Investment and International Trade. *Quarterly Journal of Economics* 80.

Von Hippel, E. 1988. *The Sources of Innovation*. New York: Oxford University Press.

Detecting Technological Performance and Variety: An Empirical Approach

Uwe Cantner, Horst Hanusch, and Georg Westermann

The modern economic theory of innovation stresses that industry structures are affected by the coexistence and competition of several different technologies. Our investigation introduces a nonparametric method suitable for detecting those structures and tracking their development. Moreover, we show that the results obtained are significantly dependent on the innovative activities of firms.

Introduction

Recent advances in the economics of technological change increasingly stress that the observed industry structure may also be the result of the coexistence and competition of several different technologes.[1] This diversity is even a major force pushing forward technological progress. Consequently, a variety of technological approaches may prevail within an industry and several technology leaders might be identified.

Within this evolutionary context our chapter attempts (1) to detect heterogeneous industry structures, as well as their development over time, and (2) to explain those findings by the innovative behavior of firms. With re-

---

We are very grateful to the "Stifterverband für die Deutsche Wissenschaft," who made it possible to relate our results on relative firm productivity to firm-specific R&D expenditures. We are especially grateful to Christoph Grenzmann from the "SV-Wissenschaftsstatistik" at Essen, who provided the technical assistance as well as the respective computations that are presented in the third section.

We thank Jean Bernard, Elias Dinopoulos, Rinaldo Evangelista, Steven Klepper, and Heinrich Oppenländer for their remarks and suggestions. Remaining errors are still our responsibility.

Finally, financial support by the European Commission for the SPES-project "Comparative Economics of R&D: The Case of France and Germany," as well as by the DAAD-programme PROCOPE is gratefully acknowledged.

1. See, for example, Dosi 1988; Nelson and Winter 1982.

spect to our first goal, however, we face a very crucial problem: Empirical analyses within evolutionary economics still lack adequate analytical and statistical tools. Borrowing well-elaborated methods out of the rich pool of neoclassical economics, however, also implies adoption of the respective underlying assumptions. In our context this is especially relevant for the most prominent feature of evolutionary modeling, the heterogeneity of agents, which then—by and large—is boiled down to the average behavior of the representative agent. Identical production functions for all firms and only stochastic deviations from a single best-practice technology are the obvious and well-known outcome.

Instead, in order to tackle the problem of heterogeneity we suggest a nonparametric linear programming approach,[2] the Data-Envelopment-Analysis (DEA),[3] to investigate heterogeneous performances and technological variety that neither needs a special type of production function nor relies on general equilibrium assumptions. Quite the contrary, based on the broad definition of Leontief-type production functions, this procedure allows us to detect a large number of specific "technologies" defined and approximated by specific input ratios. Moreover, they can be compared, delivering a number of best-practice technologies as well as measures of technical inefficiencies. The former will be used to define certain technological fields with one or several technological leaders and a larger number of technically backward firms.

Our empirical analysis focuses on the machinery and electronics sectors in Germany. In a first step we concentrate on the industry structure and its development. Here we detect several best-practice technologies, as well as a measure for technical inefficiency. Coupled with a traditional cluster analysis, technology leaders can be assigned to specific "technology fields." In a second step the influence of innovative activities on the occurrence and development of these structures is investigated. Using firm-specific R&D capital stocks on the one hand and patenting activities of the firms on the other, it is shown that these technological indicators are able to explain the intraindustry heterogeneity.

The investigation contains the following steps: The next section briefly delivers the theoretical foundation of our analysis. Additionally, the DEA method is introduced. The third section delivers our results with respect to technical inefficiency, which are then related to R&D capital stocks and patent activity in the fourth section. The fifth section concludes our analysis.

---

2. For an overview see Färe, Grosskopf, and Lovell 1993.

3. See Charnes and Cooper 1962, 1985. For an excellent overview see Charnes, Cooper, Lewin, and Seiford 1994.

Theoretical Basis and Analytical Model

Technological Variety—A Theoretical Foundation

The modern theory of new technology and innovation attempts to explain differences or asymmetries among firms by their respective technological performance. The core of this approach is the emphasis on the fact that opportunities of and advances in technology (tend to) dominate any economic determinant of a firm's choice of technology.

Conventional neoclassical theory, however, does not share this view, as there the path along which technological progress develops is mainly determined by changes in relative factor prices, where technological possibilities are open to all economic agents. Consequently, assuming a well-functioning market mechanism, heterogeneity of firms within a sector is not to be expected.

This neoclassical concept of factor price-induced technological progress has been challenged by the well-known Salter (1960) and Fellner (1961) critiques and developed further by Ahmad (1966, p. 345), who states that "only technological considerations and not a change in the relative price of the factor may influence the nature of invention. . . ." In the broad research field of modern innovation theory, besides others, a major point of criticism focuses on the standard neoclassical assumption that technological knowledge is considered as a public good, which—in turn—implies technological uniformity between firms as a core hypothesis.[4] Instead, the modern approach distinguishes between public knowledge on the one hand and private, often tacit, technological knowledge on the other. It is this private-good character of technological know-how that allows firms to develop along a certain technological path, often described as cumulative, selective, and finalized.[5] The public-good feature of know-how, on the other hand, reduces variety by giving different firms access to common technological principles.

Consequently, the twofold character of technological know-how provides for an industry structure consisting of several technology fields. Firms within a certain technology field apply very similar or even identical production functions, whereas firms attached to different technology fields use quite distinct technologies although they are all engaged in the production of the same class of goods.

The reason for building up a private stock of technological knowledge leading to technological diversity is that the technological capability a firm

---

4. As a by-product, the use of a representative agent is justified on methodological grounds.

5. See Dosi 1988.

has accumulated is determined by past investment and learning effects, as well as R&D engagements. This kind of technological progress is considered to be local.[6] And by reverse causation, these capabilities are decisive for further successful technological improvements, as well as for successful adoption of new techniques developed elsewhere.

A major consequence of this view is that relative factor prices play only a minor role in the development of new technologies. Employing the standard textbook isoquant, only a (small) number of all techniques on an isoquant are practiced, and substitution processes—which are to be considered as resource-using search processes—due to changes in relative factor prices are not cost-less. Therefore, if the technological opportunities of a firm are considerably high, search costs will be devoted to innovation, not to substitution. In the case of local technological advances, the development path of a firm will be characterized by fairly constant factor-input ratios independent of the prevailing relative factor prices. And further, changes in the relative factor prices will not cause the transition to the new technology to be reversable; that is, technological change is characterized by irreversibilities, at least in the short and medium run.

Based on this theoretical background we assume a special form of production structure on the sectoral level that we use for our empirical investigation:

1. An industry consists of firms that employ different production functions, each one representing the respective firm-specific technique. Since these techniques are the outcome of a localized technological progress, we consider the resulting techniques—at least in the short run—to be of zero elasticity of substitution at the outset. This suggests a Leontief-type production function. Firm diversity is then represented by a number of different Leontief production functions, that is, different factor input ratios.
2. For the medium and long run one still could assume the development path to be characterized by a constant factor input ratio. However, we do not need this restrictive assumption but rather suggest the development path to be constrained within elastic barriers.[7] The observation of an increasing mechanization of the production processes is thus taken into account.[8]

With this formulation of a sector's production structure, it is interesting to compare the firms in the sector with respect to their technological performance. Such an investigation has to take into account the following aspects:

6. See Atkinson and Stiglitz 1969.
7. See David 1975.
8. See Dosi and Soete 1983; Dosi, Pavitt, and Soete 1990.

1. Due to different firm-specific technological approaches, there may appear to be more than one best-practice technique, which cannot necessarily be ranked as being better and worse.
2. Despite this, quite a number of practiced techniques can be ranked as unequivocally better or worse. These differences can be measured by index numbers for traditional technical inefficiency.

Summarizing these two factors, our empirical analysis attempts to account (*a*) for variety represented by certain technological fields within an industry and (*b*) for the relative technical performance of firms.

The Analytical Model

The analytical approach we apply is nonparametric and based on a linear programming procedure. In operations research and management science this analysis has become well known as the *Data Envelopment Analysis* (DEA),[9] whereas in the economics literature on frontier production functions this method has diffused much more slowly.[10] To ease the presentation, throughout the chapter we will refer to this procedure as DEA.

DEA allows us to compute an index for relative technical inefficiency for each firm within a sample. The choice of a nonparametric approach helps to take account of technological variety by allowing for several parametrically different production functions. Principally this procedure relies on the traditional index numbers for productivity analysis. For each firm j ($j = 1, \ldots, n$) a productivity index h_j is given by

$$h_j = \frac{u^T Y_j}{v^T X_j}. \tag{1}$$

Here Y_j is an s-vector of outputs and X_j an m-vector of inputs of firm j. s-vector u and m-vector v contain the aggregation weights, u_r ($r = 1, \ldots, s$) and v_i ($i = 1, \ldots, m$), respectively. h_j in equation (1) is nothing other than an index of *total factor productivity*. The respective aggregation functions (for inputs and outputs respectively) are of a linear arithmetic type, as also employed in the well-known Kendrick-Ott productivity index.[11] There, however, by special assumptions the aggregation weights, u_r and v_i, are given exogenously.

DEA does not rely on such assumptions. In particular, it is not assumed that all firms in the sample have an identical production function. The specific aggregation weights are determined endogenously and can differ from firm to

---

9. See Charnes and Cooper 1962, 1985; Charnes, Cooper, Lewin, and Seiford 1994.
10. See Färe, Grosskopf, and Lovell 1993.
11. See Kendrick 1956 and Ott 1959.

firm. They are the solution to a specific optimization problem (as discussed in the following), and therefore they are dependent on the empirical data of our sample.

The basic principle of DEA is to determine the indexes h_j in such a way that they can be interpreted as efficiency parameters. The (relatively) most efficient firms of a sample should be characterized by an h-value equal to unity, and all less efficient firms by an h-value of less than unity. The following constrained maximization problem is used to determine such an h-value for a particular firm l, $l \in \{1, \ldots, n\}$, out of the sample:

$$\max h_l = \frac{u^T Y_l}{v^t X_l}$$

s.t.

$$\frac{u^T Y_j}{v^T X_j} \leq 1; \quad j = 1, \ldots, n;$$

$$u, v \quad > 0.$$

(2)

Problem (2) determines h_l of firm l subject to the constraint that the h_j of all firms of the sample are less than or equal to 1. The constraints provide that h is indexed on $]0,1]$. Moreover the elements of u and v have to be strictly positive. This requirement means that for all inputs and outputs used, there exists a positive value.

Since we employ linear arithmetic aggregation functions for inputs and outputs, equation (2) is to be rendered as a problem of linear fractional programming. To solve such optimizations, there exist a number of methods, the best known of which is due to Charnes and Cooper 1962. They suggest transforming equation (2) into a standard linear program by claiming the denominator in the objective function to be constant. The resulting linear program can then be solved by the simplex algorithm

$$\max \mu^T Y_l$$

s.t.

$$\mu^T Y_j - \omega^T X_j \leq 0; \quad j = 1, \ldots, n;$$

$$\omega^T X_l = 1$$

$$\mu, \omega > 0.$$

(3)

Y_l and X_l are the r- and s-vectors of outputs and inputs, respectively, of firm l. In equation (3) the vectors μ and ω are the transformed aggregation weights, which also have to be strictly positive.

Problem (3) represents a version of efficiency analysis that is known as the "production" or "efficiency technology" form: Here, one attempts to maximize the output of firm l where input is normalized, the solution is to be positive, and the efficiency indexes[12] of all firms are restricted to]0,1]. Equation (4) is known as the "envelopment" form since here a frontier function (containing several linear parts) can be determined. This obviously relates our analysis to that of Farrell 1957. The corresponding dual program then reads[13]

$$\min \theta_l$$

$$s.t.$$

$$Y\lambda_l \geq y_{rl}; \quad r = 1, \ldots, s; \tag{4}$$

$$\theta x_{il} - X_i\lambda_l \geq 0; \quad i = 1, \ldots, m;$$

$$\lambda_l \geq 0$$

where y_{rl} and x_{il} are the output r and input i of firm l, respectively. Y, and X_l are the n-vectors of outputs and inputs. The parameter θ_l to be minimized expresses the percentage level to which the inputs of firm l have to be reduced proportionally in order to produce efficiently. With $\theta_l = 1$ the respective firm belongs to the efficient firms on the frontier. The n-vector λ_l states the weights of all (efficient) firms that serve as reference for firm l. For the efficient firm l (with $\theta_l = 1$), we obtain 1 for the lth element of λ_l and 0 for all other elements.

Using the envelopment form of equation (4), it is easy to select efficient and inefficient firms directly. Principally, the Pareto-Koopmanns criterion is employed, which allows us to compare vectors. The linear programming procedure as performed by equation (4), however, may result in selecting a firm as DEA-efficient although it is clearly dominated by another firm on the frontier. This may happen when the parts of the frontier are parallel to one of the axes. To avoid such results, the linear program in equation (4) must be modified as follows:

---

12. The ratios are stated here as differences that are not allowed to be positive.
13. See Charnes, Cooper, and Thrall 1986.

$$\min \; \theta_l - \epsilon e^T s_l^+ - \epsilon e^T s_l^-$$

$s.t.$

$$Y\lambda_l - s_l^- = y_{rl}; \quad r = 1, \ldots, s; \tag{5}$$

$$\theta x_{il} - X_i\lambda_l - s_l^+ = 0; \quad i = 1, \ldots, m;$$

$$\lambda_l, \; s_l^+, \; s_l^- \geq 0.$$

This modification provides that for all firms that are on the frontier ($\theta_l = 1$) but that are dominated by other firms of the frontier, the respective slacks (s_l^+ for excess inputs and s_l^- for output slacks) are taken into account in the objective function.[14] Vector e^T contains only elements 1.[15] ϵ is a positive constant smaller than any other variable of the program. This guarantees that slacks are only taken into account when a strictly convex envelope has already been determined.[16]

For efficiency analyses additional to θ one has to take remaining slacks into account. Only then is a clear-cut selection of efficient and inefficient firms possible. For simple qualitative statements this procedure is sufficient. For a quantitative analysis, however, it would be helpful to combine the proportional reduction θ_l, as well as s_l^+ and s_l^-, into a single measure. This is done by a method suggested by Ali and Lerme (1990):

As is known from index numbers for total factor productivity, the input factors have to be aggregated in a single number. Similarly, in DEA the respective weights are given by the marginal productivities of the input factors of the reference firm. These marginal productivities are the solution of the primal program (3). Using the marginal productivities of the respective reference firms (determined by the nonzero elements of the vector λ_l) one can weight the inputs on the one hand and the s_l^+ and s_l^- of firm l on the other hand. The ratio between these delivers the amount of the additional inefficiency. Subtracting this measure from θ_l delivers an adjusted aggregate measure of inefficiency ι_l. In the following empirical analysis we rely solely on ι_l.

---

14. The variable ϵ has to be smaller than any other measure of the optimization. This implies that first the frontier has to be determined and then the slack variables can enter the basic solution.

15. Of course, one should here distinguish two vectors e^T for inputs and output that contain s and i elements, respectively. To ease notation we do not take account of this. Further analysis is not affected.

16. This condition is equivalent to the statement that the aggregation weight or prices of the primal program must be strictly positive.

Data Set, Procedure of Investigation, and Empirical Results

Data Set and Procedure of Investigation

The data set we investigate contains time series data of 78 German machinery and 39 German electronic firms of different subbranches. This data set is time consistent, in the sense that we have neither entries nor exits of firms over the period of investigation, from 1985 to 1991. All firms under consideration are of the legal form "shareholder's company."

In order to compute the efficiency score "ι," we define some suitable variables for inputs and output:

As an output measure we construct a total output consisting of the sum of total sales, inventory changes, and internal used firm services from the profit and loss accounts. This output is deflated by a composed price index for German investment goods.

On the input side we distinguish between capital, labor, and material. Capital is captured by the balance sheet position fixed assets (net value at the beginning of the year). Since we have no information about the age structure of capital, this measure is not deflated. For labor we compute the effective worker hours per year by multiplying the number of workers of a firm by an index of effective worker hours for the German machinery industry. Material consists of the deflated profit and loss position of raw materials and supplies

Our empirical analysis proceeds in three main steps. The first is related (*a*) to the technological structure, (*b*) to the dynamics of this structure, and (*c*) to the aspect of technological variety. For this investigation the efficiency scores of DEA are used and interpreted. In a second step our efficiency indices will be related to firm-specific R&D. For this data we rely on a database of the Stifterverband. From our 78/39 firms above, only 59 firms in machinery and 26 firms in electronics have reported their R&D. Finally, we also relate our productivity results to the patenting activity of the firms within the years 1985–88. The respective patent data are drawn from the database of the European Patent Office.

Technical Efficiency

According to our route of investigation in "Data Set and Procedure of Investigation" the first step of our analysis attempts (1) to detect the efficient firms in a certain year, and (2) to answer the question of whether the set of efficient firms is stable over time.

The results show that in a year-by-year analysis there are only three machinery and two electronics firms that are continuously members of the efficient set. Other firms lose their leading position after some years or appear for only a short period on the frontier. The number of efficient firms varies from five to ten (three to eight) firms per year with a slightly decreasing (increasing) tendency in the machinery (electronics) sector. We assume that only the technically best firms stay and stamp the envelope for a longer time.

With respect to the dynamics of the above-described technological structure, we ask these additional three questions:

1. Do the inefficient firms get closer to the frontier over time; that is, is there a catching-up?
2. Has technological progress been driven by the efficiency leaders?
3. Compared to the "all-time best-practice" frontier, does the efficiency of the whole sector increase?

These questions lead to dividing the sample of firms into two subgroups. The first one includes only the efficient firms, while the other one consists of the inefficient firms. Figure 1 shows the average year-by-year ι-value of the inefficient group (NEFFSTAT) together with the average year-by-year ι-value of the efficient firms (EFFSTAT) (which, of course, has to be 1.0 by definition). To obtain a measure of the movement of the frontier we compute another average ι-value for the efficient sub-sample (EFFDYN) as a comparison with the "all-time best-practice" frontier.

For the period from 1988 to 1990, figure 1a illustrates that the decreasing efficiency of the nonefficient machinery firms was mainly the result of an increasing efficiency of the frontier sample. In this period the pursuing firms were not able to follow the shifting of the frontier.

Quite a contrary result can be observed for the electronics sector in the same period (1988 to 1990). The increasing relative efficiency of the inefficient firms is not an outcome of a movement of the frontier. This is obvious because from 1988 to 1990 the actual frontier's efficiency compared to the all-time best-practice frontier does not change. The inefficient firms really do catch up.

With respect to the "all-time best-practice" frontier for the efficient firms of both sectors (for the electronics sector at least from 1986), a slight but obviously increasing tendency can be noticed. Consequently, the year-by-year efficiency leaders are pushing forward the technological development.

Another calculation not shown in figure 1 is the following: The average ι values for the group of inefficient firms (calculated in the same way with reference to the "all-time best-practice" frontier) also show an increasing trend, from 0.49 (1985) to 0.55 (1991) for the machinery sector and from 0.30 (1985) to 0.37 (1991) for the electronics sector. Therefore, both sectors shift toward more technical efficiency.

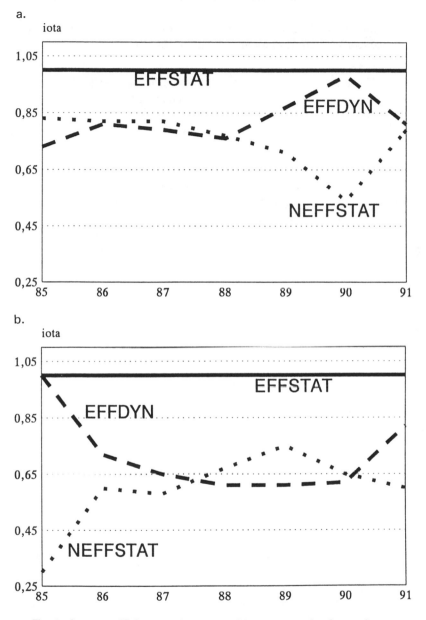

Fig. 1. Average efficiency series: a, machinery sector; b, electronics sector

Finally we want to take account of technological variety. The following three questions are addressed with respect to this issue:

1. What are the differences between the efficiency leaders?
2. Do the efficiency leaders define "technology fields" within their industry?
3. How does the technical efficiency and importance of these "technology fields" develop over time?

As a concession to clearness and size of the analysis we present with respect to the intrasector investigation only the results for the machinery firms.[17]

For 1985 we discover ten machinery firms with an ι-value of 1,0. Closer inspection of the input structure of these firms clearly shows that some of them differ extremely in the proportions of their use of the three inputs necessary to produce one unit of output. Such different proportions of inputs will help us to define different technologies—each one characterized by a certain input ratio and represented by a Leontief production function as stated in our previous discussion of technological variety. The efficient firms #52 and #101, for example, are two opposite sides in the usage of capital. Firm #52 and firm #193 mark the opposite ends of the labor use continuum. So it is obvious that there exists more than one efficient technology for producing machinery goods.

The fact that we detect some firms applying extremely differing technologies quite successfully leads to the question of whether it is possible to define them as the protagonists of different technology fields. This seems adequate because the DEA method evaluates the inefficient firms using the facets of the frontier built by linear combinations of the efficient ones. Consequently, we apply the λ values delivered by DEA to group the inefficient firms around the technology leaders. To verify this assignment defined by the DEA method, we additionally run a traditional (K-means) cluster analysis using input ratios as factors. This delivers four different clusters of input ratios which we label technology fields F1 to F4.

With respect to the input ratios, technology field F1 can be characterized as capital intensive. In field F4 we find an extraordinary high material intensity coupled with high capital intensity. An intensive use of labor, differing only in extent (F2's labor intensity is two times higher than F3's) characterizes the clusters F2 and F3.

Table 1 gives an account of the number of firms joining the four technol-

---

17. The results are of course available for interested readers from the authors.

TABLE 1. Number of Firms in Each Technology Field (F1–F4)

Year		Field		
	F1	F2	F3	F4
85		5	73	
86		5	72	1
87		8	69	1
88	1	7	70	
89		9	69	
90	1	12	65	
91	2	13	63	

ogy fields. It is evident that the main fields are F2 and F3, where the importance of the first is increasing and that of the latter decreasing over time.

The average ι-value of the technology fields could give an account of the technological level of these fields.[18] Table 2 delivers these measures for each field and each year.

Here, however, one has to be very cautious, as (in a cross-section comparison) this value tends to be higher for a lower number of firms. Taking this into account, comparing F2 and F3 suggests that the (average) technological level of F2 is constantly higher than the level of F3, with an increasing tendency for both. A reason for this result might be that we find technological progress in each of the fields, but F2 is more dense in the sense that the inefficient firms are closer to the leaders.

Table 3 shows the number of movements between the fields during the period 1985–91. Evidently most of the movements occur between technology fields F2 and F3. This again furthers the observation that the technologies in F1 and F4 are rather extreme and cannot be easily applied by "outsiders."

Table 4 gives an account of the average ι-change of the moving firms. These numbers, however, have to be interpreted carefully. A switch over into technology field F3 from F2 leads to a slight decrease in relative technical efficiency.

A contrary result is found for a "jump" into F2 from F3. One reason for this is the fact that the gap between the technology leaders and the followers in F3 is larger compared to F2. A deeper investigation into why firms nevertheless change from F2 to F3 has to be accomplished in further steps. Economic reasons as well as reasons for dynamic efficiency must then be considered. However, three of the six technology switches do fit into the concept of

18. For this measure see Forsund and Hjalmarrson 1987; Carlsson 1972.

TABLE 2. Average ι for Each Technology Field

Year	Field			
	F1	F2	F3	F4
85		0.666	0.517	
86		0.619	0.540	1.000
87		0.621	0.517	1.000
88	0.714	0.695	0.523	
89		0.625	0.539	
90	0.638	0.699	0.546	
91	0.846	0.694	0.557	

TABLE 3. Movements between Technology Fields during the Period 1985–91

Movement from	Movement to			
	F1	F2	F3	F4
F1		1		
F2	2		6	1
F3		16		
F4	1			

TABLE 4. Average ι Change of Moving Firms

Movement from	Movement to			
	F1	F2	F3	F4
F1		−0.453		
F2	0.329		−0.001	0.440
F3		0.019		
F4	−0.286			

"elastic barriers" (David 1975), where a switch into a considerably different technology is accompanied by a loss in technical efficiency.

Technical (In)efficiency and Technological Progress

In this section we focus on the relationship between the inefficiency measures obtained in the previous paragraph and proxy variables for the firm-specific technological progress. To make the latter concept operational for empirical analyses, one can distinguish between technology input measures such as R&D expenditures and technology output indicators such as patents. We will use both in the following analysis, well aware of the apparent difficulties of both indicators to give a satisfactory account of the technological performance on the firm level. Let us start with R&D expenditures.

R&D Expenditures and Relative Efficiency

In order to relate our ι-measures to R&D expenditures we apply traditional OLS, where ι is the dependent variable and the R&D capital stock and other measures are independent. Some qualifications toward these measures have to be made. One is related to ι when it is used in regression analyses in the following form

$$\iota = Z\beta + \epsilon. \tag{6}$$

Z is the matrix of independent variables, β is the vector of regression coefficients, and ϵ is the vector of error terms.

Since the efficiency scores are restricted on $]0,1]$, the error term ϵ is dependent on Z and thus biased and inconsistent estimates for β are to be expected. A proof of this is found in Holvad and Hougaard 1993, who correct for this by transforming ι onto an unrestricted range

$$\ln\left(\frac{1-\iota}{\iota}\right). \tag{7}$$

Consequently, the dependent variable is unrestricted and OLS can be applied. For interpreting the regression results, however, one has to keep in mind that the sign of the estimates for β is just opposite because it is related to the transformed ι.

In our estimation we relate different independent variables to our efficiency measure. One of these is the R&D capital stock, RDS_t, which we use instead of yearly R&D expenditures, RD_t, because R&D expenditures cannot be expected to improve productivity at once, but only after a certain lapse of time, and technological progress is considered as a cumulative activity.

Therefore we suggest that the technological level of a firm that is supposed to have a positive impact of productivity can be approximated by the accumulated R&D expenditures of the past. For this reason we calculate this stock for each firm by the perpetual inventory method, where we apply degressive depreciation by a rate of 15 percent:[19]

$$RDS_t = RDS_{t-1} * 0.85 + RD. \tag{8}$$

The measured relative inefficiency of firms naturally has more than this single determinant.[20] In the context of our analysis we are mainly interested in whether technological factors can be attributed to determine the relative position of firms. The following OLS results are therefore to be taken as a test of the sign of the investigated relations, rather than as an estimate of a complete theoretical model. Therefore we proceed step-by-step, adding technological and other related variables. Here we include RDS/L as the R&D capital stock per amount of labor; K/L, the capital/labor ratio, which takes into account the effects of the increasing mechanization of the production process; RD/Y, the R&D intensity; the time variable, ETP, which should cover trend effects not already specified, such as exogenous technological progress; and finally, in certain runs we include the dummy variables DCL for the respective technology fields in order to capture technology-specific fixed effects.

For RDS/L and ETP, we expect a negative coefficient because R&D and exogenous technological progress should improve the relative position of a firm with respect to the all-time best-practice frontier. RD/Y is expected to have a positive sign because the R&D expenditures in year t are assumed to increase productivity only in later years. The coefficient of K/L can have either sign; however, whenever process innovations are embodied in investment the sign should be negative.[21]

Tables 5 and 6 deliver our result for the coefficients, the t-values (in parentheses) and the R^2 measures for various model variants in both sectors.

For the machinery sector, considering variants 1 to 4, we find that the signs of RDS/L and K/L are both significantly negative, which implies that a higher R&D capital stock per unit labor and a higher degree of mechanization implies a higher relative efficiency score. The signs of RD/Y and ETP are as expected but the coefficients are not significant.

Including dummy variables (variants 5 and 6) for the four technology fields considerably improves the regression fit (R^2 improves from about 0.13

19. This is a rate very often used in empirical investigations where R&D capitals stocks are used. See, for example, Meyer-Krahmer and Wessels 1989 for the German manufacturing industry.

20. See Caves and Barton 1990.

21. It would be interesting to include investment data here in order to take into account vintage effects. As yet, our data do not allow us to take this into account.

TABLE 5. Regression Results for the Machinery Sector

Variant	Const.	RDS/L	K/L	RD/Y	ETP	DCL	R^2
1	6.666	−0.0059					0.11
	(108.8)	(−7.306					
2	6.684	−0.0041	−0.00001				0.13
	(109.1)	(−3.756)	(−2.556)				
3	6.684	−0.0041	−0.00001	0.0002			0.13
	(108.5)	(−3.749)	(−2.553)	(0.042)			
4	6.761	−0.0040	−0.00001	0.0002	−0.0196		0.13
	(52.84)	(−3.661)	(−2.579)	(0.048)	(−0.688)		
5		−0.0064	0.00003			3 sign.	0.39
		(−6.126)	(7.103)				
6		−0.0063	0.00003	0.0047	−0.0319	3 sign.	0.40
		(−5.951)	(7.163)	(1.331)	(−1.303)		
7	3.163	−0.0340	0.00008				0.49
only F2	(5.488)	(−4.493)	(5.566)				
8	3.923	−0.0332	0.00008	0.0009	−0.1810		0.51
only F2	(4.390)	(−4.281)	(5.550)	(0.119)	(−1.126)		
9	6.305	−0.0052	0.00003				0.18
only F3	(65.174)	(−6.280)	(5.609)				
10	6.372	−0.0050	0.00003	−0.0019	−0.0298		0.19
only F3	(59.162)	(−6.035)	(5.813)	(−0.256)	(−1.529)		

to 0.40)—only one of four dummies is insignificant at 5 percent. Additional runs specific to the two main technology fields F2 and F3 (variants 7, 8, 9, and 10) only partially repeat this result. For F2 we get an even higher R^2 of about 0.50 and for F3 it sharply decreases to 0.19. Again, the coefficients of RDS/L and K/L are significant; however, the sign of the influence of K/L has changed, implying that increased mechanization within these technology fields leads to lower efficiency scores. A reason for this result is most probably that these two main technology fields within the machinery sector are characterized by a remarkably low K/L ratio (see our previous discussion of technical efficiency).

For variants 1 to 4 of the electronics sector (table 6) the estimates for the RDS/L coefficient are significant and, as expected, negative. The mechanization variable K/L is positive in sign but not significant. The estimate for R&D intensity shows a significant positive sign, which is to be interpreted as meaning that increasing current R&D expenditures do not improve a firm's relative position at once. Finally, exogenous technological progress is not significant here.

As with the machinery industry, including dummies for the various technology fields improves the results considerably, with R^2 increasing to about 0.87. Investigating the most "crowded" technology fields, F4 and F5 (charac-

TABLE 6.   Regression Results for the Electronics Sector

Variant	Const.	RDS/L	K/L	RD/Y	ETP	DCL	R^2
1	7.600	−0.00047					0.08
	(82.562)	(−3.964)					
2	7.298	−0.00054	0.00001				0.09
	(32.090)	(−4.229)	(1.453)				
3	7.441	−0.00118	0.00001	0.73618			0.21
	(34.620)	(−6.796)	(0.693)	(5.089)			
4	7.432	−0.00118	0.00001	0.73772	0.0034		0.21
	(30.588)	(−6.748)	(0.627)	(5.037)	(0.076)		
5		−0.00116	0.00001			sign.	0.81
		(−13.09)	(0.845)				
6		−0.00119	0.00001	0.4215	0.0269	sign.	0.82
		(−14.01)	(0.865)	(1.600)	(1.199)		
7	7.410	−0.00117	0.00001				0.85
only F4	(36.073)	(−20.34)	(1.548)				
8	7.193	−0.00117	0.00001	2.802	0.0046		0.87
only F4	(31.046)	(−21.195)	(2.057)	(3.290)	(0.199)		
9	7.977	−0.0008	0.00000				0.15
only F5	(74.36)	(−3.930)	(0.151)				
10	7.871	−0.003	0.00001	1.317	0.0068		0.25
only F5	(67.86)	(−4.358)	(0.724)	(3.361)	(0.497)		

terized by comparably low K/L ratios of all technology fields within this sector) leads to a slight improvement for F4 and a drastic decline in the regression fit of F5.

Comparing both sectors, we can conclude that in both cases the accumulated R&D capital stock has a considerable positive impact on the firm's relative position toward the all-time best-practice frontier.[22] Moreover, the various technology fields have a specific (fixed) effect. Besides these common features, both sectors, however, differ with respect to the following

1. The different significance of the variable RD/Y in the two sectors can be explained by the fact that electronic firms, at the average, invest five times more R&D per unit labor than do machinery firms, so that the effect on current year's position, that is, relative efficiency, is more severe and tends to dominate other factors.
2. For the differing results with respect to K/L the following explanation seems appropriate: The machinery sector—compared to electronics— is considered mostly to be a sector purchasing technological progress

---

22. Also comparing the magnitude of the respective coefficients does not lead to additional insights because the efficiency scores are a relative concept, applicable only on an intrasectoral basis.

embodied in investment, and the increasing K/L and its effect on efficiency account for this.

These results are more or less consistent with the sector classification of Pavitt 1984. The electronics industry is there considered to be science-based, relying very much on its own R&D efforts. The machinery industry, instead, is classified as production-intensive, with intensive scale and specialized suppliers. High capital intensities are a main feature of such productions.[23]

Patenting Activity and Relative Efficiency
We capture the patent activities of the firms in our sample by simply counting the number of patents they raised within a certain period for the German market. The data are taken from the 1991 publication of the INPADOC database by the "Ifo-Institut für Wirtschaftsforschung."[24]

Certainly aware of the well-known difficulties in accounting and weighting patents,[25] we accept the rough procedure of Ifo and consider only those firms (a) who have applied for patents in at least two countries and (b) who had at least five applications during the years 1985–88. The relatively high costs for patenting abroad can be used as a yardstick (and lower bound) for the importance of the patents.

We are also aware of the fact that between patenting and a possible increase in productivity a certain lapse of time has to pass. This time lag should be not longer (or even shorter) than the one between R&D expenditure and productivity change. By comparing the patents of the years 1985 to 1988 with the efficiency measures of the year 1991, we lag our data between three and six years.

For the above-mentioned period we select from our sample 24 machinery firms and 10 firms in the electronics sector with patent activities for Germany and at least one other country. This very small number and the fact that exactly weighting the patents was not possible until now prevents us from performing regressions to relate them to efficiency measures. So we simply divide our sample into a patenting and a nonpatenting group of firms and concentrate on the differences between these subsamples. And even without a precisely measured relationship our results as stated in table 7 seem to be remarkable.

There it is shown that the average efficiency of the patenting firms is higher in both branches than the average efficiency of nonpatenting firms. For

---

23. "Technological leads are reflected in the capacity to design, build and operate large-scale continuous processes, or to design and integrate large-scale assembly systems in order to produce a complex final product." See Dosi, Pavitt and Soete (1990, p. 96).

24. See Faust and Buckel 1991.

25. See, e.g., Pavitt 1985; Griliches 1990; or Kleinknecht 1993.

TABLE 7.   Efficiency of Patenting and Nonpatenting Firms in 1991

	Electronics	Machinery
Av. efficiency of patenting firms	0.46	0.61
Av. efficiency of nonpatenting firms	0.40	0.58
% of efficient firms within patenting firms	10%	0%
% of eff. firms within nonpatenting firms	3%	4%

the electronics sector even the percentage of technology leaders is three times higher in the patenting sample than in the nonpatenting group.

Finally we take account of the relevance of patenting for the respective technology fields in both sectors. Tables 8 and 9 give an overview.

The main result for machinery is that technology field F2, with the higher average efficiency, compared to F3 (see table 2), also leads in the percentage of patenting. This statement also applies to the electronics sector's most "crowded" fields, F4 and F5.

This simple calculation supports the results for R&D as discussed in the previous section by indicating a positive correlation between patenting (as the output of R&D) and the relative efficiency of a firm and pointing to the differences between the two sectors. Again we find a slightly stronger link between patents (as the result of R&D) and the firm efficiency for the (science-based) electronics sector. This outcome can be interpreted in different ways:

1. In order to be in the top group of firms performance with respect to technological progress is more important in the electronics sector than in the machinery sector. This interpretation, however, does not take patent-specific aspects into account.
2. In this respect Scherer (1983) makes the point that the "propensity to patent" can differ between industries because of different expectations of the advantages of patenting. The respective propensities might

TABLE 8.   Patenting and Technology Fields in Machinery

Technology Field	Patenting Firms	Nonpatenting Firms	Total	% Patenting
F1	0	2	2	0
F2	6	7	13	46
F3	18	45	63	29
Total	24	54	78	31

TABLE 9. Patenting and Technology Fields in Electronics

Technology Field	Patenting Firms	Nonpatenting Firms	Total	% Patenting
F1	0	3	3	0
F2	0	2	2	0
F3	0	2	2	0
F4	9	13	22	41
F5	1	9	10	10
Total	10	29	39	26

differ between our two sectors, so that machinery relies more on other means of appropriation such as secrecy, first-mover-advantage, and so on.

3. Finally, and related to the last point, one might think of looking at the principle kind of innovation performed in both sectors. Levin et al. (1987) have stressed the fact that product innovations tend to be patented whereas for process innovations secrecy is a more appropriate means of protection. These aspects might be important for our results, since machinery might be more associated with process improvements, whereas electronics tends to develop new products.[26]

Conclusion

This chapter has reported on an empirical study of the technological performance and diversity of firms in the German machinery and electronics manufacturing sectors for the years between 1985 and 1991. Recognizing the lack of appropriate empirical tools in evolutionary economics, we suggest a nonparametric linear programming procedure, DEA, which allows us to get an account of the heterogeneity of agents. In this respect we (a) compute an index for the relative technical inefficiency of firms and (b) determine certain technology fields differing by their relative use of input factors.

Our study shows that it is possible (a) to find a structure of technical inefficiencies characterized by several technological leaders and (b) to detect several technology fields that take technological diversity into account. A dynamic analysis shows (c) that the total efficiency of the sectors improves over time and (d) that there are differences among the respective technology fields.

---

26. Since our electronics sector also includes consumer electronics, this argument is even more persuasive.

In a second step these results are related to measures of firms' technological performance. We find that for both sectors the efficiency position of firms is determined by their innovative behavior. This result seems to be independent of whether we use the R&D capital stock as a technology input measure or patenting activity as a technology output proxy.

Although our results do very much confirm the notion that technological progress is an important determinant of firm performance, some qualifications necessarily have to be made. First, all that we know about the technology of a firm is deduced by a very rough procedure, that is, technologies are distinguished by their factor input ratios. An analysis related to more technical aspects would be very much appreciated here. For future work we consider the use of more information on the production structure as well as qualitative innovation data to improve our results. Second, quite crucial for our results is obviously the definition of the factor "capital." Vintage effects, capacity utilization, technical life cycle, and so on have not yet been considered. Some improvement on this is expected when longer time series data, completed with more reliable investment figures, are available. Last but not least, the analysis of efficiency scores has to be worked on in order to distinguish between the top firms, which are as yet not comparable ($\iota = 1$). Those improved measures might then help—in a longer time series analysis—to directly compare different technology fields and their development.

REFERENCES

Ahmad, S. 1966. On the Theory of Induced Invention. *Economic Journal* 76:344–57.
Ali, A. I., and C. S. Lerme. 1990. *Data Envelopment Analysis Models: A Framework.* Working Paper, School of Management, University of Massachusetts at Amherst.
Atkinson, A., and J. E. Stiglitz. 1969. A New View of Technological Change. *Economic Journal* 79:573–78.
Cantner, U., H. Hanusch, and G. Westermann. 1993. Technological Inefficiencies in Asymmetric Industries. SPES working paper no. 5, "Comparative Economics of R&D."
Carlsson, B. 1972. The Measurement of Efficiency in Production: An Application to Swedish Manufacturing Industries 1968. *Swedish Journal of Economics* 74:468–85.
Caves, R. E., and D. R. Barton. 1990. *Efficiency in U.S. Manufacturing Industries.* Cambridge: MIT Press.
Charnes, A., and W. W. Cooper. 1962. Programming with Linear Fractional Functionals. *Naval Research Logistics Quarterly* 9:181–86.
———. 1985. Preface to Topics in Data Envelopment Analysis. *Journal of Operations Research* 2:59–94.
Charnes, A., W. W. Cooper, A. Y. Lewin, and L. M. Seiford. 1994. *Data Envelopment Analysis: The Theory, the Method and the Process.* Boston: Kluwer Academic.

Charnes, A., W. W. Cooper, and R. M. Thrall. 1986. Classifying and Characterizing Efficiencies and Inefficiencies in Data Envelopment Analysis. *Operations Research Letters* 5, no. 3: 105–10.

David, P. 1975. *Technical Choice, Innovation and Economic Growth.* Cambridge: Cambridge University Press.

Dosi, G. 1988. The Nature of the Innovative Process. In Dosi et al., *Technical Change and Economic Theory,* 221–38. London, New York: Pinter Publishers.

Dosi, G., C. Freeman, R. Nelson, G. Silverberg, and L. Soete. 1988. *Technical Change and Economic Theory.* London, New York: Pinter Publishers.

Dosi, G., K. Pavitt, and L. Soete. 1990. *The Economics of Technical Change and International Trade.* New York: Harvester Wheatsheaf.

Dosi, G., and L. Soete. 1983. Technology Gaps and Cost-based Adjustment: Some Explorations on the Determinants of International Competitiveness. *Metroeconomica* 12, no. 3:357–82.

Färe, R., S. Grosskopf, and C. A. K. Lovell. 1993. *Production Frontiers.* Cambridge: Cambridge University Press.

Farrell, M. J. 1957. The Measurement of Productive Efficiency. *Journal of the Royal Statistical Society,* Series A 120:253–81.

Faust, K., and E. Buckel. 1991. Ifo-Patentstatistik, Im Wettbewerb um die Technologie von morgen, Unternehmensreport 1991. München: Ifo-Institut für Wirtschaftsforschung.

Fellner, W. 1961. Two Propositions in Theory of Induced Innovation. *Economic Journal* 71:305–8.

Forsund, F. R., and L. Hjalmarsson. 1987. *Analysis of Industrial Structure: A Putty-Clay Approach.* Stockholm: Almqvist & Wiksell International.

Griliches, Z. 1990. Patent Statistics as Economic Indicators: A Survey. *Journal of Economic Literature* 27:1661–1707.

Holvad, T., and J. L. Hougaard. 1993. Measuring Technical Input Efficiency for Similar Production Units: A Survey of the Non-Parametric Approach. EUI Working Paper, European University Institute, Florence, ECO 93/20.

Kendrick, J. W. 1956. Productivity Trends: Capital and Labor. *Review of Economics and Statistics* 38:248–57.

Kleinknecht, A. 1993. Why Do We Need New Innovation Output Indicators? In A. Kleinknecht and Bain, *New Concepts in Innovation Output Measurement,* 1–9. New York.

Levin, R., A. Klevorick, R. R. Nelson, and S. G. Winter. 1987. Appropriating the Results of Industrial Research and Development. *Brookings Papers on Economic Activity.* 3:783–831.

Meyer-Krahmer, F., and H. Wessels. 1989. Intersektorale Verflechtung von Technologiegebern und Technologienehmern. *Jahrbuch für Nationalökonomie und Statistik,* 206, no. 6: 563–82.

Nelson, R. R. and S. G. Winter. 1982. *An Evolutionary Theory of Economic Change.* Cambridge, Mass. and London: The Belknap Press of Harvard University Press.

Ott, A. E. 1959. Technischer Fortschritt. In V. Beckerath, et al. eds. Handwörterbuch der Sozialwissenschaften, Bd. 10, 302–16. Stuttgart: Gustav Fischer.

Pavitt, K. 1984. Sectoral Patterns of Technical Change: Towards a Taxonomy and a Theory. *Research Policy* 13, no. 6: 343–73.

———. 1985. Patent Statistics as Indicators of Innovative Activities: Possibilities and Problems. *Scientometrics* 7:77–99.

Salter, W. 1960. *Productivity and Technical Change*. Cambridge: Cambridge University Press.

Scherer, F. M. 1983. The Propensity to Patent. *International Journal of Industrial Organisation* 1 (March): 107–28.

Learning-by-Doing and International Trade in Semiconductors

Frederic M. Scherer

This chapter examines some economic principles underlying the behavior of integrated circuit manufacturers and traces how their application led to a major international trade dispute whose repercussions continue. It begins by investigating the economies of scale, static and dynamic, that permeate semiconductor production. Especially important is the phenomenon of learning-by-doing, under which batch costs fall by approximately 28 percent with each doubling and redoubling of cumulative output. The first firm to race down its learning curve enjoys a substantial cost advantage over laggards. This has encouraged aggressive pricing strategies to capture the benefits of leadership, first by Texas Instruments during the 1970s and then by Japanese producers during the 1980s. Aggressive pricing of 256-kilobit DRAMs precipitated charges that Japanese firms were "dumping" their chips at prices below full cost—rational behavior in a learning curve environment. To settle the dispute, the Japanese chip makers agreed in 1986 not to charge prices below their full costs in the previous quarter, which meant that prices were well above current-quarter costs. The output restrictions this strategy required adversely affected computer makers and spurred a European complaint before GATT. A side letter to the agreement set a vaguely specified target of 20 percent for foreign semiconductor makers' share of sales in Japan. This in turn became a precedent in U.S. "managed trade" efforts to improve access to the Japanese market.

The semiconductor industry has experienced extraordinarily rapid technological advance. Many national governments have sought to have their national champion enterprises master the art of developing and producing these extremely intricate "chips" that integrate thousands or even millions of individual electronic functions. Fewer have been successful in the game, which combines unusually strong economies of scale, static and dynamic, with unique pricing strategies implemented to capture the advantages associated with being a first mover. The pursuit of those strategies led to a major international trade dispute during the 1980s. This chapter, drawn from a more encompassing study of the semiconductor industry,[1] lays out the background of that dispute and traces its history and consequences.

Economies of Scale, Static and Dynamic

Paralleling advances in semiconductor technology has been a dramatic change in the character of scale economies. In the industry's early days, a firm such as Transitron could rent an abandoned textile factory, install fairly rudimentary equipment, and begin producing transistors on a labor-intensive assembly line. Transitron's initial investment is reported to have been $1 million.[2] But as the density of functions packed onto a single chip increased, the costs of a semiconductor fabricating plant—called a "fab" in the trade—rose apace. Because specks of dust, bacteria, or other unwanted contaminants can ruin the product, one must begin with a clean room, whose air purity and vibration avoidance standards have become increasingly stringent over time as circuit densities have risen.[3] The equipment needed to project ever-finer circuit details onto photoresists—by the late 1980s, to one-hundredth of the thickness of a human hair—also became increasingly expensive, as did gaseous diffusion chambers and other apparatus. In 1972, a fully equipped high-volume integrated circuit production line required an investment of roughly $10 million. By 1980, the needed outlay had risen to $100 million.[4] Plants for four-megabit dynamic random access memory (DRAM) chips, produced experimentally in 1988, cost approximately $350 million.[5] A new plant producing Intel's 80486 microprocessor family, introduced commercially in 1989, is said to have cost $400 million.[6] Each 80486 chip contained the equivalent of 1.2 million transistors. Billion-dollar investments were projected for "fabs" of 1990s generation integrated circuits. Unless a high volume of output is achieved in these expensive plants, capital costs per unit of product will be prohibitively high.

Front-end investments in the research and development underlying the introduction of new semiconductor devices have risen commensurately. Com-

---

1. That chapter in turn is part of F. M. Scherer, *Industry Structure, Strategy and Public Policy* (New York: Harper Collins, 1996). All rights are reserved.

2. John E. Tilton, *International Diffusion of Technology* (Washington, D.C.: Brookings, 1971), 87–88.

3. "Superchip Plants: Where 'Clean' Has a Whole New Meaning," *Business Week,* September 26, 1988, 77.

4. U.S. Office of Technology Assessment, *International Competitiveness in Electronics* (Washington, D.C.: USGPO, 1983), 271.

5. "The Costly Race Chipmakers Can't Afford To Lose," *Business Week,* December 10, 1990, 185.

6. "Make It Fast—and Make It Right," *Business Week,* special Quality 1991 edition, 76.

plex circuit plans must be laid out—in the early days of integrated circuits, on room-size sheets of paper, but more recently, with computer programs that also check for erroneous interconnections. The circuit details must be reduced to a set of extremely precise photoresist masks. New production methods must be worked out, and when the first experimental chips have been fabricated, extensive testing and (frequently) reworking of masks follow. Intel is said to have spent $10 million to develop its first 4-bit microprocessor during the early 1970s; $20 million on its 16-bit 8086 microprocessor (introduced in 1978); $100 million to develop its 32-bit 80386 microprocessor family (launched in 1985); and $250 million on the 80486 family.[7] The cost (ignoring interest charges) of amortizing the 80486 R&D investment across its life cycle would be $250 per chip if a million chips could be sold, $25 per chip with sales of 10 million, and $5 per chip if cumulative sales of 50 million could be achieved.[8]

To be sure, more flexible, lower-cost design methods have been devised for special-purpose and other low-volume chips. But quite generally, the semiconductor industry has become one of the most R&D-intensive industries. In 1977, company-financed R&D expenditures averaged 6.1 percent of sales—the sixth-highest such ratio among 238 industry categories for which comparable data have been compiled.[9] Less comprehensive surveys for the late 1980s have put the R&D/sales ratio in semiconductors between 11 and 13 percent.[10]

An equally important set of scale economies comes from the phenomenon known as "learning by doing." Solving the complex problems of producing a new semiconductor device entails much "art" acquired by trial and error. When a new design enters production, the manufacturing transition team is thankful if 2 percent of the chips pass quality control tests. Production must be halted to study why problems are emerging, and solutions must be tested and verified. Gradually, the team learns how to adjust the process parameters so that yields eventually rise to as high as 90 percent and the time lost between batches is reduced. Unit batch costs fall concurrently along what is called a *learning curve*. There is considerable evidence that until the production pro-

7. Richard N. Langlois, *Microelectronics: An Industry in Transition* (Rensselaer Polytechnic Institute Center for Science and Technology Policy, July 1987), 39; and "Make It Fast," *Business Week*, special Quality 1991 edition, 76.

8. In 1987, according the Census of Manufactures, U.S. semiconductor plants shipped 133 million microprocessors. Between 1988 and 1991, Intel sold approximately 25 million 80386 chips. See "Intel's Chip Monopoly Is Facing Challengers," *New York Times*, September 5, 1990, D9.

9. U.S. Federal Trade Commission, *Statistical Report: Annual Line of Business Report: 1977* (Washington: U.S. Federal Trade Commission, April 1985), 21.

10. Kenneth Flamm, *Mismanaged Trade? Strategic Policy and the Semiconductor Industry* (Washington, D.C.: Brookings Institution, 1996), chap. 1.

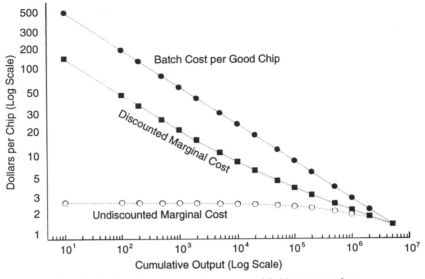

Fig. 1. Semiconductor learning curve with 28 percent slope

cess matures, the decline of unit costs is well characterized by a learning curve that is linear in the logarithms of unit cost (on the vertical axis) and the *cumulative* number of units produced (on the horizontal axis), as illustrated in figure 1. The "slope" of the typical semiconductor device learning curve appears to be approximately 28 percent, which means that unit costs fall by 28 percent, on average, with each doubling and redoubling of cumulative output.[11] Thus, the tenth unit produced (10^1) has a unit cost of roughly $536; the 100th unit $180; the thousandth unit $60.15; the ten-thousandth unit (10^4) $20.15;[12] the one hundred-thousandth unit $3.14;[12] the millionth chip $2.26; and so on. Only at some quite high cumulative output scale does the cost curve bottom out, with no further savings from learning. Until that scale is reached, chip production is, at least as a first approximation, a natural monopoly: unit costs fall more or less continuously as output is increased to levels that may well exhaust the market's absorptive capacity.

When learning-by-doing occurs, the marginal cost of a batch is not simply the out-of-pocket cost incurred for producing that batch. Rather, the

---

11. See Flamm, *Mismanaged Trade?*, chap. 6. Although learning curves are often written as $UC = a\, Q_{CUM}^{-\beta}$, the "slope" as used in normal learning curve parlance is not β. Rather, β is the exponent to which the value 2 (reflecting a doubling of output) is raised to yield (1 minus the fraction by which unit cost is reduced).

12. Technological progress in dynamic random access memory chips is sometimes characterized by what is called the "Pi rule." That is, no matter how high chip function density is, unit costs fall to approximately $\pi = \$3.14$ when a substantial production volume has been achieved. See Flamm, *Mismanaged Trade?*, chap. 1.

experience gained in producing the batch will help reduce costs on additional batches produced in the future. Thus, marginal cost is below, and possibly well below, current out-of-pocket cost (which, in turn, is below conventionally calculated average total cost because of the substantial investments sunk in research, development, and production facilities). Under certain limiting conditions, marginal cost in a learning curve environment can be viewed as the out-of-pocket cost incurred for the *last* unit to be produced—that is, the unit at the foot of the learning curve.[13] But since the savings from learning accrue only in the future, their discounted value at the moment when learning occurs is less, and hence the marginal cost at that moment is higher than at the learning curve's foot, but converges upon the terminal value. Also, the cumulative quantity that will eventually be produced is uncertain, and so also must be the terminal cost values. The undiscounted marginal cost curve in figure 1 assumes that production can end with equal probability at any output between the cumulative volume most recently attained and five million units. A zero time discount rate is assumed. The discounted marginal cost curve is a numerical approximation assuming output timing patterns estimated by Flaherty[14] and a 12 percent discount rate.

Learning Curve Pricing

The existence of learning-by-doing scale economies may lead companies to engage in a dynamic form of limit pricing with most important implications for the way market structures evolve. The first firm to race down the learning curve gains a cost advantage over its tardier rivals. The greater its lead, the larger its cost advantage, all else being equal. A cost advantage is the sine qua non for limit pricing. If it is sufficiently large, its possessor may choose to set prices so low as to deter the entry of other competitors. For example, in figure 1, if one firm succeeds in reaching a cumulative volume of one million chips while its rivals are still at the 100,000 mark, the leader will enjoy unit costs of $2.30 per batch while rival costs are $6.52. By setting its price at, say, $3.00, the leader can realize an appreciable profit (ignoring fixed costs) while inflicting substantial losses upon its rivals, who may perceive their handicap to be insuperable and drop out of the race. The result may be an increasing asymmetry of positions and perhaps monopoly, at which point the remaining in-

---

13. See A. Michael Spence, "The Learning Curve and Competition," *Bell Journal of Economics* 12(Spring 1981): 51.

14. Marie Therese Flaherty, "Manufacturing and Firm Performance in Technology-Intensive Industries: U.S. and Japanese DRAM Experience," *Review of Industrial Organization* 7(1992): 283.

cumbent can realize substantial profits without inducing new entry or reentry.[15]

There is more. Recognizing the advantage of being the first down the learning curve, firms have an incentive to lead the way in introducing the new product whose production entails learning-by-doing. And once they gain early production leadership positions, they may price their product aggressively to stimulate demand, which permits more production and hence more learning, and also to win the lion's share of orders away from rivals, which again leads to more production and hence an enhanced cost advantage. Indeed, pricing may be so aggressive in the early learning stages that out-of-pocket losses are incurred, but if a monopoly position is the prize once a high cumulative production volume is attained, the early losses could be a worthwhile strategic investment in securing future monopoly profits.

These possibilities are interesting not only because learning-by-doing is so important in semiconductor device production, but also because Texas Instruments, the U.S. industry leader during the 1960s and 1970s, openly avowed its commitment to aggressive learning curve pricing strategies. TI's philosophy was described by its president in 1973 as follows:[16]

> Follow an aggressive pricing policy, focus on continuing cost reduction and productivity improvement, build on shared experience (gained in making related products), and keep capacity growing ahead of demand.

The ultimate goal was to be "No. 1 in each product field it enters."[17] It was advised in this strategy choice by the Boston Consulting Group, which preached passionately that seizing the low-cost position on what it called "experience curves" was the key to superior profitability.[18]

Carried to their logical conclusion, these policies could end with the first or most aggressive firm securing a monopoly position in the specific products it chooses to emphasize. However, three considerations may prevent such extreme outcomes.

First and perhaps most important, as products mature, learning curves sooner or later flatten out when most of the opportunities for further improve-

---

15. See, e.g., Kenneth Flamm, "Strategic Arguments for Semiconductor Trade Policy," *Review of Industrial Organization* 7(1992): 295–326; and David R. Ross, "Learning To Dominate," *Journal of Industrial Economics* 34(June 1986): 337–54.

16. "Selling Business a Theory of Economics," *Business Week*, September 8, 1973, 87.

17. "Texas Instruments: Pushing Hard into the Consumer Markets," *Business Week*, August 24, 1974, 40.

18. See Bruce D. Henderson, *The Logic of Business Strategy* (Cambridge, MA: Ballinger, 1984), chaps. 2 and 3.

ment have been exploited. The best evidence on this point exists for aircraft production, on which the most abundant data are available.[19] Less is known about the semiconductor device volumes at which learning ebbs. If the learning curve bottoms out at volumes well below the maximum quantity demanded, semiconductor production is not a natural monopoly, and disadvantaged rivals may stay in the game, despite early losses, in the expectation that they can eventually compete on equal terms with the leader.

Second, the companies designing their electronic products around some key chip often insist upon a "second source" to ensure that supplies will not be interrupted by strikes, fires, or other plant-level catastrophes, and also exert competitive pressure on the first source's pricing. Even when learning continues out to the last batch produced and second sourcing forces chip makers to forgo one last cumulative doubling of their output, costs may not rise by the amount implied by the learning curve slope. There is evidence from aircraft production experience that competition induces rivals to intensify their cost reduction efforts, and hence to steepen the learning curve slope.[20]

Finally, the learning achieved by the first producer may "spill over" to laggard rival firms, for example, as production engineers change jobs and bring with them the know-how they have acquired in the leader's plant, or, less plausibly, as production techniques become public knowledge. How important this spillover effect is in semiconductors is unknown. Although the turnover of Silicon Valley employees is extraordinarily rapid, a move by some key engineer to work on a directly competing product would probably provoke a lawsuit seeking to bar the job changer from assuming a position that jeopardizes trade secrets.

Although horizontal spillover—from one company to others producing essentially the same chip—is probably modest, there may also be intergenerational spillovers, that is, from one generation of semiconductor devices within a company to the next generation. Learning to solve the problems of producing one chip design probably reduces the initial costs of producing more advanced chips. To the extent that this is true, the strategic advantage of being first down the learning curve on a new kind of semiconductor is all the greater.

Despite the attractions of aggressive learning-curve pricing, its use may be constrained by capacity limitations. It takes time to "ramp up" the output of an integrated circuit production line to its full capacity. Until substantial learning occurs, yields are low, and equipment rigidities may permit output to

---

19. See Harold Asher, *Cost-Quantity Relationships in the Airframe Industry,* RAND Corporation Study R-291 (Santa Monica: July 1956), chaps. 4 and 7.

20. F. M. Scherer, *The Weapons Acquisition Process: Economic Incentives* (Cambridge, MA: Harvard Business School Division of Research, 1964), 119–26.

increase only as rapidly as yields improve. If only a limited number of workable chips can be produced, cutting prices to stimulate the demand for additional chips will not increase sales, and hence will yield no learning benefit. Thus, prices will be set at the market-clearing level. Kenneth Flamm argues that pricing was in fact constrained mainly by supply-side rigidities in the early stages of DRAM production during the 1980s.[21] His analysis assumes, however, that the demand curve for new chips is smoothly convex downward, so that some demand will be forthcoming even at very high prices. The assumption is debatable. New chips must be priced low enough to induce substitution away from older generation chips that have already run far down their learning curves. The aggressive strategies Texas Instruments and others claim to have adopted may have been motivated both by the desire to get the substitution process going and to move more rapidly down learning curves. That early prices are below market-clearing levels is shown by frequent shortages of new chips, which are rationed out to computer assemblers on nonprice bases. Also, there is evidence that "ramp-up" rates are not governed solely by rigid technological constraints. Some firms appear able to increase their output more rapidly than others. Japanese producers experienced particularly rapid ramp-up rates on the 64K DRAM generation.[22] Far too little is known, at least by economists, about the factors influencing ramp-up rates and, in particular, about the role that aggressiveness (in either pricing or investment) plays.

Aggressive learning curve pricing also encounters a quite different set of problems. If one firm races down the learning curve ahead of its rivals, it (although perhaps not its consumers) will live happily ever after—or at least, until the next technological generation appears. But if several firms price aggressively in an effort to be the leader, a bloodbath may ensue. Contrary to their initial expectations in adopting the strategy, the rivals may end up sharing the market at costs too high, and prices too low, to repay their original investments in research, development, equipment, and learning.

This seems to be what happened in the early days of single-chip calculators. Texas Instruments sought to dominate the new, rapidly growing, market.[23] At first its aggressive policies curbed the market shares of Japanese firms, which were having problems producing the needed microprocessors at home, but were not allowed by Japan's Ministry of Trade and Industry (MITI) to import enough U.S. chips to sustain their desired production rates.[24] In

21. Flamm, *Mismanaged Trade?*, chaps. 6 and 7.

22. See Flaherty, "Manufacturing and Firm Performance in Technology-Intensive Industries," 273–94.

23. See F. M. Scherer, *International High-Technology Competition* (Cambridge, MA: Harvard University Press, 1992), 64–67.

24. See Flamm, *Mismanaged Trade?*, chap. 2.

1973 and 1974, however, the situation changed. Japanese companies improved their microprocessor yields and quality, and MITI's restraints on the importation of chips from the United States were relaxed. Equally importantly, the Japanese firms emulated Texas Instruments' strategy of pricing aggressively to sell their calculators in the U.S. market. As a result, their exports soared, prices plunged, and Texas Instruments found it necessary to close its Fort Walton, Florida, calculator plant, reporting calculator line write-offs of $16 million in early 1975. Both TI and Hewlett-Packard, another leading U.S. calculator supplier, exited from the low-price calculator business and retreated to a higher-price programmable calculator market niche.

Similar experiences followed in DRAM chips and Texas Instruments' first venture into personal computers. By 1983, a leading business journal reported that "TI left its rivals with no option but to fight back with their own lower prices"—a practice that was said by an executive of a rival chip maker to have "wrecked the industry."[25] However, there is reason to believe that TI recognized the dangers of widespread learning curve pricing and changed its strategy during the early 1980s, trying hard to avoid overly aggressive behavior.[26] The president of rival Intel stated in 1983 that "I don't think it's being applied as broadly and with the same fervor as in the early 1970s. . . . We are all applying more business judgment now."[27]

However, Japanese semiconductor makers apparently persisted in the pursuit of learning curve pricing strategies. As the president of Nippon Electric Corporation's U.S. electronics subsidiary stated, "The Japanese perspective is that when you are still making inroads into a market, you can't afford the luxury of making money."[28] Japanese firms gained a 40 percent share of the 16K U.S. merchant DRAM market during the late 1970s and increased their share of 64K merchant DRAMS during the early 1980s to 70 percent.[29] In 1982 some U.S. companies complained to Washington of dumping, but did not follow through when MITI (the Ministry of Trade and Industry) intervened and apparently persuaded its wards to raise their export prices. The Japanese continued to advance. By 1985, Nippon Electric had displaced Texas Instruments as the world merchant sales leader. TI fell to third rank, behind Motorola but still ahead of Hitachi and Toshiba. By 1986, NEC, Hitachi, and Toshiba held first, second, and third ranks worldwide, and Japanese producers collectively surpassed U.S. companies for the first time ever in world merchant semiconductor sales volume, capturing 46 percent of the estimated

25. "Chip Wars: The Japanese Threat," *Business Week,* May 23, 1983, 83.
26. This was verified in a private conversation between the author and a TI executive.
27. "Chip Wars," 83.
28. "Chip Wars," 83.
29. "The Selling of the 256K RAM," *New York Times,* June 3, 1983, D1.

world total.[30] Profits turned negative for many U.S. manufacturers,[31] and the crisis-ridden industry turned to Washington for protection.

The 1986 International Trade Agreement and Its Sequel

The continuing ascent of Japanese firms' world market shares and a cyclical decline in integrated circuit demand interacted to plunge the semiconductor industry into crisis during 1985 and 1986. Intel, National Semiconductor, and Mostek announced that they were exiting from DRAM production. Others followed suit, so that by mid-1986 only three U.S. companies (Texas Instruments, Micron Technology, and [mostly for internal use] AT&T) continued to produce DRAMs for the merchant market. Japanese companies reported losses along with their U.S. counterparts.[32] Responding to formal and informal complaints alleging Japanese dumping and denial of market access, the U.S. Department of Commerce initiated dumping and Section 301 investigations, first on 64K DRAMs and then on the relatively new 256K DRAMs and EPROMs (erasable programmable read-only memories).[33] Although Japanese firms reduced their exports and raised their prices, intergovernmental negotiations continued during the first half of 1986.

It is important to recognize exactly what the dumping allegations entailed. The main charge was not that Japanese producers were selling at lower prices in the U.S. market than at home, for they almost surely were not, at least not on direct contract sales.[34] Rather, they were said to be selling their chips at less than "constructed value"—that is, fully allocated production cost, including the amortization of R&D and plant outlays, plus 10 percent general selling and administration overhead, plus 8 percent profit.[35] The U.S. trade laws attempt in this respect to repeal the law of supply and demand, for one would not expect competitive producers to maintain an 8 percent profit margin during a recession. Learning-by-doing, which was still occurring at a rapid rate on the 256K chips introduced commercially only in 1984, complicated matters further. Even without aggressive learning curve pricing, a ratio-

---

30. Flamm, *Mismanaged Trade?*, fig. 1–5; and David B. Yoffie, "The Global Semiconductor Industry, 1987," Harvard Business School case 9-388-052 (1987), 18–21.

31. See "The Bloodbath in Chips," *Business Week,* May 20, 1985, 63; and "2 Chip Makers' Losses Widen," *New York Times,* October 11, 1986, 39.

32. "Japan Chip Makers in Crunch," *New York Times,* November 17, 1986, D1.

33. The best history of this series of events is Flamm, *Mismanaged Trade?*, chap. 4.

34. Flamm, *Mismanaged Trade?*, chap. 6.

35. See Tracy Murray, "The Administration of the Antidumping Duty Law by the Department of Commerce," in *Down in the Dumps: Administration of the Unfair Trade Laws,* Richard Boltuck and Robert E. Litan, eds. (Washington, D.C.: Brookings, 1991), chap. 2.

nal profit-maximizing firm will almost always set its prices below its out-of-pocket batch costs in the early stages of production.[36] If it did not do so, new products would have difficulty replacing technologically inferior substitutes. Thus, "constructed value" is a senseless test in learning curve situations. As Dickens' Mr. Bumble would have appreciated, there was only one ground for its application to the semiconductor dispute: it was the law.

In July of 1986 the trade officials of the United States and Japan reached an agreement scheduled to apply for five years.[37] The U.S. government would suspend all pending 256K memory dumping cases, and the government of Japan would monitor the costs and prices of all relevant products exported to the United States and third-country markets "to prevent exports at prices less than company-specific fair value." "Fair value" in this sense meant "constructed value," as defined under U.S. trade law. To implement the agreement, MITI was to gather data from all Japanese memory chip exporters on their fully allocated costs of production by standard product for the previous quarter and forward the data to the Department of Commerce. The Department of Commerce would check actual import prices against the cost data and, if imports of any company's product occurred at less than the company's reported costs, infer that dumping had occurred. Because the reported costs were for the *previous* quarter, the constructed value triggers lagged current costs by at least three months and in the limit by six months. Because learning occurred and costs fell in the interim, the Japanese firms were required not only to price *at* fully allocated cost, but *above* it.

The initial round of 256K DRAM cost submissions, effective until October 15, 1986, ranged from $2.50 (for Nippon Electric) to $8.70 (allegedly for Fujitsu).[38] Prior to that time, large-volume buyers were purchasing DRAMs at approximately $2.40 per chip, whether (as one would expect in a competitive market) they came from a low-cost supplier or a high-cost firm. Following the agreement, prices rose to at least $5 per chip, and perhaps to the cost floor of the high-cost producers.[39] U.S. personal computer manufacturers were furious, because under the agreement their rivals in Japan could continue to purchase memories at competitive market prices. European governments were equally angry, because the Japanese government had agreed to monitor export

36. See Flamm, "Strategic Arguments," 311–12; and Andrew R. Dick, "Learning by Doing and Dumping in the Semiconductor Industry," *Journal of Law & Economics* 34 (April 1991): 144–48.

37. "U.S. and Japan Resolve Dispute on Microchips," *New York Times,* July 31, 1986, 1.

38. See "The Chip Market Goes Haywire," *Business Week,* September 1, 1986, 25. See also Flamm, *Mismanaged Trade?,* chap. 4, note 49. For the last quarter of 1986, the range of prices was said to be between $2.50 and $4. See "Japan Chip Values Set," *New York Times,* October 13, 1986, D3.

39. "Chip Pact Angers Computer Firms," *Philadelphia Inquirer,* September 7, 1986, 1C.

prices to all nations, and not merely to the United States, so prices to Europe were set on the basis of an accord from which the Europeans had been excluded. They complained to GATT, which in 1988 ruled that the agreement was in fact illegal. Remedial action was delayed until 1989.[40] In the meantime, Japanese memory producers enjoyed record-setting profits, in part because no U.S. DRAM producers reentered the market to compete with them.

The temptation to chisel on prices held high above marginal cost is strong. A million dollars worth of integrated circuits can be packed into a modest-sized crate. Persons still unknown bought DRAMs at low prices on the uncontrolled Japanese market and smuggled them to Hong Kong and other southeast Asian entrepôts, whence they found their way to other world markets at prices below the reported "fair values." In March of 1987 President Reagan announced that the United States would retaliate against violations of the July 1986 agreement by levying 100 percent duties on Japanese electronic products (e.g., laptop computers, color television sets, and power tools), with an estimated total value of $300 million.[41] Some of the retaliatory tariffs remained in force until 1991. To correct the situation, MITI intervened even more vigorously, adding 1 MB DRAMs to its control agenda, setting individual company quotas, and monitoring export shipments in detail to suppress grey market transactions. The sanctions took hold. Production fell, prices rose, and as the demand for chips boomed again, computer makers had to cut back their output because the needed memory chips could not be obtained.[42]

Prices continued to be high and supplies tight even after MITI shifted in late 1987 from imposing individual company production quotas in advance to "forecasting" demand in the forthcoming quarter, supposedly letting companies draw their own conclusions. One possible interpretation of the evidence is that MITI's "forecasts" served as a focal point for restricting industry output—in effect, creating the basis for an effective cartel. An alternative explanation is that the Japanese semiconductor makers came to realize, as Texas Instruments did a few years before, that profits would be higher if they refrained from aggressive learning curve pricing.[43] The evidence needed to distinguish between these alternatives remains elusive.

The high prices charged for DRAMs during the late 1980s facilitated the growth of formidable new competitors—the Korean semiconductor manufac-

---

40. In June 1989, Japan agreed, in response to the European Community's GATT case decision, to cease monitoring exports to non-U.S. markets. Shortly thereafter it settled European dumping charges by instituting a cost-based reference price system similar to the one enforced for the United States.

41. "U.S. Will Retaliate Against Japanese in a Chips Dispute," *New York Times,* March 28, 1987, 1.

42. "Shortage of Memory Chips Hurts Computer Industry," *New York Times,* March 12, 1988, 1.

43. See Flamm, *Mismanaged Trade?,* chap. 4, 34–40.

turers.[44] By 1992, Samsung of Korea had displaced Toshiba as the world's leading DRAM producer.[45] Not surprisingly, charges of Korean dumping in the U.S. market accompanied the leadership change, but after announcing a 20 percent production cutback, low-cost producer Samsung was found to have set its prices below constructed value by only a trivial amount.[46] History repeats itself.

In 1991, the semiconductor trade agreement between the United States and Japan was extended for another three years.[47] Under the extension, the Japanese companies no longer submitted quarterly cost data to the U.S. Department of Commerce. Rather, they agreed to continue collecting the data, making them available only if new dumping allegations surfaced. Left unsettled was a more controversial issue. The 1986 agreement stated that "the Government of Japan will impress upon the Japanese producers and users of semiconductors the need to aggressively take advantage of increased market access opportunities in Japan for foreign-based firms." A side letter mentioned 20 percent as a target for foreign firms' Japanese market share. As the new agreement was negotiated in 1981, U.S. companies' share had risen to 12.5 percent from 8.5 percent in 1985. There was dispute over whether the 20 percent figure was in fact a commitment or only a vague goal and over how foreign firms' shares were to be measured—for example, whether the captive production of IBM plants in Japan was to be counted. The new agreement set in slightly less vague terms a 20 percent target for the end of 1992.[48] Market access was important to American semiconductor makers because an increased share of the large Japanese market meant additional progress down learning curves, and hence lower costs and greater competitiveness. As events transpired, the Japanese government redoubled its efforts to encourage U.S. chip purchases, and in the last quarter of 1992 the 20 percent target was attained, falling again in subsequent quarters.[49] Heated debate continued over whether quantitative import targets, with their implications of "managed trade," were compatible with the free-trading regime advocated in principle by the U.S. government.

---

44. On the entry of Korean producers, see Michael G. Borrus, *Competing for Control: America's Stake in Microelectronics* (Cambridge, MA: Ballinger, 1988), 206–9.

45. See "Memory Chips: Welcome Korea," *The Economist*, February 4, 1989, 66; "In Korea, All Circuits Are Go," *Business Week*, July 9, 1990, 69–71; and "Masters of the Clean Room," *Business Week*, September 27, 1993, 107–8.

46. Flamm, *Mismanaged Trade?*, chap. 4, 52.

47. "Chip Pact Set by U.S. and Japan," *New York Times*, June 4, 1991, D1.

48. "Japan Sees Chip Pact as Success; U.S. Disagrees," *New York Times*, May 22, 1992, D3.

49. "New U.S.-Japan Accord on Semiconductors," *New York Times*, June 5, 1992, D1; "Washington Says Japan Meets Goal on Chip Imports," *New York Times*, March 20, 1993, 37; and "Chip Fight Persisting with Japan," *New York Times*, December 18, 1993, 37.

Epilogue

A more fundamental recurring question in the dispute over international semi-conductor trade was whether it was vital for the United States to maintain a strong position as a producer of DRAMs, or whether its chip users should simply buy from the least-cost sources, domestic or foreign. Advocates of protection or subsidies for domestic manufacturers argued that as products requiring the most demanding fabrication tolerances, DRAMs were "technology drivers," whose production helped American firms master the techniques for making more complex application-specific and microprocessor chips. This claim appears from experience to have been fallacious, since U.S. companies continued to dominate the design and production of microprocessors, whose tolerances are at least as stringent as those of DRAMs. Second, it is argued that having strong domestic sources gives U.S. computer designers the earliest possible access to the latest memory chip layouts, and thereby facilitates technical leadership in the computer field. This "without a nail" argument is probably true for some key components, but it is unclear whether it holds for DRAM chips, whose interfaces with computers have been standardized, and for which lower-capacity chips provide a functional, even if not ideal, substitute. Third, if the United States lacks significant domestic DRAM production, it is claimed that its chip users could be forced to pay high prices for the devices sold by the cartelized producers of the dominant supplying nation.[50] The high prices paid for Japanese DRAMs during the late 1980s are cited as an example. But this example also provides its most powerful counterargument, because Japanese producers were induced to quote high prices by U.S. demands that they do so, not because they voluntarily chose to cartelize. And if they did cartelize, new entry, either in the United States or from nations such as Korea, would sooner or later undermine their efforts. Thus, the rebuttal argument insists, free trade unencumbered inter alia by ill-considered antidumping actions is the best policy. The debate will continue.

---

50. See Flamm, *Mismanaged Trade?*, chap. 7; and "Shortage of Memory Chips Hurts Computer Industry," *New York Times*, March 11, 1988, 1.

Technological Systems and Industrial Dynamics: Implications for Firms and Governments

Bo Carlsson and Staffan Jacobsson

Contrary to conventional wisdom, we argue that in a systems perspective, private and public entities share responsibility for counteracting "market failures." Policies can improve existing technological systems or build new ones. Private actors can invest in absorptive capacity, networks, bridging institutions, and competence building, while public policy can raise the awareness of new technological opportunities, increase variety, and promote the entire system, not just single elements.

Introduction

The debate over the appropriate extent, nature, and timing of government policies to foster economic growth has a long history. Almost 150 years ago, John Stuart Mill formulated the well-known infant industry argument, emphasizing the advantage of an early start in a new venture, the problems of differential social and private risk taking, and the temporary nature of intervention (Corden 1974, p. 248). In a number of developing countries, the infant industry argument has been used to justify extensive government intervention—some successful, such as in Korea and Taiwan (Jacobsson and Alam 1993, Pack and Westphal 1986, Wade 1990), and others less successful.

More recently, the classical infant industry argument has been reinvented in the form of "strategic trade policies" (Krugman 1983), extending the role of government policy in a developed economy beyond providing R&D subsidies to include trade policy as well. Policy is seen as an instrument for improving competitiveness in specific product areas, for example, integrated circuits, by creating and drawing the benefits from first-mover advantages.

This chapter was written within the framework of the research project "Sweden's Technological Systems and Future Development Potential" financed by the Swedish National Board for Industrial and Technical Development (NUTEK, formerly STU) and the Swedish Council for Planning and Coordination of Research (FRN). We are grateful to Maureen McKelvey, Charles Edquist, and Lennart Elg for useful comments on an earlier draft.

Others have emphasized the localized and path-dependent nature of learning, the close connection between national institutions and innovations, and the role of government in enhancing the learning capability of the national economy (Dosi, Pavitt, and Soete 1990, Dalum, Johnsson and Lundvall 1992). In general, in this approach it is argued that "governmental intervention should be oriented primarily at shaping the overall structure of production and the institutional set-up so that these promote self-organized learning and thereby reduce the need for fine-tuning and detailed intervention in the economy" (Dalum, Johnsson, and Lundvall 1992, p. 315). What matters here is that the economy has a production structure, technology base, and institutional setup that permit the realization of existing technological opportunities and that are flexible enough to ensure that the economy can benefit from shifting technological opportunities.

If we go one step further into a truly dynamic, uncertain, and nondeterministic world in which it is impossible to foresee the nature and direction of future changes, the challenges become even greater for policy makers at all levels, micro as well as macro. "The experimentally organized economy" (Eliasson 1991) is characterized by perennial turbulence, disequilibrium, and experimentation. With no one able to predict the future, lots of mistakes are made; it is more important to decide on a course of action than to try to ensure that it is the right action—mistakes can always be corrected later (Eliasson 1993, pp. 42–43).

So far, the work that has been done along these latter lines has resulted in few normative conclusions and has focused more on raising issues than on providing clear answers. Our policy discussion is placed within this tradition rather than in the quite restrictive infant industry and trade policy debates. Moreover, as our title suggests, we emphasize that many of the issues raised have a bearing not only on government policy, but also on firm strategy, executed in isolation or jointly with other firms.

The chapter is organized as follows. In the following section we briefly review some of the literature dealing with the nature of the innovation process and set the stage for the subsequent analysis. The third section begins with a definition and brief discussion of the concept of technological systems. This is followed by a discussion of the economic foundation of government policy. We continue by identifying and analyzing key issues with respect to three central components in a technological system: economic competence, clusters/networks, and institutions. The final section synthesizes our results with respect to both firm strategy and government policy.

The Nature of the Innovation Process

The way in which the process of innovation is conceptualized, implicitly or explicitly, is of fundamental importance. Some salient features of the innovation process will therefore be reviewed, based on recent works in the economics of innovation.

Technological change can be seen as a learning process that is gradual and cumulative in character (Lundvall 1992, p. 8).[1] A relatively ordered pattern of innovations can be observed along what Dosi (1988b, p. 1128) labels technological trajectories.

Learning and technological change are also cumulative at the level of the firm. Firms build upon their existing knowledge base and other assets when they search for new opportunities (Teece 1988; Dosi 1988a). Learning and technological change are therefore rooted in the present economic structure (path-dependent) and are local in nature (David 1988; Dosi, Teece, and Winter 1991). Still, there is a great deal of serendipity and nondeterminism in the innovation process, and more generally, in an experimental economy (Eliasson 1991). The search and innovation process can lead to a widening set of options for a firm;[2] new entrants may intensify competition, perhaps by leading a technological discontinuity; and incumbents may change their strategies; all in ways that are difficult or impossible to foresee.

Technological knowledge is, to a varying degree, tacit (person-embodied). In each technology, there are elements that cannot be written down in blueprint form, are difficult to verbalize, and can therefore not be easily diffused (Dosi 1988b, p. 1131; Landes 1991; Metcalfe 1992, p. 18). As this tacit component in the knowledge base increases, technological accumulation is more experience-based and communication as well as technology transfer take place primarily via interpersonal contacts (Metcalfe 1992, p. 19).

Consequently, formal or informal networks are important routes for the transfer of tacit knowledge (Metcalfe 1992, p. 85). Networks can partly compensate for limitations in the firm's search space on account of both bounded rationality and bounded vision (Fransman 1990). Such networks (e.g., user-supplier relations and bridging institutions) are therefore central to the innovation process. Thus, as emphasized by Lundvall (1992) and Johnsson (1992), the learning process is interactive where the institutional setup

---

1. The gradual and cumulative nature of technical change makes it difficult and misleading to make a clear-cut distinction between innovation and diffusion. Indeed, a central feature of the diffusion process is how a new product, and the technology embodied in it, alters in the course of the diffusion process (Rosenberg 1976; Gold 1981). The example of numerically controlled machine tools (NCMTs) can illustrate this feature. While the first NCMT was produced as early as 1955, it took two major changes (and twenty years) in the underlying technology base and associated price/performance characteristics and a whole range of minor improvements before NCMTs began to be diffused on a large scale (Jacobsson 1986; Ehrnberg and Jacobsson 1993). It is therefore appropriate to see the diffusion curve as an envelope curve that is superimposed on a number of minor diffusion curves (Ehrnberg and Jacobsson 1995, Metcalfe 1992).

2. Firms with a high absorptive capacity (acquired through R&D activity, experimentation, continuous learning, etc.) are in a better position to take advantage of new opportunities than those with low absorptive capacity (Cohen and Levinthal 1990).

strongly affects the process of learning.[3] Such interaction may occur across national borders and over large geographical distances, but there are good reasons to think that interaction of firms belonging to the same nation might be most efficient (Lundvall 1988, p. 355).

These networks, institutions, and actors, through their investment decisions, form highly specific national or regional innovation contexts, or systems (Freeman 1987; Carlsson and Stankiewicz 1991, Patel and Pavitt 1994). These give rise to, and rest upon, significant externalities (Dosi et al., 1990 p. 107; Carlsson and Jacobsson 1993) that lie at the heart of the innovation process. As increasing returns apply to the process of innovation, an initial specialization tends to be reproduced and strengthened, resulting in different, uneven, and divergent technological development among countries (Patel and Pavitt 1993).

These features of the innovation process strongly suggest that the spatial context (e.g., the nation or region) is not only still relevant, in spite of trends toward internationalization, but also strongly influences the rate and direction of the search activities that lead to innovations and their subsequent evolution and diffusion.

Evidence of this is found in four case studies (factory automation, electronics, materials technology, and pharmaceuticals) recently made in Sweden (Carlsson 1994, Carlsson et al. 1992). Similar evidence for a broader set of industries is reported by Patel (1993), who analyzed the geographic location of patenting activities in the United States for 569 large firms and found no systematic evidence of widespread globalization of technological activities during the 1980s. Instead, he found that for an overwhelming majority of the firms, technology production remains close to the home base.

The Economics of Policy

Technological Systems

As seen in the previous section, the national context of innovation matters for firm performance. Consequently, it is useful to discuss the factors that shape the local innovation contexts. These factors are found in the realm of government policy, as well as in firm strategy. Our approach to studying the innovation contexts for firms is summarized in the concept of technological systems. We define technological systems as

---

3. Epidemic models of diffusion emphasize that agents are imperfectly informed about a new technology and that a learning process, whereby partially tacit information is transmitted through observation and demonstration, takes place prior to adoption and diffusion. Such a learning process is, of course, interactive. Therefore, the particular characteristics, in terms of networks and institutions, of the local technological system matter for the rate of diffusion (Carlsson and Jacobsson 1994).

network(s) of agents interacting in a specific technology area under a particular institutional infrastructure [to generate, diffuse, and utilize technology.] In the presence of an entrepreneur and sufficient critical mass, such networks can be transformed into development blocs, i.e. synergistic clusters of firms and technologies within an industry or group of industries.

Technological systems have many dimensions, such as subject area (it is technology-specific), number and characteristics of actors and their interdependence, institutional infrastructure etc. This is one way in which they differ from National Systems of Innovation as defined by Nelson (1988), Freeman (1988), and Lundvall (1988), and others. Another difference is that they are not necessarily bounded by national borders, although they are certainly influenced by cultural, linguistic, and other circumstances which facilitate or impede contacts. A third difference is that technological systems place more emphasis on diffusion and utilization of technology (as distinct from creation of new technology) and therefore take micro-economic and entrepreneurial aspects into account, particularly the role of economic competence and of industrial development blocs, in conjunction with the institutional infrastructure. (Carlsson and Stankiewicz 1991, p. 111)

Technological systems thus constitute our prime unit of analysis. It is useful to pursue the policy discussion in terms of the three constituent elements of a technological system: economic competence, clusters/networks, and institutions.

Economic competence is defined as the ability to identify and commercially exploit new technology. This ability can reside in many parts of the technological system, among users as well as among component suppliers.

The character of the networks to which the firm belongs has a bearing on the type and amount of information and knowledge to which the systems give the firm access, that is, the connectivity of the constituent parts of the system matter. Buyer-seller relationships, as well as various types of bridging institutions (connecting academia and industry, institutes and industry, industry and industry), give rise to important network linkages.

Institutions refer not only to property rights and management practices, but also to the functioning of the educational units and government policy.

Market Failures and Industrial Dynamics

Industrial, trade, and technological policies are normally justified on the basis of market failure, that is, the inability of the market to achieve an efficient (Pareto-optimal) allocation, or any allocation at all. This may be due to the absence of a market, the presence of externalities, increasing returns to scale, or high transaction or information costs. But such conditions are ubiquitous in the innovation process; breaking such barriers is what innovation is all about. Thus, "innovation and Pareto optimality are fundamentally incompatible" (Metcalfe 1992, p. 4). Externalities (interdependencies that are not market-mediated) and increasing returns to scale abound in well functioning technological systems, while myopic investment behavior is a common feature of poorly functioning economies (Patel and Pavitt 1993). Hence, what static equilibrium theory denotes as "market failure" describes important features of the process of allocation of resources in a system of decentralized decision making. What role can the static concept of market failure then have in explaining industrial dynamics?

In the context of evolutionary economics, the power of the market lies not only in allocating resources, but also in serving as a powerful selection device and in providing incentives for learning and discovery, even though it may lack allocative optimality at any and every point in time (Dosi 1993, p. 22).

The selection and discovery processes can, of course, be shaped or strongly influenced by market failures. The case of videotape recorders, described by Arthur (1990), indicates that market failure (in the presence of increasing returns and network externalities) may lead to selection of an inferior technology. Similarly, lack of market institutions that shift innovation-related risks from some firms to others willing to bear the risks may lead to a too risk-adverse behavior, among smaller firms in particular (Metcalfe 1992, pp. 104–5).

These are examples of cases where decentralized decision making exhibits features that neoclassical economists label as market failure and that have important dynamic implications. These features affect both the way the economy selects (e.g., a standard for videos) and the way it generates variety (or fails to do so).

Market failures are therefore also quite relevant in a dynamic world, although they need to be liberated from the bonds of static theory (Metcalfe 1992, pp. 6–7). In a dynamic framework, market failures refer to conditions that interfere with the twin processes of selection and variety creation. The inefficiencies associated with market failures are not primarily the static ones found in equilibrium analysis (although these may be important, too). Instead, what matters most is how the mechanisms of selection and variety creation influence the process of innovation and diffusion. These mechanisms are influenced by the character of the technological systems that constitute the innovation context. Hence, market failures need to be analyzed and understood in terms of the functioning of technological systems.

There are three core elements of a technological system: economic competence, clusters/networks, and institutions. In this section we focus on the policy issues around each of these components. In the following section we discuss the implications for both government policy and firm strategy.

Economic Competence

Economic competence—the ability to identify, expand, and exploit business opportunities—is unevenly distributed among firms (asymmetric capabilities). Firms operate with different knowledge bases and under different assumptions concerning present, but most importantly, future (missing) markets.[4] The variations in the knowledge that guides management in their investment decisions, including their strategic choices, could, as previously argued, be seen as arising from long historical processes, central to which are learning processes that are local and cumulative, as well as path-dependent.

Rationality, on these assumptions, is not only limited but also quite different between firms as a result of the different experiences accumulated by management. A particularly important subset of management experience and competence refers to the firm's technology base. The technological and commercial opportunity set, as perceived by management, is presumably closely connected to this base.

When new generic technologies become available, providing vastly expanded and different technological and commercial opportunities, the bounded (and different) visions (Fransman 1990) of managers, due to varying knowledge bases, imply that firms may differ greatly in their perception of these opportunities.

"Bounded vision" is, however, not limited to the restricted vision of the individual firms. As previously argued, firms are parts of highly specific national or regional technological systems that are built up from networks, institutions, and actors. While these systems operate under increasing returns and in virtuous circles (positive feedbacks) in expansionary periods, there is a considerable risk that

1. Firms, institutions, and networks will become "locked in" to old technologies. Thus, the cumulativeness and path dependency of innovation leads to risks of lock-in into technological and institutional cul-de-sacs. This may well be the case in Sweden for mechanical engineering (Jacobsson 1993).
2. If a search is undertaken outside traditional areas, it will be done in a highly localized fashion. Thus, the particular features of firms' (and

---

4. As Eliasson (1990) argues: "agents are not marginally uninformed as in classical search theory, but grossly ignorant, and differentially informed about small subsets of an immense state space. To become informed becomes an experimental learning process" (p. 162).

other actors') absorptive capacity (Cohen and Levinthal 1990) influence their ability to evaluate new technology and shape their search processes. The cases of factory automation (Carlsson and Jacobsson 1994) and powder technology (Granberg 1993) are two illustrative cases. In the former case, there was a highly localized search from mechanical engineering to "mechatronics," and in the latter case, from iron and steel metallurgy to certain niches in the powder metallurgy field, particularly cemented carbides and other hard materials.

3. They will manage to actually hinder the process of variety creation in the local economy.[5] Electronics and computer technology in Sweden (Jacobsson 1993) is a case in which a virtuous circle in mechanical engineering seems to have prevented the emergence of a strong technological system in electronics. In other words, there may be feedback mechanisms whereby a selection process may consume variety (Metcalfe 1992, p. 103).

The risks associated with a mild or strong form of lock-in and inertia open up the most central policy issue, namely, to what extent intervention should aim at improving the functioning of existing technological systems and to what extent it should aim at building new systems.

In the former case, technology policy follows and enhances industry's current specialization pattern. This is illustrated by the creation of bridging institutions and other technology policy activities in the factory automation case, which improved the functioning of an already reasonably strong technological system. As the economic benefits of new technology are chiefly found in rapid and extensive diffusion, such intervention may have high leverage in spite of focusing on already-achieved points of strength.

In the latter case, there is a need for policy to keep options open, in the sense of stimulating and protecting technological and institutional diversity and enhancing industry's awareness of new technology.

The case of fiber optics in Sweden illustrates how a technology policy built capabilities outside industry prior to any industrial interest in that technology. This buildup proved to be quite important for Ericsson when they decided, at a later stage, to include fiber optics in their technology base (Granberg 1988). Of course, building up capabilities in the university or institute sectors means that society not only improves its awareness of the new technology, but also that the lead time is greatly reduced if and when businesses decide that they ought to expand their activities in that field.

Policy may also be aimed at enhancing industry's awareness and improving firms' vision of the opportunities for new technology. Fransman, in fact,

---

5. Metcalfe (1992, p. 85) points to the role of networks in limiting the decision horizon of firms, locking them into conventional technological attitudes that become self-reinforcing. See also Lundvall 1992, p. 310.

argues that this was the case in the Japanese collaborative research program, in which government (especially MITI) officials and researchers were able to enhance long-term economic performance as a result of their ability to compensate for the shortsightedness and blind spots of the companies (Fransman 1990, p. 286). A similar argument is made by Freeman, observing that the "not-so-invisible guiding hand of MITI shaped the long-term pattern of structural change in the Japanese economy . . . largely . . . on the basis of judgement about the *future direction of technical change* and the relative importance of various technologies" (Freeman 1988, p. 331). He further argues that while it is not possible to eliminate uncertainty, "a thorough discussion serves to mobilize resources, to expose difficulties, and bottlenecks, and above all to energize the participants, secure consensus and heighten *awareness*" (p. 334, our emphasis).

The role of MITI could thus, in part, be seen as helping firms to improve their economic competence and expand their perceived opportunity set, particularly in periods of rapidly increasing technological opportunities. Such a role is, of course, not restricted to MITI.[6] A similar case is the Swedish powder technology program that aims at establishing links between centers of excellence and prospective users, thereby raising the awareness of the latter to the opportunities of powder technology (Granberg 1993). Compensating for inadequate economic competence can, thus, constitute a major objective of policy in the process of molding a technology system.

A proactive technology policy can, however, not be pursued entirely without the active involvement of at least some firms in both the formulation of policy and its finance (Arnold and Guy 1989). It is therefore important for industry to have a broad technology base, so that there are at least a few firms with a technology base that is close enough to the new technology to enable them to understand its potential.

Vicious circles may be created if industry chooses not to go for a new technology and the universities as well as the technology policy follow suit. Eventually, this may lead to a situation where there are very few actors outside the state and the universities on which to base a proactive policy; industry can be too specialized in its technology base from the point of view of long-term growth (Soete 1988, Granstrand and Sjölander 1990). The Swedish National Micro Electronics Program illustrates the problems of a technology policy that aims at compensating for a decade of neglect of a technology, in this case semiconductors, by almost all actors.[7]

---

6. In the literature on Korea's phenomenal industrial development, a key role of the state has been to enlarge the perceived opportunity set by "field manipulation" (Jones and SaKong 1980).

7. The case of ceramics in Sweden is similar, in that the technology policy makers have difficulty finding industrial partners (Granberg 1993).

The myopic view of many firms with respect to new technology, especially technology that is "distant" from their existing technology base, therefore sets limits on what a technology policy can achieve. This is, of course, a dilemma, as the myopic view is part of the justification of policy!

Hendry (1989) describes this in the case of the British computer industry:

> The firms responded to government [subsidies] in their own terms, not in the terms of the government. . . . If a firm does not want to do something—if that something is incompatible with its own, privately developed, corporate strategy—then government money will make little real difference. . . . [It's] like trying to push mules uphill. (166–67)

One way out of this dilemma would be to use the public procurement instrument more actively, and in close coordination with other instruments, such as the educational policy. A technologically competent buyer can specify not only the price and performance of a new product, but can also contribute to its design. Moreover, by paying for the seller's R&D, the buyer reduces the risks of venturing into new technologies, and by buying the product to be developed, may give the seller a first-mover advantage. Indeed, in the electronics and computer case (Jacobsson 1993), the really successful outcomes in Sweden rely on strong user-supplier linkages with competent state buyers. The strength of the Swedish factory automation industry rests, similarly, on close interaction with a few technologically advanced users (Carlsson and Jacobsson 1994). Within the pharmaceutical field, a decisive factor behind the success of Swedish firms has been hospitals with a significant international standing in research (Carlsson et al. 1992).

Clusters/Networks

The critical role of clustering of resources and knowledge/competence networks means that a well functioning technological system depends on strongly positive and reciprocal external economies (both pecuniary and nonpecuniary) that tie together users, suppliers, and competitors.[8] Indeed, the importance of networks suggests that technological systems, and therefore the process of generating and diffusing new technology, rest heavily on reduction of transaction costs via internalization of transactions within networks. The pattern of ties between users and suppliers may overlap with those generated by market transactions. However, ties of a problem-solving nature, where more tacit knowledge is transmitted, are normally much more local in character than market ties, as demonstrated by Granberg (1993) in the case of material technology and by Oskarsson and Sjöberg (1991) in the case of mobile telephony.

---

8. Porter (1990) makes a similar observation.

In a properly functioning technological system it would be a mistake to view external economies as failures. Instead, they form an integral part of an economic organization that tends to correct for these "failures" more or less automatically—the economic organization is in these instances superior to the market. For example, in a technological system, the reciprocal flow of information may well result in a blending of visions (technological expectations) of the future among various actors. Sharing the same vision may then lead to a reduction of perceived risk and a quasi coordination of investments between formally independent actors. For instance, the interaction between the leading technological firms (in terms of factory automation) and the local supplier industry results in a blending of their visions of the future production technology. The whole development bloc then invests in technological capabilities and design developments that are interchanged within the network.

A well-functioning technological system is a result of a process characterized by increasing returns. This suggests that there may be a role for government to play in initiating such a process or in solving bottleneck problems along the way. For instance, one purpose of the Swedish technology policy in ceramics is to form links between the university sector and some firms that are in a position that makes them likely candidates for taking up the new technology.

Moreover, how well the technological system works, with respect to both selection and variety creation, depends, in part, on how well its constituent parts are connected (Metcalfe and Gibbons 1991). An improved absorptive and learning capacity for the technological system can be achieved by creating *bridging institutions* for the purpose of acting as *nodes* in different information and knowledge networks. Such bridging institutions are not limited to transferring technology from institutions specializing in basic research to industry but, as was argued above in the factory automation case, they may also play a decisive role in the diffusion process among buyers.[9]

When the rate at which information flows through the technological system is enhanced (increasing the connectivity), the general awareness of technological opportunities is raised and the visions are blended. Both innovation and diffusion are affected. The connectivity of the system also affects how quickly learning (from both failures and successes) takes place at the level of the technological system. Indeed, one of the most important functions of technological systems is to facilitate the sharing of knowledge among actors.

In some cases—for example, in the Swedish pharmaceutical industry—the information flows among users, suppliers, research labs, and so on, arise

---

9. The discussion here is limited to formal bridging institutions. Technology policy could possibly also be directed toward informal institutions.

spontaneously, without government intervention. In other cases, government policy may play an important role by improving the connectivity of the technological system and thereby enhancing the information and knowledge sharing within the system.

Institutions

Technical change depends not only on the behavior of individual firms; institutions matter, too. One of the most important institutions is the educational system. Universities have a critical role to play in identifying new emerging technologies, creating awareness of their potential, and rapidly increasing society's absorptive capacity by accelerating research and education in new technologies when they are judged to be on the verge of becoming economically interesting.[10] The universities therefore need to be proactive and flexible: proactive in order to be able to supply industry with specialized skills and new knowledge in emerging technological fields in time; flexible in order to adjust the orientation of education from old technologies (e.g., shipbuilding technologies) to new (e.g., microelectronics).

The lead time from the point when a new technology shows a good economic potential to "volume production" of engineers and Ph.D.'s with an orientation toward the new technology is very long if the universities have to start from scratch. It is therefore of utmost importance that the universities move into new technologies early and with great force, increasing variety and creating a better response capacity. This does not always happen, however. For example, in the case of electronics and computer technology in Sweden, the expansion in training of engineers in electronics and computer science was about 10 years behind that in the United States and lagged 15 years behind the key inventions in electronics (Jacobsson 1993). Of course, some new technologies never become economically interesting (e.g., the bubble memory technology) and resources will then need to leave that field, but in order for society to have a good response capacity, resources need to be allocated to many of those technologies that have the potential to become economically interesting.

In those technologies that do prove to be economically viable, society then has a competence base to rely on as demand for specialized personnel accelerates in that area. The lead time is therefore reduced significantly, albeit at the price of an overinvestment at any given point in time. But in an evolutionary world, this is the normal state of affairs; "waste" is always

---

10. In the case of factory automation (as well as in some other cases studied—see Carlsson 1994; Carlsson et al. 1992), the universities have not performed well. Other government bodies, in particular the Swedish Board for Industrial and Technical Development, have had to compensate for a slow and inadequate adjustment by the universities.

present: "static inefficiencies are the necessary cost which must be incurred if economic systems are to develop and evolve" (Metcalfe 1992, pp. 7–8).

But is it really appropriate to regard such static inefficiencies as waste? Clearly it is possible, and even likely, that mistakes are made in targeting areas for expansion within the academic system. But is it more costly than the alternative? Getting a late start and trying to catch up is likely to prove even more costly. Studies have shown that the adjustment costs are much higher when a technology is imposed from outside than when it is developed inside (see, e.g., Eliasson 1980), and in extreme cases, catch-up may no longer be feasible. Moreover, reactive policies are more likely to require efforts aimed at slowing down the adjustment process; efforts that may carry enormous price tags. For example, the firm-specific industrial subsidies to the steel and shipbuilding companies in Sweden during the period 1975–79 cost the tax-payers about 28 billion SEK (in current prices, about U.S. $5 billion). This is more than the entire R&D expenditures of Swedish firms during the same period, and roughly twice the amount spent on academic R&D.[11] It seems reasonable to think that if only a fraction of that money had been spent on academic research and higher education (particularly in engineering) in the period prior to 1975, the ability of the Swedish economy to absorb new technology and of Swedish companies to compete in new product areas would have been significantly enhanced. Consequently, the need to slow down the adjustment process would have been reduced.

A proactive educational policy is therefore central to any technology policy. But this is not to be construed as an argument for always developing new competence to replace part of the existing skills. Technical change is, of course, to a degree a process whereby new knowledge replaces old. But the dominant feature of technical change is probably one where new knowledge complements existing knowledge (Granstrand and Jacobsson 1991; Patel and Pavitt 1994; Oskarsson 1993). This implies that as new technological areas are born (e.g., electronic circuit design), they will have to be included in the curriculum of the universities not initially at the expense of the existing technological areas (e.g., solid mechanics), but in addition to them. This necessarily means that educational establishments need to expand, to a degree, just as firms' R&D expenditures need to expand to incorporate a growing number of technologies in their technology base (Oskarsson 1993).

A second critical institutional aspect is that of *bridging institutions* that act as information exchanges within the technological system, thereby improving the absorptive capacity of the system. Examples in the factory automation case are the Institute for Production Engineering Research (IVF), the

---

11. Calculated on the basis of material obtained from Carlsson, Bergholm, and Lindberg 1981, p. 29 and SCB 1992.

Swedish National Board for Industrial and Technical Development (NUTEK, formerly STU), and the Engineering Industry Association (Mekanförbundet). Some bridging institutions may initially need support, but once they are functioning they can be financed by those who discover the usefulness of their bridging work.

Other institutions that play a role within the technological system are the financial system (especially the supply of venture capital and other long-term capital for new types of business ventures and the rules under which such funds are allocated), the existence and nature of business groups and their ability to allocate financial, technical, and managerial resources, and the degree to which business activity is internationally oriented (particularly via multinational firms). These institutions can either enhance or diminish the ability of the technological system to generate and exploit new ideas. An interesting question in this context is whether loosely knit networks make it easier to break the hold of the past than *keiretsu* and other, more rigid, forms of organization. Networks could be seen as more appropriate in the long term, since they permit easier entry and exit. This may result in less homogeneity and better adaptability. The lock-in effect may be stronger in *keiretsu*-like groupings such as the Swedish "Wallenberg sphere," centered around a bank and with mutual stock ownership and board representation among the companies in the group. On the one hand, the group offers possibilities of drawing upon greater resources (financial, technical, managerial, etc.) than are available to the individual firm, but on the other hand the commonality of experience and culture may limit the group's ability to respond to new opportunities.

Implications for Firm Strategy and Government Policy

In this final section we will attempt to draw some tentative conclusions about the implications of our analysis for both firms and governments. By including firms, we want to emphasize that many of the problems identified above do not necessarily require state intervention. Obviously, the nature of the local innovation context is of great importance to the individual firm and many of the problems can be handled by firms or groups of firms.

Management Implications

There are a number of implications for firm strategy. These implications have a bearing on the content of the firm's investment portfolio. We will argue that this portfolio should include not only those investments that are internal to the firm, but also those that strengthen its linkages with other actors in the system and shape the innovation context.

No system is built up without a great deal of investment in the firm, as well as in its relations to other firms and actors. Firms need to build up their absorptive capacity, as well as their links with other actors in the technological system. In the case of industry-university links, this may mean that firms need to build up research groups at a level that makes them interesting speaking partners with academic researchers. Firms may also need to invest in building links on the personal level with the researchers in academia. These links, as well as the competence in the firm, should not be restricted to those technologies that today constitute the technology base of the firm's products; instead the search should go beyond that in order to increase awareness and reduce the risks of a "locking-in" effect. This suggests that the firm's network should be quite diverse and include weak ties to actors in more distant technologies (Alänge, Jacobsson, and Jarnehammar 1993).

Some of these investments refer to the cost of building relationships with competent and demanding users. With such links, a firm will live under constantly high pressure to innovate. Moreover, it will benefit from externalities in the form of information and competence flows from the user. These links can benefit the firm not only in its cumulative technical change, but also in handling technological discontinuities (Ehrnberg and Jacobsson 1994).

While the local context is still crucial in the process of innovation, there are good reasons to invest in building links to actors in global technological systems, as, for example, South Korea has done in building up its semiconductor sector and Japan has done in many industries.

Since the innovation and diffusion process is not a matter for the individual firm only, it follows that it is in the interest of firms to ensure that the local technological system is made up of highly competent constituent elements and is well connected. The firm's investment portfolio may therefore include not only investments to improve its absorptive capacity and its links to other actors in the system, but also investments in the technological system itself. This can be done, for example, by contributing a key technology to a joint research consortium, like IBM did with SEMATECH, or through an industry association, cofinancing the setting up of a bridging institution.

An example of a privately initiated and organized bridging institution is the 128 Venture Group in Massachusetts, a monthly forum where actors interested in creating new high-technology ventures (i.e., entrepreneurs, venture capitalists, managers, and other professionals) meet to pursue their complementary interests (Nohria 1992).

A firm could also (alone or with industry associations) be involved in financing R&D programs in institutes or universities that aim, in a proactive way, at building capabilities in new technologies. In other words, firms could finance such efforts in an attempt to reduce the risks of being locked-in to old technologies.

Finally, firms can lobby to influence the content and magnitude of industrial and technology policy. This policy should not be oriented toward saving jobs in old industries—even though that is politically difficult to avoid. Nor should it involve picking winners in terms of individual firms or industries, or a complete hands-off view of the role of the state in industrial development. Some key features of such a proactive and systems-oriented policy are outlined in the following.

Public Policy Implications

The purpose of government technology policy is to promote and shape the processes of creation, diffusion, and utilization of new technology. As argued above, it is useful to think of these processes as taking place within technological systems (and between them in the formative stage of a new system), which are therefore appropriate units of analysis not only for management, but also for public policy. The objectives of technology policy are not only to help in improving existing technological systems, but also, and perhaps primarily, to contribute to the creation of new systems. Well-functioning technological systems require that none of their important components—economic competence, networks/clusters, or institutions—constitute bottlenecks for transforming technological opportunities to growth. Consequently, a technology policy can include what are conventionally labeled industrial and scientific policies.

As our four cases demonstrate (Carlsson 1994; Carlsson et al. 1992), there is a great deal of variation among technological systems, as well as within them over time, with respect to which part of the system constitutes the prime bottleneck. The best policy shaping the technological system can therefore not be stated in general terms. Technology policy must clearly be designed to deal with the specific needs in each area. For example, an improvement in the technological system for factory automation requires an entirely different type of policy than does the case of powder technology.

In some cases it might be necessary to increase the connectivity of some of the constituent parts; the state may have to rescue a central component of the system or find compensating mechanisms; it might have to influence the visions of management and create more variety than the market forces alone would do; and it might have to initiate some institutions and networking. In other words, the precise nature of the intervention would be expected to vary from case to case, both among technological systems in a country and among countries, as well as over time, the latter adding to the need for a flexible policy.

The need for "made-to-measure" intervention is, of course, not a new finding (see, e.g., Katz 1983). A made-to-measure policy may include no intervention at all, if economic competence, networks, and institutions evolve satisfactorily from a social point of view. Perhaps firms' strategic orientations already include strong elements of technology and associated product diversification; perhaps bridging institutions are built up by the firms themselves; or perhaps investments are already made in more "distant" technologies by the firms or by industry-funded R&D institutes. A priori, it is not possible to state the extent of policy intervention necessary for a new technological system to be built; this is an empirical question that depends on the behavior of firms and other private actors, as well as on the degree of competence among state actors.

To the extent that some degree of intervention is deemed necessary, it may be useful to discuss the content of policy, in as general terms as possible, along a time axis. A first task of a technology policy is to identify new technological opportunities at an early stage and to contribute to raising the awareness of these opportunities as broadly as possible, in industry and elsewhere. Given the localized search procedures for new technology, path-dependency, and the existence of self-reinforcing patterns of specialization of regional/national technological capabilities, one should not take this task lightly. Indeed, one of the main tasks of government policy may well be precisely this.

Related to early identification of technological opportunities is the undertaking of associated investments to make sure that the natural processes of specialization do not reduce variety to such an extent that long-term economic growth is sacrificed. One aspect of the creation of variety[12] in the form of supporting the emergence of a new technology is to give it legitimacy. As Lundgren (1991) argues in the case of image-processing technology in Sweden, the early support of the state gave legitimacy to the technology in the eyes of the capital market.

At a somewhat later stage, the focus of policy is to make sure that the absorptive capacity of the economy with respect to the new technology is sufficient. This capacity determines the rate at which the new technology is diffused and the extent to which it results in new products (including new production processes).

The absorptive capacity of the technological system depends on both the competence and the functioning of the constituent parts and how well these are connected. The aim of policy is therefore to ensure that the entire system, as distinct from single elements of the system, functions well. A well-functioning system as the objective of policy means that we can leave the old and sterile debate over the ability of the state to "pick winners" in the form of individual firms. As Stewart and Ghani (1991) rightly point out, the systems

---

12. There are a number of problems associated with the proposal that policy should influence variety. For instance, for how long should investments in a particular technology be undertaken by actors other than firms? Variety may limit diffusion, and standardization may therefore at some point be a better option than continued variety.

view of the innovation process makes us instead focus on the conditions and processes whereby winners are created. This suggests that policy could be focused on any or all of the three fundamental elements of a technological system: competence, networks, and institutions.

A prime concern of the state is to stimulate technological diversity, raise awareness of new technological opportunities, and foster an improved economic competence among firms. As firms are constrained in their ability to change strategic orientation by their initial choice of trajectories, they have a limited ability to develop new businesses by exploiting these opportunities (Teece 1988, Ehrnberg and Jacobsson 1994). Product diversification based on new technology can therefore not be expected to be the norm among established firms. Indeed, in a study of 57 large Organization for Economic Cooperation and Development (OECD) firms, Oskarsson (1993) found that while most firms diversified their technology base in the 1980s, only a small number exploited it in the form of an expanding product range. While the "stick to the knitting" (lock-in) behavior dominates, as expected, it is noteworthy that about 20 percent of the firms behaved differently, and these firms exhibited the best growth performance.

Advanced procurement policies may be useful instruments to induce firms to diversify both technology-wise and product-wise. Of course, advanced procurement policies require highly competent users. A wise technology policy would aim at fostering such user competence, as well as utilizing it to enhance the economic competence of suppliers.

A competently handled procurement policy could also have a major influence on the growth of small technology-based firms. Together with technology and product diversification by the larger firms, this growth, or the absence of it, will shape the transformation of industry. Indeed, the leverage (in terms of inducing new behavior) of any public resources spent on procurement may be much higher if they are focused on smaller firms, since these are more apt to change strategy in response to a given-sized "carrot." A procurement policy that is limited to smaller firms may have the additional benefit of intensifying competition for the larger firms, thereby providing a "stick" for them to change their behavior. Thus, procurement can be a policy instrument that focuses on improving the economic competence of both large and small firms.

Institutions can also constitute a focal point for policy. We previously pointed out a whole set of institutions that are central to the functioning of technological systems: educational units, bridging institutions, the capital market, the organization of ownership and control in terms of *keiretsu* groups or in networks, and so on. In particular, we argued that, to a degree, the educational institutions need to be proactive in relation to industry's demand for new skills and that some "waste," in the form of short-term inefficiencies, is part of the price of achieving a high adjustment capacity and medium/long-term flexibility. Policy may also aim at creating institutions, such as the centers of excellence involving both academic and industrial participants currently being promoted by the Swedish National Board for Industrial and Technical Development (NUTEK).

A third focal point is networks. Just as in the case of economic competence and institutions, private actors may develop, on their own, the kind of networks that are conducive to dynamic behavior. However, problems associated with lock-in effects and increasing returns may warrant intervention, where the role of the state is more of a broker than an investor or procurer. That is, policy may have the primary function of "matching" firms that previously have had little or no contact with one another.

All of this means that technology policy in a relatively new but economically promising field may have to be comprehensive, in that it focuses on the functioning and strengthening of the whole technological system. This has not always been the case with respect to Swedish policy.[13] For instance, as was argued in the case of electronics and computer technology (Jacobsson 1993; Stenberg 1993), while military procurement policies in the United States were combined with fostering both R&D and education at the universities, the Swedish programs were aimed only at the supplier of military aircraft. A technology policy may also have to be nonmarginal in character, in that, if it is deemed necessary, it will aim to influence the investment decisions of private actors. Such influence should, of course, be only temporary in nature, but should be large enough to make sure that a self-reinforcing process gets under way.

REFERENCES

Alänge, Sverker, and Staffan Jacobsson. 1994. "Erfarenheter från det svenska teko-programmet—en syntes i ett näringspolitiskt perspektiv." Report submitted to NUTEK.

Alänge, Sverker, Staffan Jacobsson, and Annika Jarnehammar. 1993. "Some Aspects of an Analytical Framework for Studying the Diffusion of Organizational Innovations." Department of Industrial Management and Economics, Chalmers University of Technology, Göteborg, Sweden. Mimeo.

Arnold, Erik, and Ken Guy. 1989. *The Evaluation of the IT Programme, Phase 1.* Stockholm: Booz Allen & Hamilton.

Arthur, Brian. 1990. "Positive Feedbacks in the Economy." *Scientific American* 262(2):92–99.

Carlsson, Bo. 1994. "Technological Systems and Economic Development Potential. Four Swedish Case Studies." In *Innovation in Technology, Industries, and Institu-*

---

13. Alänge and Jacobsson (1994) review the Swedish textile industry policy with respect to the extent that it had a systems perspective.

tions. *Studies in Schumpeterian Perspectives,* Y. Shionoya and M. Perlman, eds., 49–69. Ann Arbor, MI: University of Michigan Press.

Carlsson, Bo, Fredrik Bergholm, and Thomas Lindberg. 1981. *Industristödspolitiken och dess inverkan på samhällsekonomin.* Stockholm: IUI.

Carlsson, Bo, Gunnar Eliasson, Anders Granberg, Staffan Jacobsson, and Rikard Stankiewicz. 1992. *"Sveriges teknologiska system och framtida konkurrenskraft."* Report submitted to NUTEK.

Carlsson, Bo, and Staffan Jacobsson. 1993. "Technological Systems and Industrial Policy." In *Technology and the Wealth of Nations. The Dynamics of Constructed Advantage,* C. Freeman and D. Foray, eds., 77–92. London: Pinter Publishers.

———. 1994. "Technological Systems and Economic Policy. The Diffusion of Factory Automation in Sweden." *Research Policy* 23(3):235–48.

Carlsson, Bo, and Rikard Stankiewicz. 1991. "On the Nature, Function, and Composition of Technological Systems." *Journal of Evolutionary Economics* 1(2):93–118.

Cohen, Wesley, and Daniel Levinthal. 1990. "Absorptive Capacity. A New Perspective on Learning and Innovation." *Administrative Science Quarterly* 35:128–52.

Corden, W. H. 1974. *Trade Policy and Economic Welfare.* Oxford: Oxford University Press.

Dalum, Bengt, Björn Johnsson, and Bengt-Åke Lundvall. 1992. "Public Policy in the Learning Society." In *National Systems of Innovation. Towards a Theory of Innovation and Interactive Learning,* B.-Å. Lundvall, ed., 296–317. London: Francis Pinter.

David, Paul A. 1988. "Path-Dependency. Putting the Past into the Future." Stanford University, Institute for Mathematical Studies in the Social Sciences, Economic Series, Technical Report No 553, November.

Dosi, Giovanni. 1988a. "The Nature of the Innovative Process." In *Technical Change and Economic Theory,* G. Dosi, C. Freeman, R. Nelson, G. Silverberg, and L. Soete, eds., 221–38. London: Francis Pinter.

———. 1988b. "Sources, Procedures and Microeconomic Effects of Innovation." *Journal of Economic Literature* 26(3):1120–71.

———. 1993. Comments by Giovanni Dosi in UNCTAD, Report of Ad Hoc Expert Group on Technology Policies in Open Developing Country Economies, UNCTAD/ITD/TEC/3.

Dosi, Giovanni, Keith Pavitt, and Luc Soete. 1990. *The Economics of Technical Change and International Trade.* New York: Harvester/Wheatsheaf.

Dosi, Giovanni, David Teece, and Sidney Winter. 1991. "Toward a Theory of Corporate Coherence." In *Technology and the Enterprise in a Historical Perspective,* G. Dosi, R. Giannetti, and P. A. Toninelli, eds. Oxford: Oxford University Press.

Ehrnberg, Ellinor, and Staffan Jacobsson. 1993. "Technological Discontinuity and Competitive Strategy—Revival through FMS for the European Machine Tool Industry?" *Technological Forecasting and Social Change* 44:27–48.

———. 1994. "Managing Technological Discontinuities by Exploiting the Technological System." Department of Industrial Management and Economics, Chalmers University of Technology, Göteborg, Sweden. Mimeo.

———. 1995. "A Theoretical Framework for the Analysis of Supplier Industries." In *Technological Systems and Economic Performance: The Case of Factory Automation*, B. Carlsson, ed., 263–72. Boston: Kluwer.

Eliasson, Gunnar. 1980. "Elektronik, teknisk förändring och utveckling" i *Datateknik, ekonomisk tillväxt och sysselsättning* (DEK). Stockholm.

———. 1990. "Commentary. Economies of Scale through Network Technologies and the Size of the State Space." Booklet No. 306, Industriens Utredningsinstitut, Stockholm.

———. 1991. "Modeling the Experimentally Organized Economy." *Journal of Economic Behavior and Organization* 16(1–2):153–82.

Eliasson, Gunnar. 1993. "Den stökiga marknadsekonomin." In *Forskningsrådsnämnden, Tvivlet på nationalekonomin. Fyra ekonomer diskuterar vetenskapen och verkligheten*. Källa/40. Stockholm.

Fransman, Martin. 1990. *The Market and Beyond*. Cambridge: Cambridge University Press.

Freeman, Christopher. 1987. *Technology and Economic Performance. Lessons from Japan*. London: Pinter Publishers.

———. 1988. "Japan: A New National System of Innovation?" In *Technical Change and Economic Theory*, G. Dosi, C. Freeman, R. Nelson, G. Silverberg, and L. Soete, eds., 330–48. London: Francis Pinter.

Gold, Bela. 1981. "Technological Diffusion in Industry: Research Needs and Shortcomings." *Journal of Industrial Economics* 29:247–69.

Granberg, Anders. 1988. "Fiber Optics as a Technological Field—A Case Study Report." Discussion paper No. 182, Research Policy Institute, Lund.

———. 1993. "Mapping the Cognitive and Institutional Structures of an Evolving Advanced Materials Field. The Case of Powder Technology." Paper presented at the 20th annual E.A.R.I.E. Conference, Tel Aviv, September.

Granstrand, Ove, and Staffan Jacobsson. 1991. "When Are Technological Changes Disruptive?—A Preliminary Analysis of Intervening Variables between Technological and Economic Changes." Paper presented at the Marstrand Symposium on Economics of Technology, Marstrand, August.

Granstrand, Ove, and Sören Sjölander. 1990. "Managing Innovation in Multi-technology Corporations." *Research Policy* 19(1):25–60.

Hendry, J. 1989. *Innovating for Failure. Government Policy and the Early British Computer Industry*. Cambridge, MA: MIT Press.

Jacobsson, Staffan. 1986. *Electronics and Industrial Policy. The Case of Computer Controlled Lathes*. World Industry Studies 5. London: Allen & Unwin.

———. 1993. "Sweden's Technological System and Future Development Potential—The Case of Electronics and Computer Technology." Paper presented at the 20th annual E.A.R.I.E. Conference, Tel Aviv, September.

Jacobsson, Staffan, and Ghayur Alam. 1993. *Liberalization and Industrial Development in the Third World. A Study of Government Policy and Performance of the Indian and Korean Engineering Industries*. New Delhi: SAGE Publication.

Johnsson, Björn. 1992. "Institutional Learning." In *National Systems of Innovation*, B.-Å. Lundvall, ed., 23–44. London: Francis Pinter.

Jones, Leroy, P., and Il SaKong. 1980. *Government, Business, and Entrepreneurship in Economic Development. The Korean Case. Studies in Modernization of the Republic of Korea, 1945–1975.* Cambridge, MA: Harvard University Press.

Katz, Jorge. 1983. "Technological Change in the Latin American Metalworking Industries. Results from a Programme of Case Studies." *CEPAL Review* April, no. 19: 85–143. (Santiago, Chile).

Krugman, Paul. 1983. "New Theories of Trade under Perfect Monopolistic Competition." *American Economic Review* 73(3):343–47.

Landes, David S. 1991. Inaugural lecture at the E.A.R.I.E. 18th Annual Conference, Ferrara, Italy, September 1–3.

Lundgren, Anders. 1991. Technological Innovation and Industrial Evolution—The Emergence of Industrial Networks. Ph.D. diss., The Economic Research Institute/Stockholm School of Economics.

Lundvall, Bengt-Åke. 1988. "Innovation as an Interactive Process; From User-Supplier Interaction to the National System of Innovation." In *Technical Change and Economic Theory,* G. Dosi, C. Freeman, R. Nelson, G. Silverberg, and L. Soete, eds., 349–69. London: Francis Pinter.

———, ed. 1992. *National Systems of Innovation. Towards a Theory of Innovation and Interactive Learning.* London: Francis Pinter.

Metcalfe, J. Stanley. 1992. "The Economic Foundations of Technology Policy. Equilibrium and Evolutionary Perspectives." University of Manchester. Mimeo.

Metcalfe, J. Stanley, and Michael Gibbons. 1991. "Technology Policy in an Evolutionary World." Working paper, University of Manchester, May.

Nelson, Richard R. 1988. "Preface" to G. Dosi, C. Freeman, R. Nelson, G. Silverberg, and L. Soete, eds. *Technical Change and Economic Theory.* London: Francis Pinter.

———., ed. 1993. *National Systems of Innovation. A Comparative Analysis.* Oxford: Oxford University Press.

Nohria, Nitin. 1992. "Information and Search in the Creation of New Business Ventures. The Case of the 128 Venture Group." In *Networks and Organizations. Structure, Form and Action,* N. Nohria and R. G. Eccles, eds., 240–61. Boston: Harvard Business School Press.

Oskarsson, Christer. 1993. Technology Diversification—The Phenomenon, Its Causes and Effects. Ph.D. diss., Department of Industrial Management and Economics, Chalmers University of Technology, Göteborg, Sweden.

Oskarsson, Christer, and Niklas Sjöberg. 1991. "Bäst i Världen projektet. Produktivitet inom mobiltelefoni." Department of Industrial Management and Economics, Chalmers University of Technology, Göteborg, Sweden. Mimeo.

Pack, Howard, and Larry Westphal. 1986. "Industrial Strategy and Technological Change. Theory versus Reality." *Journal of Development Economics* 22, no. 1 (June): 87–128.

Patel, Pari. 1993. "Localized Production of Technology for Global Markets." Science Policy Research Unit, University of Sussex. Mimeo.

Patel, Pari, and Keith Pavitt. 1993. "Uneven (and Divergent) Technological Development amongst Countries and Firms. Evidence and Explanations." Science Policy Research Unit, University of Sussex, U.K. Mimeo.

———. 1994. "The Continuing, Widespread (and Neglected) Importance of Improvements in Mechanical Technologies." *Research Policy* 23(5):533–45.

Pavitt, Keith. 1991. "Key Characteristics of the Large Innovating Firm." *British Journal of Management* 2:41–50.

Porter, Michael E. 1990. "The Competitive Advantage of Nations." *Harvard Business Review* (March–April): 73–93.

Rosenberg, Nathan. 1976. *Perspectives on Technology.* Cambridge: Cambridge University Press.

SCB (Swedish National Central Bureau of Statistics). 1992. *Forskning och utvecklingsarbete i Sverige.* Stockholm: SCB.

Soete, Luc. 1988. "Technical Change and International Implications for Small Countries." In *Small Countries Facing the Technological Revolution.* C. Freeman and B.-Å. Lundvall, eds., 98–110. London: Francis Pinter.

Stenberg, Lennart. 1993. "Internationella utvecklingstendenser i statlig teknikpolitik." NUTEK-Analys, Stockholm, Sweden.

Stewart, F., and E. Ghani. 1991. "How Significant are Externalities for Development?" *World Development* 19(6):569–94.

Teece, David. 1988. "Technological Change and the Nature of the Firm." In *Technical Change and Economic Theory,* G. Dosi, C. Freeman, R. Nelson, G. Silverberg, and L. Soete, eds., 256–80. London: Francis Pinter.

Wade, R. 1990. *Governing the Market. Economic Theory and the Role of Government in East Asian Industrialization.* Princeton, NJ: Princeton University Press.

Capital Structure, Asset Specificity, and Firm Size: A Transaction Cost Analysis

Zoltan J. Acs and Steven C. Isberg

Using a new measure of asset specificity, we find that innovation is an impor tant determinant of capital structure choice and that the exact relationship depends on firm size. For large firms, asset specificity is consistent with a discretionary governance structure. For small firms, innovation is associated with a rules-based governance structure and higher levels of debt.

Introduction

Recently, the "capital structure puzzle" has been examined through the lens of transaction cost economics (TCE), where debt and equity are viewed as alternative forms of corporate governance.[1] While many agree that firms prefer internal to external financing and debt to equity, these recent theories suggest that capital structure choice is dictated by the firm's asset specificity. For example, Williamson (1988) posits that the firm's debt/equity ratio is determined by the optimal governance structure, given the redeployability of the firms assets. If assets are easily redeployed between production alternatives, debt, a rules-based governance structure, is optimal. If assets are not easily redeployed, a more flexible governance structure is appropriate. Hall (1990) analyzed the effect of several forms of corporate restructuring on R&D investment, finding that restructuring involving substantial *increases* in leverage did result in subsequent *declines* in R&D intensity.

Previous empirical studies, mostly by financial economists, have tended to focus on tax shelter effects and business risk in the presence of bankruptcy

This is a revised version of a WZB working paper, Capital Structure, Innovation, and Firm Size," (FS IV 91-24) June 1991. We wish to thank Lemma W. Senbet, Stephen A. Ross, Bo Carlsson, Edgar Norton, Bruce Kogut, Hung-Gay Fung, Josh Lerner, and seminar participants at the University of Pennsylvania, Harvard University, the University of Baltimore, and the J. A. Schumpeter Society Münster Meeting for helpful comments. We are grateful to Brett Salazar and Gisele Giles for valuable research assistance. All errors and omissions remain our responsibility.

1. For a review of the literature see Harris and Raviv 1991.

cost, as explanations for cross-section variations in leverage. Balakrishnan and Fox (1993) show that firm-specific effects contribute most to the variance in leverage, suggesting a strong link between strategy and capital structure. The purpose of this chapter is to add to the empirical literature examining capital structure by introducing a new measure of asset specificity: innovation. By employing innovation as a measure of uniqueness, this study measures both input and output specificity. Innovation is important because it represents the manifestation of a firm's commitment to investment in the production of unique products that have not been previously introduced in the market. A clear limitation in using only R&D activity as a proxy measure for asset specificity is that R&D reflects only the resources devoted to producing innovation inputs, and advertising does not necessarily measure asset or product uniqueness.[2] We present a model that investigates the degree to which capital structure is conditioned by asset specificity, and the extent to which large and small firms respond to different stimuli.[3] The econometric analysis enables the testing of two hypotheses: (1) that innovation is negatively related to capital structure; and (2) that innovation will have a disparate effect on small and large firm capital structure choice.

This study extends research on capital structure in an important way. By introducing the innovation measure we broaden the concept of asset specificity to include both input and output measures, and simultaneously investigate the importance of innovation on the capital structure choice of small and large firms, across a broad spectrum of publicly traded companies. The only study to examine the determinants of capital structure on small firms was by Wijst and Thurik (1993). They found that most of the traditional determinants of financial structure appear to be relevant for small firms; however, their sample was limited to retail establishments and they were thus unable to examine issues of asset specificity. In the second section of this chapter the data is introduced, while in the third section the empirical model is presented. The econometric results of the study are presented in the fourth section, followed by conclusions in the fifth section. We find that innovation is an important determinant of capital structure choice. For large firms, asset specificity is consistent with discretionary governance, but for small firms innovation is associated with a rules-based governance structure.

---

2. Balakrishman and Fox (1993) find that the advertising-to-sales ratio is positively related to capital structure. This result implies that firms spending more on reputational assets such as brand names can leverage more. These goods may be bought and sold without many transaction costs.

3. A firm's relative innovative advantage is likely to be roughly proportional to the number of suitably qualified people exposed to the knowledge base from which innovative ideas might be derived. The key feature of a particular environment constitutes what Winter (1984) terms a "technological regime." For a test of the Winter hypothesis, see Acs and Audretsch 1988.

The Data

The database for this study is constructed by combining three previously uncombined sources of data—the U.S. Small Business Administration Innovation Data Base (SBIDB), the Business Week Survey of Company Financed R&D expenditures, and the Standards and Poor's Compustat Annual Industrial File. The Compustat files provide all relevant balance sheet and income statement data. The Business Week data on R&D expenditures, which incorporates 95 percent of the company-financed R&D in the United States, has been used in other previous studies (Soete 1979).[4] The SBIDB provides one of the most important and unique direct measures of innovative activity.

As systematic data measuring the number of inventions patented were introduced in the mid-1960s, many scholars interpreted this new measure not only as being superior to measures of R&D, but also as reflecting innovative output. In fact, the use of patented inventions is not a measure of innovative output, but rather a measure of intermediate output. A patent reflects new technical knowledge, but it does not indicate whether this knowledge has a positive economic value. Only those inventions that have been successfully introduced in the market can claim that they are innovations as well. While innovations and inventions are related, *they are not identical*. This distinction is that an innovation is "a process that begins with an invention, proceeds with the development of the invention, and results in the introduction of a new product, process or service to the marketplace" (Edwards and Gordon 1984, p. 1).

The development and application of this new direct measure of output specificity has led to a new learning about the sources of innovative activity (Acs and Audretsch, 1987, 1988, 1990). Central to the new learning is that small firms, as well as large enterprises, play an important role in innovative activity. Small firms tend to have the innovative advantage in those industries that are highly innovative, where skilled labor is relatively important, and where large firms are present. "This suggests that, ceteris paribus, the greater the extent to which an industry is composed of large firms the greater will be the innovative activity, but the increased innovative activity will tend to emanate more from the small firms than from the large firms" (Acs and Audretsch 1988, p. 687).

---

4. The Business Week data include the company-financed R&D expenditures of 735 companies. Although the Business Week sample excludes the smallest enterprises, firms that can be considered as relatively small are included in the data. 130 firms have fewer than 500 employees, which is the standard used by the U.S. Small Business Administration to distinguish small from large firms. The mean asset size of the whole sample in 1977 was $1,164 million, with the largest being $38,453 million and the smallest $9,527 million. Slightly more than one-quarter of the sample is composed of firms with less than $100 million in sales.

Previous studies have used different measures of capital structure. In this study, three measures of capital structure are tested in an attempt to capture the effect of asset specificity on short-term, long-term, and total indebtedness. The measures are obtained by taking the book values of short-term debt, long-term debt, and total debt divided by the total market value of common equity.[5] While data availability precludes the use of market value data for debt, its book and market values are found to be highly correlated (Bowman 1980). In addition, there is no reason to assume that differences between market and book values of debt are related cross-sectionally to variables used to explain capital structure (Titman and Wessels 1988).

The mean long-term debt to equity ratio for 1982 is 46.37, with a standard deviation of 56.14. Innovations are normalized by dividing by the log of total assets, converting the variable into a measure of the concentration of a firm's investment in innovative assets. The distribution of innovations is apparently skewed, with a small number of firms making numerous innovations, and most firms contributing fewer than three innovations. In fact, of 315 firms included in our sample, the mean number of innovations was 3.22 (unnormalized), with about one-third of the firms contributing zero innovations. For each of the three debt measures, there exists a monotonic, inverse relationship between the debt/equity (D/E) ratio and the average innovation rate. A t-test indicates that the differences in mean D/E ratios between the least and most innovative firms (i.e., categories 0 and 2) are significant in the cases of long-term and total debt. While no evidence regarding a potential size effect is provided, it is interesting to note that innovation and asset size do appear to be positively correlated.

The Hypothesis

Once corporate finance views individual investment projects in terms of their asset-specificity, a departure is made from agency theory, where the unit of analysis is the individual, and a move is made toward TCE, with emphasis on the transaction. According to Williamson

> Of the several dimensions with respect to which transactions differ, the most important is the condition of asset specificity. This has a relation to the notion of sunk cost, but the organizational ramifications become evident only in an intertemporal, incomplete contracting context. . . . A condition of bilateral dependency arises when incomplete contracting and asset specificity are joined. The joining of incomplete contracting

---

5. Short-term debt does not include nondebt current liabilities, and is defined as that which matures in one year or less. Long-term debt includes capitalized leases, and is defined as that which matures in more than one year.

with asset specificity is distinctively associated with Transaction Cost Economics. This joinder has contractual ramifications both in general and specifically with reference to corporate financing. (1988, 571–72)

The ramifications for corporate finance are that each investment project has to be analyzed on its attributes. Previous work has treated investments as *undifferentiated capital.*

In contrast with the earlier literature on capital structure, which began with an *equity* financed firm and sought a special rationale for debt, the TCE approach postulates that *debt* is the natural financial instrument. Equity, the administrative form, appears as the financial instrument of last resort. The discriminating use of debt and equity is thus predicted by the foregoing. Along the lines of Williamson, we suggest a very simple model. There are only two kinds of finance, debt and equity. Projects are ranked according to their degree of specificity. Suppose that a firm is seeking to finance a project with a low level of specificity completely out of debt. Suppose further that debt is a governance structure that works almost entirely out of rules. In the event of bankruptcy, the debt holders will exercise preemptive claims against the assets in question. If all goes well interest and principal will be paid. However, failure to make scheduled payments will result in liquidation. The various debt holders will then realize differential recovery in the degree to which the assets in question are redeployable.

Since the value of preemptive claims declines as the degree of asset specificity deepens, the terms of debt financing will be adversely adjusted. Confronted with the prospect that specialized investments will be financed on adverse terms, firms might respond by sacrificing some of the specialized investment features in favor of greater redeployability.[6] In response, equity becomes the preferred financing instrument. The board of directors become a mechanism by which the cost of capital for projects that involve limited redeployability is reduced. Not only do the added controls to which equity has access have better assurance properties, but equity is more forgiving than debt. Efforts are therefore made to preserve the value of a going concern. Thus, whereas the governance structure associated with debt is based on a set of predetermined, nondiscretionary rules, "that associated with equity is much more intrusive and is akin to [discretionary] administration" (Williamson 1988, 580).

---

6. This would retard technological change because technological progress itself depends on the creation of firm-specific assets as new products or new production processes. Porter (1992, p. 66) has recently suggested that, "many American companies invest too little, particularly in those intangible assets and capabilities required for competitiveness—R&D, employee training and skills development, information systems, organizational development, and supplier relations."

Let S_i be an index of asset specificity and let the cost of debt and equity capital, expressed as a function of asset specificity, be $k_d(S_i)$ and $k_e(S_i)$, respectively. Firms will switch between debt and equity as asset specificity increases if $k_d(0) < k_e(0)$ but $k_d' > k_e' > 0$. That $k_d(0) < k_e(0)$ is because debt is a comparatively simple governance structure. Being a rules-governed relation, the setup costs of debt are relatively low. By contrast, equity finance, which is a much more complex governance relation that contemplates intrusive involvement in the oversight of a project, has higher setup costs. Allowing as it does greater discretion, it compromises incentives intensity and invites politicking.

Although the cost of both debt and equity finance increases as asset specificity deepens, debt financing rises more rapidly. This is because a rules governance regime will sometimes force liquidation or otherwise cause the firm to compromise value-enhancing decisions that a more adaptable regime, of which equity governance is one, could implement. Accordingly whereas highly redeployable assets will be financed with debt, equity is favored as assets become nonredeployable. Let S_i^* be the value of S_i for which $k_d'(S) = k_e'(S)$.[7] The optimal choice of all-or-no finance is to use debt finance for all projects for which $S < S^*$, and equity finance for all $S > S^*$. "Equity finance is thus reserved for projects where the needs for nuanced governance are great" (Williamson 1988, 581). To test the hypothesis that input- and output-specificity is negatively related to debt in a firm's capital structure, we estimate the following model

$$(1) \; D/CE_{it} = \alpha_0 + \beta_1(INNOV)_{it} + \beta_2(R\&D/S)_{it} + \beta_3(ASSETS)_{it}$$

$$+ \; \beta_4(OPM)_{it} + \beta_5 \, (D/CE)_{it-5} + e_{it}$$

where the dependent variable, D/CE is alternatively defined as the ratio of total debt to common equity, long-term debt to common equity, and short-term debt to common equity in 1982.

INNOV is the innovation rate defined as the ratio of total innovations divided by total assets in 1982. Innovation as a measure of output specificity is the exercise of the growth option represented by R&D. In many cases, investment in specific capital assets is necessary to implement production of an R&D result. Regardless of whether new assets are purchased, however, once assets are dedicated to the production of an innovation (which on aver-

---

7. The marginal cost of debt includes two components: the cost of the debt instrument itself and the change in the cost of equity capital that results from the higher debt ratio. Although the cost of debt must be lower than the cost of equity (on average) at all times, when one considers the cost of debt at the margin, including the implicit increase in the cost of equity, it is possible for the two to be equal, as assumed in this example.

age takes almost five years), they cannot be redeployed without incurring the opportunity cost of lost profits from the innovation, and thus the assets are specific. Hence, the expected relationship between innovation and debt is negative.

$(R\&D/S)$ is the ratio of research and development expenditures divided by 1982 sales. R&D can be considered a measure of input uniqueness (Titman and Wessels 1988) and agency costs (Myers 1977). In the context of asset specificity, R&D measures investment in the process of identifying and developing unique products. Since R&D generally requires specialized labor, it is directly associated with asset uniqueness. In terms of agency costs, R&D can be viewed as a risky option on future investment, whereby its findings lead to a decision regarding capital investment. If this point precedes the maturity of associated debt financing, an agency cost is created (Myers 1977). In each of these interpretations, the predicted relationship between R&D and debt is negative.

ASSETS is a proxy for diversification measured by the log of total assets in 1982. Agency costs can be offset by diversification on the part of the firm (Warner 1977). Diversification reduces volatility in expected cash flows, and hence increases debt capacity. As such, it is expected that larger firms will face lower debt costs due to their greater diversification opportunities. Hence, the log of asset size is included in the model as a measure of debt capacity, and its sign is predicted to be positive.

OPM is employed as a measure of internal cash availability. This is included in the model as a measure for the firm's position in relation to the pecking order theory of capital structure. If firms prefer to finance with internal, rather than external, funds the sign on OPM should be negative (Jensen 1986). The long payback period and the intangible nature of the asset that is created all combine to make it difficult to finance R&D using external sources of capital (Leland and Pyle 1977). Therefore, firms with ample sources of internal financing are thought to be better able to invest in R&D, ceteris paribus.

Capital structure is viewed by most firms as a long-term strategic decision. Lagged debt to common equity (D/CE_{it-5}) is included as a measure of the firm's long-term capital structure choice. Fischer et al. (1989) argue, however, that despite the long-term nature of the capital structure decision, capital market friction may cause temporary deviations from the optimal debt/equity ratio. Lagged debt is expected to be positively related to capital structure.

Williamson (1975, p. 201) has emphasized the inherent tension between hierarchical bureaucratic organizations and entrepreneurial activity: "Were it that large firms could compensate internal entrepreneurial activity in ways approximating that of the market, the large firm need experience no disadvantage in entrepreneurial respects. Violating the congruency between hierarchical position and compensation appears to generate bureaucratic strains, however, and is greatly complicated by the problem of accurately imputing causality." This leads Williamson to conclude that

> I am inclined to regard the early stage innovative disabilities of large size as serious and propose the following hypothesis: An efficient procedure by which to introduce new products is for the initial development and market testing to be performed by independent inventors and small firms (perhaps new entrants) in an industry, the successful development then to be acquired, possibly through licensing or merger, for subsequent marketing by a large multidivisional enterprise. . . . Put differently, a division of effort between the new product innovation process on the one hand, and management of proven resources on the other may well be efficient. (1975, pp. 205–6)

However, theory offers no insight into the effect of this division of labor on the firm's capital structure choice.

By estimating the model separately for large and small firms the hypothesis that asset specificity will have a disparate effect on small and large firm capital structure choice is examined. The model is estimated both with and without the lagged capital structure variable. There are two estimation issues. First, since the error terms may be related to the size of the dependent variable, the estimates of the variance of the OLS coefficients may be biased downward. The equations are reestimated and corrected for heteroskedasticity. Second, to measure the interactive impact of firm size on capital structure, a seemingly unrelated regression (SUR) technique similar to that used in Acs and Isberg (1991) is estimated. The medium and large firms are combined to form one sample, while the small firms form the second group.[8] The model in equation (1) is reestimated in SUR form as follows

$$(2)\ D/CE = \alpha + \Sigma\ \beta_{1i}(INNOV * D_i) + \Sigma\ \beta_{2i}(R\&D/S * D_i)$$

$$+ \Sigma\ \beta_{3i}\ (SIZE * D_i) + \Sigma\ \beta_{4i}(OPM * D_i)$$

$$+ \Sigma\ \beta_{5i}(D/CE_{-5} * D_i) + e$$

where D_i = a dummy variable for small firms ($i = s$: $D_s = 1$ if small firm, 0 otherwise) and for combined medium/large firms ($i = ml$: $D_{ml} = 1$ if medium or large firm, 0 otherwise), and all other variables are as defined in equation (1). The model is estimated twice; first by constraining the lagged debt/equity coefficients to zero, and then by removing that constraint.

8. The large and medium groups were combined into one group because the small firms roughly correspond to the U.S. Small Business Administration's definition of a small firm. A small firm is defined as a firm with fewer than 500 employees.

TABLE 1.   Regression Results (OLS) for Short-term, Long-term, and Total Debt to Common Equity Equations for All Firms in 1982 (*t*-statistics in parentheses)

Variable	(1) *TD/CE*	(2) *TD/CE*	(3) *LTD/CE*	(4) *LTD/CE*	(5) *STD/CE*	(6) *STD/CE*
Intercept	95.824	48.008	65.342	33.476	30.481	17.005
	(5.871)	(3.604)	(5.071)	(3.090)	(4.663)	(2.828)
INNOV	−1.944	−1.197	−3.505	−2.799	1.561	1.571
	(−0.411)	(−0.321)	(−0.939)	(−0.917)	(0.825)	(0.931)
R&D/S	−6.701[a]	−3.927[a]	−5.135[a]	−2.868[a]	−1.574[a]	−1.186[a]
	(−4.899)	(−3.578)	(−4.751)	(−3.181)	(−2.87)	(−2.419)
OPM	−1.872[a]	−1.869[a]	−1.356[a]	−1.433[a]	−0.515[a]	−0.439[a]
	(−3.872)	(−4.909)	(−3.554)	(−4.597)	(−2.664)	(−2.554)
ASSETS	0.954	2.805	2.143	2.897[a]	−1.189	−0.207
	(0.386)	(1.437)	(1.099)	(1.816)	(−1.202)	(−0.233)
STD/CE − 5						0.391[a]
						(9.036)
LTD/CE − 5				0.407[a]		
				(12.479)		
TD/CE − 5		0.424[a]				
		(13.816)				
Adj. *R*-square	0.045	0.2417	0.113	0.408	0.118	0.4526
F-statistic	4.719	21.084	11.048	44.281	11.568	53.808
Sample size	315	315	315	315	315	315

[a]Statistically significant at the 95 percent level of confidence, two-tail test.

Empirical Results

Using the ratio of total debt to common equity (*TD/CE*), long-term debt to common equity (*LTD/CE*), and short-term debt to common equity (*STD/CE*) in 1982 as the dependent variable, the cross-section regression is estimated for 315 firms. As shown in table 1, equation (1), using total debt to common equity (*TD/CE*) as the dependent variable, the emergence of a negative and statistically significant coefficient for R&D/Sales suggests that asset specificity is inversely related to debt. This is consistent with the findings of Bradley, Jarrell and Kim (1984) and Balakrishnan and Fox (1993). The negative and statistically significant coefficient of *OPM* suggests that high levels of internal cash flow are associated with lower levels of debt. This is consistent with the findings of Titman and Wessels (1988). The negative coefficient for innovation suggests that even after controlling for internal cash flow, innovative firms use less, not more, debt, relying on a discretionary governance structure as suggested by Williamson (1988), however, the results are not statistically significant. The positive coefficient on assets suggests that larger firms are more diversified than smaller ones.

When lagged D/CE is included in equation (2), neither the sign nor the significance of any of the other coefficients change. The coefficient of the lagged debt term is positive and statistically significant, implying that current capital structure is closely related to its prior characteristics. This supports the hypothesis that capital structure is stable over time, as advanced by Fischer, Heinkel, and Zechner (1989). These results are robust for different specifications of the dependent variable in equations (3)–(6). The negative and statistically significant coefficients for $R\&D/S$ in equations (5) and (6) suggests that short-term debt may be a more important strategy variable than long-term debt, since it can be increased and/or decreased more easily to "hit a target" for firms that are actively managing their capital structure.

Table 2 shows separate regression estimates for large and small firms.[9] $R\&D/S$ and OPM apparently have similar effects on small- and large-firm capital structure. The negative and significant coefficient for R&D is consistent with the hypothesis that R&D is a risky growth option. All of the arguments regarding the difficulty of using external finance, especially debt, for R&D should apply most strongly to small firms. Such firms have access to a narrower range of capital market instruments, and are less likely to be able to trade off externally financed physical investment and R&D at the margin. Although operating cash flow is negatively associated with both large- and small-firm capital structure, the coefficient for large firms is not statistically significant. The negative and statistically significant coefficient for OPM in equation (1) for small firms is consistent with previous findings that small firms rely more on retained earnings to finance investment than large firms do.

In equation (2) the coefficient for large-firm innovation is negative and statistically significant. Firms that tend to invest heavily in firm-specific assets and firm-specific know-how will find it more difficult to fund such investments with debt. The results are consistent with a discretionary governance structure (Williamson 1988). However, the negative and statically significant coefficient for innovation suggests that small firms use more, not less, long-term debt to finance innovation. These results suggest that small innovative firms must use higher levels of debt and a more simple governance structure to

---

9. In order to estimate an SUR model a balanced data set is required. Since the small-firm category used in this study is half the size of the large-firm category, a special selection process was designed to match pairs from each subsample to run the SUR regressions. First, the large-firm sample was ranked by size, and every other firm was selected. This preserves the distribution within the subsample. Each of the large firms were then matched to a firm in the small-firm sample. First, the subsample was matched by firm size, and then by innovation rate. The same process was then repeated with the large firms omitted from the first subsample. The sample size varied from run to run, depending on how it was sorted. The SUR results were virtually identical for all of the different sorts.

TABLE 2. Regression Results for Debt to Common Equity for Large and Small Firms in 1982 (*t*-statistics in parentheses)

Variable	(1) LTD/CE OLS SF	(2) LTD/CE OLS LF	(3) STD/CE OLS SF	(4) STD/CE OLS LF	(5) LTD/CE SUR SF	(6) LTD/CE SUR LF
Intercept	104.01	−3.718	81.945	18.391	82.623	6.717
	(2.431)	(−0.173)	(4.116)	(1.571)	(1.861)	(0.267)
INNOV	32.389[a]	−8.461[a]	14.636[a]	−1.818	35.931[a]	−10.377[a]
	(3.111)	(−2.168)	(3.021)	(−0.858)	(3.253)	(−1.911)
R&D/S	−5.819[a]	−5.892[a]	−2.285[a]	−0.801	−5.502[a]	−3.048[a]
	(−3.647)	(−4.087)	(−3.075)	(−1.023)	(−2.866)	(−2.014)
OPM	−3.771[a]	−0.511	−0.784[a]	−0.594[a]	−3.962[a]	−1.803[a]
	(−4.842)	(−1.155)	(−2.166)	(−2.469)	(−4.572)	(−3.555)
ASSETS	−2.109	10.481[a]	−12.222[a]	0.602	1.793	9.120[a]
	(−0.227)	(3.582)	(−2.814)	(0.378)	(0.185)	(2.543)
Sys. weighted *R*-square	—	—	—	—	0.357	0.357
Adj. *R*-square	0.242	0.146	0.201	0.028	—	—
F-statistic	8.596	10.353	6.954	2.603	—	—
Sample size	95	219	95	219	89	89

[a]Statistically significant at the 95 percent level of confidence, two-tail test.

finance investment. Governance patterns for small firms may differ from large firms because these firms tend to be more closely held, subject to greater proprietary control and different monitoring costs. However, this should indicate a lower cost of equity, resulting in the use of less debt.[10]

Equations (3)–(4) in table 2 report analogous results for short-term debt. For both large and small firms higher levels of cash flow are associated with less short-term debt. For small firms the positive and statistically significant coefficient of innovation suggests that even after holding the level of *R&D/S* constant, innovative activity results in higher levels of short-term debt. The statistically insignificant coefficient of both innovation and *R&D/S* in equation (4) suggests that for large firms, *the short-term capital structure choice is independent of long-term investment decisions.*

This somewhat surprising finding suggests that, ceteris paribus, small firms use more debt to finance innovation, but not R&D, than large firms. For

---

10. Indeed, we know that small biotechnology companies in the R&D phase have very low debt levels and are equity financed, as suggested by the theory. Biotechnology companies in the innovation phase also have low levels of debt. However, they have been the recipient of billions of dollars of venture capital investment!

small firms this result holds for both short-term and long-term debt. This result is robust for different specifications of the model. These results simply would not go away. Therefore, we cannot reject the hypothesis that innovation will have a disparate effect on small- and large-firm capital structure. Brouwer and Kleinknecht (1996) found that R&D expenditures account for only about a third of total investment for a new innovation. One possible explanation is that small firms may face binding liquidity constraints and must rely on both short- and long-term debt, as permanent capital, that is, short-term debt, is used for more than smoothing transitory shortages of internal cash flow in small firms. The amount that must be invested in new equipment and plants to produce a new product, or embody a new process, generally greatly exceeds the R&D costs. This finding is consistent with Evans and Jovanovic (1989), Fazzari, Hubbard, and Petersen (1988), and Holtz-Eakin, Joulfaian and Rosen (1994) that small firms face binding liquidity constraints.

The results in equations (5) and (6) using the SUR model are similar to the OLS results. Most of the coefficients have the hypothesized sign and are statistically significant. While not reported here, these results are robust for different sample size and specification of the model, with the exception of lagged debt. Table 3 shows regression results for large and small firms with

TABLE 3.   Regression Results for Debt to Common Equity for Large and Small Firms in 1982 Corrected for Heteroskedasticity (t-statistics in parentheses)

Variable	(1) LTD/CE OLS SF	(2) STD/CE OLS SF	(3) LTD/CE OLS LF	(4) STD/CE OLS LF
Intercept	77.902	50.246	−7.442	17.677
	(1.827)	(1.831)	(−0.405)	(1.147)
INNOV	18.856[a]	11.764[a]	−4.388[a]	−0.772
	(2.262)	(3.197)	(−2.248)	(−0.842)
R&D/S	−4.207[a]	−1.646[a]	−3.287[a]	−0.588
	(−3.464)	(−3.148)	(−3.787)	(−1.226)
OPM	−3.353[a]	−0.568[a]	−0.685	−0.586[a]
	(−4.073)	(−2.285)	(−1.860)	(−1.960)
ASSETS	−1.359	−7.510[a]	7.280[a]	−0.558
	(−0.161)	(−4.425)	(2.889)	(−0.034)
LTD/CE − 5	0.293[a]	—	0.411[a]	—
	(4.787)		(6.859)	
STD/CE − 5	—	0.335[a]	—	0.424[a]
		(3.559)		(9.449)
Adj. R-square	0.33	0.46	0.48	0.16
F-statistic	10.54	17.25	42.90	9.48
Sample size	95	95	219	219

[a]Statistically significant at the 95 percent level of confidence, two-tail test.

lagged debt to common equity corrected for heteroskedasticity. Mostly the variables have the expected sign and are statistically significant. The positive and statistically significant coefficients of lagged debt suggest that the capital structure choice of large and small firms is a long-run decision.

Conclusion

This chapter uses a new measure of specificity to examine the effect of uniqueness on capital structure choice in the context of corporate governance and firm size. The results suggest that innovation is an important determinant of capital structure choice, and that the exact relationship may depend on firm size. For small firms, innovation coincides with greater levels of debt financing, while for large firms asset specificity is associated with a more flexible governance structure.

There are at least three conclusions to be drawn from these results. First, the results for small firms may be spurious. Second, governance patterns for small firms may be different from those for large firms. Structural differences in governance costs may explain the lack of fit of the TCE model to all firms. Third, small innovative firms may face binding liquidity constraints, relying more on debt (both short- and long-term) as permanent capital, instead of equity. Liquidity constraints would suggest that capital markets may not be perfect, as assumed in much of the literature. While these findings are not without ambiguity, they do suggest that future research should examine the *impact* of leverage on the survival of small firms.

REFERENCES

Acs, Zoltan J., and David B. Audretsch. 1987. "Innovation Market Structure and Firm Size." *Review of Economics and Statistics* 69, no. 4: 567–75.
———. 1988. "Innovation in Large and Small Firms: An Empirical Analysis." *The American Economic Review* 78, no. 4: 678–90.
———. 1990. *Innovation and Small Firms.* Cambridge, Mass.: MIT Press.
Acs, Zoltan J., and Steven C. Isberg. 1991. "Innovation, Firm Size, and Corporate Finance: An Initial Inquiry." *Economics Letters* 35:323–26.
Balakrishnan, Srinivasan, and Isaac Fox. 1993. "Asset Specificity, Firm Heterogeneity and Capital Structure." *Strategic Management Journal* 14:3–16.
Bowman, J. 1980. "The Importance of a Market Value Measurement of Debt in Assessing Leverage." *Journal of Accounting Research* 18:242–54.
Bradley, Michael, Gregg Jarrell, and E. Han Kim. 1984. "On the Existence of an Optimal Capital Structure: Theory and Evidence." *Journal of Finance* 39:857–78.
Brouwer, Erik, and Alfred Kleinknecht. 1996. "Firm Size, Small Business Presence and Sales from Innovative Products." *Small Business Economics.* (forthcoming)
Edwards, Keith L., and Theodore J. Gordon. 1984. "Characterization of Innovations Introduced on the U.S. Market in 1982." *The Futures Group, U.S. Small Business Administration,* Contract No. SBA-6050-OA-82. March.

Evans, David S., and Boyan Jovanovic. 1989. "Estimates of a Model of Entrepreneurial Choice under Liquidity Constraints." *Journal of Political Economy* 4:808–27.

Fazzari, Steven R., Glenn Hubbard, and Bruce Petersen. 1988. "Financing Constraints and Corporate Investment." *Brookings Papers on Economic Activity* (March): 19–37.

Fischer, Edwin O., Robert Heinkel, and Josef Zechner. 1989. "Dynamic Capital Structure Choice: Theory and Tests." *The Journal of Finance* 44:19–40.

Hall, Bronwyn. 1990. "The Impact of Corporate Restructuring on Industrial Research and Development." *Brookings Papers on Economic Activity: Microeconomics.* 85–124.

Hao, Kenneth Y., and Adam B. Jaffe. 1990. "The Effect of Liquidity on Firms's R&D Spending." *Discussion Paper 1492.* Harvard Institute of Economic Research.

Harris, Milton, and Artur Raviv. 1991. "The Theory of Capital Structure." *Journal of Finance* 46:297–356.

Holtz-Eakin, D., D. Joulfaian, and H. S. Rosen. 1994. "Sticking It Out: Entrepreneurial Survival and Liquidity Constraints." *Journal of Political Economy* 102, no. 1: 53–75.

Jensen, Michael C. 1986. "Agency Costs of Free Cash Flow, Corporate Finance, and Takeovers." *The American Economic Review* 76:323–29.

Leland, Hayne, and D. H. Pyle. 1977. "Informational Asymmetries, Financial Structure, and Financial Intermediation." *Journal of Finance* 32:371–87.

Milgrom, Paul. 1988. "Employment Contracts, Influence Activities and Organization Design. *Journal of Political Economy* 96, no. 1: 42–60.

Myers, Stewart C. 1977. "Determinants of Corporate Borrowing." *Journal of Financial Economics* 4:147–76.

Porter, Michael E. 1992. "Capital Disadvantage: America's Failing Capital Investment System." *Harvard Business Review* 70, no. 5 (September–October): 65–82.

Soete, Luc L. G. 1979. "Firm Size and Inventive Activity: The Evidence Reconsidered." *European Economic Review* 12:319–40.

Titman, Sheridan. 1984. "The Effect of Capital Structure on a Firm's Liquidation Decision." *The Journal of Financial Economics* 13:137–51.

Titman, Sheridan, and Roberto Wessels. 1988. "The Determinants of Capital Structure Choice." *The Journal of Finance* 43:1–19.

Warner, J. 1977. "Bankruptcy Costs: Some Evidence." *The Journal of Finance* 32:337–47.

Wijst, D. van der, and Roy Thurik. 1993. "Determinants of Small Firm Debt Ratios: An Analysis of Retail Panel Data." *Small Business Economics* 5:55–65.

Williamson, Oliver E. 1975. *Markets and Hierarchies: Antitrust Analysis and Implications.* New York: Free Press.

———. 1988. "Corporate Finance and Corporate Governance." *The Journal of Finance* 43:567–91.

Winter, Sidney G. 1984. "Schumpeterian Competition in Alternative Technological Regimes." *Journal of Economic Behavior and Organization* 5:287–320.

Part 3. Economic Dynamics and Economic Evolution

Economic Dynamism: Lessons from German Experience

Herbert Giersch

While I hesitated to accept the invitation to give this address, I was too venturesome and quick to formulate the topic. In an entrepreneurial mood, I committed myself with dynamism, before really knowing what I would be able to produce. Let me therefore begin with four clarifications and qualifications, to lower the level of expectations.

- First: I take dynamism to mean spontaneous growth with technological progress in a modern capitalist economy.
- Second: This field is probably not yet over-researched. So I do hope that we can still make use of "lessons." By lessons I mean impressionistic conclusions, admittedly mixed with subjective elements; they are derived from personal experience and professional observations. Critics may take these lessons as mere hypotheses—surely as hypotheses in search of evidence, even of contradicting evidence.
- Third: The main field of my professional observations is the German economy, but widely framed—in the context of an increasing liberalization of world trade and an increasing globalization of production.
- Fourth: Though insights that may turn out to be pretty subjective do not constitute hard science, we should not ignore them altogether, not even for reasons of scientific dignity. A narrow focus would make economics much less attractive; it might prevent us economists from submitting sensible contributions to the contemporary economic policy debate. In this context, I conjecture that it is better to be controversially productive than to run into the trap of sterile perfectionism.

Thirty Propositions to Think About

Having said this, I dare to submit the following propositions. They are fairly general to begin with and will become more specific when their number approaches twenty-five.

(i) Economic dynamism arises from intensive evolutionary competition; that is, from competition in the exploitation of new (and hence risky) opportunities. Such competition is comparable to a race, the outcome of which is not determined and cannot be foreseen nor predicted. This implies, almost by definition, that conditions must be such that it is impossible to pick the winner. In the global economy, this condition tends to be fulfilled, given the fact that more and more countries have succeeded in catching up and in approaching the technological frontier. The world economy now has several centers of excellence. The game, in its outcome, is becoming more and more undetermined, the future more and more open. Governments, by still trying to pick the winner in advance, may try to push ahead. But as they actually interfere by offering protection, they are likely to give rise to moral hazards and to impair rather than foster the competitive spirit—except in the business of lobbying for government subsidies. If we had more government control over investment, and less openness toward the future, we would probably have to expect less economic dynamism. This leads to a proposition of historical dimensions: The globalization of innovative competition is likely to enhance the world economy's growth prospect, as it probably has done in the last fifty years, when the unfolding of a multipolar world economy with a liberal trade order made us forget the stagnation thesis of the 1930s. (But also consider point xxviii and the possibility that there will be more control of investment and innovation—for reasons of environmental protection—on a national and international scale, which is likely to temper dynamism and to limit economic growth.)

(ii) There can hardly be too large a number of entrepreneurs participating in the race. Dynamism thus depends on openness in the horizontal dimension, that is, on easy entry—for the young and for all sorts of nonconformists, including foreigners as owners of financial and human capital. On this account, dynamism can be enhanced by progressing toward a less constrained economy. The constraints to be removed may include bureaucratic regulations, cartel arrangements and restrictive business practices, and impediments to imports and to foreign investments. Postwar Germany greatly benefited not only from the influx of enterprising refugees from the East (i.e., from Germany's former territories and from the G.D.R.), but also from entrepreneurial people among the guest workers. The reform countries of Central and Eastern Europe would be well advised to let foreign investment and entrepreneurship come in freely and for this purpose move fairly quickly to full currency convertibility on capital accounts.

(iii) Horizontal openness also involves tolerance toward immigrant labor. There is, however, one qualification to be added. This condition is that immigration must not severely impair cultural values that are economically efficient. Such values include personal safety, property rights, loyalty under the law, trustworthiness, compliance with contracts, and similar features of business ethics. They are factors of production that help to save transaction costs. In a sense, they are valuable club goods. Immigrants will have to contribute to their maintenance and preservation in order to be readily accepted as equals.

(iv) Tolerance toward foreigners and foreign capital is related to another requirement for economic dynamism. I mean the suppression of envy. Envy gives rise to xenophobia, but also to quests for redistributive taxation. Instead, envy should be turned into a motivation for efforts to catch up with one's neighbors. The appropriate means is moral suasion. Moreover, excessive envy can be tempered by demonstrating that individuals can expect positive externalities from other people's success. The individual must learn to trust that, in some way, he or she will benefit from the neighbor's achievements, either directly or through the price mechanism. The poor in the neighborhood of the rich can and often will be absolutely better off than the poor in the neighborhood of the poor. It is true that housing rents are higher where people benefit from saving of transportation costs, but prospering agglomerations offer increasing income and sales opportunities for suppliers of local goods and services, including services for the rich. These opportunities can help to transform envy into effort and to make people aware that they participate in a positive-sum game. Such an interpretation of economic life is essential for creating a social atmosphere that is progressive and free of distributive quarrels and conflicts. I claim to have observed such an atmosphere during the period of postwar reconstruction in West Germany. Ludwig Erhard spoke of "Wealth for all."

(v) In the same vein, there is reason for attributing a positive social value to tolerance vis-à-vis winners of all sorts. Those who are sufficiently lucky, eager, and skillful to win should be free to keep much of the gain for their own disposition. In a competitive environment, they will in any case devote much of it to investment. If marginal income taxes are high, the expected gains (before tax) must be correspondingly larger for the same excitement to be aroused. Even if gaining profits was attributed to sheer luck—as in a lottery— profits would still be useful, as, like lottery gains, they induce people to participate in the game. The huge profit has an exciting influence; it makes many people move or run faster. Nonpecuniary prizes may be a substitute, but not a perfect one: the Nobel Prize owes its high reputation at least partially to the large sum of money attached to it.

(vi) As a main proposition I submit that dynamism goes along with inequality. The reasoning is as follows: There is a given distribution of talents; if people are completely free to use them—within the legal constraints imposed to protect private property rights—there will quickly be a maximum number of activities in a wide division of labor, limited only by transportation and communication costs. Activities may be constrained, to be sure, by abstract rules of conduct as they have emerged in a Lamarckian process of evolution, but as long as these rules remain abstract and nondiscriminatory, they will merely lower the overall motivation level and will not affect the distribution of outcomes and incomes, which is essentially determined by differences in talents and tastes. Only specific interferences in the market—designed to suppress the activities of the talented achievers—and outright measures to redistribute incomes from the achievers to the nonachievers (and losers) will produce more equality. Such discriminatory interferences require coercion that will reduce dynamism. (There is only one redistributive device that is likely not to impair economic dynamism: It is the taxation of pure talent. Yet pure talent cannot be assessed independently of the person's will to develop it. Like beauty, it would quickly disappear from this world if it became a tax base.) A metaphor may help us to understand the complex system of interdependence. Imagine traffic congestion on the road, for example, in the face of a railway barrier. When the road is closed, all cars waiting in the queue are equal at speed zero. The distances between them are minimal. The drivers' talents and the cars' motive power and brakes do not matter. But once the barrier is lifted and the traffic is deregulated, the cars soon move at different speeds, with varying distances between them. Compared to the previous orderly queue the acceleration that follows liberalization looks like chaos. People not accustomed to the complexities of freedom and inequality will be irritated. The greater the average speed, the greater will be the dispersion. At full average speed, the inequality will reach its maximum, and the "cohesion" its minimum. A speed limit will appear sensible. It will limit the dispersion together with the average speed. If fixed low enough, the speed limit will transform a competitive crowd into a slow convoy, and the convoy will stop once a single car happens to break down. In this sense, dynamism and equality are surely at odds with each other.

(vii) Globalization that promotes worldwide dynamism increases inequality in the advanced countries, as well as in newly industrializing economies. In advanced countries, globalization depresses the incomes of unskilled workers. In the less advanced poorer countries, it is entrepreneurs and skilled workers who see their income opportunities improved. This is a trade-off between equality and progress (or growth). As a dynamic trade-off, I consider it to be more relevant for economic policy than the static trade-off between "equality and efficiency" that is the subject of Arthur Okun's celebrated 1975 book (published by the Brookings Institution). Okun's perspective was neoclassical rather than Schumpeterian. The evolutionary perspective I prefer is less focused on factor endowments and on an efficient factor allocation and more concentrated on factor augmentation; that is, on saving and investment, on the formation of human capital, on the process of innovation, and on the growth of knowledge. Inequality may be indispensable in a system of incentives for such factor augmentation, and hence for an acceleration of economic growth in the present circumstances.

(viii) From an evolutionary perspective, competition is not so much a mechanism for factor allocation as a growth race. Even more important, competition is a process of discovery (Hayek) that enables us to find out what we did not, and could not, know before. The knowledge that counts is the knowledge that will be considered useful in the future. It is the future that determines the evaluation. Time will show and appreciate what is useful; and time will depreciate what is becoming obsolete under the impact of new knowledge. Only a society that is forward looking in this sense and is prepared to welcome new discoveries as potentially useful, will fully test and effectively expand its dynamic properties. A precondition is full freedom of thought and research mixed with a minimum of protection for old values as it seems necessary to conserve the stability that even an evolutionary society needs. What is most required is optimism—technological and environmental optimism in particular. I consider this in tune with Popper, who is reported to have said: "Optimism is duty."

(ix) The outcome of dynamic competition may often be some form of cooperation. I mean first of all the cooperation that evolves within the pattern of a deepening division of labor. People want to make use of their comparative advantages once they have discovered their relative strengths and weaknesses in a competitive and stormy process of trial and error. They want to specialize and thus to deepen their knowledge and expertise in the division of labor. They are likely to pursue the path of learning-by-doing. And they have some interest in cultivating their complementary relations with customers and suppliers for improved (factorial) terms of trade—undisturbed by elements of substitution and competition. Competitive self-organization thus leads to cooperation. Such competition for subsequent cooperation may be called "co-opetition," more specifically: co-opetition in time.

(x) Co-opetition in time—as a general notion—may also be useful for describing the two distinct phases of the business cycle.

There is tough competition in periods of recession, when efforts are concentrated on cutting costs, improving the product mix, and searching for new markets. Sclerotic firms go bankrupt, and new combinations and alliances are formed. People speak of a crisis because the future appears most uncertain and can hardly be ascertained by extrapolating past trends. The market coordination through price signals seems to have broken down. Relative prices seem to change too fast.

These competitive irritations disappear in the course of the new upswing, when price and cost competition give way to output expansion and when the fruits of the new division of labor among firms show up in increased company profits. Such output dynamism resembles cooperation and cartel-like behavior, but it is really nothing more than the period of harvest following the time of competitive sowing and intensive cultivation. Our national accounts ignore this as they focus on output, thus creating the illusion that the recession is merely a slowdown, a temporary stagnation or decline. In actual fact, there are, of course, such mini-recessions. But we also recognize deeper structural declines, perhaps once in a decade. They serve as phases of restructuring or preparation for the spurt of economic development that is bound to come afterward. The unemployment that arises in such structural recessions under the impact of globalization is likely to persist, if the labor market—including the wage system—is as inflexible and sclerotic as in Europe, and not prepared to accept what appear to be the new inequalities.

(xi) Co-opetition in time has its parallel in space and geography: You observe how centralized production plants cater to dispersed markets; you see hierarchically organized firms having horizontal relations with customers and suppliers for "just in time delivery"; you notice office districts in central cities bringing together people who commute to and from their homes in surrounding rural areas. Most nuclear families cultivate reciprocal altruism within a narrow realm and have fewer intimate relationships with more distant relatives, friends, or anonymous markets. And small teams share their knowledge internally, and simultaneously take part in extensive research networks worldwide. The point to be made in this context is that the center or nucleus or team serves as the locus of creation, while the surrounding area and the periphery are the field of application, testing, and marketing. The nucleus is a kind of volcano, a powerhouse for the dynamism of the spatial economy. Look at Stanford and Silicon Valley or at MIT and Route 128 near Boston! Or consider how a few chemical research centers in Germany gave birth and nutrition to the chemical industry on the River Rhine!

(xii) Central places are in competition with each other—just as families and firms, teams and universities compete with their likes. We call this locational competition. It includes competition among jurisdictions and political systems, among institutions and fiscal authorities. The ultimate objective in each case is excellence—for a better standing, a better living, or mere survival. What these central places are competing for in locational competition is mobile resources such as physical capital or human capital, including technological knowledge. These factors of production are hoped to contribute to raising the income of local residents and to broadening the local tax base for lower tax rates or for better public services. Locational competition deserves more attention among scholars than it has attracted in the past. It is most likely to bring competitive pressure to bear on national and regional governments and on local communities. More civil servants will have to study business administration.

(xiii) The driving force behind locational competition is the increase in the worldwide mobility of capital and human capital, including embodied and disembodied knowledge (Giersch 1982). Globalization, as a step toward openness, may be considered to have followed from liberalization, a policy mistake in the judgment of some observers. On this policy interpretation, the change appears quite reversible. But there are deeper causes: the decline of transportation costs and, perhaps more important, the decline of long-distance communication costs. This process toward openness brought down east European socialism and is likely to prevent the reemergence of closed systems for a long time to come. "Fortress Europe," for example, will turn out to have been an anachronistic conception or ideological monster.

(xiv) The lowering of communication costs is greatly increasing the size of the market for ideas. From decade to decade, tens and hundreds of millions more people are becoming part of Western civilization. The talent pool, on which the centers of research have to rely in recruiting personnel, is becoming larger and larger. From this I draw the heroic conclusion that the process of knowledge creation will accelerate. The same will hold for the stream of inventions and innovations. What technical progress gained from Japan's integration into the progressive world order appears to me immense. A repetition can be expected when China and India become an integral part of the world economy.

(xv) This acceleration is likely to raise the demand for investible funds relative to the supply of savings and thus to drive up the real rate of interest. Financial analysts and fund managers please listen! You will have to learn (or relearn) the lesson that the real rate of interest is the price of time (rather than of liquidity) and that time becomes short in supply when the growth of knowledge accelerates.

(xvi) The tendency for the rate of interest to rise under such conditions may create disorientation or irritation in designing monetary policy. What is the tolerable inflation rate when the basket of goods and services used as a yardstick improves in quality rather than in quantity and contains more and more services that have no physical property to dissociate from their nominal value when one wants to identify their contribution to price inflation? And if one does not know today's true inflation rate, how can one formulate substantive views on the inflation rate expected by the bond market to find out what today's rate of interest really is? What is, and what will be, the true rate of productivity advance to be used for judging wage increases if output mainly consists of intangible services? How much should I deduct from the official inflation rate in order to take account of the additional flow of information and knowledge that comes to me in exchange for what I pay to the print media and the electronic media?

Should it become more and more difficult to answer such questions, we may have to give up price-level stability as a goal of monetary policy and use a more simple yardstick. Perhaps we may have to again tie money to the price of gold.

(xvii) If capital is scarce and affords a high price, the wage rate as the price for complementary labor will have to be relatively low—in line with the abundance of labor, and especially of unskilled labor. In the years to come, wages in Europe will have to lag behind the advance of labor productivity until the pool of structurally unemployed labor has been exhausted.

(xviii) An important lesson can be learned from comparing the West German employment miracle of the 1950s with the labor market failure in East Germany in the present decade. In both cases there was domestic liberalization, the removal of import controls, substantial aid from outside, and a stable monetary policy. The main difference—apart from the restoration of property rights in former Soviet East Germany—was in wage policy. Wage moderation in West Germany, in the first experiment, led to the miraculous return to full employment in the late 1950s. This is in stark contrast to the wage explosion in the name of equality that accompanied East Germany's social unification with the West in the 1990s. That explosion made much of the capital stock economically obsolete, as if it had been physically destroyed. The remedy is now expected to come from investment subsidies. Reduced investment costs are to compensate for excessive labor costs, as if capital were abundant and labor were the scarce factor. The outcome can only be excess capital deepening, a waste of capital in a process of jobless growth. We will also observe excessive commuting within Germany from East to West and will witness the emergence of a dual economy in Germany's new territories. Compared to a scenario with undistorted factor prices, East Germany will require more aid, will gain less from trade, and will need more time for wholly catching up with the West and with its own long-run development potential.

(xix) Wage moderation in West Germany in the postwar period was partly due to the mystery of continuous gains from trade. These gains from trade were the result of a favorable export mix—with a high income elasticity of demand—and of fast income growth in industrial countries. And "wage policy allowed firms to keep their terms of trade gains for investment purposes" (Giersch, Paqué, Schmieding 1992, p. 72). The explanation for this mystery is sheer ignorance. Until late 1964, when the newly created German Council of Economic Experts submitted its first report, hardly anybody was aware of the fact that terms of trade gains (losses) raised (depressed) the potential for wage increases in the same way as the increase (decline) of physical productivity that used to be in the center of the wage policy discussion. The terms of trade gains thus accrued to exporters and importers and were mostly invested for further growth when postwar Germany became an integral part of the expanding world economy. This was positive feedback at the expense of income equality.

(xx) Another factor contributing to wage moderation was Ludwig Erhard's mode of moral suasion. In contrast to modern monetarist views, he held wage setting responsible for inflation (rather than for employment), thus mobilizing the public's fear of inflation in his fight against excessive wage claims. In the same vein, business was persuaded to expand volumes at constant prices. Thus a kind of decency—in contrast to greed—became the moral characteristic of what is being labeled the "Social Market Economy."

(xxi) We can also speak of a "morally repressed inflation" to indicate the existence of a macroeconomic disequilibrium, a disequilibrium that was associated with the undervaluation of the D-Mark from the beginning to the end of the 1960s. This disequilibrium produced high growth rates, especially in 1968 and 1969, similar to the rates achieved in the 1950s. The disequilibrium had its parallel in an excess demand for labor, which induced an inflow of guest workers who were flexible and mobile. Thanks to this imported flexibility, West Germany enjoyed an absence of structural unemployment despite structural change. The labor market disequilibrium also induced employers to unfold search activities and to engage in labor hoarding, notably for training workers on the job. The market thus made private enterprise bring about what would otherwise have been public labor market policies. The labor market performed smoothly, and firms in search of labor often invested in backward regions with pockets of unemployment.

(xxii) This disequilibrium system not only attracted immigrant workers for faster GDP growth; it was also accompanied by a balance of payments disequilibrium of the following sort: German capital exports were too low to match the current account surplus, not to mention the inflow of speculative short-term funds that looked for revaluation gains. Pulling in even more guest workers and using more resources for faster growth of the capital stock might have stabilized the economy on a steep growth path, though only for a couple of years and perhaps at the expense of growth in countries at the periphery of Western Europe. This alternative was not considered as a policy option. Instead, the twin disequilibria led to a currency revaluation and a wage explosion (at the end of the decade). Nevertheless, it is still worth considering the twin disequilibria as a possible growth strategy in the game of locational competition. How—and for how long—can domestic labor and land underprice themselves in order to make domestic locations more attractive for mobile capital and for complementary immigrant labor? How can domestic resources be kept undervalued for faster growth in worldwide competition?

(xxiii) The West German case of growth acceleration raises the question as to what kind of exchange rate would be suitable for speeding up economic growth in less developed countries. My conclusion boils down to the following advice: (1) Have an exchange rate sufficiently undervalued in terms of production costs for traditional goods (Heckscher-Ohlin goods), so that domestic exporters gain market shares in expanding world markets. (2) If this goes along with an import of capital and a deficit in the balance of payments on current account, please do not get worried: The capital inflow is needed to build up production facilities for a fast growth of exports. And consider that foreign capital would not come in without a high profitability of investment for export production. In that case you are not living beyond your means; instead, you are merely investing in excess of domestic savings. The deficit in your current balance of payments testifies to your locational advantages in a world economy with a global capital market. And you test the country's potential for real growth. The country may be underindustrialized, given its catching-up potential, its labor force, or its raw material deposits; or the country may count on an excess supply of potential entrepreneurship. If entrepreneurship happens to be in short supply, you may pull in entrepreneurs—together with foreign capital—in the form of foreign direct investment. If such complementarities are not perceived as strong enough to warrant the inflow of long-term capital, the deficit on current account will come under criticism. The answer, then, is to reduce domestic absorption by fiscal austerity. This will release resources for exports and/or depress the flow of imports. The quick reaction of the trade balance will show you (and convince the IMF) that the deficit in the balance of payments does not represent a fundamental disequilibrium. The criterion for an ex ante judgment is whether the deficit is small enough in relation not to exports, but to the rate of growth of exports. With fast export growth, the inflow of capital can be taken to enhance export capacity rather than consumption.

(xxiv) Promoting the inflow of capital will certainly be criticized as being a patent case of Beggar-thy-Neighbour policies. The answer to this is in a sense yes; but in this broad sense one could denounce almost all supply-side policies unless they had been sanctioned before in consultations, in harmonization efforts, or in other cartel-like arrangements euphemistically called cooperation. Using a more objective language, we better call such supply-side measures competitive behavior in the context of locational competition—thereby admitting that competition in this field is bound to be imperfect or oligopolistic and may harm others unless these others also make themselves more attractive to internationally mobile resources. My advice toward an undervaluation of domestic resources as a means of attracting foreign resources is exactly what we have to conceive as being the essence of locational competition. Should all countries happen to follow such a strategy, there would of course be less to gain for any single one. But an overall acceleration of growth worldwide would result as a free good benefiting all.

(xxv) The best policy to attract forward-looking resources from abroad is to grant them freedom from coercion, including guaranteed property rights, unlimited outmigration, and fair taxation in return for the supply of public goods; in short, a policy of openness. Such a policy may benefit capital and other mobile resources in the short run. In the long run it will be to the (absolute) advantage of immobile domestic resources, notably land and labor, thanks to a leaner government and to a more efficient use of capital, including human capital and knowledge.

(xxvi) Acceleration will be followed by deceleration once the economy's potential and driving force have been exhausted. In the medium run, that is, after several business cycles, one may say in very general terms that deceleration is likely to occur when the politicians' time horizon is shortening, when people's time preference is markedly increasing, and when impatience becomes characteristic of the public's mood. We observed this in Germany in the early 1970s. In general it appears that deceleration is around the corner

- when people resent new knowledge and innovation and the costs of adjustment to structural change;
- when the demand for economic security expands at the cost of entrepreneurship and competition,
- when the demand for equality leads to wage pressures and a profit squeeze, to a compression of the vertical wage spread, and to a more progressive tax system; and
- when government and bureaucracy pervade and regulate the market system, perhaps under the pressure of special interest groups, so that the economic system becomes more and more sclerotic—or socialist.

(xxvii) Such deceleration can be postponed for a while if it is possible to exploit a stock of money illusion. This is what the government tried in Germany in the 1970s (after the explosion of wages and oil prices) under the slogan "Five percent inflation is better than five percent unemployment." The inflationary "trick" behind this is a compression of real interest rates under the impact of unanticipated inflation. This compression of the costs of capital serves the purpose of compensating firms for excessive wage costs. Such a twist of the two decisive factor prices, however, leads to a serious distortion of the growth process; it leads to excessive capital deepening and—after a while—to a capital shortage in the sense that the capital stock contains some very capital-intensive jobs, but necessarily too few of them (Herbert Giersch, *Socialist Elements as Limits to Economic Growth,* 1983, reprinted in *The World Economy in Perspective,* 1991).

(xxviii) The most popular reason suggested for a deceleration of growth is a shortage of natural resources. While the fast growth of the world economy in the third quarter of this century can be interpreted as a march into an oil-intensive society, the slowdown of growth in the 1970s is often associated with the oil price explosions of 1973 and 1979. Whether the Club of Rome was right or wrong in its 1972 predictions is not the point in this context; but a major change in relative resource prices is bound to indicate the need for a redirection of economic activity, including R&D. This cannot but result in less output growth, if growth is measured on the basis of past—rather than current—relative values. But our statistics might show more growth, perhaps even an acceleration, if we could and would properly assess the gains in utility that we derive from the computer.

(xxix) Since the oil price shocks, world economic growth seems to have taken a new direction: It has turned into a move toward the information society, where the communication of ideas and knowledge will become even more important relative to the transformation and transportation of materials. The growth of knowledge does not seem to have any limits at all, but it will be very difficult to subject it to any form of precise measurement (though there are people who believe that science *is* measurement—and little more or nothing else). And how will we evaluate—other than by its cost—the progress we will believe to be making in approaching or ascertaining the truth in such fields as cosmology, astronomy, medicine, history, or even economics? Will the impossibility of disentangling quantity elements and price changes, and thus real growth and inflation, ultimately mean the end of economic growth as a topic of interest to the public?

(xxx) As a central field of economic dynamics, economic growth may soon be replaced by structural change. Let me mention two reasons. The first one is that growth almost inevitably goes along with structural change. The second point is that structural change often tends to harm as many inhabitants and voters as it benefits. Insurance against harmful changes will then play an increasing role in public policy. The fundamental conflict between social values will then not be growth versus equality, but progress versus security. The ghost of protectionism is raising its head. We will have to find intelligent responses.

Concluding Remarks

Socialism lost the competitive race between socioeconomic systems mainly because of its lack of freedom in the market of ideas and knowledge. Social democracy surely has a role to play in the competition among beliefs, to the extent that it takes care of those who can gain from greater equality. But once the equality issue fades into the background and the security aspect dominates the concerns of people, it appears that there remains little difference between social democracy and conservatism—that is, conservatism in the European sense of conserving traditional values and structures against the forces of innovation and structural change. Individuals will then have to choose between halting or promoting progress, and between technological pessimism or evolutionary optimism.

As for myself, I have several times come out in favor of long-run optimism. We will be able to solve the problems that we create, just as mankind has done in the past. I feel happy that I happened to live in this century rather than in any previous period, and I feel sorry that I will not be able to observe the dynamism to be expected from the growth of knowledge in the future. These are admittedly very personal judgments, but they seem to be quite in order, and pertinent in a broad, though impressionistic and very preliminary assessment of economic dynamism before an audience with an evolutionary mind.

REFERENCES

Giersch, Herbert. 1982. *Emerging Technologies: Consequences for Economic Growth, Structural Change, and Unemployment.* Philadelphia: Coronet.
————. 1991. "Socialist Elements as Limits to Growth." In Herbert Giersch, *The World Economy in Perspective.: Essays on International Trade and European Integration.* Brookfield, Vt.: Ashgate Publishers.
Giersch, Herbert, Karl-Heinz Paqué, and Holger Schmieding. 1992. *The Fading Miracle: Four Decades of Market Economy in Germany.* New York: Cambridge University Press.
Hayek, Friedrich A. von. 1949. *Individualism and Economic Order.* London: Routledge and Kegan Paul.
Okun, Arthur. 1975. *Equality and Efficiency: The Big Tradeoff.* Washington, D.C.: The Brookings Institution.
Popper, Karl. 1966. *The Open Society and Its Enemies.* Princeton: Princeton University Press.
————. 1994. Alles Leben ist Problemlösen. Munich: Pibes.

Economic Dynamism: Durability, Learning, and Time-Differentiated Demand

Christopher Green

The chapter explores some postinnovation dynamics at the firm level: the combination of time-differentiated demand, a feature of products where new models are expected to be introduced periodically, and production characterized by decreasing costs. The chapter takes off from the "Coase conjecture" and concludes with applications to predatory pricing, "dumping," and Japanese success in penetrating and holding foreign markets.

Introduction

Joseph A. Schumpeter believed that "vision" is an important starting point in economic theorizing. The vision of the present chapter is that economic dynamism not only flows from new products and new processes—or, (much) more generally, "new combinations"—but from the nature of the demand and production-distribution processes themselves. In fact, in some cases the dynamic properties of market demand and production-distribution processes are *complements* to innovation, in particular to the introduction and diffusion of new products and production technologies.

The focus of the chapter is on market demand-production processes with the following characteristics: (1) demand is time-differentiated, that is, demand is segmented in time, either because of (*a*) differences among consumers in their degree of impatience to acquire the good or (*b*) differences among consumers in the time it takes to learn about the qualities of, or acquire a taste for, the good or service; (2) heavy fixed (or set-up) costs (F) that cause average costs (C/Q) to decline substantially as total output (Q) increases; and (3) variable (and marginal) costs that decline because of learning-by-doing. The first and last characteristics explicitly invoke (historical) time; the second

The author is indebted to his colleague, Seamus Hogan, for many helpful suggestions and insights.

one can, too, if we think of output in terms of the length of the production run rather than the rate of output per unit time.

The production technology described in the preceding stands in contrast to three others in the economic literature. Neoclassical economic theory emphasizes constant returns to scale, the most mathematically tractable of forms. The field of industrial organization has given substantial attention to increasing returns to (economies of large) scale, where the scale factor is defined in terms of the rate of output per unit time and scale is measured in terms of plant capacity. Recently Milgrom and Roberts (1990) have called attention to flexible manufacturing systems (FMS) technology that operates in the opposite direction from scale economies. FMS technology employs "flexible machine tools and programmable, multitask production equipment" (Milgrom and Roberts 1990, 511), giving it the capability of quickly and cheaply "changing gears"—or switching tasks—thereby permitting the firm to produce a variety of outputs in small batches, that is, in very short production runs. The purpose of FMS technology is to meet increasingly variegated consumer preferences and produce input requirements for custom-made goods and services without suffering the increased costs associated with short production runs.

Although FMS technology may well be the wave of the future—and in some cases FMS technologies are already well established (see Milgrom and Roberts 1990 for examples)—it is too early to render the role of long production runs to the scrap heap of business-industrial history. As this chapter will show, the importance of long production runs is enhanced if the demand side is time-differentiated. It is, in fact, the aim of this chapter to bring together time-segmented demand and long production runs into a framework that reveals the dynamic properties of the duo and their potential role in shedding light on some issues of public interest and policy.

Theoretical Backdrop

An unlikely starting place for the chapter is Coase's "conjecture" in "Durability and Monopoly" (1972). In his seminal paper, Coase conjectured that, with production technologies characterized by decreasing or constant returns to scale, the equilibrium price set by a durable goods monopolist will be the competitive price. The basic argument is that a durable goods monopolist that sells its output is unable to exploit its monopoly power because it is unable to commit itself not to expand output in the future. After selling the monopoly quantity, the monopolist has an incentive to lower its price and sell more. Because consumers will recognize this incentive, they will delay their purchases until the price is lowered. Thus, Coase observed, the standard determination of the monopoly price is time-inconsistent (Bizer and De Marzo 1993).

The crucial assumptions underlying this nonintuitive result are that the durable goods monopolist is unable to credibly commit not to sell output beyond the monopoly level and that consumers are (infinitely) patient. Or to put it another way, if the durable goods monopolist can make offers arbitrarily frequently, the market will be quickly "saturated" at the competitive price. To make this point (and perhaps demonstrate the limited scope of his result), Coase used the example of a land monopolist whose perfectly durable commodity is naturally given and the buyers of which are patient enough to wait until the offer price falls to the level at which the monopolist's supply is equated with prospective demand.

Initially, there was something of a delayed response to Coase's paper and its conjecture. By 1980, however, the potential importance of Coase's insight began to attract economic theorists. Early contributions attempted to see if Coase's intuition could be proved using formal techniques. Stokey (1981) and Bulow (1982) showed that it could. Subsequent work focused on conditions in which the Coase intuition fails. Gul (1987) and Ausubel and Deneckere (1989) show that the competitive results of the durable-goods monopoly case may be substantially altered in the case of durable-goods oligopoly. Nonintuitively, durable-goods oligopolists without commitment powers may be able to attain the profits that Coase showed a durable goods monopolist without commitment power could not attain. The explanation—or intuition—for this paradoxical result is that the threat of a price war between the oligopolistic rivals may be sufficient incentive for them to restrict output and earn monopoly profits. The commitment power that a true monopolist lacks may reside in the actions (i.e., punishment for price cutting) that an oligopolist rival can exact.

Closer to the purpose of this chapter, Olsen (1992) shows that the "Coase conjecture" is refuted when the production technology exhibits increasing returns to scale of the type associated with learning-by-doing. In Olsen's model, marginal costs decrease with cumulative production. Olsen shows that, while price is still set at marginal cost *at each date*, price declines over time. Moreover, the market is not quickly saturated. If buyers' strategies are specified by reservation prices depending continuously on the stock of the durable good, the producer has an incentive to produce slowly in order to appropriate the learning benefits generated by its own production (Olsen 1992, 159).

The "twist" that the present chapter adds is one that seems particularly appropriate in the presence of many innovations. In the case of fashion goods, and more generally sequential product improvements such as those found in computer hardware and software (the move, say, from 386 to 486 technology), consumers can be differentiated by their patience—or impatience. That is, consumers' preferences for the new product are time-differentiated. Some consumers want the product (or service) immediately and are willing to pay a high price to obtain it now. Others are prepared to wait, believing that in time the price will fall. (In fact, one might think of differences among consumers in their reservation prices as resulting largely from how quickly—from the point of its introduction on the market—they wish to obtain the good.) One reason why some consumers are prepared to wait is that the previous model or fashion has some durability and thus can be used during (i.e., overlaps) the introduction of the new technology or fashion.

Why is the durability literature applicable to such goods? The reason is that although these goods are not long-lived, they have a *physical* durability that substantially exceeds their economic life, the time period for which they are in demand. What distinguishes the goods treated in this chapter from those in the Coase literature is that the ones considered here by their nature create varying degrees of consumer impatience for them. It is varying degrees of impatience, rather than repeat sales of the same model (or version) that allow producers to spread both sales and production over time.

In this chapter's model, as in the Olsen model, costs of producing the good decline as length of production run increases. What are added are time-differentiated demands, for the reasons explained above. Moreover, because long production runs take time to complete, prices must be set higher at first in order to ration demand (to the impatient), even though the average cost of the output over the planned production run is far below the price charged. Over time, as production increases, prices decline toward the cost of producing the last unit in the run. In this way, the producer earns a substantial profit or rent on its inframarginal production. This rent acts as both a reward for past and an inducement to future innovation. The result is quite Schumpeterian and supports the "Schumpeter conjecture" about the role that (temporary) monopoly plays in the innovative process.

Casual observation suggests that numerous goods are priced in such a way that early consumers pay considerably more than do later consumers. This is particularly true where it is predictable that after a time the good in question will be replaced by another—typically an improved or more "fashionable"—version of the existing one. Perhaps some of these goods are not "durable" enough to meet the stringent requirements of the "Coase conjecture." But to think in these terms would miss the point. What is crucial is that the production technology and the impatience of some consumers would rule out Coasian pricing even if the goods were highly durable. Innovators, particularly those producing fashion goods or, more importantly, those goods subject to sequential improvements over time, know this. One of the inducements to innovation is that, if successful, planned production runs will be long enough to reduce to a minimum the fixed costs of launching the product, while sale of inframarginal units will be at prices above the long-run per unit costs of their development and production. Moreover, the prospect of declining prices helps promote sales, assuring that production plans will be fulfilled. The combination of decreasing costs and intertemporal nonlinear pricing therefore provides an important complement to the innovation process.

The chapter has two parts. The first part sets out the model and discusses its component parts. The second part suggests some applications of the model. Two of the applications relate to the issues of predatory pricing and dumping. Another application is to an understanding of the success of Japanese "sunrise" firms in capturing international as well as domestic markets, and the role MITI may have played in that success.

The Model

Consider a firm with the following demand, cost, and industry characteristics, that produces a good x_j, where j indicates model or version, $j = 1 \ldots k$.

1. There are two important demand characteristics

   (a) There are many customers, but each buys only 1 unit of *durable* good x_j, which lasts for a period whose length is τ, where $\tau > t$, the length of time over which the firm actually produces x_j, prior to turning to the production of a new model of x. In other words, the life of any given version of good x exceeds the period over which the firm produces that version.

   (b) Consumers differ in their impatience to purchase x_j. Some consumers purchase early in time period t, others later. Those who wait (i.e., are relatively patient) *expect* to be "rewarded" with lower prices. For convenience, it is assumed that customers buy at one of a number (we use four in a graphical example below) of points during period t.

2. Average cost (AC) declines as total output of x_j increases. AC falls for two reasons:

   (a) there are large fixed (setup) costs of launching and distributing the product

   (b) learning-by-doing reduces average variable and marginal costs (at least up to a point) as the quantity of output (length of production run) increases

3. The industry setting is one in which the firm producing x_j is initially a monopolist, although as production continues other firms may enter the "industry"—that is, enter into the production of a close substitute, or clone, for x_j.

It is useful to briefly assess the implications of each of these assumptions one at a time, prior to considering them together. In doing so, the approach taken is verbal rather than mathematical, intuitive rather than technically rigorous. A "soft" approach is dictated by the assumed discontinuities and nonconvexities that limit the model's mathematical tractability.

Demand Impatience

The first assumption, that there are a large number of consumers who differ in the degree to which they are impatient to purchase good x_j, is crucial. Consider the case where the firm selling x_j is a monopolist. We now have the market setting for the Coase conjecture. But the impatience assumption assures that we will not have the Coase result, in which all buyers wait until the monopolist finally offers the good at cost. The monopolist can exploit the impatience of even perfectly forward-looking consumers, and thereby earn inframarginal rents (monopoly profits). It can do so even though (a) total sales ultimately match the competitive level, and (b) the terminal price, the one paid for the last units of output sold, approximates (or equals) AC, as in the Coase case.

In the model developed here, prices decline with cumulative output and time. The non-Coase result in attributable to the ability of the monopolist to charge impatient (early) consumers more than it can charge patient (later) consumers. This is so regardless of the shape of the cost function(s)—decreasing, constant, or increasing. Our result is, therefore, clearly distinguished from that of Olsen (1992), who accepted the Coase conjecture in the case of increasing or constant costs, but showed that the conjecture would be vitiated if there were decreasing (marginal) costs due to learning-by-doing.

While the impatience assumption assures that, ceteris paribus, prices will tend to decline over time, the amount by which they decline will be sensitive to market structural assumptions. Suppose that the firm is a monopolist in period one, but in subsequent periods becomes a product-differentiated oligopolist, a change in setting that is foreseen by the firm. Intuitively, the threat of competition in subsequent periods would lead the first period monopolist to lower its period 1 price in order to induce more consumers to buy while it is still a monopoly.

Decreasing Costs

The second assumption is that large set-up costs and learning-by-doing cause unit and marginal costs to decrease with cumulative output. This assumption reinforces the conclusion that prices will tend to decline over time if some but not all consumers are impatient. The decreasing cost assumption also influences whether the firm will adopt a strategy of setting a cumulative output target. The assumption may also affect the extent of the product cycle over which price may lie below *current* cost, marginal or average.

It is useful to give some formalization to the cost function. Let

$$C_i(q_i) = \alpha(Q_i)q_i$$

where $C_i(q_i)$ is the cost in period i of producing q_i units, $\alpha(Q_i)$ is the constant marginal cost of producing in period i, a marginal cost that depends negatively on Q_i, the sum of all production in previous periods:

$$Q_i = \sum_{j=1}^{i-1} q_j \quad i \geq 2 \quad Q_1 = 0$$

That is, the more production there has been in previous periods, the more learning-by-doing there has been and thus the lower the marginal cost will be in the present period. The cost over all periods then would be:

$$C = F + \sum_{i=1}^{t} C_i(q_i) = F + \alpha(Q_i)q_i$$

Unit cost, C/Q_i, declines because F/Q_i and αq_i decline as cumulative output Q_i, increases.

Under the conditions described, the relationship between price and current cost, marginal or average, no longer has the definiteness that characterizes standard price theory, where demand is continuous and the shape of the cost curve, whether increasing, constant, or decreasing is uniquely related to the rate of output, not its cumulative value. Here, whether price will be above, equal to, or below current unit or marginal cost will depend on the slope of the average and marginal cost curves and the prevailing and expected competitive conditions.

Industry Setting

Many, if not most, of the goods, the demands for which are time-differentiated, originate as innovations (new or improved goods). It is natural, therefore, to assume the industry begins as a monopoly. But even the existence of patents and other forms of intellectual property rarely prevent the appearance of Schumpeterian competition. Thus, it is also natural to assume that after an initial period of monopoly, an innovator will face competition, however imperfect, in the form of competing, if somewhat differentiated, goods and that the firm knows ahead of time that this will be so. This knowledge creates an incentive to be the first, and for an initial period, the only (monopoly) producer of a new good. If more than one firm has this incentive, there will be competition to be first—to innovate.

What are the implications of competition to be first to introduce new or improved products? There is long Schumpeterian literature on the effect that competition has on innovation, among which papers by Arrow (1962) and Dasgupta and Stiglitz (1980) are particularly relevant. Arrow's model predicts that (otherwise perfect) competitors have a greater (profit) incentive to innovate than does a monopolist. Dasgupta and Stiglitz show that the picture is less clear where the industry is oligopolistic. Using a game-theoretic framework, Dasgupta and Stiglitz show that as oligopolistic rivalry increases, the incentive to imitate rather than innovate increases. However, the Arrow and Dasgupta-Stiglitz models assume constant returns to scale. What might happen in the presence of increasing returns to scale?

The intuition is as follows. The dynamic economies of scale produced by a combination of large set-up cost and learning-by-doing give an incentive for a monopolist seller of product x_j to stick with an existing model (or version) of x for a long time before bringing out a new model. The existence of competition in later periods, however, creates an incentive to innovate earlier than would otherwise be the case. These conclusions parallel those reached by Arrow (1962). But in the presence of product differentiation an interesting question is whether free-market competition produces too much product diversity, in what is a dynamic analogy to Dixit and Stiglitz (1977). If it does so, the results are at some variance with Dasgupta and Stiglitz (1980), who conclude that, after a point, increased oligopolistic rivalry raises the incentive to imitate rather than innovate. Why the difference? One answer resides with decreasing costs. As Ross (1986) shows, learning-by-doing increases the incentive to be the first to innovate and thereby move down the learning curve ahead of prospective competitors. Learning curves give first movers the opportunity to dominate their markets and reap whatever rewards are associated with dominance. Thus, in the presence of decreasing costs, a decision to imitate rather than innovate may put the imitator behind the scale or learning curve eight ball. A decision to innovate may, if successful, permit the innovator to dominate, and for a time to hold the competition at bay while it earns supranormal profits.

We now state the following proposition

PROPOSITION. *If the firm producing x_j can plan the length of its production run, and is confident that its plan will be fulfilled, its pricing policy will have the following qualitative characteristics:*

(a) *the price of x_j falls over period t*

(b) *The price of x_j may be greater than, less than, or equal to the AC of producing x_j, up to that point. The greater the vigor of competition and the greater the importance of (fixed) set-up costs, the more likely it is that $P \leq$ current AC.*

(c) *even in the absence of strategic behavior (vis-à-vis other producers), the price of x_j may from time to time be less than its current MC.*

(*d*) *unless the firm is prevented from fulfilling its output plan, or loses its competitive edge, the firm will earn supranormal profits on all but the last units of the total output it produces.*

These propositions can be restated in somewhat expanded form as follows

1. A firm offering a differentiated product that is purchased by consumers with varying degrees of patience, or, if you will, impatience, will progressively reduce the price it charges as its sales increase, with the final units sold at cost.

2. The firm, producing under conditions of decreasing cost as length of production run increases, will earn supranormal profits over its production run, even though the price at which it sells a unit of output is less than the per unit cost and, at times, the *MC* (marginal cost) of producing that unit of output.

3. The pricing strategy described is not only profitable, but may provide a natural barrier to entry to, or expansion of, any firm that cannot improve on the quality of the good from the viewpoint of consumers.

4. Even if the product is physically long-lived (physically durable), it may pay to limit its economic life ("economic durability") by providing for a sequence of improvements over (historical) time.

The intuition behind these four propositions can be demonstrated with a (relatively) simple diagram (fig. 1). The key elements of figure 1 are:

(*a*) A continuously declining *AC* curve reflecting (1) declining *MC* due to learning-by-doing and (2) the ability to spread the substantial fixed costs of launching a new product over a long production run.

(*b*) Time-differentiated demand with four demand segments: D_1, D_2, D_3, and D_4.

(*c*) Each successive demand curve has an ordinate at the previous period's output and price. For example, D_2 begins at the price at which the previous period's quantity was sold. Thus the starting point for the second period's demand curve, D_2, is at P_1, on an (imaginary) ordinate extending vertically from Q_1.

(*d*) Since cumulative output is measured along the abscissa, each period's output can be found by subtracting the present period's output from that of the previous period. Thus the first period's output is Q_1, the second period's is $Q_2 - Q_1$, and so on.

(*e*) Price declines from one period to the next. Each period's price is chosen in a way that leads to the expectation that at the end of period t, planned output (in this case Q_4) will be sold so that ex post supranormal profits are earned on inframarginal sales.

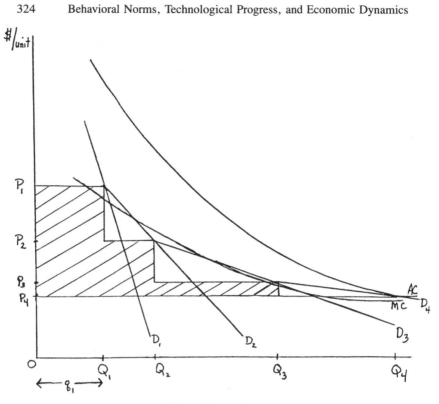

Fig. 1. Demand curves

Evidence

What evidence is there that at least some products have the cost, demand, and pricing attributes described above? The cost side is easier to evaluate. It is obvious that large set-up costs cause average cost to decline as output (length of production run) increases. Not so obvious, perhaps, is the importance of learning-by-doing, with its implication of decreasing marginal costs over time. Until Spense's (1981) pathbreaking paper, learning curves remained largely outside the ambit of economic theory, belonging mainly to the work of industry consultants and occasional industry studies. Among the earliest studies are ones of airframe production (Wright 1936) and ship construction (Searle 1945; see also Lucas 1993). Lieberman's (1984) empirical study of the learning curve in the chemical-processing industry confirms the relative (to static scale economies) importance of cost reductions due to learning. Noteworthy is its indication that the learning curve appears to steepen in the presence of R&D expenditures. However, Lieberman's dependence on publicly available price data as a surrogate for proprietary cost data rules out drawing any conclusions from his results about the relationship between price and cost over the product cycle.

With respect to the time-differentiated demand attribute, the evidence is chiefly anecdotal, representing generalizations of specific observations of widely observed industry behavior. The personal computer and fashion goods industries are examples. In the case of personal computers, purchasers appear to vary in their impatience for updated versions, and prices are observed to decline over the lifetime of a version.

One important industry that has been studied in depth and that exhibits both the cost and pricing, and by inference, the demand characteristics described here is the semiconductor industry. Flamm (1993), Scherer (1994), and Irwin and Klenow (1994) find evidence of decreasing costs, learning-by-doing, and prices that fall over time. Figure 2 shows cost curves that are qualitatively similar to those derived empirically in the Flamm and Irwin-Klenow studies. The several curves indicate that each new generation of dynamic random access memory (DRAM) experiences sharply declining prices over most of its life. In addition, the DRAM case illustrates one of the important characteristics of the type of good described in this chapter: its economic life is kept short by the introduction of a new generation (model, version)—one of greater quality, power, capacity, or versatility than that of the preceding generation.

Implications

The model described in this chapter has several implications—some more obvious and less controversial than others. Three implications that will be briefly discussed in the following are: (*a*) for tests of predatory pricing; (*b*) for evaluating allegations of dumping: and (*c*) for explaining the strategy of MITI (Japan's Ministry of International Trade and Industry) in promoting specific Japanese firms within certain industries.

Predatory Pricing

Beginning in the 1970s there was a vigorous debate, following the appearance of the famous Areeda-Turner (1975) article, over criteria for establishing the existence of "predatory pricing." Although the debate cooled somewhat in the 1980s, game theorists using models with asymmetric information had a field day with predation. For the courts, and economists who advise lawyers and judges, the issue of predation remains controversial.

The Areeda-Turner (A-T) rule establishes that if a firm sets price (P) less than short-run marginal cost (SMC), it is engaging in predatory pricing. Because it is typically difficult to observe MC, $P < AVC$ (average variable cost)

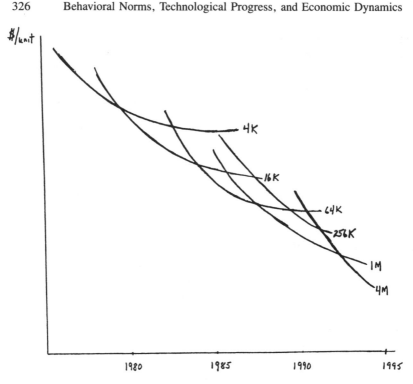

Fig. 2. DRAM price contours

can be employed as a proxy criterion. The analysis set out above, however, requires us to ask, *MC* (or *AVC*) at what level of output? The relevant level is the unobservable "planned" level of output rather than the "current," and presumably observable, level. As we have seen, a firm could temporarily set price below current *SMC* or *AVC* and be profitable, even though future prices are anticipated to decline. This configuration is at variance with one of the cardinal requirements for predatory pricing, the temporary (intertemporal) sacrifice of profits in return for supranormal ones earned in the future after prices are raised. In the present case both per unit profitability and prices decline over time—as the production run approaches its planned level.

Dumping

The analytical framework developed in the chapter has implications for charges of "dumping." Traditionally, dumping has implied selling in foreign markets at prices lower than in home markets. However, as Flamm (1993) notes, since the mid-1970s, more than 60 percent of dumping cases in the United States have been handled under an alternative standard: whether sales at cost were less than some constructed "fair value." In short, the increasingly used U.S. standard for finding that goods have been dumped is whether the foreign firm is selling at a price below some constructed average cost.

Flamm (1993) investigates the case of Japanese DRAM's, exports of which to the United States have brought numerous charges of dumping. Flamm's paper is relevant to our study because it clearly analyzes the case of "forward pricing" under conditions in which large up-front costs and learning-by-doing reduce average, marginal, and average variable costs as production runs are lengthened. Flamm's analysis, like our own, establishes that a firm that "forward prices" on the basis of long production runs, could rationally—and profitably—set its price below current marginal, as well as average, cost. His empirical analysis indicates, however, that in the case of DRAMs, non-strategic (nonpredatory) pricing below MC is likely to be observed only in the very "earliest stages of the product cycle" (1993, 80), although price may consistently fall below average cost. At the very least, Flamm's study and our analysis throw into question a dumping criterion based on average cost concepts.

But in an important respect, Flamm does not go as far as the present chapter. Yun-Wing Sung (Flamm 1993, 94), in a brief comment, aptly notes that "Flamm's model assumes a constant elasticity of demand over time and thus cannot take into account the postponement of purchases on the part of buyers." But buyers, in fact, are likely to anticipate a decline in chip prices over the product cycle. As a result the more patient of them will postpone their purchases. What postponement implies for the proportion of the product cycle over which it may be profitable to price below (current) MC is more difficult to say. But willingness to wait should be an integral part of any full-blown analysis of pricing over the product cycle.

The Japanese "Miracle"

Much has been made of the strategy of Japan's Ministry of International Trade and Industry (MITI) of identifying and targeting "sunrise" industries with increasing returns technologies and capabilities. Promotion of certain firms in these industries—specifically direct or indirect means of stimulating demand—allowed them to expand their capacities and thereby move down their (decreasing) average cost curves. In this way industrial "infants" became, with some initial aid or protection from the government, cost-competitive and able to stand on their own in international as well as domestic markets.

It is difficult, perhaps impossible, to determine to what extent the reduction in average costs experienced by Japanese firms is attributable to learning and other product-specific (length of production run) economies of scale, as opposed to the more traditional plant-specific (rate of output per unit of time) economies of scale. Undoubtedly, both types of scale economy played a role in reducing unit costs. Moreover, there is a certain degree of interdependence between the two, in that a large-scale plant implies an increase in output that adds to the length of the production run.

What is crucial to the analysis here is the extent to which the amount of output produced over time influences unit costs. While it is not possible to give a precise estimate for the relative importance of these two types of scale, it is hard to believe that product-specific economies of scale are unimportant in the Japanese case. In addition to evidence on learning curves, one rough indicator of the importance of the length of production run is the level of unit costs associated with nonfabrication assembly activities. These activities include innovation; product development, design, and improvement; marketing and promotion; and quality control. Taken together, the per unit cost of these nonfabrication assembly activities depends upon total output rather than the rate of output per unit time (plant scale) as such. The unit costs of these activities are reduced as total output rises, whatever the scale of plant.

It seems likely, then, that MITI could count on unit costs falling as *cumulative* output of the most capable firms in "sunrise" industries rose. The problem for MITI was to assure that these leading firms priced in such a way as to assure they could reach large cumulative output targets. Reaching these targets could be achieved by pricing below the "immediate" unit cost of production—that is, below the unit cost of producing cumulative output at any given point. MITI's strategy also implied that the firm would continuously reduce real prices over time, even if such a pricing scheme implied short-term paper losses. If the firm successfully achieved its target, the losses would, of course, be transformed into substantial profits. This is the process pictured above in figure 1.

In order to facilitate its strategy MITI supported "sunrise" industries or firms by temporarily providing them with various types of subsidies and protection. At first these helped Japanese firms to capture and hold the Japanese market, but in time (but not too much time) they also helped them to capture the international market as well. One could interpret this step-by-step process in terms of our model. In the case of export-oriented Japanese firms, demand was time-differentiated because it took time for prospective foreign customers to learn about, become familiar with, and acquire a "taste" for the qualities of Japanese products. In the meantime, Japanese firms could take advantage of temporary protection, increasingly free trade, and decreasing unit costs to establish pricing strategies that would eventually permit them to capture foreign markets and profitably fulfill their long-run production plans. To the extent that this is an accurate account of the behavior of Japanese firms, our model is consistent with and provides a theoretical underpinning for MITI's industrial strategy.

Conclusion

This chapter is an exploration of some postinnovation economic dynamics at the firm and/or industry levels. A unique feature of the chapter is its introduction of time-differentiated demand, a feature of industries where new models or versions of the product are expected to be periodically introduced. The fashion, the computer hardware and software, and some other telecommunications/electronics industries are examples. However, the interesting applications are ones that also include decreasing cost function features, such as that associated with learning-by-doing, that have dynamic implications of their own.

Another feature of the chapter is that it takes off from the "Coase conjecture," using that interesting thought experiment to motivate the time-differentiated demand feature. The chapter thus supplies another limitation on the ambit of the Coase conjecture, while owing much to one of Coase's lesser-known ideas as a useful starting point for the analysis.

Some applications of the model are provided in the penultimate section of the chapter. Given the nature of the model, applications to predatory pricing and dumping are predictable and, in their learning-by-doing aspect, have been anticipated in the literature (see, for example, Ross 1986; Flamm 1993). Not so predictable, and perhaps more controversial, is the potential the model has for helping to explain Japanese industrial strategy. An implication of the chapter is that Japanese success in penetrating and holding foreign markets may be chiefly attributable to an implicit recognition of certain demand and cost features, too long ignored in the West. If so, Japanese industrial success may owe more to planned production runs of great length and a pricing strategy based on the demand and cost features described here than on subsidies, protection, or alleged "unfair trading" behavior.

REFERENCES

Areeda, P., and D. Turner. 1975. "Predatory Pricing and Related Practices under Section 2 of the Sherman Act." *Harvard Law Review* 88 (February): 697–733.

Arrow, K. J. 1962. "Economic Welfare and the Allocation of Resources for Invention." In *The Rate and Direction of Inventive Activity,* R. Nelson ed. Princeton: Princeton University Press.

Ausubel, L., and R. Deneckere. 1989. "Reputation in Bargaining and Durable Goods Monopoly." *Econometrica* 57:511–31.

Bizer, D. S., and P. M. De Marzo. 1993. "Sequential Trade and the Coase Conjecture: A General Model of Durable Goods Monopoly with Applications to Finance." Working Paper no. 157, Kellogg Graduate School of Management, Northwestern University. Mimeo.

Bulow, J. I. 1982. "Durable-Goods Monopolists." *Journal of Political Economy* 90, no. 2 (April): 314–32.

Coase, R. H. 1972. "Durability and Monopoly." *Journal of Law and Economics* 15 (April): 143–49.

Dasgupta, P., and J. Stiglitz. 1980. "Industrial Structure and the Nature of Innovative Activity." *Economic Journal,* 90 (June): 266–93.

Dixit, A., and J. Stiglitz. 1977. "Monopolistic Competition and Optimum Product Diversity." *American Economic Review* 67 (June): 297–308.

Flamm, K. 1993. "Forward Pricing versus Fair Value: An Analytic Assessment of 'Dumping' in DRAMS." In *Trade and Protectionism,* T. Ito and A. O. Krueger, eds., 47–95. Chicago: University of Chicago Press.

Gul, F. 1987. "Noncooperative Collusion in Durable Goods Oligopoly." *Rand Journal of Economics* 18 (Summer): 248–54.

Irwin, D. A., and P. J. Klenow. 1994. "Learning-by-Doing Spillovers in the Semiconductor Industry." Graduate School of Business, University of Chicago, March. Mimeo.

Lieberman, M. B. 1984. "The Learning Curve and Pricing in the Chemical Processing Industries." *Rand Journal of Economics* 15 (Summer): 213–28.

Lucas, R. E. 1993. "Making a Miracle." *Econometrica* 61 (March): 251–72.

Milgrom, P., and J. Roberts. 1990. "The Economics of Modern Manufacturing: Technology, Strategy, and Organization." *American Economic Review* 80 (June): 511–28.

Olsen, T. E. 1992. "Durable Goods Monopoly, Learning by Doing and the Coase Conjecture." *European Economic Review* 36, no. 1 (January): 157–77.

Ross, D. R. 1986. "Learning to Dominate." *The Journal of Industrial Economics* 36 (June): 337–54.

Scherer, F. M. 1994. "Learning-by-Doing and International Trade in Semiconductors." Harvard University. Mimeo.

Searle, A. D. 1945. "Productivity Changes in Selected Wartime Shipbuilding Programs." *Monthly Labour Review* 61:1132–47.

Spence, A. M. 1981. "The Learning Curve and Competition." *Bell Journal of Economics* 12 (Spring): 49–70.

Stokey, N. L. 1981. "Rational Expectations and Durable Goods Pricing." *Bell Journal of Economics* 12 (Spring): 112–28.

Wright, T. P. 1936. "Factors Affecting the Cost of Airplanes." *Journal of Aeronautical Sciences* 3, no. 4: 122–28.

From the Artificial to the Endogenous: Modeling Evolutionary Adaptation and Economic Growth

Gerald Silverberg and Bart Verspagen

We develop an "artificial worlds" disequilibrium model incorporating inter firm rivalry, technological uncertainty, diffusion, spillovers, and learning. We demonstrate that R&D strategies in the long run converge to a target R&D/value-added ratio comparable to values observed in some sectors and nations, and that history matters.

Introduction

The process of economic growth and development strikes us as messy and anything but a clean steady state. Firms evolve strategies over time and are heterogeneous within and across industries and national economies. Growth and cycles overlap and interact in ways that are still controversial. Structural shifts occur, often rather suddenly on a historical time scale, and without any apparent exogenous cause. The rate of technical change is not God-given, but rather results from the collective but largely uncoordinated decision of numerous economic agents to pursue and implement innovation, primarily motivated by the expectation of realizing profits. The conditions under which this can be reliably done are anything but transparent in terms of the directions in which to search, the probabilities of success, and the ability to appropriate a return in the face of competition, temporal lags, and informational spillovers.

Yet the economy can often be characterized by certain regularities of behavior, both over time and cross-sectionally. Firms may come to adopt similar behavioral rules, such as price markups, investment payback periods, or target levels for inventories and R&D spending. Such relatively simple rules have been the object of study of the behavioral theory of the firm first

Maastricht Economic Research Institute on Innovation and Technology, University of Limburg, P.O. Box 616, NL-6200 MD Maastricht, The Netherlands. The research of Bart Verspagen has been made possible by a fellowship of the Royal Netherlands Academy of Arts and Sciences.

outlined by Cyert and March (1963), who very early on advocated empirical study of actual business procedures on the one hand, and computer-based simulation as a research tool on the other. In this tradition, Nelson and Winter (1982) introduced the concept of routines as a "genetical" description of the gamut of behavioral traits internal to and integral to the firm. The inheritability or persistence of such rules may be motivated by limited information-processing ability and "menu costs," or Simon's notion of satisficing as a common denominator of boundedly rational behavior: agents only change their strategies when the gap between aspirations and realizations exceeds a certain threshold.

However, the rejection of fully optimizing behavior as an explanation of economic activity does not single out any precise alternative as a theory of boundedly rational behavior. It is probably for this reason—the absence of an operationalizable alternative based on "first principles"—that economists continue to cling so tenaciously to the standard paradigm.

In the model we present in the following, firms must determine how much to spend on R&D in relation to either their profits or their sales.[1] In contrast to the more neoclassical approaches, we investigate this decision problem in the context of *bounded rationality,* where agents can have only vague ideas about the relationship between their actions and outcomes. To provide some anecdotal evidence, we recall an interview with the director of R&D of the Japanese firm Canon published in *The Financial Times* a number of years ago. The director reported that the firm had some time before raised its R&D/turnover ratio from 11 to $11\frac{1}{2}$ percent. This appeared to have been beneficial to the firm, so the directors were debating whether to cautiously raise it even further. There in fact did not seem to be any way to determine where an upper limit might lie, and what the optimum policy might be, short of actually trying it out, but the firm was set to continue in this direction. Given that firms may operate in a trial-and-error mode in some areas of their strategic behavior, and moreover that they interact, is there any modeling approach that promises to capture this form of collective "learning" in a scientifically reproducible way?

The perspective we adopt to address this question simulates a model economy consisting of "artificial" agents endowed with limited but nonnegligible abilities to update their behavior in interaction with each other on the basis of their performance. Their environment is such that the product of their efforts is a pattern of economy-wide growth as they learn to undertake the R&D necessary to induce innovation and generate profitable avenues of investment. Hence this is a model of endogenous growth in the sense of Romer

---

1. This chapter extends Silverberg and Verspagen 1994a,b, where the decision rule is based on only the R&D to profits ratio.

(1986, 1990), but without an aggregate production function, a representative agent, and intertemporal optimization.

In the next section we discuss recent work on learning and evolutionary games, as well as the more computationally based artificial worlds approach. We then outline the details of the model before introducing the methods we have developed to evaluate its behavior. The last section compares the implications of the modeling exercise with some causal observations about real economies and locates them within the general research agenda on growth theorizing and economic history.

Selection, Learning, and the Artificial Worlds Modeling Philosophy

Selten (1989) presents a provocative discussion of the tensions between the boundedly rational perspective and perfect rationality as traditionally used in economics. The traditional "as if" argument of Milton Friedman (1953) holds that regardless of the boundedness of individual agents in their decision making, market selection will ensure that the traditional optimization result will prevail. This seems to absolve the economist of any necessity for explaining in detail how an equilibrium comes about, given arbitrary and out-of-equilibrium initial conditions. And in the event of multiple equilibria, as is common in many interesting problems in game theory, it provides no help at all. A bridge between a theory based on causal mechanism and outcomes based on equilibrium has been sought in learning or evolutionary game models, often inspired by biological applications (cf. Friedman 1991 for a survey). The static notion of *evolutionary stable strategy* is the biologist's refinement of a Nash equilibrium, while dynamic versions have usually been based on replicator dynamics (cf. Hofbauer and Sigmund 1988). The key biological stability concept is *uninvadability,* the inability of a small number of mutants to invade an equilibrium population. But evolutionary game theory reflects just one-half of the evolutionary process, namely selection, and has focused on the equilibria as once-and-for-all asymptotic states.

Recently, attention has shifted to the role of mutation and stochasticity in further refining the notion of stability in evolutionary games (Foster and Young 1990; Young 1993; Kandori, Mailath, and Rob 1993). In contrast to conventional evolutionary game theory, agents or species are allowed to mutate continually over time before an equilibrium is attained. In general, the equilibria that remain (usually in the limit as the mutation probability goes to zero) will be a significant further refinement of the limiting states. This framework has been proposed as a model of learning by ongoing trial and error with selection. Once again, though, the focus has been on asymptotic states and the refinement of equilibrium concepts.

Approaching learning from another extreme is work based on artificial intelligence and computer science, such as neural nets, genetic algorithms, and classifier systems. While these approaches are also based on complex interdependence of interacting subunits, as in game theory, selection, and stochastic perturbations, the complexity of the problems workers have addressed has made analytical results difficult to come by. Whereas in the beginning, most work focused on computing standard optimization problems and thus converging to a hopefully unique point, more recent efforts have been directed at using these tools open-endedly to simulate the self-organization and evolution of lifelike systems, whether they be abstract ecosystems, microorganisms, individual behavior, or human economies (cf. the work in Langton 1989; Langton et al. 1992; Arthur 1991; and Lane 1993).

For systems exceeding a certain complexity in their organization, if not in the nature of their constituent parts and their interactions, the existence and uniqueness of an asymptotic steady state may be less interesting than two heuristic phenomena that have often been commented on without precise definition. The first is *emergent properties,* that is, complex but identifiable patterns of behavior that emerge spontaneously at some point in the history of the system and are not in any obvious way inherent in the constitution of its parts. The second is *punctuated equilibria,* periods of quasi-stable behavior separated by usually very rapid periods of transition and disorder. Evolutionary game theory, by focusing on very low-dimensional game structures, may well provide an explanation of the emergence and stability of a single such behavior, but has deliberately excluded the complexity apparently necessary to generate an ongoing sequence of such states. There is obviously a trade-off here between analytic tractability and behavioral richness. Lane (1993) argues that the artificial world framework differs from conventional approaches in one or more of the following ways

1. Transients are at least as important as steady states;
2. The concept of stability must be relativized to some notion of meta-stability, that is, one that may contain the seeds of its own destruction;
3. New statistical methods will have to be developed to enable meta-stable states and emergent properties to be identified and characterized; and
4. Computational methods will attain a scientific status equal to that reserved until now for analytical ones.

Most of the work in artificial worlds has been based on discrete genetic codings of strategies, such as are called for by genetic algorithms or classifier systems. One may ask whether this perspective, borrowed from biological genetics, should not be made more congruent with the way agents may be interpreted to formulate and modify their strategies in reality. In our case—the determination of firms' R&D investment—it may make more sense to mutate locally around existing values than to allow for jumps across the entire parameter space. This "realistic" approach to evolutionary modeling based on stylized behavior is characteristic of the work initiated by Nelson and Winter (1982) and in the computer science realm to the real-valued evolutionary algorithms of Schwefel (1981). Thus mutation or trial and error will be represented in our model by a draw from a normal distribution centered around the current value of the R&D to investment ratio. Imitation, in contrast, does permit large discrete jumps in parameter space, but will be modified here to reflect a satisficing principle—only firms with relatively poorer performance will imitate.

The Model

Our model has much in common with recent work on "endogenous growth" (cf. Romer 1986, 1990; Lucas 1988; Aghion and Howitt 1992; and Helpman 1992), where technical change comes about as a result of the profit-seeking activities of individual agents, and increasing returns, spillovers, and other phenomena known from the economics of innovation may be present. While recognizing that innovation is associated with many imponderables and uncertainties, these models still hinge on the standard tools of market clearing, classical rationality, intertemporal optimization, rational (technological) expectations, and the identification of steady-state equilibria.

Moreover, their representation of technology has often been oversimplified to correspond to known and tractable special cases. Thus, in the model most closely related to the structure of our own, Aghion and Howitt (1992) assume that at any time only one technology prevails in the economy. When a new innovation is made, it instantly and costlessly (except for the sunk cost of the R&D that went to invent it) replaces its predecessor. The monopoly returns associated with it, for as long as it prevails, are completely recouped by the single innovator, with no imitation or spillovers. Thus the appropriate stochastic decision problem to determine the level of R&D spending, they argue, can be represented as a patent race with a commonly known probability of making an innovation as a function of R&D effort.

As any student of the history of technology knows, however, this is a far cry from anything that has ever prevailed economy-wide. And even in some particular industries where a monopoly of a truly key innovation has been defended for as long as possible (one thinks of the Boulton and Watt patent on the condensing steam engine), earlier technologies (such as the Newcomen engine and water power) retained a significant place in production for a considerable time (partly because of the monopoly, no doubt).

These cursory reflections suggest a number of requirements for an endogenous growth model regarding a model's representation of both technology and the problem confronting the innovator

1. At any given time, a number of technologies will be concurrently in use, particularly if these technologies are capital-embodied (the vintage effect);
2. Even at the investment "frontier," different technologies may be adopted simultaneously;
3. The aggregate rate of technical change will be a function of the rate of diffusion of new technologies, and not of the rate of instantaneous innovation;
4. Even if one may accept that the return to innovative effort is representable as a draw from a stationary random process, the parameters of this process are not a priori known to agents, and their subjective priors may differ widely. Moreover, even if they are Bayesians, they may not live long enough to draw more precise conclusions. Their problem is not dissimilar to that of the multiarmed bandit;
5. Technological knowledge, like information in general, can have a public and codifiable, a private, and a tacit character. It can only be imperfectly protected as private property (the mere knowledge that something can be done, which a patient discloses, can already be very useful information). This state of affairs will certainly influence innovative activity, but in ways that are difficult to anticipate.[2]

The Evolution of the Artificial Economy with a Given Set of Firms and Technologies

The basic framework of the model is taken from Silverberg and Lehnert (1993), which in turn draws on Silverberg (1984) and Goodwin (1967). Let hats above variables denote proportional growth rates, w be the (real) wage rate, v the employment rate (persons employed as a fraction of the labor force), and m and n parameters (both positive). Then the wage rate is determined by the following differential equation

$$\hat{w} = -m + nv. \tag{1}$$

It is assumed that there is a fixed number, q, of firms in the economy, while each of these firms has a variable number, p_q, of different types of capital

---

2. In classic articles Nelson (1959) and Arrow (1962) underscored the disparity that may exist between the social and the private rates of return and incentives to innovation. Recent literature has uncovered the possibility of both insufficient as well as socially excessive, redundant R&D, depending on the precise assumptions made. Cohen and Levinthal (1989) and Nelson (1990) argue that substantial R&D efforts are necessary even to imitate.

goods that it utilizes to produce a homogeneous product. New capital arises from the accumulation of profits, a process described by the following equation

$$\hat{k}_{ij} = (1 - \gamma_{1i})r_{ij} - \frac{\gamma_{2i}}{c} + \alpha(r_{ij} - r_i) - \sigma. \tag{2}$$

The capital stock is denoted by k, r stands for the profit rate, and σ is the exogenous rate of *physical* depreciation of capital (technological obsolescence is an endogenous component of the model itself). The subscript i $(1 \ldots q)$ denotes the firm, and j $(1 \ldots p_q)$ the type of capital (the absence of any of these indices indicates an aggregation over this particular dimension). Equation (2) assumes that the principal source for type ij capital accumulation is profits generated by ij capital. This is modeled by the first term on the right-hand side of equation (2), that is $(1 - \gamma_i)r_{ij}$. A firm-specific portion of profits (denoted by γ_{1i}) plus a firm-specific portion of total output (denoted by γ_{2i}) is used for the development of knowledge (R&D) (when $r_i < 0$, γ_{1i} is set to zero).

However, profits may also be redistributed in such a way that more profitable types of capital accumulate even faster, less profitable types even slower, than would otherwise be the case. The mechanism used to model this was first proposed by Soete and Turner (1984), and is represented by the second term on the right hand side of equation (2). By changing the value of α, redistribution of profits takes place faster (larger α) or slower (smaller α).

It is assumed that each type of capital is characterized by fixed technical coefficients, c and a (for capital coefficient and labor productivity, respectively). The capital coefficient is assumed to be fixed throughout the economy (and time), while labor productivity is assumed to change under the influence of technical progress. The profit rate of ij capital is then given by $(1 - w/a_{ij})/c$.

The principal variable used to describe firm dynamics is the share of the labor force employed on each capital stock. Production is assumed to always be equal to production capacity (the influence of effective demand is absent), so that the amount of labor employed by each capital stock is equal to $k_{ij}/(a_{ij}c)$. Dividing this by the labor force (assumed to grow at a fixed rate β) gives the share of labor employed, v_{ij}, whose growth rate is

$$\hat{v}_{ij} = \hat{k}_{ij} - \beta = (1 - \gamma_{1i})r_{ij} - \frac{\gamma_{2i}}{c} + \alpha(r_{ij} - r_i) - (\beta + \sigma). \tag{3}$$

R&D also has an employment effect. We assume that the ratio between R&D expenditures and R&D labor input is equal to a fraction δ of the economy-wide labor productivity. The employment rate v_q resulting from production is then found by summing v_{ij} over i and j. Under these assumptions, it can then be shown that the overall employment rate v is equal to $[1 + \delta(\gamma_1 rc + \gamma_2)]v_q$.

Equations (1) and (3) together create a selection mechanism in our artificial economy. Equation (3) describes how more profitable technologies (i.e., those with above-average labor productivity) tend to increase their employment share, whereas more backward (below-average) technologies tend to vanish. The real Phillips curve equation (1) ensures that real wages tend to track labor productivity in the long run. In a situation in which new technologies are continually being introduced, this implies that all technologies, after an initial phase of market penetration and diffusion, will eventually vanish from the production system.

The Introduction of New Technologies and Firms into the Economy

It is assumed that in each time period, firms devote resources (R&D) to the systematic search for new production possibilities (i.e., new types of capital). The outcome of this search process is assumed to be stochastic. The structure of the *technological space* is assumed to be a simple directed graph. More complicated graphs could well be imagined with branching and even merging nodes; this remains a subject for future research.

Each time an innovation occurs, the firm creates a new type of capital. The labor productivity of this type of capital is given by the following process

$$a_{i,t}^* = (1 + \tau)a_{i,t-1}^*, \tag{4}$$

where τ is the fixed proportional increase in labor productivity between innovations and $a_{i,t}^*$ is the firm-specific best practice labor productivity. The new type of capital is seeded with a small employment share (say 0.0001). In order to keep the total employment rate constant, this seed value is (proportionally) removed from the other types of capital of the innovating firm. The number of technologies employed by any given firm may vary in time.

As real wages rise over time, every technology will eventually generate negative profits and enter the scrapping phase. When a technology's employment share falls below a specified (very small) value E, it is scrapped completely.

A firm's R&D activities, as well as possibly those of its rivals, enter an innovation potential function T_i. This in turn determines the firm's probability of making an innovation according to a Poisson process with arrival rate ρ_i. The simplest relation is simply linear

$$\rho_i = AT_i + \rho_{\min}, \tag{5}$$

where ρ_{min} is the (small) autonomous probability of making a fortuitous innovation without doing formal R&D and A is the innovation function slope. One can also posit a nonlinear relationship with both increasing and decreasing returns to R&D, such as a logistic

$$\rho_i = \frac{\rho_{min}\rho_{max}}{\rho_{min} + (\rho_{max} - \rho_{min})e^{-AT_i}} . \tag{6}$$

This logistic function has intercept ρ_{min} and (asymptotic) saturation level ρ_{max}. In this case, the parameter A determines the speed at which the saturation level is approached.

T_i, the innovation potential, is determined both by the firm's own R&D level (h_i, to be defined in the following) and its ability to profit from other firms' R&D (technological spillovers, where the parameters ϕ_1 and ϕ_2 determine the importance of each spillover mode[3])

$$T_i = h_i + \phi_1 h + \phi_2 h h_i. \tag{7}$$

The firm-specific R&D level h_i is defined to be the ratio of a moving average of firm R&D investment to its total physical capital stock. A ratio is used to normalize for firm size, since otherwise such a strong positive feedback between R&D and firm growth exists that monopoly becomes inevitable. While a priori it is by no means clear why the size of individual R&D effort should not directly relate to innovative success, a pure scale effect must be ruled out by the continuing existence of competition and the ability of small countries to remain or even advance in the technology race. The exponential moving average RD_i on R&D for a lag of L (or a depreciation rate of $1/L$) is given by the following differential equation

$$\frac{d}{dt} RD_i = [(\gamma_{1i} r_i + \gamma_{2i}/c)k_i - RD_i]/L . \tag{8}$$

Hence the firm-specific R&D level is

$$h_i = RD_i/k_i. \tag{9}$$

An innovation can be defined in either a narrow or a wide sense. In the wide sense, the adoption of any technology not yet employed by a firm (or a country) is an innovation to that unit. In the narrow sense, only technologies that have never been employed before anywhere are considered innovations at

---

3. Spillovers will not be dealt with in this chapter. They are examined within the context of one-parameter strategies in Silverberg and Verspagen 1994a,b.

their time of introduction. If firms innovate according to the above Poisson arrival rates in the narrow sense, however, a very considerable intertemporal externality is created, because firms' innovations always build on each other. Thus there can be no duplication of effort and, as long as firms maintain a minimal level of R&D, no cumulative falling behind. On the other hand, once an innovation has been introduced into the economy somewhere, it should be progressively easier for other firms to imitate or duplicate it; it should not be necessary to reinvent the wheel. We capture this by introducing a catching-up effect. Let the labor productivity of the economy-wide best practice technology be a^* and the best practice technology of firm i, a_i^*. Then firm i's innovation potential, T_i, will be augmented by a measure of its distance from the best practice frontier

$$T_i' = T_i[1 + \kappa \ln (a^*/a_i^*)]. \tag{10}$$

Thus, adopting an old innovation is facilitated for backward firms, but they are still required to invest in their technological capacity to reap these catch-up benefits. Here, however, R&D efforts should be interpreted in the larger sense of technological training and licensing, reverse engineering, or even industrial espionage (all costly activities, if not as costly as doing state-of-the-art R&D).

We have also experimented with innovations in the narrow sense, but the results on strategic selection are rather ambiguous. This is not surprising, since the import of the intertemporal externality is indeed quite large. We consider the Ansatz in equation 10, therefore, to be a justifiable first formulation, since technology adoption decisions are never passive, but rather require technological efforts by the adopting firm. However, this does place too much of the burden of catching up onto R&D.

In the artificial economy modeled here, entry of a new firm occurs only as a result of exit of an incumbent firm. Exit occurs whenever a firm's employment share (excluding its R&D employment) falls below a fixed level E. While exit of incumbent firms is completely endogenous, entry only occurs in case of exit, so that the total number of firms is constant. While this feature of the model is not very realistic, it is not the aim of this model to describe the phenomena of entry and exit as such. Instead, the main function of entry and exit is to maintain potential variety in the population of firms while providing for firm elimination.

Whenever entry occurs, the entrant is assigned a single technology with an amount of capital corresponding to an employment share of $2E$ (the remaining employment is proportionally removed from other firms so that total employment remains constant). The labor productivity of this technology is drawn uniformly from the range $[(1 - b)A,(1 + b)A]$, where A is the unweighted mean value of labor productivity of all the firms in the economy, and b is a parameter. The values for h and γ are (uniformly) drawn from the range existing in the economy at the time of entry.

Firm Strategies for Innovation

Learning now enters the picture in the form of two "genetic" operators, mutation and imitation. With probability Π each decision period, which is set exogenously and is equal for all firms, a firm will draw from a normal distribution and alter one or both of its strategy parameters γ within the admissible range $[0,1]$ (mutation). Given that mutation occurs, each possibility (change in either one or both parameters) occurs with equal probability

$$\gamma_{1it} = \min\,[1,\max\,(\gamma_{1it-1} + \epsilon,0)], \quad \epsilon \sim N(0,s), \quad \text{or}$$

$$\gamma_{2it} = \min\,[1,\max\,(\gamma_{2it-1} + \epsilon,0)], \quad \epsilon \sim N(0,s), \quad \text{or} \qquad (11)$$

$$\gamma_{lit} = \min\,[1,\max\,(\gamma_{lit-1} + \epsilon_l,0)], \quad \epsilon_l \sim N(0,s), \quad l = 1,2.$$

With variable probability Π_i^c, the firm simply imitates the strategy of another firm. Again, given that imitation occurs, each possibility (imitate either one or both parameters) occurs with equal probability

$$\gamma_{1it} = \gamma_{1jt-1}, \quad j(\neq i) \in [1 \ldots q]_i, \quad \text{or}$$

$$\gamma_{2it} = \gamma_{2jt-1}, \quad j(\neq i) \in [1 \ldots q]_i, \quad \text{or} \qquad (12)$$

$$\gamma_{lit} = \gamma_{ljt-1}, \quad j(\neq i) \in [1 \ldots q]_i, \quad l = 1,2.$$

The imitation probability is partly endogenous, to reflect satisficing behavior. Only firms with unsatisfactory rates of profit with respect to economy leaders will choose or be forced (for example, by their stockholders or by hostile takeovers) to adopt the strategy of a competitor

$$\Pi_i^c = \mu \left(1 - \frac{y_i - y_{\min}}{y_{\max} - y_{\min}} \right). \qquad (13)$$

y_i is the firm's rate of expansion of physical capital (defined as $\min\,[r_i - \gamma_{2i}/c, (1 - \gamma_i)r_{1i} - \gamma_{2i}/c)]$, $y_{\max}$ and $y_{\min}$ are the maximum and minimum values of y in the sample, and μ is the (exogenously determined) maximum imitation probability. Thus, the more profitable a firm is, the less likely it will change its strategy by imitating another firm. The most profitable firm has an imitation probability equal to zero; the least profitable has the maximum probability, μ. Once a firm has decided to imitate, it randomly selects a firm to imitate from the industry with weight equal to the target firm's market share in output. If neither imitation nor mutation occur, the firm simply retains its strategy from the previous period.

Identification of Steady States by Random and Spontaneous Generation

The main feature of the model we will investigate is the existence and nature of an "evolutionary attractor" in the dynamics, that is whether a "stable" configuration of firm R&D strategies exists to which our artificial economy will converge from particular classes of initial conditions. We have initialized the system in two ways: first in a "grapeshot" mode we term random generation in which the initial γ's are drawn from a uniform distribution over [0,1] and [0,0.2] (respectively for γ_1 and γ_2); and second, in a "spontaneous generation" mode in which all initial γ's are set to zero.[4] We present the results of these experiments by means of density plots made on the basis of three-dimensional histograms of the two γ's. On the horizontal axis we plot the experimental parameter that is being varied through different simulation runs (A or μ). The (market share weighted) mean value of the strategy parameter over the firms in each run is shown on the vertical axis. The data are pooled from the last 1,000 years of five simulation runs for each value of the experimental parameter, each generated with a different random seed. Darker shading indicates higher frequencies.

In figure 1, we plot the results for the runs initialized by random generation. The figure clearly shows that the converging behavior of the two strategy parameters is quite different. Parameter 1 (the targeted R&D to profits ratio) does not converge very clearly, except for higher values of the innovation slope, when relatively high frequencies are found at values near zero. Parameter 2, targeting R&D to sales, shows a more tight convergence, although there are still high frequencies near zero (the white band between the horizontal axis and the attractor is quite narrow). Thus, firms show a tendency to select a relatively tight range of values for parameter 2, while parameter 1 tends to drift or, if anything, go to zero. Summarizing, firms seem to display a tendency to select tightly defined strategies based upon parameter 2 and show indifference to parameter 1.

Figure 2 shows corresponding results for the case of spontaneous generation, that is, a situation in which firms have to discover R&D as an activity *ad initio*. As firms explore the strategy space by mutation and imitation, they

---

4. The parameters of the model and the values used in the simulations are summarized in the Appendix.

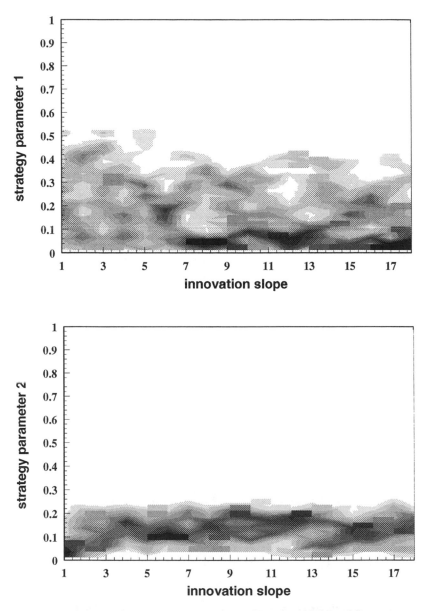

Fig. 1. Histograms of strategy parameters from pooled data of five runs per value, last 1,000 years of 8,000-year runs (random generation), for a linear innovation function

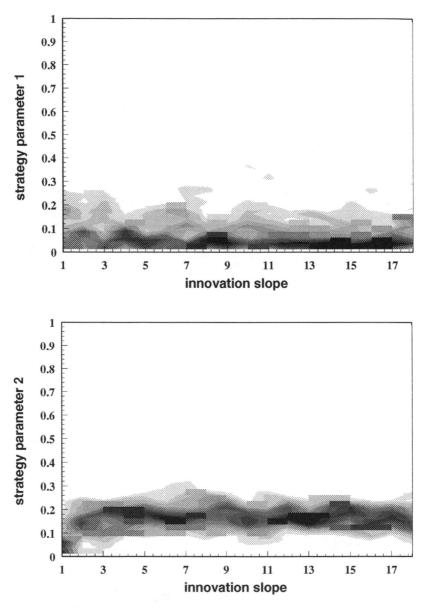

Fig. 2. Histograms of strategy parameters from pooled data of five runs per value, last 1,000 years of 8,000-year runs (spontaneous generation), for a linear innovation function

may (or may not) find R&D a useful activity. The density plots show that in this case, the evolutionary attractor is much more clearly defined. The type 1 strategy parameter remains near zero (in our interpretation, the positive values found are largely attributable to random "evolutionary" noise). The type 2 strategy parameter, however, shows a well-defined peak significantly distant from zero, as indicated by the white space bordering it from below.

This behavior of the system can be interpreted as a particular form of lock-in or path dependence. When the system is started "clean," without any form of commitment to any type of R&D strategy, it will select a much more unambiguous evolutionary attractor than in the random generation case. This is not the case when only the type 1 strategy parameter is employed (compare Silverberg and Verspagen 1994a,b). There the asymptotic steady states of the two initializations are identical.

For a logistic innovation function (eq. 6) we obtain similar patterns from the histograms over innovation opportunity (fig. 3). In contrast to the linear case, however, the steady-state value of parameter 2 does seem to decline somewhat with increasing technological opportunity. What is also remarkable is the sudden collapse of the technological regime below values of A of about 40. The steady-state values of parameter 2, in the range 20–30 percent, are also higher than in the linear case.

Why is strategy parameter 2 subject to positive selection, while parameter 1 displays either drift or is constrained to zero? Our interpretation is that R&D comes to be regarded as a "core" business activity in the model, for, due to the "Goodwin" business cycles of the underlying economy, profits are more variable than sales. Thus, firms that base their R&D expenditures upon profits will have more fluctuating R&D stocks than firms that base their R&D on sales. The selection environment seems to favor the latter firms because, in the long run, their R&D behavior provides a more reliable stream of innovations.

Whereas the steady-state values of the strategy parameters do not appear to depend on technological opportunity, as represented by the value of A,[5] the realized rate of technical change is a simple linearly increasing function of it. The transient time paths in the spontaneous generation case on the way to steady-state growth are also of interest in themselves. Figure 4 displays the market-share-weighted values of the two strategy parameters for a single run over 8,000 years. Convergence is relatively rapid in comparison with the single-parameter case. Figure 5 shows the time paths of the rate of technical change and the Herfindahl concentration index.[6] Viewed as a process in

---

5. This is not true when only parameter 1 is used. In this case, the value gradually *falls* with increasing A.

6. This is defined as $H = \Sigma f_i^2$, where f_i is the market share of the ith firm. It ranges from $1/n$, for n equally sized firms, to 1, for a complete monopoly.

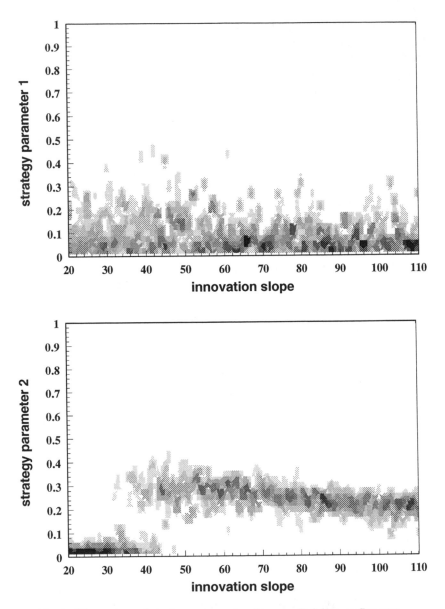

Fig. 3. Histograms of strategy parameters from pooled data on five runs
per value, last 1,000 years of 8,000-year runs (spontaneous generation),
for a logistic innovation function

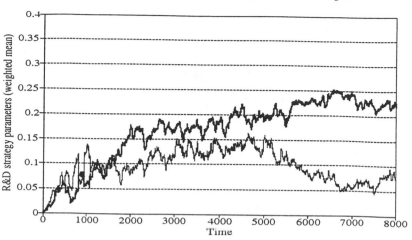

Fig. 4. Time paths of market-share-weighted strategy parameters in a spontaneous generation run (50 firms, $\tau = 0.04$). The light line is γ_1, the heavy line is γ_2.

historical time and not just as an out-of-equilibrium transient, this figure recapitulates a piece of virtual economic history. The economy starts off with no R&D and an essentially vanishing rate of technical change. Within this regime the rate of market concentration is quite high, although the identity of the near monopolist changes at almost regular intervals, as indicated by the breaks in the level of concentration. As the γ's rise with time and with them the overall rate of technical change, this market regime breaks down. It is replaced by low levels of concentration and considerable market turnover.

We have also begun to investigate how the structure of the evolutionary learning process affects the outcomes of these experiments. Recall that the variables Π and μ, representing the probability of mutation and imitation, are exogenously imposed. We have compiled histograms for the two strategy parameters by varying each of these rates separately. Varying the mutation probability does not change the results in any essential way. In contrast, increasing the ceiling on the imitation probability leads to a progressive collapse of γ_2 selection (fig. 6). If firms imitate each other too strongly, they become involved in an evolutionary game of musical chairs, and no nontrivial strategy is able to establish itself.

Discussion and Conclusions

In this chapter we have developed an evolutionary model describing the relation between endogenous technological change and economic growth along

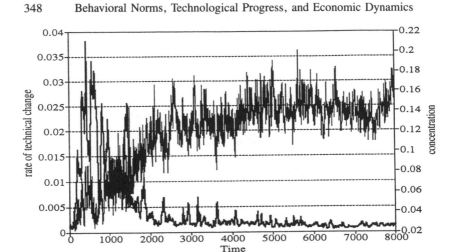

Fig. 5. Time paths of rate of technical change (light line) and Herfindahl index of concentration (heavy line) for the same run as in fig. 4

the lines of an "artificial world" modeling philosophy. By this we mean that the economy is disaggregated into individual behavioral subunits (instead of the representative agent so prevalent in most macroeconomic modeling) connected by nontrivial nonlinear dynamic interactions based on plausible notions of disequilibrium competition and investment. Rather than search for a strategic equilibrium based on a concept of rationality, we have assumed that these agents use boundedly rational behavioral procedures. In the present case this is an extremely simple rule for the R&D/profits (or gross investment) and R&D/sales ratios, which are parameterized by two real numbers between 0 and 1. Learning is modeled by allowing for mutation and imitation rules operating on the agents' strategy parameters. An element of behavioral realism is injected into the model by insisting that mutations are local in the strategic "genotype" space, and that imitation is only prompted by less than satisfactory performance.

Using both a linear and a logistic innovation function, we were able to show that evolutionary steady states exist that are attractive in the behavioral space, but may differ depending on "history." Thus, the model does establish a case for endogenous growth in the sense of demonstrating that economic competition, even with very relaxed assumptions about individual goal-seeking behavior and profit maximization, leads to an approximately steady-state growth path with a positive rate of technical change and R&D investment.

However, the spontaneous generation experiments underline the fact that the mere existence of such a steady state does not mean that history does not matter. Quite the contrary. A society starting with no or low rates of R&D will

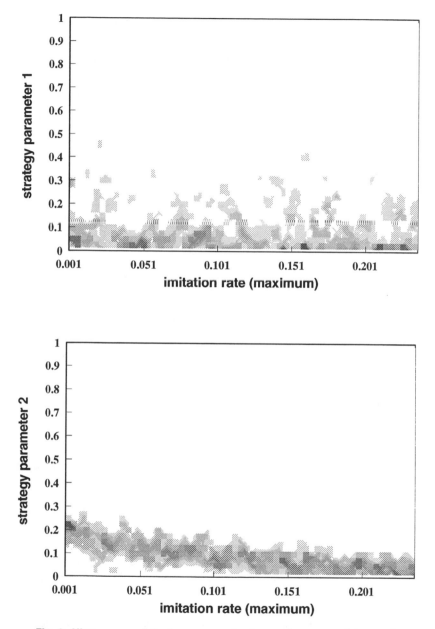

Fig. 6. Histograms of strategy parameter for varying rates of the maximum imitation parameter ($A = 10$, random generation)

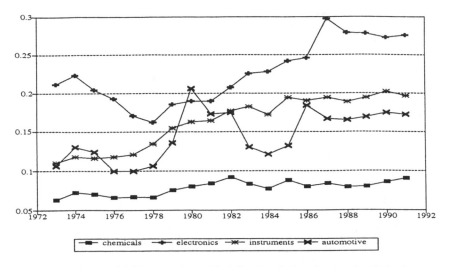

Fig. 7. Ratio of R&D to value added for five industries in the United States. (Note: chemicals does not include pharmaceuticals.)

pass through a phase of very high market concentration, but with periodic upheavals or "palace revolts" of market leadership on a time scale of centuries. Eventually such an economy will "bootstrap" itself to higher rates of R&D and technical change.[7]

To demonstrate that the levels of R&D to which the model points are by no means unrealistic, figures 7 and 8 present OECD data on the share of R&D expenditures in value added[8] for five industries in the United States and Japan, respectively. These data are representative of the extreme cases of a mature and a catch-up economy. The evidence for convergence to a high and stable level of R&D is striking, both over time and between these countries. Even more remarkable is the fact that these values correspond very closely with those predicted by our model. The range of 10–25 percent of R&D to value added, independent of technological opportunity, thus seems to be both a long-period invariant of capitalist development, as captured in our model, and an empirically verifiable phenomenon.

While we do not wish to overburden such a simple model with historical interpretations, the point must still be made that it would be unfortunate to restrict the concept of endogenous growth to steady-state growth paths with no

---

7. This should be compared with the one-parameter strategy case, where the evolution is slower and passes through at least three distinct historical phases.

8. We employ value added instead of sales to reflect more accurately the proper interpretation of our model, where firms are assumed to be completely vertically integrated, and thus sales and value added are assumed to be identical.

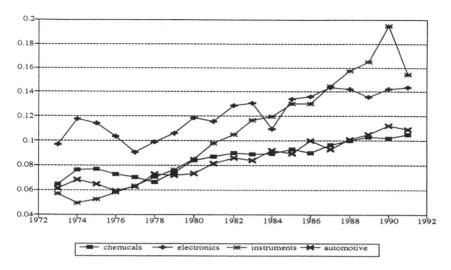

Fig. 8. Ratio of R&D to value added for five industries in Japan. (Note: chemicals does not include pharmaceuticals.)

real structural development, social learning, and historical contingency. For this reason an evolutionary approach appears to offer an attractive alternative explanation of how an economy can bootstrap itself in historical time through a succession of growth phases and market structures. The concepts of growth or development stages, takeoffs, and changes of regime were prominent in a classical line of thought associated with Marx, Schumpeter, and Rostow. The criticism that these theories smacked of rigid mechanistic determinism is overcome by the artificial worlds methodology, which demonstrates that reversions, variable delays, and path dependence resulting from underlying stochasticity and nonlinearity cannot be excluded. Needless to say, such a broad and differentiated perspective on economic growth has mostly fallen by the wayside in the postwar literature on growth and development (cf. Rostow 1990).

Our model also demonstrates that a bounded rationality approach to the theory of the firm, coupled with an evolutionary framework for analyzing market selection and collective learning, does yield dividends, in terms of explaining both how identifiable patterns of behavior emerge from *profit-seeking* rather than completely rational *profit-maximizing* assumptions, and how market structures and growth regimes may be simultaneously endogenized. We believe that the apparent inconvenience of bounded rationality and an artificial worlds, computer-based modeling strategy is more than outweighed by the ability to go far beyond the mere reproduction of conventional wisdom and open up a range of phenomena and relationships to theoretical and quantitative empirical study that historians have repeatedly emphasized but economists have for the most part ignored.

APPENDIX

A summary of the parameters and the values employed in the runs analyzed in the chapter is presented in the following

$q = 10$	number of firms
$m = 0.9$, $n = 1$	parameters of the Phillips curve in equation (1)
$\alpha = 1$	Soete-Turner coefficient in equation (2)
γ (endogenous)	R&D/investment ratio in equation (2)
$c = 3$	capital-output ratio
$\sigma = 0$	rate of physical depreciation in equations (2) and (3)
$\beta = 0.01$	rate of growth of labor force in equation (3)
$\delta = 1$	ratio of productivity in goods and R&D sectors
$\tau = 0.06$	proportional jump in labor productivity in equation (4)
A (variable)	innovation slope in equation (5)
$\rho_{min} = 0.01$	autonomous rate of innovation in equation (5)
ϕ_1 (variable)	type 1 spillover coefficient in equation (7)
ϕ_2 (variable)	type 2 spillover coefficient in equation (7)
$L = 5$	lag for R&D moving average in equation (8)
$\kappa = 4$	catch-up parameter in equation (10)
$\Pi = 0.02$	mutation probability in equation (11)
$s = 0.02$	standard deviation of mutation step size in equation (11)
$\mu = 0.02$	maximum imitation probability in equation (12)
$E = 0.005$	exit level in employment share
$b = 0.1$	labor productivity bandwidth for entrants

REFERENCES

Aghion, P., and P. Howitt. 1992. A Model of Growth through Creative Destruction. *Econometrica* 60:323–51.

Arrow, K. 1962. Economic Welfare and Allocation of Resources for Invention. In *The Rate and Direction of Inventive Activity,* ed. R. Nelson. Princeton, NJ: NBER/ Princeton University Press.

Arthur, W. B. 1991. Designing Economic Agents that Act Like Human Agents: A Behavioral Approach to Bounded Rationality. *American Economic Review. Papers and Proceedings* 81:353–59.

Cohen, W. M., and D. A. Levinthal. 1989. Innovation and Learning: The Two Faces of R&D. *Economic Journal* 99:569–96.

Cyert, R. M., and J. G. March. 1963. *A Behavioral Theory of the Firm.* Englewood Cliff, NJ: Prentice-Hall.

Foster, D., and P. Young. 1990. Stochastic Evolutionary Game Dynamics. *Theoretical Population Biology* 38:219–32.

Friedman, D. 1991. Evolutionary Games in Economics. *Econometrica* 59:637–66.

Friedman, M. 1953. The Methodology of Positive Economics. In *Essays in Positive Economics.* Chicago: University of Chicago Press.

Goodwin, R. M. 1967. A Growth Cycle. In *Socialism, Capitalism and Economic Growth,* ed. C. H. Feinstein. London: Macmillan.

Helpman, E. 1992. Endogenous Macroeconomic Growth Theory. *European Economic Review* 36:237–67.

Hofbauer, J., and K. Sigmund. 1988. *The Theory of Evolution and Dynamical Systems.* Cambridge: Cambridge University Press.

Kamien, M. I., and N. L. Schwartz. 1982. *Market Structure and Innovation.* Cambridge: Cambridge University Press.

Kandori, M., G. J. Mailath, and R. Rob. 1993. Learning, Mutations, and Long-Run Equilibrium in Games. *Econometrica* 61:29–56.

Lane, D. A. 1993. Artificial Worlds and Economics. Parts 1 and 2. *Journal of Evolutionary Economics* 3:89–108, 177–97.

Langton, C. G., ed. 1989. *Artificial Life.* Redwood City, CA: Addison-Wesley.

Langton, C. G., C. Taylor, J. D. Farmer, and S. Rasmussen, eds. 1992. *Artificial Life II.* Redwood City, CA: Addison-Wesley.

Lucas, R. 1988. On the Mechanisms of Economic Development. *Journal of Monetary Economics* 22:3–42.

Nelson, R. R. 1959. The Simple Economics of Basic Scientific Research. *Journal of Political Economy* 67:297–306.

Nelson, R. R. 1990. What is Public and What is Private about Technology? CCC Working Paper No. 90-9, Berkeley, CA.

Nelson, R. R., and S. G. Winter. 1982. *An Evolutionary Theory of Economic Change.* Cambridge, MA: Belknap Press of Harvard University Press.

Romer, P. M. 1986. Increasing Returns and Long-Run Growth. *Journal of Political Economy* 94:1002–37.

Romer, P. M. 1990. Endogenous Technological Change. *Journal of Political Economy* 98:71–102.

Rostow, W. W. 1990. *Theorists of Economic Growth.* Oxford: Oxford University Press.

Scherer, F. M., and D. Ross. 1990. *Industrial Market Structure and Economic Performance,* 3d ed. Boston: Houghton Mifflin Company.

Schwefel, H. P. 1981. *Numerical Optimization of Computer Models.* Chichester: John Wiley.

Selten, R. 1989. Evolution, Learning, and Economic Behavior. *Games and Economic Behaviour* 3:3–24.

Silverberg, G. 1984. Embodied Technical Progress in a Dynamic Economic Model:

The Self-Organization Paradigm. In *Nonlinear Models of Fluctuating Growth,* ed. R. Goodwin, M. Krüger, and A. Vercelli. Berlin, Heidelberg, New York: Springer Verlag.

Silverberg, G., and D. Lehnert. 1993. Long Waves and "Evolutionary Chaos" in a Simple Schumpeterian Model of Embodied Technical Change. *Structural Change and Economic Dynamics* 4:9–37.

Silverberg, G., and B. Verspagen. 1994a. Learning, Innovation and Economic Growth: A Long-Run Model of Industrial Dynamics. *Industrial and Corporate Change* 3:199–223.

Silverberg, G., and B. Verspagen. 1994b. Collective Learning, Innovation and Growth in a Boundedly Rational, Evolutionary World. *Journal of Evolutionary Economics* 4:207–26.

Simon, H. A. 1986a. Rationality in Psychology and Economics. In *The Behavioral Foundations of Economic Theory,* ed. R. M. Hogarth and M. W. Reder, special issue of *The Journal of Economics* 59:209–24.

Simon, H. A. 1986b. On the Behavioral and Rational Foundations of Economic Dynamics. In *The Dynamics of Market Economies,* ed. R. H. Day and G. Eliasson. Amsterdam: North Holland.

Soete, L., and R. Turner. 1984. Technology Diffusion and the Rate of Technical Change. *Economic Journal* 94:612–23.

Young, H. P. 1993. The Evolution of Conventions, *Econometrica* 61:57–84.

Economic Evolution and Transformation of the Economic Order

Maria Brouwer

Schumpeter had a largely implicit theory of social evolution. Evolution is spurred by social mobility. Politics determines the capabilities that are promoted. Socialism can outperform capitalism, if it adheres to free trade and rational selection of entrepreneurs. The introduction of Knightian uncertainty interferes with Schumpeter's ideas on selection and business cycles.

Introduction

Schumpeter predicted that the capitalist economic order would not survive in spite of its great economic successes. This prediction is based on the distinction he made between the capitalist order and the capitalist system. The competitive capitalist order is characterized by private property, production for a market, and credit. The capitalist system, characterized by a market-clearing price mechanism, although evolving in a wavelike manner, was—in his view—inherently stable. Static economic equilibria will be upset periodically by bunches of innovation, but these disturbances can be absorbed and incorporated in new market equilibria (Schumpeter 1928).

In spite of its innate economic stability, the capitalist institutional order—in his view—had gradually succumbed to trustified or regulated capitalism, which in turn would give way to socialism. Competitive capitalism prevailed during the nineteenth century, after which it transformed into managed or organized capitalism (Schumpeter 1928, 362). Consequently, capitalism constituted a transitory, historical state located between feudalism and socialism.

In this chapter I want to explore Schumpeter's view on the question of transition. Can his analysis of the transition from feudalism into capitalism be put on a par with the envisioned subsequent transitions of the economic order, that is, from capitalism into trustified capitalism and socialism?

Another question involves the nature of his evolutionary theory. Did he see economic evolution as linearly progressive, so that each new equilibrium situation outperforms the previous one, or did he also include possible stagnation or leaps backward? The answers to these questions hinge on the alleged innovativeness of various economic orders. Can innovation proceed unhampered and can business cycles be discarded under socialist conditions?

Schumpeter's view on the economic performance of socialism derives from his ideas on investment selection and social mobility. A fundamental question in this respect involves whether the quality of investment proposals can be determined ex ante or only ex post. Schumpeter's ideas will be confronted with those of Knight.

The Demise of Competitive Capitalism

Schumpeter viewed (competitive) capitalism as a transitory period that had to give way under the weight of opposing forces that were the product of capitalism itself. His *History of Economic Analysis* (Schumpeter 1954; hereafter HEA) is the richest source for constructing Schumpeter's vision on the evolution of the economic order.

He viewed the defeat of both economic and political liberalism as the main reason for the demise of the competitive capitalist order. Economic liberalism underlines the prevalence of laissez-faire policies (HEA, 761). Political liberalism refers to the "sponsorship of parliamentary government, freedom to vote and extension of the right to vote, freedom of the press, divorce of secular from spiritual government, trial by jury, and so on." Liberalism in both senses reigned from the end of the eighteenth century until about 1900 (HEA, 761). From that time onward, liberalism gave way to the attacks launched upon it by its multiplying ideological adversaries.

The defeat of political liberalism set in from the 1880s onward, but this did not immediately show at the polls, except for in Germany and Austria, where liberal parties met with open defeat.[1] The state bureaucracy that before had sponsored economic liberalism now also grew hostile toward it, and linked up with other social strata such as the peasants, the artisans, and the landlords, who all felt threatened by the rise of the bourgeoisie (HEA, 763).

> Finally, individuals and sub-groups of all classes broke loose from economic and political liberalism—though often retaining the label. And they had one thing in common in spite of all the differences in interests and cultural preconceptions that no doubt existed between them: the central or controlling position that they allocated to the State and the Nation—the National State. (HEA, 764)

---

1. Schumpeter was of the opinion that liberal parties in other countries, particularly in England, only held their own by "radicalizing" their programs (HEA, 761).

Hence, capitalism failed because liberalism was too feeble an ideological shield to take refuge behind.

Schumpeter described the politics of nineteenth-century capitalism as follows: competitive capitalism is characterized by a division of labor between the bourgeoisie and the aristocracy, in which politics is the domain of the aristocracy and all things economical are the preserve of the bourgeoisie. Capitalism thus constitutes an economic order in which politics is subordinated to commerce.

Competitive Capitalism, Feudalism, and the State

Liberalism was preceded by a period wherein nationalism had reigned. Capitalist institutions, such as big business, stock and commodity speculation, and "high finance" had already established themselves firmly at the end of the fifteenth century, and had entailed the ascent of the bourgeoisie (HEA, 78). Capitalism had first emerged in the Italian cities and had then spread to the low countries. But capitalism could not unfold unfettered, because of the rise of the nation-states that ascended from the fifteenth century onward. The rising bourgeoisie had to submit for centuries to come to the rule of a warrior class of feudal origins that milked the bourgeoisie to fight their endless series of wars. The breakdown of the empire contributed to this aggression, in Schumpeter's view (HEA, 144–46). The emergence of the nation-states was strengthened by the threat of a Turkish invasion, which prompted the rise of mercenary armies. Consequently, England could largely maintain its feudal framework and transcend into liberalism without the intermezzo of the mercantilist nation-state.

Moreover, continental aristocracies needed to be appeased by the splendor of the monarchial courts, which also took a financial toll. Furthermore, nation-states could tap a torrent of precious metals that were the product of the conquest of South America to feed their aggression.

The ascent of the nation-state was not inevitable, but was the result of the unusual strength of the feudal social framework, which Schumpeter categorizes as accidental (HEA, 144). This exploitation of the bourgeoisie, in Schumpeter's view, hampered economic development until the national bureaucracies had withered away as a consequence of bourgeois revolutions, particularly the French Revolution.[2]

---

2. Capitalistic progress was hampered in the sixteenth century by the rise of (Spanish) colonial ventures, which expanded the circulating medium and caused rapid inflation that inflicted grave suffering on the peasants, whose revolts and defeat strengthened the position of the warrior classes. In other countries (with the exceptions of England, The Netherlands and Hungary), all classes were appeased and fitted into the state organ. The ascending bourgeoisie was exploited (and protected) to pay for the splendor of the prince, the court, and the army (BC, 235).

In contrast to seventeenth- and eighteenth-century practices, downsized nineteenth-century bureaucracies did not appropriate the larger part of entrepreneurial profits, but wholeheartedly endorsed the interests of the bourgeoisie. This made the nineteenth century unique in history, in Schumpeter's view: "a ruling stratum that did not defend its own interests, but that of the business class and consequently a government that was no longer prepared to go to war at the slightest occasion" (Schumpeter, 1955, pp. 66–72).

Economic and political liberalism thus only constituted a short intermezzo in Western developed countries (but most spectacularly in England), which then gave rise to a pace of economic development that was unprecedented in history (HEA, 396). Free trade was generally practiced, although only wholeheartedly embraced by the English. French, German, and U.S. policies were more reluctant on this issue, but they all shared the new attitude toward international affairs: that of an understanding between nations (HEA, 397–99). But from the 1880s onward, the state bureaucracy grew increasingly hostile toward liberalism, as the contours of the tax state emerged.

The Role of Rational Utilitarianism and Leadership

Liberalism, in Schumpeter's view, could not sustain capitalism, because of its shallow philosophical basis. The utilitarian philosophy on whose foundations it stood, with its Benthamite calculus of pleasure and pain, reduced the whole world of human values to the pursuit of a freedom that does not go far beyond beefsteaks, ruling out as contrary to reason all that really matters to man (HEA, 131–33). Utilitarian philosophy tried to impose a logical scheme of their own making on people with disregard for what *they are and think and feel* (HEA, 420).

Capitalism fosters rationalism, because it makes economic success central. Economic reasoning, however, due to its quantitative character and its emphasis on learning from experience, stands in sharp contrast to all other realms in life, where magic and prerational thought prevail (Schumpeter 1942, 121).

These features of logical reasoning and learning from experiment were responsible for a rapid pace of scientific and cultural advance, which took off during the sixteenth and seventeenth centuries, together with the rise of capitalism (Schumpeter 1974, 124; hereafter CSD).

Capitalism, therefore, triggered both scientific and economic progress. It stands afar from warrior ideology and is essentially pacifist, as it insists on the application of moral precepts of private life into international relations.

But utilitarianism, due to its rationalism and antiheroism, cannot survive ideological attacks, because it lacks the extrarational justifications that people demand. This also explains the lack of success of the bourgeoisie in the political arena. The bourgeoisie never provided people eligible for leadership. One of the causes for the demise of (competitive) capitalism, therefore, lay in its incapacity to generate successful politicians of its own making. Nineteenth-century politicians were of a precapitalist fabric, and when bourgeois politicians tried to rule they generally failed, because they lacked the glamour and the mystique that came natural to the aristocrat (CSD, 137).

Hence the bourgeoisie were incapable of pleading their cause and lacked self-confidence. The demise of capitalism was hastened by the bourgeoisie's failure to produce political and intellectual leaders, who could have extended their purely economic leadership into a broader social one.

Economic leadership, hence, does not qualify a person for political leadership. This also explains the long ruling of the aristocracy and the short-lived historical intermezzo of competitive capitalism. Consequently, the bourgeoisie's ascent lost its force because of political rather than economic reasons. The presumed rationality of capitalism could not prevent its collapse, but hastened it. It gave due weight to hostile arguments but failed to produce an appropriate set of values. In contrast, the bourgeoisie hailed the products of a spirit hostile to its civilization. This was not primarily Marxism. Schumpeter comments that Marx was read vicariously by the nineteenth-century bourgeoisie, but not really understood. Marxist rationalistic attitude was not opposed to capitalist civilization, in Schumpeter's view (HEA, 774). His main culprits are the philosophies that emerged during the nineteenth century and stood against the liberal cult of rationality and progress and its democratic humanitarianism. The first category consisted of pragmatism, which identifies truth with beliefs that are accepted as true. Another antirational strand saw truth (in a Hegelian spirit) reveal itself in the course of history (HEA, 778). Georges Sorel, the ideologue of syndicalism, was also considered a representative of the antirational strand of philosophical thinking (CSD, 340).

Hence, capitalism did not need a revolution to be discarded, but gave up its political and economic power voluntarily. The business class had lost its confidence in the virtues of laissez-faire, and its good conscience had gone when the attacks cumulated. Liberal parties could not hold their own, but succumbed to either reformers or political parties of a different creed.

We might conclude from this condensed version of Schumpeter's vision of social and political evolution that Schumpeter's views on economic and political/cultural evolution are not on a par. Economic development can only emerge when it has political support. This support is, however, not self-evident. The liberal nineteenth century seems to constitute a pinnacle of political/cultural evolution that was unfortunately unable to sustain itself.

This might lead to the conclusion that Schumpeter saw the defeat of liberalism and the period of neomercantilism that set in from the close of the nineteenth century onward as a historical leap backward. This corresponds with his view that the rise of the nation-state and the defeat of liberalism were mainly the result of antidemocratic policies and anti-intellectualist philosophies. The return of the nation-state would then signal a return to precapitalist political conditions. However, socialism, as the logical successor of capitalism, inherited the rationality of its predecessor. The transition to socialism therefore did not need to impair economic performance. The latter interpretation seems to suit Schumpeter best. He never contended that socialism meant a leap backward or would entail a retardation of economic progress similar to the precapitalist era.

His most popular work, *Capitalism, Socialism and Democracy,* portrays a rather optimistic picture of socialism's capacity for innovation and democracy. Innovation becomes increasingly mechanized, but will not be impeded under trustified capitalist and socialist conditions. In contrast, business cycles can be curbed and democracy maintained under socialism.

Capitalism fostered economic progress because of its rational attitudes and the absence of a rent-absorbing state apparatus, both of which promoted innovative investment. No compelling reason can be found for economic progress to flounder if trustified capitalism and socialism also feature rationalism and governmental austerity. But Schumpeter, being mainly preoccupied with the spacing of innovative investment in time, ignored the uncertainty that is inherent to innovative investment. Selection of innovation is, therefore, a neglected issue in his analysis.

Innovation under Trustified Capitalism and Socialism

Schumpeter's model of competitive capitalism involves a world in which innovations are introduced by new firms. Schumpeter compares the founders of these firms to the leaders of feudal times. The entrepreneurial role is summarized as: "His role though less glamorous than that of medieval warlords, great or small, also is or was just another form of personal leadership acting by virtue of personal force and personal responsibility for success" (CSD, 133).

His rudimentary sketches of trustified capitalism depict an economy wherein large incumbent firms innovate in a mechanical manner. The entrepreneurial role has now become obsolete and a different kind of leader—the politician—has come to the fore. He, in contrast to the entrepreneur, is a master in the dealing with men and makes it his full-time occupation in his competition for votes.

The borderline between trustified capitalism and socialism is not clearly marked. Increasing state interference with the economy lets capitalism gradually fade into socialism. The latter is defined as an institutional pattern in which the control over means of production and over production itself is vested with a central authority (CSD, 167). The main borderline already seems to have been passed at the end of the First World War, when competitive capitalism gave way to trustified capitalism.

The politicians who hold the helm of the ship of state will, however, delegate all economic decisions to appointed managers (CSD, 299). These managers are recruited from all classes and are mainly selected on the basis of capability. Willpower and leadership are no longer required, since leadership has been appropriated by the political body. The main difference between competitive and trustified capitalism, therefore, consists of the kind of people that will be selected as leaders. "Trustified capitalism allows other types of persons to rise and as a corollary other types will be kept under than in a competitive capitalist society" (Schumpeter 1928, 385).

However, as long as bureaucracies are given the freedom to develop their own professional codes, progress can proceed unhampered (CSD, 293–94).

Schumpeter mentioned some drawbacks of bureaucracies, but did not consider them unsurmountable obstacles.

> Bureaucracy has some draw-backs, such as the moral atmosphere it spreads, which exerts a depressing influence on the most active minds. Mainly this is due to the difficulty, inherent in the bureaucratic machine, of reconciling individual initiative with the mechanics of its working. Often the machine gives little scope for initiative and much scope for vicious attempts at smothering it. From this a sense of frustration and of futility may result which in turn induces a habit of mind that revels in blighting criticism of the efforts of others. (CSD, 207)

Schumpeter might have had doubts about actual socialist performance, as William Fellner recorded.[3] It must, therefore, be kept in mind that his statements on socialism only referred to an imagined state of affairs, where the central authority was democratically elected and where prices guided allocative decisions.

Schumpeter was convinced that such a socialism could perform the job of innovation and further economic progress. Precisely because it was more rational than capitalism, it could evade the painful method of creative destruction to discard obsolete capital goods, and reallocate capital and labor to more profitable lines of business. Production factors would be reallocated by a central authority instead of by a decentralized market mechanism (CSD, 195).

---

3. William Fellner, "March into Socialism," in Schumpeter's Vision; Capitalism, Socialism and Democracy after 40 Years, A. Heertje, ed., 1983. London: Praeger.

Social Mobility and Social Classes

We can wonder why Schumpeter was so optimistic about the performance of socialism. In my view, Schumpeter's vision of historical evolution, that is, the evolution of the social and economic order, was heavily imbued with his theory of social classes, which linked economic progress and social mobility. The kernel of his theory of social classes consisted of the idea that only those people who were most capable of fulfilling the leadership role required by their times would be called to power. Hence, the feudal era called for warriors, and selected leaders among those most capable at the job of fighting. Capitalism called for entrepreneurial capability and selected entrepreneurs accordingly. Moreover, capability (or its absence) allowed social climbing (or descending) of individuals and their families. The family aspect came in to explain the longevity of social rise (and decline). Individuals who had proven their prowess at arms would first rise within their class, and only with time would their family join the ranks of a higher social stratum. The concept of the family is thus used to assuage the divergence between class position and capability that—in his words—is often observed (CSD, 204).

Hence, classes can erect barriers to entry for outsiders, but these barriers are permeable (Schumpeter 1955). This results from the fact that new blood needs to be infused into the leading ranks of society in order for them to sustain their position. Within classes, families rise and fall. This applies to feudalism and (especially) to capitalism, where it generally only takes three generations from shirt sleeves to shirt sleeves. Schumpeter's position is clearly anti-Marxian when he points out that change in general does not benefit the establishment, but—in contrast—opens up opportunities for everyone, irrespective of former class position (Schumpeter 1955, 118).

We can, therefore, conclude that Schumpeter saw social and economic inequalities as the result of differences in ability and willpower. Societies, however, differ with respect to the qualities they value most. These can range from military prowess to political proficiency and to entrepreneurship. Every society will, therefore, promote those persons who possess the capabilities that are held in highest esteem.

A few comments can be made regarding Schumpeter's theory of social classes. His idea that social classes act as brakes on social mobility seems fully applicable to feudal times, in which ascent into knighthood was a lengthy process. However, its relevance for capitalism seems questionable. His business cycle theory implies that innovations will be introduced at regular intervals. Only basic innovations, engendering Kondratieff waves of 55-years length would cause a two-generational social rise. The Juglar waves, spanning only 8 years, would require an uninterrupted series of entrepreneurial successes by members of one family.

His grand historical scheme implied that every society required a ruling stratum. Professional politicians were needed to fill the political vacuum that had emerged after the defending walls put up by the aristocracy had crumbled. Those politicians would resemble the knights and aristocrats of earlier times, who were not hesitant in grasping and using power. Democratic leadership required persuasive skills, instead of mere physical power. Selection in corporate industry already helped people possessing such skills to rise. "In corporate industry it is necessary to woo support, to negotiate with and handle men with consummate skill" (Schumpeter 1955, 123). The bourgeoisie, however, were never able to convince people of the beneficial nature of capitalist rule. The political scene favorable to unfettered capitalism was, therefore, only of short duration.

"The feudal master class was once—and the bourgeoisie was never—the supreme pinnacle of a uniformly constructed social pyramid. The feudal lord was once lord and master in every sphere of life. It was not only the sole possessor of physical power; it was physical power incarnate" (Schumpeter 1955, 153).

Schumpeter's political theory hinges on the idea that politicians constitute a distinct class. Consequently, politics needs to provide career opportunities that span more than one lifetime. The concept of the professional politician is not devoid of realism, although recurrent elections can break off a political career. It seems rather far-fetched to assume, however, that politics constitutes a multigenerational family affair. The ballot box is a mechanism that would make such a series of successes rather unlikely. Hence, in accordance with the chances of a string of entrepreneurial successes, the odds seem against longevity of familial political power.

Schumpeter's analysis of competitive capitalism seems surely inspired by his admiration for its economic achievements. His historical view, however, is strictly positivistic. He only wants to predict future events, instead of trying to persuade people to change course. His sympathies might have wavered between the aristocrat/diplomat and the creative entrepreneur. He started out as a theoretician of capitalism, emphasizing its virtues. Later he turned into a detached observer of things political and economic who was careful not to mingle personal preferences with theory.

Schumpeterian Selection of Entrepreneurs

Schumpeter's positive opinion of the innovative performance of socialism is based on his expectation that the central economic authority will not hesitate to introduce new production functions, when they are available. Hence, planned economic progress can outperform unplanned economic progress, because it is not inhibited by former investment (CSD, 195). Selection of innovation does not pose problems, because entrepreneurial quality is easily observable.

Innovation is the sole source of profit (and interest) in competitive capitalist society. Ultimately, innovators in competitive capitalism are selected and rewarded by the market, but only after potential innovators have passed the test imposed on them by the financial markets. Bankers decide on the granting of credit, and they are thus the selectors in competitive capitalism. Bankers grant credit to those projects whose expected revenues exceed their costs. These expectations are largely shaped by the state of economy. Both inflation and deflation dampen expected profits to the extent that no innovative credit is supplied at all. These assumptions are central to Schumpeter's contention, that innovative credit will only be provided in situations of (Walrasian) equilibrium. A situation of inflation will refrain bankers from investing, because it favors incumbents (old debtors). Periods of deflation, on the other hand, will depress investment of any sort, but will stimulate consumption spending (nominal wages are assumed rigid over the whole business cycle).

Hence, only at certain points in time can bankers be induced to furnish entrepreneurs with credit. Schumpeter's position can be criticized for its waste of entrepreneurial talent. Because entrepreneurs can only obtain credit at certain points in time, entrepreneurial talent is only partly utilized.

In Schumpeter's first model of the business cycle, bankers are assumed to be gifted with perfect foresight, so that no selection errors are made. The second approximation allows for selection errors, but these entail purely negative consequences. Excessive credit creation entails excessive inflation and, accordingly, excessive deflation in the downturn of the business cycle. The economy may then fail to reach its equilibrium position and fall prey to depression. An additional recovery phase is then required in order to restore profits before a new round of innovations can appear.

Hence, Schumpeter's view on selection is clearly biased toward the negative effects of too lax a selection, whereas the potentially negative effects of too harsh a selection are ignored. Entrepreneurial talent is always abundantly available, but the economy cannot absorb this entrepreneurial talent at a continuous rate. Consequently, potential entrepreneurs will be frustrated most of the time, so that socialism might easily outperform it.

Capitalism requires (equally spaced) intervals between bursts of innovative investment, because physical capital goods cannot be replaced immediately. Novelty can, therefore, only be absorbed gradually. Otherwise, the costs of progress—creative destruction—will exceed the benefits of increased productivity. Innovation reduces the economic lifespan of capital goods and so spurs investment spending. The rate of obsolescence is, however, curtailed by the need for total profits and losses to balance in time. Entrepreneurial investment triggers inflation, which reduces real wages. These painful processes of forced saving and creative destruction are, however, distributed over the whole length of a business cycle, which can span 8 or even 50 years, depending on the importance of the innovation.

Schumpeter's theory differs from that of Böhm-Bawerk and other Austrian theorists on the subject, who put waiting—or the degree of roundaboutness of production—central.

The Vanishing of Depressions

Schumpeter was of the opinion that increased knowledge of the business cycle would eventually even out cyclical fluctuations. Recurrent waves of prosperity and recession feature prominently in his analysis of competitive capitalism. Investments expand in prosperity at the expense of consumption expenditures, whereas the reverse occurs during recession. Net investments—and profits—revolve around a zero mean; the zero-profit Walrasian equilibrium. Net profits occur during prosperity, whereas business incurs net losses during recession. The process of creative destruction is then at work at its fullest force. Only the innovative firms are profitable in recession. Noninnovative incumbents are forced to disappear from the scene. Consequently, profits and losses will exactly balance over the full length of the business cycle.

Depression, in Schumpeter's view, is the result of overinvestment spending during prosperity, which then entails excessive deflation in the downward phase. This causes the disappearance of otherwise healthy firms. Depression prompts an additional recovery phase to compensate for the losses incurred during depression.

In Schumpeter's view, trustification raises overall profitability and curbs losses. This makes trustified capitalism less susceptible to business cycles than its competitive capitalist counterpart.

> We all know the characteristics of former crisis, f.i. that of 1873: the dramatic panics, the blindfolded destruction of both good and bad firms, situations that seemed to contemporaries both incomprehensible and hopeless, and the desperateness of the central bankers. All these phenomena do not hardly occur anymore. The working of the capitalist machine are better understood. The banks are aware of the nature and scope of their duties, and the leaders of the banking community do not lose their head that easily anymore.
>
> Prospective depressions are bound to lose their sharpness and risk for two reasons: firstly because of the concentration movement in manufacturing and banking, by which economic life is ever more subjugated to the power of the large corporations, that are so strong, that no depression can imperil their existence, so that their investment policy will become in-

dependent from actual economic situations. Second, did we, as is known, make good progress in obtaining such a precise knowledge of the business cycle, and obtaining such detailed meteorology, that the most common business man can avoid errors that derive from the general economic situation in the near future. For this reason, almost anything that appears evil about business cycles will be neutralized. (Schumpeter 1925, 575)

Schumpeter thus held the view that increased predictability of the course of economic events could attenuate business cycles.

This view, which was presented in the 1920s, was not shocked by the severeness of the depression of the 1930s. In contrast, this depression, and especially the policies it evoked, strengthened his belief that capitalism had become more and more untenable, not for economic, but for political reasons. He blamed wrongly conceived policies—protectionism and the New Deal—for the deepness of the depression.

But Schumpeter's position on business cycles is fraught with difficulties. If mere knowledge of business cycles can prevent their occurrence, the quality of the theory, and not the prevailing economic order, is decisive in forestalling them.

Moreover, we can doubt whether a better understanding of business cycles can ever cause their disappearance. A correct understanding of business cycles implies that they can be anticipated and warded off by countercyclical policies. Consequently, business cycles will never emerge, according to prediction, and no business cycle theory can ever be borne out by the facts. From this point of view all theories of business cycles are incorrect, because they can never be corroborated.

This was the position of F. H. Knight, who pointed out that irregularity and unpredictability of business cycles lie at the heart of cyclical profits (and losses). All efforts to depict regular business cycles are in vain, according to Knight. "If any of these changes take place regularly, whether progressively or periodically or according to whatever known law, their consequences in the price system and the economic organization can be briefly disposed of" (Knight 1921, 147–48). This conclusion obviously spells disaster for all theories of business cycles, including Schumpeter's.

Knight's position on business cycles echoes his more elaborate theory on the causes of profits and losses, in which uncertainty is put central. All profits and losses that are predictable will vanish before they can emerge because competitors will pour in and desiccate profit flows.

Schumpeter and Knight on Entrepreneurial Profits

Schumpeter's theory is diametrically opposed to Knight's theory of innovation and entrepreneurship, which puts the unpredictability of economic outcomes—with respect to the state of both the whole economy and individual ventures—central to his explanation of profits (and losses). Average (excess) profitability—in his view—did not need to be positive. Investment could occur in the absence of excess profits, if individual ventures were expected to be profitable.

It was previously noted that Schumpeter's assumption of business cycles of a fixed periodicity runs counter to this essential uncertain character of competitive market economies and its capacity to generate unexpected profits and losses. Arguably, if incumbents know that their capital goods will become obsolete after 8 or 50 years, they will refrain from investing in capital goods that endure beyond that length of time.

The same line of argument can be applied to Schumpeter's hypothesis on entrepreneurial selection. If the quality of a potential entrepreneur can be easily observed by bankers, profits will disappear before the event. Competition among bankers will then erode prospective returns on investment. Schumpeter's theory is rather ambiguous on this point. Bankers—in his view—are rewarded by interest payments, an idea that is compatible with his view that investors run no risks. Entrepreneurs pay interest out of innovative profits. Schumpeterian entrepreneurs are also not exposed to risk or uncertainty. Their profits (over interest payments) can be seen as a premium collected for quality. If quality does not differ among those chosen for entrepreneurship, all entrepreneurs will be equally profitable. However, this would imply that the supply of entrepreneurship is limited, which runs counter to his idea that entrepreneurship is amply available and has been queuing up for a number of years. Schumpeterian entrepreneurs can reap profits exceeding interest payments, due to the losses inflicted on incumbents. Average profitability will equal the interest rate, if profits and losses exactly balance.

Schumpeter's theory can be described as a theory without errors and consequently without entrepreneurial losses. This is diametrically opposed to Knight's view of the matter. He—in accordance with his theory on business cycles—emphasizes that profits can only result from uncertainty. Knight argues that capabilities of potential entrepreneurs are not clearly discernible. Selection of innovative projects is, therefore, essentially an uncertain affair and only above-average perceptive investors can earn rents, whereas others will run into losses. Hence, only investors whose judgment is superior to that of their peers can earn (excess) profits.

Knight holds the view that average profitability is determined by the balance of power between capital and labor (Knight 1921, 283). He also contends that average profitability equals the interest rate (Knight 1934, 262). This leads to the unorthodox conclusion that the balance of power between capital and labor determines the (real) interest rate.

It seems straightforward, in a Schumpeterian world, that bankers are only rewarded by interest payments. Entrepreneurial quality is easily observable and does not deserve excess profits. Why entrepreneurs should get a premium for quality is questionable, as previously indicated.

In Knight's theory only the investor qualifies as an entrepreneur, because only he is subject to uncertainty. This reduces the Schumpeterian entrepreneur to a manager who is rewarded by wage payments. The transition to socialism seems easier to achieve in a Schumpeterian world than in a Knightian world. Easily observable quality will turn entrepreneurs into managers, which does not violate the core of his theory. Knight's theory, however, presumes competition among investors, which seems much harder to realize under socialism. Moreover, many investors will lose out on their projects, so that capital is constantly reallocated among sectors and firms.

The capitalist rules of the game—according to Knight—imply that the tipped winner can succeed, but he will generate no profits to the investors, who, in a herdlike manner, run to provide him with capital. If everybody places his bets on the same person, nobody can win. Perfect foresight will thus eliminate profits. Success can only accrue to those who play the game, but not all who partake can win. Only those managers (and projects) that are relatively undervalued can generate (excess) profits. Profits thus only accrue to those investors who can see capability where others do not. Hence, investment thrives on unexpected capability, which prevents the prices of production factors from being bidden up to their "true" value. Knight's theory, therefore, has interesting implications for the division of profits between managers and investors. If managerial qualities are easily discernible, profits will be fully appropriated by managers. Schumpeter's position that bankers are rewarded by interest payments does fit into this theoretical framework. Both Knight and Schumpeter agree on the importance of capability as a source of profits.

However, in Knight's view it is above-average capability *of a chosen set of entrepreneurs* that matters. If overall capability of the chosen set increases, average efficiency gains from innovative investment will also increase, but average profitability can either increase or decline. This will depend on the rashness or timidity of entrepreneurs as a class, which determines average profitability. Profits need to equal losses, if average (excess) profitability amounts to zero. Hence, in Knight's theory entrepreneurs can incur both profits and losses.

Knightian competition occurs between entrepreneurs, whereas Schumpeterian competition involves a redistribution of profits between innovative and noninnovative firms. Knight ignores the hindering effect of former investment. This can be explained by his present-value approach to investment spending, which excludes competition between investments of various vintages.

Knight agrees with Schumpeter on the issue of the beneficial effect of increasing firm size. Large corporations can mitigate uncertainty, because they can invest in a variety of ventures. This investment portfolio enables them to absorb losses without risking bankruptcy.

Knight's theory of entrepreneurial profits thus points at an idea overlooked by Schumpeter. In Knight's theory, capability cannot prevent failure, as Schumpeter has assumed. Knightian uncertainty does not need a theory of classes to signal expected quality. If uncertainty can be so reduced, it will also affect profitability. My interpretation of Knight makes me, therefore, conclude that improved selection of entrepreneurs might enhance efficiency, but not profitability.

Knight's theory of social mobility is not so much a question of quality, but of under- and overvaluation. Investors benefit (or suffer) from their judgments on future profits of a variety of ventures. In Schumpeter's view, social mobility is determined by quality and by timing. Knight's profit theory seems superior due to its greater realism with respect to investment selection. His theory lacks an explanation of the spacing of investment in time, however, which Schumpeter put central in his analysis of creative destruction.

Schumpeter did not adhere to Austrian capital theory, since he denounced the increasing roundaboutness or waiting explanations of interest. Capital intensity is constant over the full length of the business cycle and the interest rate is determined by profitability and not by waiting, in his scheme.

Knight is a fierce critic of Austrian capital theory. He contends that all investment projects whose discounted present value exceed investment outlays will be carried through (Knight 1934). The durability of capital goods will depend on their expected economic lifespan. Hence, more will be invested if the revenue stream is expected to be of relatively long duration. Sticking to our interpretation of Knight's uncertainty principle as generating a distribution of profits and losses grouped around a mean (the interest rate), we can conclude that those investment projects whose actual lifespan exceeds expectations will be profitable (and vice versa).

Conclusion

Schumpeter's theories of economic and social evolution are interrelated. Only those people who are most capable will attain both political and economic power. The type of capability that is rewarded differs from one society to another. Feudalism rewarded warrior capacity, whereas capitalism rewards entrepreneurial talents. The warrior function became obsolete in time and the same happened to entrepreneurial capacity. The entrepreneurial era was extraordinarily brief, due to the bourgeoisie's lack of interest and talent for politics. Instead, professional politicians appropriated the political realm.

Politicians delegate the management of the economy to bureaucrats, which—in Schumpeter's view—will inevitably lead to socialism. Socialism can work and innovation can continue unhampered, as long as bureaucracies are allowed to set their own professional codes.

This, however, ignores the uncertainty inherent in innovative investment. Quality as such will never generate excess profits, as we may conclude from Knight. Only above-average perceptiveness can achieve this. Knightian entrepreneurial profits are dispersed around a mean, which is determined by the strength of capitalists as a class.

Schumpeter's theory of profits is related to his theory of social classes and social mobility. His position, however, differs from that of Knight in several respects. Both authors see innovative investment as the main carrier of mobility, but Schumpeter views entrepreneurial income as the result of capability, whereas Knight's theory points at the discrepancy between perceived and proven/signaled capability as the source of profits.

REFERENCES

Heertje, A., ed. 1983. *Schumpeter's Vision: Capitalism Socialism and Democracy after 40 years*. London: Praeger Publications.
Knight, F. H. 1921. *Risk, Uncertainty and Profit*. Reprint, New York: Augustus M. Kelley, Bookseller, 1964.
Knight, F. H. 1934. Capital, Time and the Interest Rate. *Economica* 1 (August): 257–86.
Schumpeter, J. A. 1925. Oude en Nieuwe Bankpolitiek. *Economisch Statistische Berichten*. July 1 (pp. 552–554); July 8 (pp. 574–577); July 15 (pp. 600–601).
Schumpeter, J. A. 1928. The Instability of Capitalism. *Economic Journal,* 38, no. 151 (Sept.): 361–86.
Schumpeter, J. A. 1954. *History of Economic Analysis*. New York: Oxford University Press.
Schumpeter, J. A. 1955. *Imperialism and Social Classes: Two Essays*. Edited by Bert Hoselitz. New York: Meridan Books.
Schumpeter, J. A. 1974. *Capitalism, Socialism and Democracy,* 13th ed. London: Unwin University Books.

Schumpeterian Growth Theory: An Overview

Elias Dinopoulos

Since the early 1990s, several studies have provided an elegant formalization of economic growth through creative destruction. The Schumpeterian features of the new theory are presented, and a basic formal model is developed to highlight its analytical structure. The implications of Schumpeterian growth theory are briefly discussed.

Introduction

The traditional theory of growth, pioneered by Solow (1956), which focused on economic expansion caused by exogenous population growth, has come under increasing scrutiny. Its main implication that policy cannot affect long-run growth rates was at odds with recent country experiences. Under the heading of endogenous growth, new approaches to growth theory have emerged. These approaches have brought technological progress to the center of growth theory and have demonstrated how economic policies can affect long-run growth. The impact of the new theories has been profound. The concept of growth, as well as the theory of growth, have undergone a permanent transformation. *Economic expansion* might be a better term for the type of growth that neoclassical theory has analyzed for the last 35 years. *Economic progress* can characterize the component of growth that is based on endogenous technological change.[1] The present chapter is concerned with Schumpeterian growth theory, which has formalized Schumpeter's (1942) insights into endogenous technological change that in turn leads to economic progress.

This paper was prepared for a lecture at Osaka City University in September 1993. An earlier version of the paper was originally published in *Osaka City University Economic Review* 29:1–21, January 1994. I would like to thank Patrick Conway, James Oehmke, Paul Pecorino, Costas Syropoulos, Paul Segerstrom, Peter Thompson, Doug Waldo, two anonymous referees, and participants in seminars at the University of Florida and Osaka City University for useful comments and suggestions.

1. Schumpeter (1928) has used this terminology and emphasized the distinction between economic expansion caused by accumulation of factors of production and economic progress, which is based on endogenous technological change.

If, in fact, Schumpeterian growth theory formalizes Schumpeter's description of technological progress, why did it take so long to develop? One answer to this question is that the analytical tools that were necessary for the development of the new theory only became available in the mid-1980s. It was not until the 1970s that dynamic game theory and industrial organization developed analytical tools for the study of dynamic imperfect competition.[2] In the early 1980s, trade theorists pioneered in the development of general equilibrium models with imperfect competition that examined issues related to patterns of trade.[3] The next important step was taken by Romer (1986, 1990), who constructed models based on dynamic imperfect competition and focused on technological externalities as a mechanism of economic growth. Other studies quickly followed and identified a variety of endogenous growth patterns. Lucas (1988) developed a model where human capital accumulation and external economies provide the engine of growth. Young (1991) analyzed learning-by-doing mechanisms of endogenous growth. Grossman and Helpman (1991), Feenstra (1996), and Rivera-Batiz and Romer (1991), among others, analyzed endogenous growth through the accumulation of new varieties of goods.

The development of Schumpeterian growth theory started with two studies. Segerstrom, Anant, and Dinopoulos 1990 was the first study to model the process of Schumpeterian growth in a dynamic general equilibrium model of North-South trade. This study modeled sequential innovation races that resulted in growth through product quality improvements. New products replaced old ones and were imitated after an exogenous imitation lag. Aghion and Howitt (1990) developed a closed-economy model of Schumpeterian growth based on stochastic R&D races that resulted in process innovation. New and better intermediate products endogenously replaced old ones. These two studies have been extended and generalized in several important dimensions.[4]

The next section of this chapter makes an attempt to identify the Schumpeterian characteristics of what Cheng and Dinopoulos (1992) and Romer (1994) have called the neo-Schumpeterian approach to growth. The third section develops a simple model of Schumpeterian growth. The fourth section presents an overview of the implications of the new theory for international

---

2. Reinganum (1989) provides an excellent survey of the industrial organization literature on innovation.

3. Krugman (1979a, 1979b) developed general equilibrium models of the product cycle and of monopolistic competition and intraindustry trade. Eithier (1982) analyzed issues of external scale economies and international trade.

4. The fourth section of this chapter presents the contributions of other Schumpeterian growth studies. For a recent survey of Schumpeterian growth models, see Aghion and Howitt 1993.

economics, macroeconomics, and empirical research. The final section presents my conclusions.

Growth through the Process of Creative Destruction

Schumpeter described the mechanics of economic progress (i.e., growth) in detail in two studies: "The Instability of Capitalism" (1928) and *Capitalism, Socialism and Democracy* (1942). Instead of stating the basic features of creative destruction, let me present Schumpeter's thoughts through his own words

> Economic progress, in capitalist society, means turmoil. And, . . . in this turmoil competition works in a manner completely different from the way it would work in a stationary process, however perfectly competitive. Possibilities of gains to be reaped by producing old things more cheaply are constantly materializing and calling for new investments. These new products and new methods compete with the old methods not on equal terms but at a decisive advantage that may mean death to the latter. This is how "progress" comes about in capitalist society. (Schumpeter 1942, p. 32)

> The introduction of new methods of production and the new commodities is hardly conceivable with perfect competition from the start. And this means that the bulk of what we call economic progress is incompatible with it. As a matter of fact, perfect competition is and always has been temporarily suspended whenever anything new is being introduced. (Schumpeter 1942, p. 105)

> What we, unscientifically, call economic progress means essentially putting productive resources to uses hitherto untried in practice, and withdrawing them from the uses they have served so far. This is what we call "innovation." (Schumpeter 1928, p. 64)

> Successful innovation is, as said before, a task suis generis. It is a feat not of intellect, but of will. Its difficulty consisting in the resistances and uncertainties incident to doing what has not been done before, it is accessible for, and appeals to, only a distinct type which is rare. . . . It is this entrepreneur's profit which is the primary source of industrial fortunes, the history of every one of which consists of, or leads back to, successful acts of innovation. And as the rise and decay of industrial fortunes is the essential fact about the social structure of capitalist society, both the emergence of what is, in any single instance, as essentially temporary gain, and the elimination of it by the working of the competi-

tive mechanism, obviously are more than "frictional" phenomena, as is that process of underselling by which industrial progress comes about in capitalist society and by which its achievements result in higher incomes all around. (Schumpeter 1928, pp. 66–67)

Segerstrom, Anant, and Dinopoulos (1990) and Aghion and Howitt (1990) developed the first two models of Schumpeterian growth, which captured three main features of the process of creative destruction. First, both studies built models using a dynamic general-equilibrium framework. Second, product obsolescence based on quality improvements, coupled with imperfect competition, formalized Schumpeter's notion of temporary market power. Third, R&D races were used to capture the entrepreneurial risk and uncertainty that are inherent in the process of innovation. These three features constituted the skeleton of all subsequent Schumpeterian growth studies.

I would like to emphasize that the new theory does not claim exclusive rights to all of Schumpeter's thoughts. Indeed, several normative implications of the new theory do not always coincide with views advocated by Schumpeter. However, this theory is closer to Schumpeter's notion of creative destruction than any other existing approach to economic growth.

A Simple Model of Schumpeterian Growth

This section develops a simple closed-economy model of Schumpeterian growth by combining the taste structure of Segerstrom, Anant, and Dinopoulos (1990) with the R&D structure of Aghion and Howitt (1990). The analysis in this section follows the spirit of Grossman and Helpman (1991, chap. 4), who integrated the two original studies.[5] There is only one final good, whose quality can be improved through the introduction of better products. Labor is the only factor of production; it is supplied inelastically and the aggregate endowment of labor is fixed over time. In other words, unlike the neoclassical growth model, there is no population growth in this model. Labor can be allocated between two economic activities, manufacturing of the high-quality goods and R&D services that are used to discover new products of higher quality. There is instantaneous free mobility of labor between manufacturing and R&D services, which ensures that the wage rate is equalized across the two activities. For simplicity of exposition and notation, I assume that one unit of labor can produce either one unit of manufacturing output or one unit

---

5. The basic model differs from the "quality ladders" model developed by Grossman and Helpman in at least two important aspects. First, it abstracts from the continuum of industries framework. Second, it introduces instantaneous diminishing returns to R&D. The first feature enhances the intuitive understanding of the theory and allows me to focus on how financial markets deal with aggregate uncertainty. The second feature has implications for the welfare properties of the model that differ from the original "quality ladders" model.

of R&D services. Using labor as the numeraire, I can normalize the wage rate to unity.

The process of endogenous innovation is modeled through stochastic and sequential R&D races. Individual firms hire labor that performs R&D services. By devoting more resources to R&D, each firm participating in a race increases the probability of discovering the next higher-quality product. The sole winner of each R&D race enjoys temporary market power until it is replaced by the firm that wins the next R&D race. The arrival of innovations follows a Poisson process whose intensity depends on resources devoted to R&D. The random time intervals between innovations, which follow the exponential distribution, serve as market-determined "patents" for the winners of R&D races. This formalization of Schumpeterian innovation has two desirable features: It captures the risk associated with discovering new goods and it formalizes the notion that increasing resources devoted to R&D shortens the expected time between innovations, which results in higher Schumpeterian growth.

R&D investment is financed through consumer savings. Consumers allocate their income between consumption and savings by maximizing their discounted lifetime utility. There is a stock market that channels consumer savings to firms engaged in R&D activities. The instantaneous interest rate clears the stock market at each instant in time.

The preference structure of the model is captured by the following standard intertemporal utility function of the representative consumer

$$U = \int_0^\infty e^{-\rho t} \ln [z(\cdot)] dt \tag{1}$$

where $\rho > 0$ is the consumer's subjective discount rate and $z(\cdot)$ is a subutility function that takes the following form:

$$z(x_0, x_1, x_2, \dots) = \sum_{q=0}^\infty \alpha^q x_q, \quad \alpha > 1. \tag{2}$$

The subutility function (2) introduces product obsolescence, which is essential for Schumpeterian growth. In this economy, there is a countably infinite set of products $\{x_0, x_1, x_2, \dots\}$. The parameter $\alpha > 1$ captures the degree of quality improvement of a product relative to its immediate predecessor. The functional form of $z(\cdot)$ implies that products are perfect substitutes.

To illustrate the product replacement mechanism embodied in (2), assume for the time being that each product is priced at marginal costs. At time zero, the economy starts with good x_0, because the rest have not yet been discovered. The consumer maximizes $z(x_0, 0, 0, \ldots) = x_0$. When good x_1 is discovered, the consumer maximizes $z(x_0, x_1, 0, \ldots) = x_0 + \alpha x_1$. If both goods command the price of unity, then no consumer buys good x_0: one unit of good x_1 gives $\alpha > 1$ units of utility, whereas one unit of good x_0 gives only one unit of utility. The endogenous substitution of higher quality products for lower quality ones allows the economy to shift resources from old uses to new ones. Unless the new products are better than the old ones, growth cannot be sustained in the long run.[6]

The above reasoning can be readily applied to the case of goods x_q and x_{q-1}. Because goods are perfect substitutes, consumers allocate their consumption expenditure E on a single good. Thus $x_q = E/p_q$ and $x_{q-1} = E_{q-1}/p_{q-1}$, where p_q and p_{q-1} are prices of goods x_q and x_{q-1}, respectively. Consumers switch to good x_q from x_{q-1} if $z(0, \ldots, x_q, 0 \ldots) > z(0, \ldots, x_{q-1}, 0, \ldots)$. Substituting x_q and x_{q-1} into (2) we obtain the following product replacement condition:

$$\alpha p_{q-1} > p_q. \tag{3}$$

Thus, the price of the state-of-the-art quality product cannot exceed the price of its immediate predecessor times the quality increment α. I will assume that even if (3) holds as an equality, each consumer switches her expenditure to the higher quality product, although formally she is indifferent.

Innovation, which results in higher-quality products, is modeled through sequential R&D races. Denote with L the aggregate amount of labor devoted to an arbitrary R&D race. Then $\mu(L)dt = L^\gamma dt$ is the probability that if the next higher-quality product has not been discovered at time t, it will be discovered at time $(t + dt)$, where dt is an infinitesimal increment of time. The returns to R&D races are assumed to be independently distributed over time. The parameter $0 < \gamma \leq 1$ captures the degree of instantaneous diminishing returns to R&D.[7] In the balanced-growth equilibrium, the duration of each innovation race is exponentially distributed. This implies that the expected

---

6. Stokey (1988) has an excellent discussion of the importance of obsolescence in models of growth through the introduction of new goods.

7. The standard argument for constant returns of scale, which is based on replication of plants, does not apply to R&D. Replicating an R&D plant creates the possibility of duplicating the effort of the existing plant. Strong diminishing returns to R&D investment are required for sensible comparative steady-state analysis in Schumpeterian growth models with a continuum of industries and linear manufacturing technology. Over time, each R&D race is characterized by a common pool problem that arises from the "winner takes all" assumption. This property implies diminishing returns to R&D investment because when a firm increases its R&D investment, the aggregate hazard rate increases and every firm in the race faces a shorter expected duration. When γ is strictly less than unity, there is also a similar common pool property across rivals at each instant in time, which captures possible interdependencies of R&D strategies. Instantaneous diminishing returns to R&D can be generated by industry-specific factors. Houser (1994) and Segerstrom (1995) provide more details on issues related to diminishing returns to R&D.

time of innovation arrival becomes shorter with the more resources devoted to R&D.[8]

The preceding paragraphs described the structure of tastes and technology of the model. I will concentrate on the balanced-growth equilibrium, defined as the equilibrium path in which the allocation of resources remains constant over time. Consider the product market first. The winner of an R&D race becomes the only firm that knows how to produce the state-of-the-art quality product. The demand for that product is

$$
x_q = \begin{cases} \dfrac{E}{p_q} & \text{if } p_q \leq \alpha \\[2mm] 0 & \text{if } p_q > \alpha \end{cases}
\tag{4}
$$

where E is consumer expenditure and p_q is the price of good x_q. Because product x_q is competing with product x_{q-1}, condition (3) implies that the producer of x_q can charge at most a price that is α times the marginal costs (equal to unity by assumption) of its closest competitor.

The maximum instantaneous profit for the winner of an R&D race is

$$
\pi = (p_q - 1)\frac{E}{p_q} = \frac{(\alpha - 1)}{\alpha} E ,
\tag{5}
$$

where $p_q = \alpha$ is the maximum price that drives the immediate predecessor out of business.

Let $\mu_j dt$ be firm j's instantaneous probability of discovering the next higher quality product. Then $\mu(L)dt = (\Sigma_j \mu_j)dt = L^\gamma dt$ is the aggregate probability of success. Let L_j be the amount of labor firm j devotes to an R&D race. Then $L = \Sigma_j L_j$ is the aggregate amount of labor in R&D. Assume that each firm participating in a race behaves competitively and treats the aggregate labor in R&D as given when it chooses its own R&D labor level. Assume also that $\mu_j/\mu = L_j/L$, which states that firm j's relative instantaneous probability of success equals its share of R&D resources. These assumptions imply that firm j's instantaneous probability of success is $\mu_j dt$, where $\mu_j = L_j \mu/L = L_j L^{\gamma-1}$.

Denote with $V(t)$ the expected discounted profits of a *successful* innovator, which serves as a reward to R&D investment. The expected discounted profits of a typical firm j in an R&D race are

$$
VL_j L^{\gamma-1}dt - L_j dt.
\tag{6}
$$

---

8. The arrival of innovations is governed by a Poisson process with parameter $\mu(L)$. The interarrival time of innovations is exponentially distributed with mean $1/\mu(L)$ and variance $1/[\mu(L)]^2$. The expected number of innovations from time zero to time t equals $\mu(L)t$, which equals the variance of the number of innovations as well. Taylor and Karlin (1984, chap. 5) provide an exposition of the Poisson process.

Firm j earns V with instantaneous probability $L_j L^{\gamma-1} dt$ and incurs L_j costs (the wage of labor serves as the numeraire) for a time interval dt. Each firm in the race is infinitesimally small, and chooses L_j to maximize equation (6), taking L as given. Thus there are constant returns to scale in L_j for each individual firm, but decreasing returns to scale for the industry as a whole. Following the Schumpeterian growth literature, assume that there is free entry into each R&D race, which implies that equation (6) becomes zero

$$V(t) = L^{1-\gamma}. \tag{7}$$

The free-entry condition renders the size of each firm L_j indeterminate, but establishes a positive relationship between the reward to innovation, $V(t)$, and the aggregate amount of resources devoted to innovation, L.[9]

The next step is to establish a relationship between $V(t)$ and π. Following Segerstrom, Anant, and Dinopoulos 1990, let me introduce the stock market, which plays a pivotal role in financing the R&D investment. Each firm participating in an R&D race does not earn any revenues for the duration of the race, and each needs to borrow in order to pay its R&D workers. At each instant in time, each firm issues a risky Arrow-Debreu security that pays the flow of monopoly profits if the firm wins the race instantaneously and pays zero otherwise. Although from the point of view of each firm there is uncertainty, from the point of view of the economy, firm-level risk remains idiosyncratic. The representative consumer knows that there is a single firm that earns profits, π, and that there are many firms engaged in R&D to discover a better product. If a new product is discovered, only the *identity* of the firm earning profits changes, and nothing else.[10] Because the utility function is logarithmic and the uncertainty is industry-specific, there exists monetary separation in portfolio allocation.[11] Thus, it is possible to construct many mutual funds, each of which yields the same return, $r(t)$, in every state of nature, with $r(t)$ remaining constant over time.

For simplicity of exposition, let me construct an economy-wide (industry-specific) mutual fund with a riskless rate of return. At each instant in time, the mutual fund manager lends L amount of dollars, which cover the R&D

---

9. Consider the case of $\gamma = 1$, which corresponds to constant returns of scale in R&D in the presence of linear R&D costs. Condition (6) becomes $(V - 1)L_j dt$, and implies that each firm has an incentive to engage in infinite R&D if $V > 1$ and in zero R&D if $V < 1$. Segerstrom (1995) has shown that in the case of $\gamma = 1$ and in a continuum of industries framework, the unique symmetric steady-state equilibrium with $L > 0$ is unstable, and all stable equilibria result in a no-growth trap. Diminishing returns to R&D resolve this type of instability problem.

10. Cheng and Dinopoulos (1993) have analyzed a similar model using stochastic optimal control techniques to deal with aggregate uncertainty. In the case of equal quality increments, the instantaneous interest rate $r(t)$ remains constant in the balanced growth equilibrium.

11. For more details on separation theorems, see Cass and Stiglitz 1970.

costs of *all* firms in the race. Because in the steady-state equilibrium one of these firms will discover the new good, the net income flow of this portfolio is $\pi - L$, which equals $r(t)\bar{N}A$, where A is per capita wealth. If and when an R&D race ends, the mutual fund manager finances the next R&D race. At the steady-state equilibrium, the net income flow, $\pi - L$, can be obtained with certainty and does not vary over time. The riskless rate of return, $r(t) = (\pi - L)/A\bar{N}$, is independent of which firm wins the race. Any mutual fund that invests in all firms engaged in R&D obtains the same rate of return as the economy-wide mutual fund.[12]

At each instant in time, there are two types of firms in the economy. The existing dominant firm and firms engaged in R&D to discover the next higher-quality product. Portfolio efficiency requires that the expected return to the security of the existing monopolist be equal to the riskless rate of return, which equals the instantaneous interest rate. Consider the stock market valuation of the firm that produces the state-of-the-art quality product. Over the time interval dt, the shareholder receives a dividend equal to $\pi(t)dt$ and the value of the firm appreciates by $\dot{V}(t)dt = (\partial V(t)/\partial t)dt$. Because the firm is targeted by other firms engaged in R&D to discover the next higher-quality product, this shareholder suffers a total capital loss of $V(t)$ if further innovation occurs. The latter event occurs with probability $\mu(L)dt = L^{\gamma}dt$, whereas the former event occurs with probability $1 - L^{\gamma}dt$. The shareholder could have earned the riskless rate of return $r(t)dt$, and it must be that

$$\frac{\pi(t)}{V(t)}\, dt + \frac{V(t)}{V(t)}\, (1 - L^{\gamma}dt)dt - \left\lfloor \frac{V(t) - 0}{V(t)} \right\rfloor L^{\gamma}dt = r(t)dt \,. \tag{8}$$

Taking the limit as dt goes to zero we obtain

$$\frac{\dot{V}(t)}{V(t)} + \frac{\pi(t)}{V(t)} = r(t) + L^{\gamma} \,. \tag{9}$$

Equation (9) states that, in the steady-state equilibrium where $\dot{V}(t) = 0$, the rate of return of a dollar invested in the existing monopolist exceeds the instantaneous interest rate by a risk factor that equals the probability that the monopolist will be replaced by the next innovator.

The next equilibrium condition is derived from the requirement that, at each instant in time, the amount of labor demanded by firms engaged in R&D

---

12. One can check the consistency of the above analysis by considering the GNP identity $E \equiv r(t)A\bar{N} + \bar{N}$, which states that aggregate consumption expenditure equals income from assets plus wages at the steady-state equilibrium. Substitute $r(t) = (\pi - L)/A\bar{N}$ to obtain $E \equiv \pi + (\bar{N} - L)$, which states that GNP equals aggregate profits plus manufacturing costs, which is the goods-market definition of GNP.

and the firm manufacturing the final good must equal the aggregate endowment of labor,

$$L + \frac{E}{\alpha} = \bar{N}, \tag{10}$$

where (E/α) is the quantity of a typical product produced and equals the number of workers engaged in manufacturing. $\bar{N}$ is the aggregate endowment of labor. Equation (10) is the resource constraint of the economy and defines a trade-off between consumption, E, and investment, L, at each instant in time.

The solution to the consumer intertemporal maximization problem determines the supply of savings. Denote with $C(t) = E(t)/\bar{N}$ the per capita consumption expenditure. Substituting $z(\cdot) = [\alpha^q C(t)/\alpha]$ into equation (1), I can express the consumer problem as

$$\max_{C(t)} \left\{ \int_0^\infty e^{-\rho t} \ln C(t) dt + \text{Exp} \int_0^\infty e^{-\mu}(q - 1) \ln \alpha \, dt \right\},$$

subject to $\dot{A}(t) = r(t)A(t) + 1 - C(t)$. The term Exp denotes the expectation operator, $A(t)$ stands for consumer assets, and $r(t)$ is the instantaneous interest rate. Because the second integral does not depend on consumption expenditure or assets, the consumer problem is equivalent to maximizing the first integral, subject to a differential equation describing the evolution of assets.

Since there is no aggregate risk, I can use standard optimal control techniques to solve the consumer problem. Define the current value Hamiltonian

$$H = \ln C(t) + \lambda(t)[r(t)A(t) + 1 - C(t)], \tag{11}$$

where $\lambda(t)$ is the multiplier. The necessary conditions for a maximum are

$$\frac{\partial H}{\partial C} = \frac{1}{C} - \lambda = 0, \tag{12a}$$

and

$$\dot{\lambda} = \rho\lambda - \frac{\partial H}{\partial A} = \rho\lambda - r(t)\lambda; \tag{12b}$$

equations (12a) and (12b) imply

$$\frac{\dot{C}}{C} = \frac{\dot{E}}{E} = r(t) - \rho. \tag{13}$$

In the balanced-growth equilibrium, consumption expenditure is constant over time and equation (13) implies that $r(t) = \rho$. In other words, the instantaneous interest rate equals the subjective discount rate.

Substituting $r(t) = \rho$, π from equation (5) and $V(t)$ from equation (7) into equation (9) with $\dot{V}(t) = 0$ we obtain the R&D equilibrium condition[13]

$$(\alpha - 1)E = \rho\alpha L^{1-\gamma} + \alpha L, \tag{14}$$

which defines a positive relationship between R&D investment L and consumption expenditure E. The resource constraint (10) and the R&D equilibrium condition (14) determine the market equilibrium values of L and E. Figure 1 illustrates the balanced-growth equilibrium in the R&D investment and consumption expenditure space. The full employment of labor condition (10) defines a negatively sloped line, NN, and equation (14) defines the positively sloped locus, OR, which starts at the origin. The intersection of the two curves at point A defines the unique market equilibrium values $\bar{E}$ and $\bar{L}$.

What are the properties of the balanced-growth equilibrium? The incumbent monopolist does not have any incentive to engage in R&D investment to discover the next higher-quality product. This result depends on the free-entry condition for each R&D race and on the absence of differences in the technology and costs of R&D between the incumbent and the challengers.[14] The values of R&D investment, consumption expenditure, and assets are all constant when measured in units of labor. New products are discovered through

---

13. Equation (14) can be derived by calculating the net expected benefits of winning an arbitrary race discounted to the beginning of the race, and setting the expression equal to zero because of free entry. See Cheng and Dinopoulos (1993) for this alternative methodology.

14. The argument for the absence of incentives for the incumbent to engage in further R&D can be summarized as follows: Suppose the incumbent were to win the next R&D race. This firm would be two quality levels above its immediate competitor and could have charged a price equal to α^2, earning an instantaneous flow of profits equal to $\pi' = [1 - 1/\alpha^2]E$, which is higher than $\pi = [1 - 1/\alpha]E$. However, a fraction of π' equal to π has to be paid as a dividend to investors who have financed the first of the two R&D races the incumbent won. Thus, the additional R&D investment by the incumbent has to be justified by the difference in profits, $\pi' - \pi = [1 - 1/\alpha](E/\alpha)$, this firm would make if it won the next R&D race. Each challenger, on the other hand, obtains profits π if it wins the next race and zero otherwise, and consequently the difference in profits is $\pi = [1 - 1/\alpha]E$, which exceeds $\pi' - \pi$. Thus, each challenger has an incentive to invest more in R&D than the incumbent firm, given symmetry in R&D technology and costs between challengers and the incumbent. Reinganum (1985, proposition 5) has shown this result under more general market-structure conditions than those of the present chapter. The free-entry condition in each R&D race implies that a challenger makes zero discounted expected profits. Consequently, an incumbent makes negative discounted expected profits if it engages in the next R&D race.

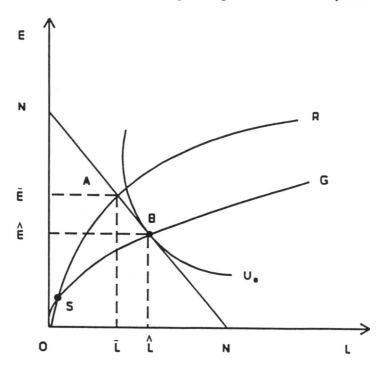

Fig. 1. Social optimum and market equilibrium

R&D races, old products are replaced by higher-quality ones, and firms are born and die. Temporary monopoly profits fuel innovation and technological progress. The arrival of new products is governed by a Poisson process whose intensity depends positively on R&D investment. The random time intervals between innovations are exponentially distributed.

There are no transitional dynamics in this simple model of Schumpeterian growth. At time zero the economy jumps immediately to point A in figure 1 because consumers choose E and firms choose L instantaneously. Thus, point A is the unique perfect foresight steady-state equilibrium consistent with optimizing behavior of consumers and firms. Dinopoulos (1994, appendix) provides a formal analysis of perfect foresight dynamics. This simple model captures all basic features of Schumpeterian growth through creative destruction: Firms chase temporary economic profits and face considerable uncertainty. In the meantime, every time a new product is discovered the utility of the representative consumer jumps by an increment equal to ln α.

I can obtain simple expressions of Schumpeterian growth and welfare by concentrating on the steady-state behavior of the economy. The indirect subutility at time t is given by $z(\cdot) = \alpha^q E/\alpha$, where $q(t)$ denotes the number of innovations between time zero (when the economy jumps to the steady-state equilibrium) and time t. Taking logarithms and denoting with $F(t,E) =$ Exp[ln (z)] the expected aggregate instantaneous utility at time t, I obtain $F(t,E) = \ln E - \ln \alpha + \ln \alpha$[Exp (q)] because aggregate expenditure is constant over time. The number of innovations is governed by a Poisson process with intensity L^γ, and therefore Exp$(q) = tL^\gamma$, and

$$F(t,E) = \ln E - \ln \alpha + tL^\gamma \ln \alpha. \tag{15}$$

The long-run Schumpeterian growth is defined as

$$g = \frac{dF(t, E)}{dt} = L^\gamma \ln \alpha, \tag{16}$$

which equals the expected growth rate of the quality weighted index of consumption. In other words, g is the expected growth rate of subutility $z(\cdot)$ defined in equation (2).

The expected growth rate of the economy increases in the quality increment, α, and in the amount of R&D investment, L, and decreases in the degree of instantaneous diminishing returns to R&D, which is related to γ. The dependence of the expected growth rate on R&D investment generates the endogenous growth feature of the model. A variety of policies (trade, investment, or consumption taxes) can alter the equilibrium level of R&D investment and long-run growth. Because the population in the economy is fixed, g represents the per capita expected long-run growth. Finally, notice that L^γ is the intensity of the Poisson process that governs the arrival of innovations. The higher the R&D investment, the higher the "frequency" of innovations per unit of time, and the lower the expected lifespan of each new product.

Comparative statics results can be obtained easily by totally differentiating equations (10) and (14), or by utilizing figure 1. An increase in $\bar{N}$ shifts the NN curve to the right, resulting in higher $\tilde{E}$ and $\tilde{L}$. An increase in $\bar{N}$ should be interpreted as an increase in market size and not as population growth. Larger economies experience higher growth rates and higher consumption per capita. More complicated versions of the simple model can demonstrate that international trade has a similar potential effect on long-run growth. Trade results in larger market size, which increases profits and R&D investment. An increase in α rotates both curves OR and NN clockwise and results in higher $\tilde{E}$ and $\tilde{L}$. Economies facing larger technological opportunities experience higher long-run growth. An increase in ρ rotates the OR curve counterclockwise without affecting curve NN. Economies that value the future less invest less and consume more. Finally, an increase in γ rotates the OR curve clockwise, resulting in higher investment and long-run growth and in lower consumption expenditure. The lower the degree of diminishing returns to R&D, the higher the level of Schumpeterian growth.

The above-mentioned comparative statics results are remarkably intuitive. However, the policy implications of the present model are more complicated. How does the market solution compare to the socially optimal one? Aghion and Howitt (1990) provide an excellent analysis and discussion of the nature of the distortions inherent in Schumpeterian growth models. The following discussion follows the spirit of their analysis.

Substituting equation (15) into equation (1), I obtain a simple expression for the expected welfare discounted to time zero

$$U = \int_0^\infty e^{-\rho t} F(t, E) \, dt$$

$$= \frac{1}{\rho} \left(\ln E - \ln \alpha + \frac{L^\gamma \ln \alpha}{\rho} \right).$$

(17)

Expression (17) was obtained under the assumption that each manufacturing firm charges a price equal to α. In principle, there are two ways of viewing the government's problem: The government can maximize equation (17) subject to the resource constraint (10). This approach confines the government to the use of instruments that alter the market incentives faced by firms. Following the analysis of existing Schumpeterian growth models, I will present the case of private R&D. Alternatively, the government can engage in R&D and finance it through lump-sum taxes. The present model allows the analysis of public R&D as well. Because in this case the government engages in marginal-cost pricing, the second term inside the parentheses in equation (17) becomes zero, and the resource constraint (10) becomes $\bar{N} = L + E$.

Because U is an increasing and concave function of consumption E and investment L, the solution to the government's problem can be obtained and illustrated with the use of welfare indifference curves. Totally differentiating equation (17) and setting $dU = 0$, I obtain $dE/dL = -(\gamma E \ln \alpha)/(\rho L^{1-\gamma}) < 0$, which states that welfare indifference curves are downward sloping and convex to the origin in the consumption-investment space. At the social optimum, the slope of an indifference curve equals the slope of the market resource constraint (10), which is $dE/dL = -\alpha$, and therefore I have

$$\frac{(\gamma \ln \alpha) \hat{E}}{\rho \hat{L}^{1-\gamma}} = \alpha.$$

(18)

Equations (18) and (10) determine the optimal consumption $\hat{E}$ and R&D investment $\hat{L}$. The right-hand side of equation (18) can be thought of as the market rate of technical transformation, and it is equal to the monopoly price, α. In the case of public R&D, the right-hand side of equation (18) equals unity. The left-hand side of equation (18) is the marginal rate of substitution between consumption and investment.

To compare the socially optimal solution to the market equilibrium for the case of private R&D, note that the resource constraint (10) is identical for both problems. The market R&D equilibrium condition (14) can be written as

$$\frac{(\alpha - 1)\bar{E}}{(\rho + \bar{L}\gamma)\bar{L}^{(1-\gamma)}} = \alpha. \tag{19}$$

The right-hand side of equation (18) is identical to the right-hand side of equation (19). The social planner allows each firm to charge a monopoly price in order to allow product replacement to take place. However, there are three differences between equations (19) and (18).

First, the parameter $\gamma < 1$, which captures the degree of diminishing returns to R&D, appears in the numerator of equation (18) but not in equation (19). The social planner takes into account the fact that, at the margin, the social value of R&D diminishes as more resources are devoted to R&D. In the market equilibrium, each firm in an R&D race is small, so this effect is ignored by the firms. Thus, the higher the degree of diminishing returns to R&D (i.e., the lower the value of γ), the higher the bias of the private sector toward R&D investment.

Second, the numerator of equation (19) has the term $(\alpha - 1)$, whereas the numerator of equation (18) has the term $\ln \alpha$ instead. This is the monopoly distortion effect. The winner of each R&D race is concerned about the profit margin, $\alpha - 1$, associated with each new product, whereas the social planner is concerned with the change in consumer surplus due to an innovation that equals $\ln \alpha < \alpha - 1$ for $\alpha > 1$. This effect tends to create a private sector bias toward R&D investment.

Finally, there is the intertemporal spillover effect, which is reflected in the denominators of equations (18) and (19). The social planner discounts each innovation by using ρ instead of $\rho + L\gamma$, which is the private discount rate. The social planner takes into account the fact that the benefits of an innovation continue forever, whereas private firms discount future profits by taking into account the probability that these profits will disappear. This effect tends to increase the level of R&D investment of the planner relative to the market solution at each level of expenditure.

The above discussion and analysis are illustrated in figure 1. The downward-sloping line NN is the resource constraint (10), and the upward-sloping concave curve OSAR is the market R&D equilibrium condition, with point A being the market equilibrium. The positively sloped concave curve OSBG is the graph of equation (18), and its intersection with NN at point B determines the optimal consumption and investment levels. Point B corresponds to the tangency of a welfare indifference curve U_0 and the resource constraint, NN. It is easy to see that the graph of equation (18) lies above the graph of equation (19) for low values of R&D investment, and below the graph of equation (19) for high values of R&D investment.[15] Point S corresponds to the intersection point of the two curves. If the resource constraint NN just happens to pass through point S, then the market and social solutions coincide. There is no scope for government intervention. Thus, point S is loosely associated with Schumpeter's view of no government intervention in the absence of various macroeconomic frictions. At point S, however, it is simply the case that the various externalities and distortions exactly offset each other. Small economies should move resources toward more consumption and avoid risky R&D investments. Economies with lots of resources should encourage even more R&D investment than the market is willing to undertake.

One lesson from this simple Schumpeterian growth model is that, depending on the parameters of the model, either R&D taxes or subsidies are optimal. This insight has been robust in more general versions of the model, and it is similar in spirit to that of static models with imperfect competition.

Accomplishments and Implications

Many studies have constructed more sophisticated versions of the basic Schumpeterian growth model to address a variety of issues. These studies have increased the number of analytical techniques and have provided valuable insights into the mechanics of Schumpeterian progress. Because the Schumpeterian growth literature is still evolving, it is premature to provide a complete survey. I will confine my attention to several representative studies that highlight the accomplishments and implications of the new theory.

A popular version of Schumpeterian growth theory is the "quality ladders" model of economic growth developed by Grossman and Helpman (1991, chap. 4) and refined by Segerstrom (1991, 1995) and Houser (1994). Instead of one sector, the quality ladders model has a continuum of industries

---

15. Dividing equation (18) by equation (19), I obtain $\hat{E}/\bar{E} = [(\alpha - 1)/\gamma \ln \alpha][\rho/(\rho + L\gamma)]$. The first bracket is always greater than one. For L close to zero, $\hat{E} > \bar{E}$. As L increases, $\hat{E}/\bar{E}$ declines monotonically, and approaches zero as L approaches infinity.

and no aggregate uncertainty. Thompson and Waldo (1994) formalized another version of Schumpeterian growth based on Schumpeter's notion of "trustified capitalism," where innovating firms are infinitely lived and compete in market shares through the introduction of better products.

Several studies constructed multisectoral dynamic general equilibrium models to analyze the implications of Schumpeterian growth theory for patterns of trade, gains from trade, and trade restrictions. Segerstrom, Anant, and Dinopoulos (1990), Grossman and Helpman (1991), Dinopoulos, Oehmke, and Segerstrom (1993), and Taylor (1993), among others, have analyzed dynamic patterns of trade and investment through the perspective of Schumpeterian growth models. These studies emphasized the sectoral composition of aggregate growth and the relevance of comparative advantage to dynamic trade patterns. Segerstrom, Anant, and Dinopoulos (1990), Grossman and Helpman (1991), Taylor (1994), and Dinopoulos and Syropoulos (1995) analyzed the effects of trade liberalization and tariffs on Schumpeterian growth and/or welfare. These studies revealed the complex general-equilibrium interactions between trade restrictions and growth based on intersectoral shifts of resources caused by trade intervention. Romer (1994) and Dinopoulos and Syropoulos (1994) highlighted the risks of trade intervention by recalculating the costs of protection using neo-Schumpeterian models of growth.

The area of macroeconomics has also benefited from developments in Schumpeterian growth theory. Aghion and Howitt (1990) and Cheng and Dinopoulos (1992, 1993, 1996) have applied the insights of the new theory to issues of economic fluctuations. These models managed to provide a unified framework to study the interactions between long-run Schumpeterian growth and economic fluctuations. The latter are generated as a result of multiple perfect foresight equilibria, or can emerge in the presence of asymmetric technological opportunities in the form of technological breakthroughs and improvements. Aghion and Howitt (1994) introduced frictions in the labor market and analyzed the interactions between long-run Schumpeterian growth and involuntary unemployment.

Finally, several empirical studies have tested implications of the theory. Phillips (1993) reported a positive correlation between R&D investment and technological change measured by Solow residuals. Thompson (1995) has utilized U.S. firm-level data to estimate a Schumpeterian growth model of trustified capitalism. Arroyo, Dinopoulos, and Donald (1994) introduced population growth and neoclassical physical capital accumulation in the model of the previous section and estimated it using U.S. macroeconomic data. These studies provided very encouraging signals for the empirical relevance of Schumpeterian growth theory.

Conclusions

In the preface to Japanese edition of "Theorie der wirtschaftlichen Ent-wicklung," Schumpeter (1937) was searching for a theory of endogenous technological change

> There must be a purely economic theory of economic change which does not merely rely on external factors propelling the economic system from one equilibrium to another. It is such a theory . . . that I have tried to build . . . [and that] explains a number of phenomena, in particular the business cycle, more satisfactorily than it is possible to explain them by means of either the Walrasian or the Marshallian apparatus.

Fifty years later, Schumpeter's description of endogenous growth through creative destruction was formalized using state-of-the-art modeling tech-niques.

The goal of the present chapter was to describe the basic features, devel-opments, and implications of Schumpeterian growth theory. The autonomy of the new theory is based on the distinct features of creative destruction. Schumpeterian growth models utilize a dynamic general-equilibrium frame-work, model temporary market power through dynamic imperfect competi-tion, and focus on the risks associated with endogenous introduction of better products and processes. Although the spirit and basic assumptions of Schum-peterian growth models are definitely Schumpeterian, as the extensive quota-tions in the second section establish, several normative implications of the new theory do not always coincide with Schumpeter's views. The new theory has provided one of many possible formalizations of the process of creative destruction, and it is more Schumpeterian in spirit and implications than other existing models of economic growth.

The Schumpeterian growth theory is still evolving, following the general law of creative destruction. Better new models replace old ones, empirical testing modifies the original assumptions of some models, and more powerful analytical techniques push the boundaries of the new theory. More research is needed on the stability properties of Schumpeterian growth models with state variables such as physical or human capital accumulation. In addition, inter-national transfer of technology, unemployment caused by business fluctua-tions, personal income distribution, multiproduct firms, and empirical testing of Schumpeterian growth models are unexplored important issues that await further research.

REFERENCES

Aghion, Philippe, and Peter Howitt. 1990. "A Model of Growth through Creative Destruction." Document No. 90-91, DELTA and HEC, Paris, April; *Econometrica* 60, no. 2: 323–52, 1992.

Aghion, Philippe, and Peter Howitt. 1993. "The Schumpeterian Approach to Technical Change and Growth." In *Economic Growth in the World Economy,* Horst Siebert, ed., Institut für Weltwirtschaft, Universität Kiel, Tübingen: J. C. B. Mohr.

Aghion, Philippe, and Peter Howitt. 1994. "Growth and Unemployment," *Review of Economic Studies* 61:477–94.

Arroyo, Cristino, Elias Dinopoulos, and Stephen Donald. 1994. "Schumpeterian Growth and Capital Accumulation: Theory and Evidence." University of Florida. Mimeo.

Cass, David, and Joseph E. Stiglitz. 1970. "The Structure of Investor Preferences and Asset Returns, and Separability in Portfolio Allocation: A Contribution to the Pure Theory of Mutual Funds," *Journal of Economic Theory* 2:122–60.

Cheng, Leonard K., and Elias Dinopoulos. 1992. "Schumpeterian Growth and International Business Cycles." *American Economic Review* 82 (May): 409–14.

Cheng, Leonard K., and Elias Dinopoulos. 1993. "Schumpeterian Growth and Stochastic Economic Fluctuations." University of Florida. Mimeo.

Cheng, Leonard K., and Elias Dinopoulos. (1996). "A Multisectoral General Equilibrium Model of Schumpeterian Growth and Fluctuations." *Journal of Economic Dynamics and Control* forthcoming.

Dinopoulos, Elias. 1994. "Schumpeterian Growth Theory: An Overview." *Osaka City University Economic Review* 29 (January): 1–21.

Dinopoulos, Elias, James Oehmke, and Paul Segerstrom. 1993. "High-Technology Trade and Investment: The Role of Factor Endowments." *Journal of International Economics* 34:49–71.

Dinopoulos, Elias, and Constantinos Syropoulos. 1996. "Growth-Creating Trading Blocs." *The Canadian Economic Association Annual* forthcoming.

Dinopoulos, Elias, and Constantinos Syropoulos. 1995. "Tariffs and Schumpeterian Growth." University of Florida. Mimeo.

Eithier, Wilfred J. 1982. "National and International Returns to Scale in the Modern Theory of International Trade." *American Economic Review,* 72 (June): 389–405.

Feenstra, Robert C. 1996. "Trade and Uneven Growth." *Journal of Development Economics* forthcoming.

Grossman, Gene, and Elhanan Helpman. 1991. *Innovation and Growth in Global Economy.* Cambridge, MA: MIT Press.

Houser, Cynthia. 1994. "Stability in Neo-Schumpeterian Models of Growth." University of Florida. Mimeo.

Krugman, Paul. 1979a. "Increasing Returns, Monopolistic Competition, and International Trade." *Journal of International Economics* 9, no. 4: 469–70.

Krugman, Paul. 1979b. "A Model of Innovation, Technology Transfer and the World Distribution of Income." *Journal of Political Economy* vol. 87, no. 2 (April): 253–66.

Lucas, Robert Jr. 1988. "On the Mechanics of Economic Development." *Journal of Monetary Economics,* 22:3–32.

Phillips, Kerk. 1993. "Quality Ladders, Growth and R&D: An Assessment from U.S. Industry." Carnegie-Rochester Conference Series on Public Policy 38, 239–74.

Reinganum, Jennifer F. 1985. "Innovation and Industry Evolution." *Quarterly Journal of Economics* 100, no. 1 (February): 81–99.

Reinganum, Jennifer F. 1989. "The Timing of Innovation: Research, Development, and Diffusion." In *Handbook of Industrial Organization,* Vol. 1, R. Schmaleusee and R. D. Willig, eds., 849–908. New York: Elsevier Science Publishers B.V.

Rivera-Batiz, Luis A., and Paul M. Romer. 1991. "Economic Integration and Endogenous Growth." *Quarterly Journal of Economics* 106 (May): 531–55.

Romer, Paul M. 1986. "Increasing Returns and Long-Run Growth." *Journal of Political Economy* 94:1002–37.

Romer, Paul. 1990. "Endogenous Technological Change." *Journal of Political Economy* 98:S71–S102.

Romer, Paul. 1994. "New Goods, Old Theory, and the Welfare Costs of Trade Restrictions." *Journal of Development Economics* 43:5–38.

Schumpeter, Joseph A. 1928. "The Instability of Capitalism." In *Joseph A. Schumpeter: Essays on Entrepreneurs, Innovations, Business Cycles, and the Evolution of Capitalism,* Richard V. Clemence, ed. New Brunswick, NJ: Transaction Publishers, 1989.

Schumpeter, Joseph A. 1937. Preface to Japanese edition of "Theory Der Wirtschaftlichen Entwicklung." In *Joseph A. Schumpeter: Essays on Entrepreneurs, Innovations, Business Cycles, and the Evolution of Capitalism,* Richard V. Clemence, ed. New Brunswick, NJ: Transaction Publishers, 1989.

Schumpeter, Joseph A. 1942. *Capitalism, Socialism and Democracy.* New York: Harper and Row.

Segerstrom, Paul S. 1991. "Innovation, Imitation and Economic Growth." *Journal of Political Economy* 99, no. 4: 190–207.

Segerstrom, Paul S. 1995. "A Quality Ladders Growth Model with Decreasing Returns to R&D." Michigan State University. Mimeo.

Segerstrom, Paul S., T. C. A. Anant, and Elias Dinopoulos. 1990. "A Schumpeterian Model of the Product Life Cycle." *American Economic Review* 80 (December): 1077–91.

Solow, Robert M. 1956. "A Contribution to the Theory of Economic Growth." *Quarterly Journal of Economics* 70:65–94.

Stokey, Nancy L. 1988. "Learning by Doing and the Introduction of New Goods." *Journal of Political Economy* 96:701–17.

Taylor, Howard M., and Samuel Karlin. 1984. *An Introduction to Stochastic Modeling.* New York: Academic Press.

Taylor, Scott. 1993. "Quality Ladders and Ricardian Trade." *Journal of International Economics* 34:225-43.

Taylor, Scott. 1994. "Once-off and Continuing Gains from Trade." *Review of Economic Studies* 61:589–601.

Thompson, Peter. 1995. "Technological Opportunity and the Growth of Knowledge: A

Schumpeterian Approach to Measurement." *Journal of Evolutionary Economics* 5:1–21.

Thompson, Peter, and Doug Waldo. 1994. "Growth and Trustified Capitalism." *Journal of Monetary Economics* 34:445–62.

Young, Alwyn. 1991. "Learning by Doing and the Dynamic Effects of International Trade." *Quarterly Journal of Economics* 106:369–405.

Financial Institutions, Economic Policy, and the Dynamic Behavior of the Economy

Domenico Delli Gatti, Mauro Gallegati,
and Hyman P. Minsky

Introduction

When Schumpeter asserted that there are only two "fundamentally different groups of Business Cycle theories" (Schumpeter 1939) he undoubtedly had the then-current formal theories in mind, which allowed for only damped (monotonic or oscillating) behavior, on the one hand, and explosive (monotonic or oscillating) behavior, on the other, with a border between the damped and the explosive. In one common form this border required that the accelerator coefficient equal one for the generation of a constant amplitude (nondamped, nonexplosive) cycle (Hicks 1950; Minsky 1959).

Schumpeter, in his obituary of Mitchell, associated his own position with Mitchell in holding that "cycles are the form of capitalist evolution." Schumpeter's Kitchin, Juglar, and Kondratieff cycles reflected his views that there were a number of facets to the generation of economic evolution and that these cycles, along with their synchronization one to the other, reflected the special economic factors that were involved in the generation of a particular type of cycle. To Schumpeter, Kitchen cycles were mainly inventory and investment cycles, Juglar cycles were investment cycles with monetary or financial market involvement, and Kondratiev cycles were the result of the rise and then the decline of the exploitation of major technological innovations. Great depressions, such as that of the 1930s, occurred when the low points of Kitchen, Juglar, and Kondratiev cycles coincided. In this chapter we integrate the intertemporal behavior of profits, investment, indebtedness, and interest rates: we are modeling what Schumpeter would have considered Juglar cycles (Schumpeter 1939).

Even as we agree with Schumpeter in holding that cycles are the form of capitalist dynamics and evolution, we differ with him: we expand the alternative intertemporal behaviors to three. It is not necessary for the interactions of economic variables through time to yield either a nonoscillatory time series or a wavelike motion. The endogenously determined path through calendar time of the complexly interrelated markets of a capitalist economy can take the form not only of nonoscillatory time series and wavelike motions, but in addition it can become incoherent. The incoherence of runaway inflations and debt deflations are facts of economic history. In general it is accepted that the incoherent behavior of the economy has dire consequences, and in modern economies incipient or realized incoherence will lead to governmental interventions. These governmental interventions can be by the government, strictly speaking, or by a "semi-independent" central bank. We can now visualize a third set of business cycle theories in which cycles result from the combination of endogenous interactions that can lead to incoherence and the impact of institutions and interventions that aim to contain these thrusts toward incoherence.

We note that this third set of models finds that government-sponsored institutions and government interventions can play a positive role, in that, if well used, they contain the degenerative tendencies of capitalist economies (Ferri and Minsky 1992). We need but recall that the capitalisms of the winter of 1932–33 were rather complete failures and that the capitalisms of the main capitalist economies were quite successful in the first quarter century after World War Two.

The starting point of our extension of Schumpeter's insight is the linear accelerator multiplier model that had a run during the 1940s and 1950s and then faded from the scene as growth theory replaced cycle theory as a focus of research. In the Hicks-Hansen-Samuelson linear accelerator multiplier model the path through time of the system depended upon an accelerator coefficient that linked investment demand to the change in income and a consumption coefficient—the marginal propensity to consume—that linked consumption to income. The accelerator was taken to be a technical attribute of the economy and the consumption coefficient was taken to be a deep-rooted psychological law.[1]

In a series of exercises, Minsky explored the properties of an accelerator-multiplier setup where the values of the accelerator and multiplier generated explosive time series. These explosive time series were constrained by floors and ceilings that broke the ongoing process and established a new process with new initial conditions.[2] In one article (Minsky 1957a), ceilings and floors

---

1. We view the accelerator and marginal propensity to consume coefficients as economic variables. In particular, we model the economic determinants of the investment coefficient. We find ample reason to believe that the volatility of the investment coefficient leads to incoherent behavior in a system where investment determines profits and the financing of investment commits future profit flows to the servicing of liabilities.

2. In the special case where the ceiling's rate of change is less than the smaller of the two positive real roots that generate the explosive series (these roots are transformations of the

were determined by the behavior of the monetary system, that is, by an aspect of the institutional structure, which determined the maximum rates of investment and disinvestment by setting limits on the acquisition of assets by the banking system.

Because the power of computers enables us to discover characteristics of time series that are generated by mathematically nontractable systems, we can set up our analytical structure without being unduly concerned with the tractability of the resulting model.

Schumpeter's assertion that began this essay reflected the state of knowledge at the time he was writing. Today's knowledge enables us to take a third approach, in which the complex structure of an economy yields time series that can generate smooth growth and well-behaved cycles as possible transitory results of the economic process, but that also allow for the intermittent emergence of conditions conducive to the emergence of incoherence or turbulence. Such emerging incoherent or turbulent behavior results from the cumulative effect of the ordinary behavior of the agents of the economy upon variables that affect the behavior of the economy. In the early stages of the process these cumulating variables are not a significant influence on the qualitative characteristics of the time series that are generated: their effect is, so to speak, suppressed. However, when the cumulative changes pass some threshold, qualitative changes occur in the economy's performance.

In the second section of this chapter, "Some Principles of the Formulation," some principles underlying the formulation are presented. In the third section, "Institutional Structure," we discuss the impact of institutions upon the behavior of the processes that generate our time series. In our argument, institutions can act as the equivalent of circuit breakers. If the system is very turbulent then the time series actually generated can be dominated by the impact of institutional characteristics that set maximas and minimas to variables. In the fourth section, "The Model Stated," the model is presented. We go over the nine equations that make up our rather simple extension of the accelerator multiplier model. In the fifth section, "The Reduced Form," we examine the reduced form equations. In the fourth and fifth sections, references are made to a series of figures that illustrate the equations and the simulations of the model. The final section draws out some implications of what remains an evolving work in progress.

---

accelerator and multiplier coefficients), the new initial conditions lead to a small negative coefficient for the larger (major) root and a large positive coefficient for the smaller (minor) root. As a result, the dynamic process begins by generating an increasing income but, as the large major root with its negative coefficient takes over, the rate of increase of income first decreases and then becomes negative: income decreases. A setup that has two positive real roots can, with appropriate initial conditions, generate one turning point: the business cycle that results is due to the system bouncing between "floors" and "ceilings."

Some Principles of the Formulation

As our agents possess incomplete (and in particular asymmetric) information, the hypothesis of complete and perfect markets, which is the cornerstone of the Arrow-Debreu general equilibrium framework, is rejected.[3] Once liberated from Arrow-Debreu, we are free to emphasize the role of time and conditionality in the economy. Debt, that is, promises made at one date by an economic unit (firm, household, government, or financial institution) to pay a certain (or contingent) sum of money to specified other (or bearer) units at some future dates, provides a natural way to link time periods for capitalist economies.[4] Because, in the aggregate, the ability of units to fulfill the commitments on their debts depends upon the endogenously determined paths of profits and debts, the commitments on debts may or may not be fulfilled.

Debt is specialized to corporate debt to banks: the liability structure sets up a time series of gross cash payments that corporations must pay to banks. This is a great simplification of the debt structure of modern economies. Household and government debts, as well as a complex layering of debts, exist and undoubtedly affect the behavior of a modern economy.

In the following we explore the complex interrelations of financial and real variables with the help of an analytical framework that is a simplified (and slightly modified) version of a class of macrodynamic models published elsewhere (Delli Gatti, Gallegati, and Gardini 1993, 1994; Delli Gatti and Gallegati 1994) that have been extensively analyzed and simulated in order to gain new insights about business fluctuations in financially complex economies. A model per se, however, is nothing other than a device for organizing thoughts. When deemed necessary, our description of financial developments will be richer and more detailed than that incorporated into the model.

In macrodynamic models such as the one discussed here, we can obtain a wide range of different dynamic processes. Depending upon the parameter configuration, the reduced form can yield a wide array of time paths, ranging from oscillations of the Slutsky-Frisch-Lucas type, which are due to stochastic disturbances affecting an otherwise nonoscillatory framework, to more or less regular endogenously determined wavelike motions, from aperiodic dynamics

---

3. Since information is asymmetric, agents differ one from another (Stiglitz 1992), and therefore the representative-agent assumption is not valid. Macroeconomic models cannot be built upon a representative-agent microfoundation (Kirman 1992).

4. This also implies that we cannot get meaningful results by abstracting from financial markets and then adding money or finance to the model. Note that as debts are of private units, there is no certainty that commitments will be fulfilled. Also note that among the proximate holders of debts are banks: this implies that nonfulfillment of debt contracts compromises the liquidity and the ability to finance of the economy.

Fulfillment of private, and even public, debts is contingent upon outcomes whose likelihood cannot be known. Once the Arrow-Debreu hypothesis of complete and perfect markets is rejected then the world becomes Keynesian, in that intractable uncertainty exists.

to financial instability and time-dependent fluctuations. The actual outcome depends not only upon the behavior of firms, households, and financial institutions, but also upon the structural characteristics of the economy, ruling parameters, institutional regime, and policy interventions.

Institutional Structure

Schumpeter characterized the banker as the *ephor* of developing capitalist economies. At an earlier meeting of the Schumpeter Society, Minsky characterized central bankers as the *"ephor of the ephors"* of capitalism (Minsky 1990).[5] The difficulties in getting capitalism well started in Eastern Europe center around the problems of developing a financial system in societies where there are no significant financial institutions and where the population is mainly non-numeric in a financial sense.

The recognition that market economies are unstable did not wait for the demonstration that complex interactive nonlinear equation systems can yield incoherent or turbulent time series. The historic experience of runaway inflations and debt deflations served as evidence that the behavior of market systems is not necessarily benevolent. As capitalism developed, responsible policy makers always took Adam Smith's dictum in regard to the power of the invisible hand with the proverbial grain of salt.

One of the most evident evils of the market-economy way of organizing affairs was the periodic eruption of financial crises followed by hard times. To contain the evils that market systems can inflict, capitalist economies have developed sets of institutions and authorities that can be characterized as the equivalent of circuit breakers. These institutions, in effect, stop the economic processes that breed the incoherence and restart the economy with new initial conditions and perhaps with new reaction coefficients.

Even though there are many devices in modern capitalist economies that constrain and regulate market processes, the guidance of the economy by participating in and constraining market outcomes is perhaps most evident in banking systems and financial markets. Without going into details, in recent years we have seen various effective and ineffective central bank "lender of last resort" interventions, as well as some interventions that can be best interpreted as government equity infusions into financial institutions to prevent their liabilities from falling to a discount.[6] The deficits that big governments run, minimum-wage laws, unemployment compensation, and government-sponsored social insurance are further examples of devices that do not

---

5. Ephors were elected magistrates of Sparta whose function was to keep the kings in line.

6. In the United States the so-called bailout of Savings and Loan Associations, as well as of many commercial banks, is an instance of an equity infusion. Similar refinancings, perhaps not at the same scale and perhaps without similar systemic causes, have taken place in almost all advanced capitalist economies.

permit the unconstrained market determination of economic outcomes, but set boundary values to the permissible values for some variables.

In the nonlinear systems that can breed incoherence there are terms that initially have small impact upon system behavior, but that accumulate as the processes "mature." As the accumulating variables approach critical values, incoherent behavior looms as a likely outcome. Whether such an incipient incoherence blossoms into realized incoherence depends upon the institutions, regulations, and government interventions that set or constrain the values of economic variables.[7]

The institutional structure at any date reflects legislation, administrative actions, and the evolution of institutions and usages that are due to the past behavior of market participants.[8] The legislation reflects the understanding of the economy (i.e., the maintained economic theory) that ruled among the policy establishment at the time the institutions were created. Administrative interventions that aim to steer the economy or to contain what is believed to be incipient incoherent behavior reflect the maintained economic theory of the relevant authorities at the time they intervene. It is worth noting that the two sets of theories can be markedly different. The institutions could have been set in place when the policy-making agents of the economy believed that instability verging on incoherence was an inescapable attribute of a capitalist economy, whereas the interventions may be implemented by agents who believe in the inherent stability of capitalist economies.[9]

Thus the time path of economic variables reflects the behavior of self-seeking market agents, the impact of the institutional structure, and the interventions by policy authorities: the interventions reflect a maintained economic theory. The values of variables that the unconstrained and noninterventionist economy would generate are replaced by values that reflect the immediate impact of interventions, controls, and constraints: what happens reflects the impact of the economic thinking of different times. Such replacements of endogenously determined variables, which are formally equivalent to the imposition of new initial conditions, reset the dynamics of the economy.

---

7. As interventions set off interactive processes with new initial conditions, the outcome depends upon interventions that occur at different dates. Thus the outcome, as determined by endogenous forces and the resetting of the process with new initial conditions, is time-dependent.

8. See Minsky 1957b for an application of these ideas to the interrelations between banks and central banks in determining the evolution of banking practices.

9. The legislation of 1935–36, which set up the basic structure of the financial system for the United States, was strongly affected by ideas that held that breakdowns are "normal" outcomes of "laissez-faire" capitalism, whereas the various monetarisms that have influenced policy and institution building over the past two decades are based upon the assumption that market capitalisms, even intensely financial variants, are inherently stable and seek out an outcome that can be characterized as optimal.

Thus initial conditions are not set once and for all, but are imposed from time to time as institutional usages become binding or the authorities react to their view of the state of the economy and its future. Thus the behavior of the economy depends not only upon endogenous dynamic processes, institutional structures, and interventions by the authorities, but also upon the model of the economy that guides the authorities.

A ruling conjecture that follows from the previous discussion is that the aptness of institutions and interventions will largely determine the extent to which the path of the economy through time is tranquil or turbulent; that is, whether it is progressive, stagnant, or deteriorating.

The Model Stated

Our base model is a closed economy with four types of agents: firms, households, banks, and governments. Households supply labor services, demand consumption goods, and hold bank liabilities (demand deposits). Firms supply consumption and investment goods and demand labor services, investment goods, and bank loans. Banks supply their liabilities (deposits) and demand financial assets (i.e., they supply loans).

Fiscal authorities and the central bank—which we lump together under the heading of the "public sector," or the government—supply nonmarket goods and services; underwrite minimum living standards; and guarantee, explicitly or implicitly, select private contracts. Government expenditures, underwritings, and guarantees are paid for either through tax collection, by selling government bonds, or by the issuance of central bank liabilities.

There are balance sheet as well as income relations among the units. There can be no balance sheet loose ends in analyzing a capitalist economy: all financial instruments need to appear as assets on one balance sheet and liabilities on another. A simplified balance sheet is shown in table 1, where the symbol "+" represents assets, while "−" stands for liabilities.

We postulate three markets: labor, credit, and goods. We do not deal explicitly with the labor market. We assume that employment is a positive function of effective demand at a given wage.

There is no stock market. Equity investment grows by means of retained earnings. Credit and the rate of interest are determined in the loan market. The price level is constant and normalized to unity: no distinction can be made between nominal and real variables.

There are nine equations in our basic model.

According to the Kalecki-Levy equation, gross profits (Π) at time t equals

$$\Pi_t = I_t + G, \tag{1}$$

TABLE 1. The Balance Sheet Structure of the Economy

Households	Firms	Banks	Government
Deposits (+)	Deposits (+)	Deposits (−)	Deposits (+)
Bank equity (+)		Bank equity (−)	
Corporate equity (+)	Corporate equity (−)		
Government bonds (+)		Government bonds (+)	Government bonds (−)
	Loans (−)	Loans (+)	
		Reserves (+)	Reserves (−)
Wealth (−)	Capital assets (+)		

Note: The present value of tax revenues is an implicit asset on the government's balance sheet and an implicit liability of households' balance sheets. The ability of popular governments to tax to support their funded debts and current operations is the main issue in the crisis of democratic welfare capitalism.

where I is gross investment and G is gross government deficit, which in our simplified framework coincides with gross government expenditure. Heroically, we ignore taxes and interest payments on public debt.[10] Therefore, we can focus on the impact of the government's budget on gross profits.[11]

In this chapter, current investment does not explicitly contribute to future capacity: it is a component of aggregate demand, a determinant of profits, and an absorber of financing. In other words, we rule out any capital capacity constraint to output: we are tracking the path through time of gross capital income, private debt, and the interest rate. The demand for investment is

$$I_t = av_t + b_t IF_t. \tag{2}$$

Equation (2) is an algebraic statement of figure 1, a graph used by Minsky (1975, 1982, 1986) to explain the determination of investment. v is the price of capital assets (Minsky's P_K), IF is the internal finance, to be defined in equation (3).

Since the price of current output (in both the consumption and the investment goods sectors, by assumption) is constant and normalized to 1, v can also be conceived of as the ratio of the price of capital assets to the current

---

10. An obvious extension consists of endogenizing taxes and introducing a government budget constraint. This is left to future developments of our research program.

11. Schumpeter's view that, in the absence of investment, profits are zero is consistent with the Kalecki-Levy equations after allowing that the impact upon profits of government deficits is equivalent to that of financed investment. As a "Walrasian," he had difficulty in explaining this view.

Perhaps the most difficult of the Keynes, Kalecki, Levy, and Schumpeter views to get across to a modern economist is that capital is a value term: it is the value placed upon the current expectations of mainly future income flows.

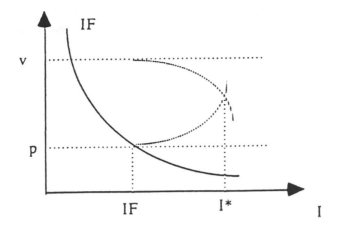

equation 2: $I_t = a\ v_t + b_t\ IF_t$

Fig. 1. The determination of investment

supply price of investment output,[12] that is, "average q" in Tobin's terminology.[13]

The (nonnegative) parameter a reflects the sensitivity of investment to v, the current valuation of capital assets, while b reflects the extent to which

---

12. Since the price level of capital assets and the price level of investment output are determined by different sets of variables, we expect them to behave differently; in particular, the former is expected to be more volatile than the latter (Minsky 1975). For investment to take place, the expected cash flows from operating investment outputs as capital assets have to service liabilities that reflect what was paid for the investment: an implication of this is $v > 1$.

13. Tobin (1989) believes Minsky's theory of investment to be indistinguishable from his own. As has been correctly pointed out by Dymski and Pollin (1992), Minsky's theory differs from Tobin's because he assumes the presence of private information, which means the Modigliani Miller theorem cannot be applied.

Abel and Blanchard (1986) and Fazzari, Hubbard, and Petersen (1988) show that internal finance plays a central role in investment activity on the assumption that alternative sources of finance are not perfect substitutes: in an environment of asymmetric information, a financing hierarchy that ranges from internal funds to various types of external funds emerges. One difference between internal and external finance is that internal funds do not lead to a legal binding commitment of future cash payments. Managements may feel committed to paying dividends, but in principle and in practice dividends depend upon the realization of profits. In the hierarchy of hedge, speculative, and Ponzi finance, the greater the ratio of equity to debt financing, the greater the chance that the firm will be a hedge financing unit. Note that Ponzi finance, the capitalizing of interest, involves an increase in indebtedness equal to the decrease in equity. By compromising the equity base of an organization, Ponzi financing increases the likelihood that future Ponzi financing will occur.

firms lever retained earnings in the financing of investment. In other words, *b* is a *leveraging ratio* on the flow of equity capital in the form of retained earnings.[14]

Internal finance available at time *t* is the difference between lagged profits and lagged debt payments

$$IF_t = \Pi_{t-1} - r_{t-1}D_{t-1}, \tag{3}$$

where *r* is the ratio of gross payments due on outstanding debt (interest and principal) to the stock of corporate debt (loans extended by the banking system). For the sake of simplicity, in the following we will refer to it as the "interest rate."

In principle, the price of capital assets reflects the stream of expected future profits. In this chapter we adopt a simplifying shortcut that consists of representing the price of capital assets by an autoregressive process[15]

$$v_t = v_{t-1} + \epsilon_t, \tag{4}$$

where ϵ is a random variable with zero mean and finite variance.[16]

The propensity to lever internal funds is an endogenous variable. It is represented as a nonlinear increasing function of profits (fig. 2)[17]

---

14. An investment equation such as equation (2), already present—albeit implicitly—in Minsky's works, has been formalized in Delli Gatti and Gallegati 1990. Since then it has been used in different versions of the prototype framework (Delli Gatti and Gallegati 1992, 1994; Delli Gatti, Gallegati, and Gardini 1993, 1994). The empirical literature on functional forms of this type starts with Fazzari, Hubbard, and Petersen 1988. For a survey of the literature on the econometric implementation of investment equations see Chirinko 1993.

15. This specification is consistent with empirical results found by Blanchard et al. 1990, according to which average Q is a white noise random process.

16. Laibson and Friedman (1989) model capital asset prices as a Poisson distribution where the height of the tails are positively related to the debt-income ratio. As a result, crashes in the stock market and in the market valuation of firms become more likely as the fragility of the financial structure increases.

Equation (4) evades the issue of how expected future profits are transformed into the implicit price for capital assets. In the modern capitalist economies, capital assets are usually, but not always, transferred from one owner to another as a packet of assets combined with a market position. The transformation of such prices, which include a valuation of market position, into Minsky's P_k and Tobin's Q is an open question.

17. A procyclical propensity to invest or leveraging ratio can be explained by a "composition effect." According to Fazzari's empirical investigation, small firms are characterized by small capital stock, a high sales and capital growth rate, a high retention rate, and a high propensity to invest out of internal finance. Just the opposite is true for relatively large firms. As the aggregate propensity to invest is a weighted average of the propensities to invest of small and large firms, with weights equal to the share of the total cash flow generated by small and large firms, respectively, when the population of small firms increases during the stage of the expansion of business cycles, the propensity to invest by leveraging internally generated funds increases.

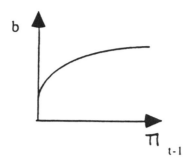

equation 5: $b_t = b_0 + b_1$ arctg Π_{t-1}

Fig. 2. The propensity to lever internal funds

$$b_t = b_0 + b_1 \text{ arctg } (\Pi_{t-1}). \tag{5}$$

The parameter b_0 represents "liquidity preference" on the part of firms. A decrease in b_0 can be interpreted as an increase in the liquidity preference of firms and for every level of (lagged) profits a fall in b_0 lowers b_t.

Informational imperfections on capital markets (for instance, asymmetric information)[18] imply that investment is constrained by the availability of external finance. We assume that the supply of (external) finance on the part of banks, F, is an increasing function of the interest rate

$$F_t = Hr_t. \tag{6}$$

the parameter H is assumed to be under the control of monetary authorities.[19]

The demand for loans equals the sum of corporate debt inherited from the past and the financing gap, that is, the difference between total investment and the amount financed by internal funds

$$D_t = D_{t-1} + I_t - IF_t. \tag{7}$$

Loan market equilibrium requires

$$D_t = F_t. \tag{8}$$

---

18. Keynes' and Kalecki's notions of borrowers' risk and lender's risk—which are incorporated into Minsky's diagrammatic representation of investment determination—can be interpreted as informational imperfections in an asymmetric information framework.

19. The Schumpeterian (and Keynesian) tradition, to which we adhere, views money as both endogenous and having an evolving composition. This is a simplifying assumption that needs to be lifted as this program advances. See Minsky 1957b.

From equations (6) and (8) we derive the following interest rate equation:

$$r_t = \frac{D_t}{H} . \tag{9}$$

In principle, present views of the future affect current investment financing, while past financing determines payment commitments due now. The willingness and the ability of banks to commit their funds at any particular time depends upon the performance of the assets they own, that is, whether commitments made in the past that are falling due today are being honored.

The Reduced Form

A modern economy has to be viewed as a time-dependent system because nearly every unit makes financial decisions every today that come due in a myriad of tomorrows. Such decisions depend upon the performance of the economy "now," the current status of financing decisions made in the past that are maturing today, and the expected performance of the economy. Because of the financing connections among units, a part of spending is previously determined by the structure of liabilities. For debts and equity, internal finance, and investment, what happens during any today can more than validate, just validate, or to a greater or lesser extent fail to validate decisions made in the past.

Rational agents know that they lack perfect foresight: they know they may be wrong. This implies that their willingness to accept particular types of assets into portfolios or particular types of funding of their operations is subject to change as history yields evidence that their past decisions were right or wrong. When past investment and funding decisions are strongly validated by current and past outcomes, then the belief in the model of the economy that guides the decisions of potential debtors and asset-holding financing agencies is reinforced. When decisions made in the past are currently barely being validated, then either no revision or minor changes of the belief in the model that guided past actions take place. When current cash flows are insufficient to validate decisions taken in the past, then the model that guided behavior is abandoned and defensive steps are taken by firms, financiers, and the ultimate owners of financial assets to contain the damage from their errors.

We study the behavior of three fundamental relations in a view of the economy that focuses upon profits, debts, and the cost of carrying debts (that is, the interest rate).

Substituting equations (2) and (4) into equation (1) gives us the following profit equation:

$$\Pi_t = av_{t-1} + a\epsilon_t + b_t IF_t + G. \tag{10}$$

Other things being equal, an increase in the leveraging ratio increases investment and leads to an increase in profits.

Substituting equations (2) and (4) into equation (7), we get the debt equation

$$D_t = D_{t-1} + [av_{t-1} + a\epsilon_t + (b_t - 1)IF_t]. \tag{11}$$

The dynamic behavior of the interest rate is linked to that of corporate debt, as shown by equation (9) above. We are now ready to derive the reduced form of the system. Substituting equations (3) and (9) into equations (10) and (11), we get

$$\Pi_t = \alpha + b_t \Pi_{t-1} - \frac{b_t}{H} D_{t-1}^2 + G \tag{10'}$$

$$D_t = D_{t-1} \alpha + (b_t - 1)\Pi_{t-1} - \frac{b_t - 1}{H} D_{t-1}^2 , \tag{11'}$$

where $\alpha = av_t$ is treated as an exogenous variable and b is represented by equation (5). The system of equations (10') and (11') is characterized by two nonlinearities: it is obviously nonlinear in D, but it is also nonlinear in Π, thanks to the interaction of the leveraging ratio—an increasing function of the profit level—and internal finance.

Systems of two nonlinear difference equations of this type have been studied extensively (see in particular Delli Gatti, Gallegati, and Gardini 1993, 1994). The procedure is as follows. First we compute the steady state of the system and assess its stability properties, treating b as a given parameter. The steady state is

$$\Pi^z = G + \frac{\alpha}{1 - b}$$

$$D^z = \sqrt{HG}$$

Simulations show that a relatively "low" value of b, that is, a value of b smaller than a critical (lower) crucial level, b^H, leads to a monotonically or cyclically damped time series, converging to the steady state. Alternatively, a relatively "high" value of b, that is, a value of b greater than a critical (upper) crucial level, b^M, leads to a monotonically or cyclically explosive time series. Between b^H and b^M the time series that are generated evolve from bounded cycles to (purely deterministic or stochastic) chaotic behavior.[20]

---

20. A stochastic disturbance affects investment through the autoregressive process that determines the price of capital assets.

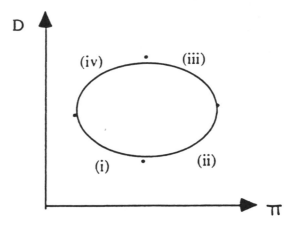

Fig. 3. A bounded cycle

In figure 3 a (bounded) cycle—a closed orbit—is depicted as reproduced by our simulation.

We can begin our examination at phase (i), where debts are falling even as profits are rising. This is a period of tranquil expansion, during which entrepreneurs are pleasantly surprised by actual profits exceeding anticipations of profits. In phase (ii) debts rise, but through most of this phase profits rise even faster. At the transition from phase (ii) to phase (iii), profits stop increasing even as debts virtually explode. In phase (iii) debts continue to rise even as profits fall. In phase (iii) the financial structure becomes fragile. At the transition from phase (iii) to phase (iv), debts begin to fall even as profits continue to decline. In phase (iv) both profits and debts fall. At the transition between phases (iv) and (i) the fall of profits stops but the fall of debts becomes almost vertical: unless contained a debt deflation could result. In a modern society government deficits can be expected to sustain profits as a debt deflation threatens.[21] With the transition to phase (i) the debt decrease tapers off and profits again begin to increase. The transition from a fragile to a robust financial system begins again.

Figure 4 shows the closed orbit on the (Π, D) plane of figure 3 and two ceilings, a maximum debt-profit ratio (D') and full employment (Π') and one floor to profits as set by the government deficit (Π_G).

The combination of the maximum debt-profit ratio and the floor to profits decreases the likelihood of a debt deflation. On the other hand, financing ceilings can prevent the exploitation of seemingly profitable opportunities.

---

21. Furthermore, as we just saw, in the United States the government may take responsibility for assuring that bank and near-bank liabilities are sustained at par.

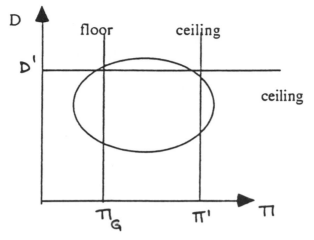

Fig. 4. The closed orbit of (Π,*D*)

Profit-seeking agents can be expected to develop innovative financing techniques that avoid the constraints. These often catch central bankers "asleep at the switch." The fragility of the financial system that results from the new ways can force central banks to ease their restrictions on available financing (Minsky 1957b). Fiscal policy measures are also ways to contain debt deflations by supporting aggregate profits.

Conclusions

The approach to business cycles and macroeconomic dynamics adopted here holds that the path of a capitalist economy through calendar time cannot be reduced to a dynamic process that started way in the past and will continue for the foreseeable future. This is so because the market processes that determine investment, employment, income, consumption, the composition of portfolios, and the myriad of individual prices and quantities take place within an institutional structure that limits the movement and values of some of the variables of the system. Whenever such institutionally determined values dominate the endogenously determined values in what actually occurs, then the path of the economy, the ongoing dynamic process, is broken and an interactive process that starts with new initial conditions generates future values.

In particular, whenever the economy behaves or even threatens to behave in an incoherent way, "stabilizers," which may be built in or require actions by authorities, kick in and prevent the economy from continuing on the prior endogenously determined dynamic path. At these times prior dynamic processes are superseded by a new process characterized by a combination of new initial conditions and new reaction coefficients. This new process will have its run in the context of a new institutional structure that incorporates market adjustments, regulatory changes, and legislative initiatives that were responses to the "crisis."

One of the advances in this chapter is that b, the leveraging ratio, which plays a role analogous to the accelerator coefficient of the multiplier accelerator models, is an endogenous variable. Swings in b can be interpreted as what Keynes characterized as changes in liquidity preference on the part of firms. The ability of a businessman to finance investment, that is, to become less liquid, requires a parallel willingness by the "external" financier to become less liquid. There is a type of self-fulfilling prophecy in the swings of liquidity preference. Cash flows, in the form of increased gross profits, accrue to business as financed investment increases and cash flows to business, in the form of aggregate profits, decrease when some real or financial asset fails to perform, which leads to a shift toward an increase in desired liquidity by bankers, portfolio managers, and businessmen.

In figure 1, which is a representation of equation (2), the leverage is determined by the way in which the external financing line falls away from the capital asset price line and the way the external financing line rises from the current price line. The first represents the reluctance of the firm to lever and the second the reluctance of the "bankers" to lend. Such risk assessments are among the main drivers of capitalist economies, and their current status at any time reflects how the past of the economy affects bankers and businessmen. It is the combined animal spirits of bankers and businessmen that determine what in fact happens.

One simple assertion—that investment has to be financed either by capitalist-retained profits or by external funds—has profound effects in making our model both time-dependent and nonlinear. This opens a rich menu of possible system behaviors, even though we greatly simplified the financing relations (debt financing was by banks and we really did not allow much influence to bank liabilities).

We assumed that the government deficit equals government spending and we kept it constant throughout the exercise. This of course has the consequence that government spending becomes an increasingly large (small) factor determining profits as investment falls (rises), but not to the same extent that would have been true if we had modeled contracyclical fiscal policy. Endogenizing tax revenues and government expenditures is an obvious extension of the work. Our intuition is that instead of only one ephor in banking that guides and directs the economy, there are at least two of them because fiscal policy provides a second ephor complementary to the banking one.

To a large extent the 45 years since Schumpeter died have been dominated by the results of Arrow and Debreu. We are now more aware of the limited applicability of general equilibrium theory than hitherto in the Arrow-Debreu era. We know that their results were based upon not only heroic, but also profoundly unacceptable assumptions: utility functions over the reals and perfect foresight being two that are especially foreign to modern capitalist economies.

One implication of Schumpeter's *Theory of Economic Development* (1934) is that the analysis of capitalist economic processes will not lead to the relegation of money, credit, and finance to a pound of details that are irrelevant for an understanding of the fundamental rules of capitalism. The monetary and financial structures provide not only an essential set of links between the past, the present, and the future, but they also provide the economy with some of its most important aborters of incoherence. The dominating functions of central banking, deposit insurance, and fiscal policy are to sustain asset values and aggregate profits and thus contain any thrust of the economy toward the incoherence of a deep debt deflation and depression. Schumpeter was never more relevant than when he identified bankers as the ephor of capitalist economies. In modern capitalism the central bank and the fiscal powers of governments are, so to speak, the ephors of the ephors of capitalism.

Thus the Schumpeterian monetary production innovative economy is a rich version of Keynes' monetary production economy (Keynes 1933). This economy is a maze of cash flows, production is always an $M > C > M'$ phenomenon—to use Marx's terminology, and profits exist not because capital assets are productive but because the composition of aggregate demand makes capital assets scarce.[22] Furthermore part of M is from and part of M' is to bankers.

Now that for the foreseeable future the world economy will be dominated by a set of financially complex capitalist economies, economists should turn from the contemplation of abstract economies to the study of the behavior of innovative monetary production economies. A marriage not of convenience but of shared insights between the economics of Keynes and of Schumpeter seems to be a fruitful program for research.

REFERENCES

Abel, A., and O. Blanchard. 1986. The Present Value of Profits and the Cyclical Movement of Investment. *Econometrica* 54, no. 2 (March): 249–73.

---

22. To Schumpeter, Keynes, Kalecki, and Jerome Levy, profits were determined by the composition of financed demand, not by any technical productivity of capital assets. They were closer to the Marshallian view that profit income is a quasi rent than to the modern view that assumes that a marginal product of capital is a meaningful concept so that profits are determined by the technical conditions of production.

Baumol, W., and J. Benhabib. 1989. Chaos and Economics. *Journal of Economic Perspectives* 3, no. 1 (Winter): 77–105.

Chirinko, R. 1993. Business Fixed Investment Spending: A Critical Survey of Modeling Strategies, Empirical Results and Policy Implications. *Journal of Economic Literature* 31, no. 4 (December): 1875–1911.

Delli Gatti, D., and M. Gallegati. 1990. Financial Instability, Income Distribution and the Stock Market. *Journal of Post Keynesian Economics* 12, no. 3 (Spring): 356–74.

———. 1992. Imperfect Information, Corporate Finance, Debt Commitments and Business Fluctuations. In S. Fazzari and D. Papadimitriou 1992.

———. 1994. External Finance, Investment Expenditure and the Business Cycle. In W. Semmler 1994.

Delli Gatti, D., M. Gallegati, and L. Gardini. 1993. Investment Confidence, Corporate Debt and Income Fluctuations. *Journal of Economic Behaviour and Organization.* 22, no. 2 (October): 161–87.

———. 1994. Complex Dynamics in a Simple Macroeconomic Model with Financing Constraints. In Dymski and Polin 1994.

Dymski, G., and R. Pollin. 1992. Minsky as a Hedgehog. In Fazzari and Papadimitriou 1992.

Dymski, G., and R. Pollin, eds. 1994. *New Perspectives in Monetary Macroeconomics.* Ann Arbor: University of Michigan Press.

Fazzari, S., G. Hubbard, and B. Petersen. 1988. Financial Constraints and Corporate Investment. *Brookings Papers on Economic Activity,* no. 1.

Fazzari, S., and D. Papadimitriou, eds. 1992. *Financial Conditions and Macroeconomic Performance.* New York: M. E. Sharpe & Co.

Ferri, P., and H. P. Minsky. 1992. Market Processes and Thwarting Systems. *Structural Change and Economic Dynamics* 3, no. 1: 79–91.

Hahn, F. 1981. *Essays on Stability and Growth.* Cambridge: Cambridge University Press.

Hicks, J. 1950. *Trade Cycle.* Oxford: Clarendon Press.

Keynes, J. M. 1933. [1973] A Monetary Theory of Production. In vol. 13 of *Collected Writings of John Maynard Keynes, The General Theory and After: Part I: Preparation.* London: Macmillan.

———. 1936. *The General Theory of Employment, Interest and Money.* London: Macmillan.

Kirman, A. 1992. Whom or What does the Representative Consumer Represent? *Journal of Economic Perspectives* 6, no. 2 (Spring): 117–36.

Ingrao, B., and G. Israel. 1989. *The Invisible Hand.* Cambridge: Cambridge University Press.

Laibson, D., and B. Friedman. 1989. Economic Implications of Extraordinary Movements in Stock Prices. *Brookings Papers in Economic Activity,* no. 2.

Minsky, H. P. 1957a. Monetary Systems and Accelerator Models. *American Economic Review* 47, no. 6 (December): 859–83.

———. 1957b. Central Banking and Money Market Changes. *Quarterly Journal of Economics* 71, no. 2 (May): 171–87.

————. 1959. A Linear Model of Cyclical Growth. *Review of Economics and Statistics* 41, no. 2 (May): 133–45.

————. 1975. *John Maynard Keynes*. New York: Columbia University Press.

————. 1982. *Can "It" Happen Again? Essays on Instability and Finance*. New York: M. E. Sharpe & Co.

————. 1986. *Stabilizing an Unstable Economy*. New Haven, Conn.: Yale University Press.

————. 1990. "Schumpeter: Finance and Evolution." In M. Perlman and A. Heertje, eds. *Evolving Technology and Market Structure: Studies in Schumpeterian Economics*. Ann Arbor: University of Michigan Press.

Schumpeter, J. A. 1939. *Business Cycles*. New York: McGraw-Hill.

————. 1934. *Theory of Economic Development*. Cambridge, MA: Harvard University Press.

————. 1950. Wesley Clair Mitchell (1874–1948). *Quarterly Journal of Economics* 44, no. 1 (February): 139–55.

————. 1951. *Ten Great Economists*. New York: Oxford University Press.

Semmler, W. 1994. *Business Cycles: Theory and Empirical Methods*. Boston: Kluwer Academic Publishers.

Stiglitz, J. E. 1992. Methodological Issues and New Keynesian Economics. In Vercelli and Dimitri 1993.

Tobin, J. 1989. Review of *Stabilizing an Unstable Economy,* by H. P. Minsky. *Journal of Economic Literature*.

Vercelli, A., and N. Dimitri. 1993. *Macroeconomics: A Survey of Research Strategies*. Oxford: Oxford University Press.

Money Creation, Profits, and Growth: Monetary Aspects of Economic Evolution

Mathias Binswanger

Evolution of modern capitalist economies is driven by the search for monetary profits. This was emphasized by Keynes, Marx, Schumpeter, and Veblen, but it is often neglected today. Economic processes might be characterized as an M-C-M' circuit, if we use Marx's terminology, that describes how firms spend money (M) on wages and capital to make more money (M') by selling their products. The search for new profit opportunities leads to a continuous expansion of the M-C-M' circuit that, in turn, induces economic growth. However, from time to time, further expansion of the M-C-M' circuit is limited by financial or real constraints. An important breakthrough in the history of the development of capitalist economies was the relaxation of the financing constraint. The financing constraint is due to the fact that firms have to finance their activities before they earn money by them, because production processes take time. In barter or commodity-money economies, firms, on an aggregate level, could only spend what had previously been saved. However, the development of modern banking systems removed this constraint as endogenous money creation by bank credits was enabled. In modern capitalist economies, which are credit-money economies, profits and growth depend on creation of additional purchasing power by bank credits, by which firms are able to finance investments in income-producing capital and, finally, to earn more money than they initially spent. Creation of additional purchasing power by bank credits is also an important, however many times neglected, part of Schumpeter's theory of economic development. Reexamination of the unorthodox monetary side of Schumpeter's contribution shows the importance of money creation for real economic development.

The *M-C-M'* Circuit and Its Dual Nature

The main goal of firms in a monetary production economy (as in all modern capitalist economies) is to make profits in nominal terms, no matter in what particular economic activity firms are engaged. Investments will only be made

413

if the total of present and future (discounted) cash flows will exceed total outlays, that is to say, if firms end up with more money than they started with. This was clearly expressed by Keynes, when he wrote

> An entrepreneur is interested, not in the amount of product, but in the amount of money which will fall to his share. He will increase his output, if by so doing he expects to increase his money profit, even though this profit represents a smaller quantity of output than before. (Keynes 1979, p. 82)

Similar remarks can be found in the writings of Marx (1936, p. 97), Schumpeter (1951, p. 222), and Veblen (1904, p. 50), who all recognized the predominant role of money. Heilbroner (1986, p. 142) describes the search for monetary profit as "the fundamental force that drives capitalist systems through history—a search on whose outcomes hinges the historical fate of the social formation as a whole."

If we use Marx's terminology (which was also used by Keynes), the whole process of profit making might be expressed by a M-C-M' circuit that captures the fundamental logic of capitalism (Heilbronner 1986, p. 36). M-C is the use of money capital (financial capital) M to purchase physical capital and the hiring of labor to produce goods and services. C-M' describes the sale of goods and services for money M', which represents firm's income. A profit is realized when M' exceeds M. Firms will not produce unless they expect M' to be above M. The M-C-M' circuit is a short version of a single firm's activities during a production period and, on an aggregate level, a description of the total nonfinancial business activities in an economy. Of course, M-C-M' circuits of different firms do not happen at the same time, nor do households spend their incomes at the same time. Firms are continuously starting new M-C-M' circuits that are interwoven with other firms' M-C-M' circuits in time. In spite of this fact, the M-C-M' circuit might serve as a representation of firms' activities in the aggregate during a certain period of time, in the same way that national income accounts represent economic activities during a certain period of time. Continuous realization of the aggregate M-C-M' circuit will lead to economic growth, as profits can only be maintained by net investments in income-producing assets (physical and financial capital).

To a noneconomist the message from the M-C-M' would hardly be surprising, but the M-C-M' circuit describes economic processes from a monetary point of view that is fundamentally different from orthodox economic theory which is built on neoclassical theory. Orthodox macroeconomic approaches (monetarism as well as Keynesian orthodoxy) accept the quantity theory of money, in which money (and therefore monetary profits) does not matter to the real economy, at least in the long run, since nominal values can matter only to those who suffer from money illusion. And in modern orthodox approaches, money illusion is ruled out by the rational expectations hypothesis (see also Minsky 1993, p. 77f). In the orthodox economic world "real" factors (labor, physical capital) determine "real" variables (real output) and money is just a veil. Therefore, the consequences of rediscovering the importance of the M-C-M' circuit as described in the works of Marx, Keynes, Schumpeter, Veblen, and others are more far-reaching than one might expect at first sight. As soon as we accept the logic of the M-C-M' circuit, financial processes and institutions become paramount to the evolution of economic systems.

The M-C-M' circuit is not an instantaneous process since cost outflows (M) always precede revenue inflows (M'). This is simply a result of the fact that production processes take time and therefore cannot initially be financed by the monetary income flows they will create. This time gap between spending and earning money may be short if, for example, the food industry spends money on wages and the employees immediately buy food with their income. But the time gap may also be many years, if, for example, the chemical industry finances basic research that will lead to marketable products at a much later date. Filling this time gap is the essential function of money in a monetary production economy, as it allows spending on wages and capital (M) before firms earn money (M') by sales of goods and services. Because of its role as credit for financing spending, some post-Keynesian economists (e.g., Minsky 1986a; Wray 1990) defined money as a debt issued primarily to transfer purchasing power from the future to the present. This definition of money is not restricted to any of the standard monetary aggregates ($M1$, $M2$, $M3$, and so on) and includes a variety of financial assets (bonds, stocks,[1] etc.) that might serve as money (or, more precisely, money capital) as they finance a firm's spending. During the evolution of modern capitalist economies, the types of assets serving as money substantially increased as financial innovations generated new kinds of assets and financial markets. The financial part of the M-C-M' circuit became increasingly sophisticated, especially during the last decades. Therefore, a broad definition of money is necessary to capture the whole monetary dimension of the M-C-M' circuit in a modern capitalist economy.[2]

As just outlined, the M-C-M' circuit is a process with a time arrow that points from M to M'. However, the actual M-C-M' circuit has to be distinguished from its ex ante valuation, which precedes any actions undertaken to start the M-C-M' circuit. Before firms will actually invest in any project, they will compare costs (M) with discounted expected revenues (M'), of which the

---

1. Stocks may be interpreted as debts of a firm against itself.

2. A more detailed description of different forms of money and their creation processes will follow later.

latter are still uncertain at the moment of decision making. Therefore, firms can only compare M with an expected value of M', which is determined by expectations of the future development of the firm's economic performance and the demand for its products (see also Keynes, chap. 12 of *The General Theory*). The result of the comparison of M with expected M' (expectations may differ a lot between economic agents) will determine whether projects or investments will be financed or not. These kinds of valuation processes take place inside firms, but are also made by banks when they decide whether they will provide credit to a firm, or by potential investors planning to purchase financial assets issued by firms. These valuation processes lead to capitalization of expected future money inflows, which, in turn, determine the market value of a whole firm. Prices of firms, as for example set in mergers and acquisitions, depend on ex ante valuations of future income expectations, which become visible by being transformed into prices of a firm's assets (especially stocks). Even though expected money inflows are still fictional at the moment of their market valuation, they are immediately reflected in current prices. The more markets for financial assets, whose valuation depends on expected future money inflows, were developed, the greater the influence of profit expectations on current asset prices became. Nowadays, a firm's value, and therefore its creditworthiness and its potential to attract investors, is mainly determined on financial markets, where price movements of financial assets reflect a firm's ability to create successful profit expectations (see also Minsky 1986b, p. 348).

Ex ante valuations of the M-C-M' circuit always precede the actual M-C-M' circuit. Not profits realized, but profit expectations, are the driving force and the motivation to keep the dynamics of the M-C-M' circuit alive. In this sense all economic activities have a speculative element, as there is always uncertainty about the profitability of investments. Speculation is an inherent part of a monetary production economy, as financial asset prices are determined by profit expectations that have not been realized so far. Profit expectations lead to a rise in a firm's value (mainly by a rise in its financial asset prices), which precedes actual money inflows (M') that become due after production and sales of products. Investors are not directly interested in the actual productive activities of a firm. They are interested in realizing capital gains on financial markets due to a successful transformation of profit expectations into current asset prices. However, profit expectations must eventually come true because otherwise frustrated economic agents (banks and investors) will lose faith in the economic system and stop financing business activities of a certain firm, as profit expectations disappear. On an aggregate level, this would cause a recession, since new investment projects would no longer be financed.

The dual nature of the M-C-M' process, that is to say, its ex ante valuation and its actual realization, became increasingly important during the evolution of modern capitalist economies and is crucial for understanding the dynamics and constraints of the M-C-M' circuit. Discrepancies between ex ante valuations and actual economic processes exist at any point in time, and actual economic production always tries to follow its anticipated trend, which ex ante results in profit expectations (otherwise a project would not have been financed at all). Successful creation of profit expectations is the first step and the major driving force for actually realizing profits.

Constraints on the *M-C-M'* Circuit

The history of the evolution of capitalist economies might be interpreted as a constant search for new ways of removing prevailing constraints to the M-C-M' circuit's further expansion. Removal of constraints is a necessity at times when further economic growth and, thus, new possibilities for profit making are limited. Constraints arise mainly due to the temporal separation of M and M', the discrepancy between monetary and real developments, and the discrepancy between actual production and ex ante valuations. Three main categories might be distinguished

- the financing constraint (M constraint)
- the real constraint (C constraint)
- the profit constraint (M' constraint)

These constraints will now be described in more depth.

The Financing Constraint[3]

The financing constraint is due to the fact that cost outflows precede revenue inflows. Firms have to finance their activities before they earn any money by these activities. Therefore, they must have money at the beginning of the production process to be able to spend on wages and capital, no matter whether they finance current costs (mainly the wage bill) or investments (purchase of physical or financial capital). For the single firm this money may come from internal funds (retained profits made in earlier periods) or it may be borrowed from banks (credits) or other potential investors (long-term financing by issuing financial assets). The relevance of the financing constraint, however, can only be seen on the aggregate level. In a closed economy[4] without any possibility of money creation, firms' spending is absolutely con-

---

3. This constraint is also described in Guttmann 1990, pp. 87–88.

4. In an open economy, firms' spending might be financed by foreign credit. However, for the world economy as a whole, financing constraints apply in the same way as to a closed economy.

strained by prior savings. This was the case in pure barter economies (in which savings were in physical goods), as well as in commodity-money (e.g., gold) economies,[5] in which economic agents in the aggregate could not spend more money than was previously saved (see next section). Due to the development of modern banking the financing constraint was removed step by step and firms' spending became increasingly independent of prior savings as money creation by bank credits allowed firms in the aggregate to continuously spend more than was earned in earlier periods (deficit spending).[6] The relaxation of the financing constraint was crucial to the development of a monetary production economy, which is not a commodity-money but a credit-money economy (Moore 1990, p. 55).

The Real Constraint

Real constraints arise if there is a scarcity of profitable investment opportunities, in relation to money capital (M), which would be available for financing profitable investments. During the evolution of capitalist economies this constraint was constantly eased by new innovations that created new profit opportunities, as emphasized in Schumpeter's theory of economic development (Schumpeter 1934). However, there are periods in economic development when a lack of profitable investment opportunities becomes a real constraint to the whole economy because existing production possibilities are no longer sufficient to create enough prospects for profits. Then the M-C-M' circuit must expand to totally new areas, in which additional profit opportunities may emerge due to new kinds of innovations. This was the case when agrarian economies developed into industrial economies and technical progress allowed fundamentally new kinds of innovations. Physical capital (operated by new energy sources) substituted for labor in physical production. By this development the real labor constraint was removed, as production could always be increased without a corresponding need for additional labor (see Hahn 1920, p. 118 ff). In modern capitalist economies there is no full employment level of production beyond which an economy cannot expand. However, modern capitalist economies are threatened by a new kind of real constraint, which is due to the fact that the removal of the financing constraint enabled a constant increase in financial capital, which increased much faster than innovations and profit opportunities in production. But, as has already been recognized by Schumpeter, innovations are not restricted to physical production

---

5. However, in a commodity-money economy, in which for example gold served as money, some economic agents could spend more money than was saved by extraction of additional gold from gold mines.

6. The process of money creation through credit and its effects on the economy will be described in detail in the following sections.

and can also take place within financial institutions (Schumpeter 1951, p. 222). Financial innovations create additional profit opportunities without a corresponding increase in production, which partially leads to delinking of the development of financial markets from the development of the "real economy." The M-C-M' circuit is combined with a fast growing M-M' circuit, which bypasses productive activity by removing the C out of the circuit (see also Dow 1993, p. 54).

The Profit Constraint

The profit constraint refers to a variety of constraining factors. The constraint mainly arises from the discrepancy between expected and actual developments of the economy. As already described above (in the first section), there is always uncertainty about future money inflows when investments are decided and, therefore, always a danger that expectations might be frustrated. On the aggregate level, this uncertainty is especially related to the development of aggregate demand, because firms never know how much consumers and investors will spend for their products in future periods and how much they will save.[7] Therefore, aggregate demand may fall behind its expected level, which means that the fictional ex ante values (and therefore financial asset prices) are not actually validated ex post. Due to the dual nature of the M-C-M' circuit, continuing unfulfilled profit expectations will have two effects. They will lead to a recession as firms reduce their investments but they will also cause an immediate decline in financial asset values and, therefore, reduce current economic wealth, which, in the extreme case, may lead to a financial crash. This was the case in 1929, when the stock market crashed in New York, leading to the following Great Depression.

Especially since World War II, severe downturns of the economy could be prevented and the profit constrained could be relaxed due to the following developments:

- An increase in government deficit spending stabilized aggregate demand and counteracted contraction dynamics from spending cutbacks (Minsky 1982, p. 37; Guttmann 1990, p. 88).[8]
- Central banks became more sophisticated in protecting financial markets as lenders-of-last-resort, which prevented general declines in asset values (Minsky 1986a).

---

7. In modern capitalist economies, saving mainly implies that economic agents leave money in their bank accounts or invest it in financial assets instead of buying goods or services for consumption or "real" investments.

8. This argument is quite contrary to the "crowding out hypothesis," which mainstream economists are very fond of. The divergency mainly arises from the different interpretation of the process of money creation (see the next section).

– The development of credit-financing possibilities kept aggregate demand on high levels, even if more money was saved, and therefore not spent again, during a certain period. Increasing credit-financing possibilities relaxed the financing constraint as well as the profit constraint.

Other developments that stimulated demand (such as marketing) might also have contributed to high spending levels. But the main point to be emphasized is the crucial role of government and the central bank, which has prevented general declines in developed capitalist economies since World War II and therefore has allowed further expansion of the M-C-M' circuit.

The remainder of this chapter will deal mainly with the financing constraint and its relaxation but, since all constraints are basically interrelated, the real constraint and the profit constrained also matter to the arguments that will be presented. In modern capitalist economies, relaxation of all constraints is related to credit expansion, which is at the heart of economic development. And economic development is intrinsically related to economic growth, as economic agents try to expand the M-C-M' circuit during their constant search for profits.

Is Money Creation Necessary for Profits and Growth?

In modern monetary production economies,[9] growth depends on the creation of profits through investments in income-producing capital, which might be net investments in physical capital (gross investments minus depreciation) or investments in financial capital (purchasing financial assets). But investments have to be financed first before they are able to produce income. Therefore, we must ask how investments might be financed on an aggregate level. Theoretically, the following possibilities exist:

– by savings
– by creation of credit money
– by savings and creation of credit money

As long as we stay in the framework of neoclassical theory, investments can only be financed by savings. Economic modeling starts with a given level of income that can either be spent on consumption goods or be saved. Investments are financed out of prior savings that may come from internal funds or are intermediated from lenders to borrowers by the banking system. Therefore, investments can only be increased by a reduction in consumptive spending, which increases savings by the same amount. Since our analysis deals

---

9. We still make the simplifying assumption that the economies described in this section are closed economies. Also, we neglect the government for the moment.

with equilibrium situations, the supply of savings will equal the demand for investments (there is no money hoarding) through an adjustment of the interest rate.[10] Banks are interpreted as institutions that intermediate savings from lenders to borrowers, but not as money-creating institutions. However, the neoclassical framework does not bear much resemblance to a modern capitalist economy, which is mainly a credit-money economy. It would aptly describe a barter economy or a commodity-money economy, but these kinds of economies are outmoded today (see the previous section about the financing constraint).[11]

The neoclassical framework is not well suited to analyze an economy characterized by the *M-C-M'* circuit, which is dominated by firms' search for monetary profits. The question of how investments and economic growth are to be financed cannot be analyzed if the crucial role of money and its creation is ignored. We have to understand how money is created and integrated into a monetary production economy. Therefore, economic modeling may not be started with a given level of income that can either be consumed or saved, since the source of this income also has to be explained. Economic analysis must start with firms (or the entrepreneur, in Schumpeter's theory) that plan to engage in some business activities but have not earned any money from these business activities so far and, therefore, face a financing constraint. Initial finance requirements of firms are determined by the amount of the wage bill and the cost of capital. If we simplify for the moment by assuming that there is no saving and all income is spent again during a production period, these finance requirements can only be met by bank credits granted to firms, which function as money as they transfer purchasing power from the future (the end of the production period) to the present (the beginning of the production period). The purchasing power, however, would never come into existence without the credit and, therefore, it might also be said that purchasing power is created by new credit. This was clearly expressed by Schumpeter

> In a capitalist economy, credit is essentially the creation of purchasing power for the purpose of transferring it to the entrepreneur. (Schumpeter 1934, p. 107)

Credits enable firms to start production of goods and services at the beginning of a production period. During the same production period, the recipients of firms' spending will spend their money again to purchase goods and services

---

10. If capital markets are not in equilibrium, as is always the case in reality, this is usually explained by market imperfections, which in modern approaches are mainly due to asymmetric information.

11. Some economists doubt whether pure barter economies or commodity-money economies ever existed (see Wray 1990).

that firms produced during the production period. With their income from sales, firms may repay their debts to banks, but the credits have to be renewed (rolled over) at the beginning of the next period of production, as firms' spending has to be financed again. Bank credits provide the "revolving fund of finance" (Wray 1991, p. 956) that finances a constant level of spending. If firms plan to expand their business activities, bank credits also have to be expanded to finance a higher level of spending. A constantly growing economy (in nominal terms) needs a constant growth in the amount of money created during every production period.

Only in two special cases does a growing economy not necessarily need an extension of credit:

1. If there is a fall in prices during a production period, credits do not have to be expanded for an expansion of business activities. However, this condition is unlikely to hold in modern production economies dominated by labor market institutions that create substantial downward rigidity of money wages (see Knodell 1988, p. 165). Additionally, falling prices lower profit expectations and discourage firms from expansion of their business activities, which would be unlikely to occur together with economic growth (Preiser 1953, p. 253).
2. If the velocity of money is increased, more transactions can be financed with the same amount of money. However, in a modern production economy, in which money is mainly credit money, the velocity of money[12] might not be increased much further.

So far, we have just described the conditions under which the M-C-M' circuit could be expanded, but have not addressed the question of how M' can exceed M. If firms on the aggregate are to make profits during a certain period of production, an increase in firm spending in every production period is not optional, but a necessity. Otherwise, the following paradox cannot be solved: *How can firms in the aggregate make monetary profits if they do not receive income that exceeds their initial outlays?* Or, formulated in a different way: *How can firms earn more money than they initially spend?*

If firms in an economy spend 100 units of money at the beginning of a production period, they cannot earn more than this 100 units at the end of the production period and, therefore, making profits (in terms of money) is not possible in the aggregate,[13] unless some additional money enters the M-C-M'

---

12. The term also loses its precise meaning if money is broadly defined and, therefore, encompasses a variety of different assets.
13. This statement also holds if the velocity of money is increased during a certain period. An increase in the velocity of money decreases the amount of money that firms need to borrow

circuit. Without new money creation, firms can maximally recapture their production costs during a certain production period if the recipients of firms' initial spending on wages and capital spend all their money received to purchase the output produced during this period. If we make our model more realistic by allowing economic agents to save, the previously described conditions are not fundamentally altered. When economic agents also decide to save money (not spend money) during a production period and there is no additional money creation, firms cannot even recapture all production costs and will have losses. Of course, this nonspending of income could be compensated for by savings from earlier periods, but this only shifts the problem backward in time, as in earlier periods the same problem applied. Firms must have had losses during earlier periods due to nonspending of money if there are prior savings available for financing current spending. Therefore, if we aggregate over several periods of time, firms on the average will just recapture what they spend by either consumption or intermediation of savings, unless there is permanent money hoarding.

However, firms will only produce if they expect to sell their products at a profit and they would not produce if they would recapture only their initial outlays. GDP must always be sold not at cost, but at cost plus a profit markup, which requires that money available for purchasing output must exceed production costs in every production period. There must be an increase of purchasing power in every period if firms are to make profits. And the additional purchasing power can only be provided by newly created credits. Prior savings cannot create purchasing power, since they represent money that has not been spent again so far and thus have reduced aggregate demand in earlier periods. Therefore, if we extend our analysis over several production periods, savings are not a source for creating purchasing power. One of the few mainstream economists who recognized this fact was Evsey Domar. He wrote

> It is not sufficient . . . that savings of yesterday be invested today, or, as it is often expressed, that investment offset savings. Investment today must always exceed the savings of yesterday. . . . An injection of new money . . . must take place every day. (Domar 1957, p. 92)

The grant of a bank credit to a firm in addition to the credits already existing and in excess of credits being repaid (net credit creation) means an increase in the money supply. When firms spend this newly created money on wages or capital, the recipient's income is increased. And if the recipients of income spend this additional money again during the same period (a rise in aggregate

from banks, as more transactions may be financed with less money. But no matter how many times money is transferred from one economic agent to another, there is no way that firms in the aggregate can earn more money than they originally spend without money creation.

demand), firms are able to make profits as their income exceeds their initial outlays. This is the case because the credit does not appear as cost in firms' income statements. The increase of firms' spending is deficit-financed (Wray 1991, p. 956). Only the interest payments that have to be paid to the bank are costs, but these outlays will also finally be recaptured by firms as banks (or their employees) spend their income for purchasing products.

Up to now, two different aspects concerning money creation and its effects on the M-C-M' circuit have been described. First, it was shown that business spending at the beginning of a production period has to be financed by bank credits, which firms are able to repay at the end of a production period. Or at least they are able to do so if saving during this period does not exceed prior savings that come from internal funds or can be intermediated to firms during this period. So, even if in reality part of firms' spending is financed by prior savings, these savings are ultimately the result of bank credits that did not flow back to firms. Savings are the result but not the cause of credits and, therefore, credits always precede savings.

Second, we demonstrated that firms in the aggregate are only able to make profits if additional money (by an extension of credits) is injected into the M-C-M' circuit in every production period. Then firms will realize profits unless all of the additionally created money is saved by its recipients (households) and therefore not spent again during the production period. In this case, the behavior of households will destroy the profit expectations of the firms.

No distinction has yet been made as to whether firms spend newly created money for financing additional current costs (mainly spending on wages) or for financing investments in income-producing capital. In all cases spending of additional money will increase national income. Additionally, national income is also increased by consumer credits or, if we include the government again in our model, by government deficit spending. All newly created money that is spent for buying goods and services increases aggregate demand. This leads to growth in nominal terms but not necessarily to growth in real (as opposed to nominal) terms. Whether firms respond to increased demand by increasing their output or by raising prices depends on many factors and cannot be stated with assurance. In a monetary production economy, creation of money is a necessary but not sufficient condition for real growth to appear.

Ultimately, profits can only be maintained by making investments in income-producing capital. This is the case because, in the long run, sustaining profits is related to innovations. Due to competition in capitalist economies, high profits cannot be sustained over long periods without innovations, by which firms gain a competitive advantage. Therefore, except in the case of a permanent monopoly, firms constantly have to innovate their business activities, because otherwise their profit expectations will be lowered as other firms enter profitable markets and destroy temporary competitive advantages. The search for profits by innovation is crucial to Schumpeter's analysis, which described how the drive for above-normal profits leads to innovation (Schumpeter 1951, p. 222). But innovations can only become economic reality by investments in income-producing capital, no matter whether the innovations are related to products, production techniques, marketing, business organization, or financial activities. Successful investments will also induce real growth by raising an economy's productive capacity as they increase production of goods, create new goods and services, or improve quality of existing goods and services. However, only the increase in production of goods can really quantitatively be measured and separated from price movements. In all other cases, which become increasingly important, the term *real* and therefore also the term *real growth* is ambiguous, because there is no exact way that real changes can be separated from price changes. If the term *real* is used in this chapter, it implies all quantitative and qualitative changes of output, which do not necessarily correspond to a change in the quantity of goods produced. Therefore, not all real aspects are reflected in changes of real GDP as measured in national income accounting. This is of special importance if we analyze investments in financial assets, which enable "profits without production" (Binswanger 1994). These profits are the result of real activities by financial institutions on financial markets, which, however, are only reflected in price movements.

Summing up, we may say that in the long run, real growth depends on innovations, which, in turn, become economic reality by investments. Therefore, money creation for financing investments is crucial for sustaining profits, as well as for inducing real growth. Only money creation used for financing investments will directly induce real growth. Other ways of spending newly created money, which have no real effect on business activities, might contribute to profit realization by relaxation of the profit constraint (see above) as they stabilize aggregate demand, but without being accompanied by investments they will only raise prices and therefore cause inflation. That is why the question of financing economic growth is mainly about financing investments. And investments, as with all spending, can ultimately only be financed by money creation and not by savings. Of course, if we restrict our analysis to only one period of production, it looks like investments can be financed by either credits or saving. However, if analysis is extended over several periods, savings cannot create purchasing power and therefore cannot be the ultimate source for financing growth. This point was made by Preiser, when he wrote

Growth of economic production would be impossible if the banking system would not grant credits for investments. (Preiser 1953, p. 253, translated by the author)

The following simple model might illustrate and summarize the arguments presented so far by expressing them in common macroeconomic terminology. However, since expected profits are the major driving force of the M-C-M' circuit, profits are treated as a separate macroeconomic variable, which is not the case in conventional macroeconomic modeling. Again we refer to a closed economy, which consists of just firms and households. Firms only receive income from selling output. Income from owning financial assets is not considered and there is no consumption out of profit income.

Let us adopt the following symbols:

Y: Aggregate demand, which equals firms' total income during the production period.

C: Consumption, which is the demand for goods of firms in the consumption goods sector.

I: Investment, which is the demand for products of firms in the investment goods sector

S: Saving (household saving)

E: Initial expenditures of firms, which equal spending on wages (the wage bill) and therefore equal income of households, which is either consumed or saved.

Π: Firms' total profits in both sectors.

M: Money

During a production period, represented by a M-C-M' circuit, firms' income Y is

$$Y = C + I$$

and firms' expenditures E are

$$E = C + S.$$

Therefore, firms' profit Π during a production period is

$$\Pi = Y - E = (C + I) - (C + S) = I - S. \quad [14] \tag{1}$$

---

14. See Kalecki 1971; Minsky 1982, p. 34 ff; or Preiser 1953 for more detailed descriptions.

Profits of firms[15] are determined by the difference between investments and savings. If investments exceed savings during a production period, firms are able to make profits. This result is due to the fact that consumption enters both costs (spending on wages) as well as demand (income of firms in the consumption goods sector) and therefore has no influence on profits. Household savings lower profits, because they diminish the income of firms in the consumption goods sector. Household savings represent the part of the wage bill that firms are not able to recapture. Investments, contrary to consumption, represent income but no cost to firms of both sectors together during one period. To understand this fact, we additionally have to consider the way in which investments are financed.

The answer to the question of how investments are financed shows the fundamental difference between a nonmonetary approach, such as the neoclassical framework, and alternative approaches, which recognize the monetary reality of the M-C-M' circuit. Therefore, we might distinguish the two following answers to the question of how investments are financed

1. Financing of investments in the neoclassical model: The neoclassical model is a timeless equilibrium model and all processes happen instantaneously. Investments are financed with income not spent for consumption (savings), which immediately flows back from households to firms and finances investments. Savings always equal investments and actually come to mean the pecuniary accountancy of investment (Ranson 1983, p. 906). Thus, firms are not able to make profits, as the profit Π in formula (1) is always zero if there are no market imperfections. Monetary constraints do not exist in the equilibrium, as market forces adjust supply and demand of financial funds.

---

15. Profits of firms in the consumption goods section and profits of firms in the investment goods sector are inversely related. The higher the wage bill in the investment goods sector, the lower the profits in the investment goods sector, but the higher the profits in the consumption goods sector, as a higher wage bill in the investment sector will increase consumptive spending. To demonstrate this, let us adopt the following symbols:
Π_I: Profits of firms in the investment goods sector
Π_C: Profits of firms in the consumption goods sector
Then,

$$\Pi_I = I - C_I - S_I$$

$$\Pi_C = C_C + C_I - C_C - S_C = C_I - S_C.$$

Therefore,

$$\Pi_I = I - \Pi_C - S.$$

2. Financing of investments in the M-C-M' circuit: Economic analysis is in historical time and money matters. Therefore, investments have to be financed before they create income and income is created before investment goods are actually produced. Investments are ultimately financed by newly created money, which immediately increases aggregate demand as additional investment goods are demanded.[16] On the aggregate, total income of firms in the consumption goods sector and the investment goods sector is increased without increasing financial outlays. This is the case because the additional outlays for investment goods, which firms of the consumption goods sector have to pay to firms of the investment goods sector, represent additional income to firms of the investment goods sector at the same amount. Therefore, they do not increase costs to the industry sector as a whole. The additional money paid to workers in the investment goods sector, however, leads to additional income in the consumption goods sector without increasing financial outlay,[17] as the credits that they used to finance the purchase of investment goods are not paid back during the production period. They might be paid back afterward out of firms' profits, however in this case they have to be renewed in the next period if further investments are planned.

Household saving, on the other hand, has no direct connection to investments and depends on households' propensity to save, which are (in this context) independent of firms' investment decisions. If all additionally created money is saved, savings will equal investments, which means that all of the new money is hoarded by households and cannot be recaptured by firms of the consumption goods sector. In this case, as in the neoclassical model, but for different reasons, firms will not make profits, which is indicated by formula (1).

Keeping in mind the different ways in which investments are financed in neoclassical models and the M-C-M' approach, we may now demonstrate how different assumptions about savings and investments affect nominal growth and profits during one period. We assume that initially there is no savings S and there are no investments I. Letting $Y = C = 100$ as the initial state of the economy, we will show how an investment of $\Delta I = 10$ will affect the economy by distinguishing three different cases (table 1). In the first case (no money creation) investments must be accompanied by a corresponding reduction of consumption, so there will be no growth. In the second case (money creation with high consumption) there is growth as firms can recapture all of

---

16. The process will be described more exactly in the next section.

17. Only interest payments to banks represent additional costs, but they normally also can be recaptured by firms, as banks and workers of banks spend their income for investment and consumption goods.

TABLE 1. The Effect of Money Creation and Savings on Nominal Growth and Profits during One Period

	Initial Conditions	Changes during Production Period	Result at the End of Production Period
No money creation (barter or commodity-money economy, the neoclassical case)	$Y = C = 100$ $I = S = 0$ $\Pi = 0$	$\Delta I = 10$ $\Delta S = 10$ $\Delta C = -10$ $\Delta M = 0$	$Y = 100$ (no growth) $C = 90$ $I = S = 10$ $\Pi = 0$
Money creation and no saving (credit-money economy with high consumption)	$Y = C = 100$ $I = S = 0$ $\Pi = 0$	$\Delta I = 10$ $\Delta S = 0$ $\Delta C = 0$ $\Delta M = 10$	$Y = 110$ (growth) $C = 100$ $I = 10$ $S = 0$ $\Pi = 10$
Money creation and saving (credit-money economy with household savings)	$Y = C = 100$ $I = S = 0$ $\Pi = 0$	$\Delta I = 10$ $\Delta S = 10$ $\Delta C = 0$ $\Delta M = 10$	$Y = 110$ (growth) $C = 100$ $I = 10$ $S = 10$ $\Pi = 0$

their outlays and all of the additionally created money accounts as firms' profit. In the third case (money creation and saving), there is also growth, but households hoard all of the additionally created money (do not spend it again during the period). Thus, firms are not able to make profits and their profit expectations are frustrated due to households' saving. Therefore, in the third case, it is unlikely that firms will continue to expand their production, while they will have an incentive to continue growing in the second case due to profits realized.

The second and third cases represent extreme conditions, as all of the additionally created money is either spent (case 2) or saved (case 3). In reality, it might be somewhere between these cases, so that part of the additionally created money is saved and part of it accounts for firms' profit, which means (see also Parguez 1988)

$$0 < S < I.$$

The main purpose of this section was to show that money creation is a necessary condition for financing investments and growth, as well as for making profits in a monetary production economy characterized by the *M-C-M'* circuit. However, we did not describe the process of money creation and how it is intertwined with economic development and growth. The way in which money affects economic evolution in a dynamic context has always been a matter of controversy among economists and will be further considered in the next section.

Endogenous Money Creation and Its Real Effects: Schumpeter Revisited

Basically, analyzing real effects of money creation involves two steps:

- the money creation process
- the expansion of the M-C-M' circuit

As far as the money-creation process is concerned, the discussion mainly centers around the question of how money can be endogenously created by the banking system. The possibility of endogenous money creation by the banking system is a main point of departure from orthodox monetary theory, in which the money supply is exogenously controllable by the central bank. If this is not the case in reality, it is because the monetary authorities are not really inclined to control the money supply. In the ideal world of orthodox monetary theory, which is strongly influenced by monetarist ideas, banks are supposed to adjust their balance sheets as the central bank increases or contracts reserves. The central bank controls reserves (or the monetary base that consists of currency held by the public and of bank reserves), which determine the money supply. The money supply is interpreted as the product of the monetary base with the so-called money multiplier.[18]

In contrast to orthodox monetary theory, theories of endogenous money creation rest on the following basic assumptions.[19]

- Money is created by new bank loans (which represent credit money) demanded by nonbanks.
- Money creation by commercial banks is generally accommodated by the central bank as the quantity of reserves is adjusted to bank needs. Therefore, money creation is endogenously determined by the banking system. The central bank is able to control interest rates but not the money supply.
- Deficit spending by economic agents is not constrained by the availability of prior savings (relaxation of the financing constraint).

---

18. The money multiplier is a function of the reserve-deposit ratio (the fraction of deposits that banks hold in reserve) and the currency-deposit ratio (the fraction of money that the public holds in the form of currency). The lower the reserve-deposit ratio and the lower the currency-deposit ratio, the higher the money multiplier.

19. I do not attempt to give a detailed description of theories of endogenous money creation in this chapter. Overviews can be found in Lavoie 1992; Moore 1988; Niggle 1990; and Wray 1990.

Theories of endogenous money creation are actually quite old and can be traced back to the Banking School as represented by Tooke (1848), or the Scottish economist Macleod (1889).[20] At the beginning of this century, the possibility of endogenous money creation was emphasized in the nonorthodox monetary writings of Keynes (in the *Treatise of Money* but not in *The General Theory*) and Wicksell, and of the German economists Schumpeter and Hahn. Later, the endogenous money approach was of major importance to the contributions of Gurely and Shaw, Kaldor, Minsky, and Preiser, to name just a few. Nowadays, the theory is especially put forward by post-Keynesians (e.g., Davidson, Moore, Rousseas, Wray) and the French-Canadian School of circuitistes (e.g., Lavoie, Parguez).

Although there are numerous contributions describing the process of endogenous money creation, few economists dealing with endogenous money creation have actually tried to link this approach to the expansion of the M-C-M' circuit in the long run. The analysis of the expansion of the M-C-M' circuit should explain

- the way that newly created money enters economic processes
- the effects of money creation on investment, aggregate demand, income, saving, prices, output, and, finally, real growth, as well as the temporal sequence of changes of the economic variables

Schumpeter was one of the few economists who tried to link endogenous money creation to the expansion of the M-C-M' circuit and the evolution of capitalist economies in the long run. He emphasized the role of money creation in economic development. Therefore, we will reexamine some important monetary aspects of Schumpeter's theory, which, however, are frequently neglected (see also Maier-Rigaud 1985, p. 26).

Schumpeter's analysis of money creation can be related to Macleod, who wrote

A bank is not an office for borrowing and lending money but it is a manufactory of credit. (Macleod 1889, p. 594)

Schumpeter, as well as Macleod, emphasizes the role of banks as credit-granting institutions. Banks create money by issuing claims (debts) against themselves, which then function as money. Banks guarantee for the borrower, who would not be trusted if he were to issue a debt against himself. However, at banks credits (loans) created deposits, which became accepted means of payment during the evolution of capitalist economies. The creation of credit is the exchange of present against future purchasing power (Schumpeter 1934,

---

20. The history of the endogenous money approach is described in Wray 1990.

p. 125). If a bank grants credit to a firm, it accepts the products the firm is expected to produce as collateral (if the firm does not own securities that can be used for this purpose). Therefore, the credit precedes the existence of the collateral, which comes into existence at a later date (Schumpeter 1934, p. 112 f).

Banks and other financial enterprises, like nonfinancial firms, are profit-seeking entrepreneurial organizations that make profits by lending their promises to pay. Banks will grant credit as long as they expect to make profits by doing so. This will be the case as long as there are borrowers who are deemed to be creditworthy. And creditworthiness, in turn, implies that borrowers are expected to make profits and, therefore, ultimately be able to repay the loans granted to them. If credit expansion is not restricted by the central bank (or if there is the possibility of refinancing credits at the discount window or through open market operations) and if there is a clearing system established among banks, banks might extend credit beyond a healthy level by lowering their safety standards of creditworthiness and, thus, generate credit inflation (which is permanent and not temporary, as the credit inflation described below). In this case, additional legal restrictions would be necessary (Schumpeter 1934, p. 114 f).[21]

Schumpeter's analysis of the link between money creation and expansion of the M-C-M' circuit especially emphasizes the creation of purchasing power.

> Without the creation of new purchasing power by bank credits . . . financing of industrial development in modern economies would have been impossible. (Schumpeter 1927, p. 86, translated by the author)

Banks create credits on demand by firms, which increases a firm's purchasing power. The increase in purchasing power is the first step, if the M-C-M' circuit is to expand. Money enters the M-C-M' circuit by firms' spending of money, which is created by new bank credits.

The main thrust of Schumpeter's theory was to explain how innovation and growth take place through the creative destruction of the competitive process. Therefore, his analysis of monetary processes is also related to economic development. Of special importance is the time sequence of the whole process that starts with innovations and ends with economic growth. The starting point of Schumpeter's analysis is a new enterprise (or a previously existing firm that expands its activities into new fields) without internal funds available to finance its planned business activities. Therefore, new purchasing power has to be created by bank credits, if there are no savings that

---

21. The analysis of endogenous money creation by Schumpeter is consistent with modern approaches by post-Keynesians or circuitistes.

can be intermediated through the banking system. Saving, however, does not create purchasing power, since it is the result of purchasing power created by new credit in an earlier period that has not yet become effective (see previous section). This is also recognized by Schumpeter, although he often remains rather vague about this subject. But in his 1927 article he makes a clear statement by referring to his contemporary, Albert Hahn, who is much clearer (and more radical):

> If the basic mechanism of economic development is analyzed . . . it is advisable to accept the view developed by A. Hahn that . . . every credit creation increases purchasing power, but that in the case when this purchasing power is accompanied by saving, the money increasing effect is neutralized by that. (Schumpeter 1927, p. 87, referring to Hahn 1920, translated by the author)

This quote shows that Schumpeter basically supports the idea that all new purchasing power must be created by credits.

The motivation of an enterprise starting new business activities is expectation of profits due to innovations that yield a transitory monopoly position. Therefore, firms use the additionally created purchasing power for demanding investment goods that are necessary for innovations to become economic reality. Investments increase aggregate demand and therefore increase prices of investment goods, since production of investment goods has not been increased so far (Schumpeter 1927, p. 93). This, in turn, will raise demand for consumption goods[22] and cause price increases in consumption goods, whose production also has not yet been expanded. At first, creation of purchasing power will increase prices but not output. This is what Schumpeter calls credit inflation due to the fact that purchasing power precedes production of new products (or improvements of products). Schumpeter argues:

> Just as when additional gas streams into a vessel the share of that space occupied by each molecule of the previously existing gas is diminished by compression, so the inflow of new purchasing power into the economic system will compress the old purchasing power. When the price changes which thus become necessary are completed, any given commodities exchange for the new units of purchasing power on the same terms as for the old, only the units of purchasing power now existing are

---

22. Schumpeter explains the increasing demand for consumption goods by an increasing demand by the owners of the already existing investment goods (Schumpeter 1927, p. 93). It could, however, also be argued that the major impulse comes from additional consumption of employees in the investment goods sector. If production in the investment sector is increased due to the higher demand for investment goods, this will raise the total wage bill of the investment good sector before the investment goods are actually produced.

all smaller than those existing before and their distribution among individuals has been shifted. This may be called credit inflation. (Schumpeter 1934, p. 109)

Up till now, only nominal income has increased, but the productive capacity is still unchanged. However, in the next step there follows a credit deflation,[23] as in the following production period, investments have increased the productive capacity of the economy and new products will come to the market. Otherwise investments would not be profitable, since, due to the competitive process, profits cannot be maintained over a longer period of time by just raising prices. This is the way that real growth is induced by money creation. Price increases are followed by output increases, which neutralize the initial inflationary effect. Schumpeter writes

> After completing business—in our conception, therefore, after a period at the end of which [new] products are on the market . . . he [the innovating entrepreneur] has, if everything has gone according to expectations enriched the social system with goods whose total price is greater than the credit received and than the total price of the goods directly and indirectly used up by him [intermediate goods]. Hence the equivalence between the money and commodity streams is more than restored, the credit inflation more than eliminated, the effect upon prices more than compensated for, so that it may be said that there is no credit inflation at all in this case—rather deflation—but only a non-synchronous appearance of purchasing power and of the commodities corresponding to it, which temporarily produces the semblance of inflation. (Schumpeter 1934, p. 110)

Ultimately, the innovating firms are also able to repay their bank loans either by profit income or by replacing the original bank credits by issuing financial assets. This enables firms to get ahold of savings, which makes it possible to finance debts (including stocks) by savings. This short reexamination of the nonorthodox monetary side of Schumpeter's theory of economic development leads to some important conclusions.

1. Without money creation, real economic growth in a monetary production economy would be impossible (this was outlined in detail in the previous section).
2. Money creation first induces nominal growth, but this nominal growth finally leads to real growth, if the newly created money was used for financing investments in income-producing capital.

---

23. This is not the case for consumer credits or government debts, which only cause inflation (Schumpeter 1927, p. 93).

3. Real growth is a logical result of firms' constant drive for profits, which lead to innovations. Therefore, economic development (or evolution) is fundamentally intertwined with growth.

Schumpeter's analysis makes clear how economic development of modern capitalist economies has been enabled by the relaxation of the financing constraint. His contribution should not be ignored if we analyze the many times neglected monetary aspects of evolution in capitalist economies. However, due to the relaxation of the real constraint (see previous section) during the last decades, economic development in modern industrial economies is increasingly related to financial innovations, and this makes it much more difficult to separate nominal from real effects, as was done by Schumpeter.

Conclusion

The development of the possibility of endogenous money creation through the banking system has been one of the major breakthroughs in the evolution of capitalist economies. It made investments independent of prior savings, which in a monetary production economy is a necessity if firms are to make profits. And making monetary profits is the main goal of firms in a monetary production economy, as was recognized by Keynes, Marx, Schumpeter, and Veblen. However, only Schumpeter linked the drive for profits to long-term economic development of capitalist economies and the way that this development could be financed by endogenous money creation.

The economic processes of a monetary production economy are characterized by the M-C-M' circuit, which describes how firms invest money in their business activities and finally receive income by selling their products. However without endogenous money creation, the M-C-M' circuit (with $M' > M$) would not be feasible on an aggregated level. Without money creation, firms cannot earn more than they initially spend. Therefore, profits are financed by money creation and this money creation expands the M-C-M' circuit over time. This is the case because the competitive process forces firms to innovate if they want to make profits in the long run, which increases the productive capacity of an economy. Economic growth is linked to money creation, which is used for financing investments in income-producing capital.

A major consequence of our analysis concerns the role of saving in economic development. Orthodox economic logic is built on the idea that a high saving rate is the key to economic success, as it is used to finance investments. But a consequent analysis of the M-C-M' circuit over several production periods shows that savings cannot create additional purchasing power, which is necessary for profits and growth. Savings are the result and not the cause of investments,[24] because the financing of investments by newly created money enables economic agents to receive additional income, which they can either spend or save. But money which is not spent (savings) lowers firms' income. Therefore, at first savings do not stimulate investments, as they lower firms' profits, which, in turn, will reduce the incentive to invest any further. In the longer run, savings help to finance investments by intermediation through financial institutions. But this intermediation of savings cannot by itself stimulate investments, as it lowered profits in an earlier period. A high saving rate is not necessarily beneficial for growth.

REFERENCES

Binswanger, Mathias. 1994. "Wirtschaftswachstum durch "Profits without Production"?" In *Geld und Wachstum*, Hans Christoph Binswanger and Paschen von Flotow, eds. Stuttgart: Weitbrecht.
Domar, Evsey. 1957. *Essays in the Theory of Economic Growth*. New York: Oxford.
Dow, Sheila. 1993. *Money and the Economic Process*. Aldershot: Edward Elgar.
Gurley, John, and Edward Shaw. 1960. *Money in a Theory of Finance*. Washington, D.C.: Brookings.
Guttmann, Robert. 1990. "The regime of credit-money and its current transition." *Economies et Sociétés. Monnaie et Production* 7:81–105.
Hahn, Albert. 1920. *Volkswirtschaftliche Theorie des Bankkredits*. Tübingen: Mohr.
Heilbroner, Robert. 1986. *The Nature and Logic of Capitalism*. New York: W. W. Norton.
Kaldor, Nicholas. 1982. *The Scourge of Monetarism*. Oxford: Oxford Economic Press.
Kalecki, Michal. 1971. *Selected Essays in the Dynamics of the Capitalist Economy*. Oxford: Basil Blackwell.
Keynes, John Maynard. 1979. *The Collected Writings*. Vol. 29. London: Macmillan.
Knodell, Jane. 1988. "Mainstream macroeconomics and the "neutrality" of finance. A critical analysis." *Economies et Sociétés* 9:155–84.
Lavoie, Marc. 1992. *Foundations of Post Keynesian Economics*. Aldershot: Edward Elgar.
Macleod, Henry Dunning. 1889. *Theory of Credit*. London: Longmans.
Maier-Rigaud, Gerhard. 1985. "Durch statisches Denken zur stationären Wirtschaft." *Kon junkturpolitik* 31:1–33.
Marx, Karl. 1936. *Capital*. Vol. 1. New York: Modern Library.
Minsky, Hyman P. 1982. *Inflation, Recession and Economic Policy*. Brighton: Wheatsheaf Books.

---

24. This conclusion seems to be similar to that of Keynes, who argued that a change in autonomous investment spending would induce the level of income to adjust, through the multiplier process, until planned saving was again equal to planned investment. However, the Keynesian multiplier is a timeless concept, in which all processes take place instantaneously. Here the connection between investment and saving is more direct and does not involve any multiplier.

————. 1986a. *Stabilizing an Unstable Economy*. New Haven and London: Yale University Press.

————. 1986b. "The evolution of financial institutions and the performance of the economy." *Journal of Economic Issues* 20(June): 345–53.

————. 1993. "On the non-neutrality of money." *FRBNY Quarterly Review* (Spring 1992–1993): 77–82.

Moore, Basil J. 1988. *Horizontalists and Verticalists: The Macroeconomics of Credit Money*. New York: Cambridge University Press.

————. 1990. "Why investment determines saving." *Challenge* 32(May–June): 55–56.

Niggle, Christopher J. 1991. "The endogenous money supply theory." *Journal of Economic Issues* 1(March): 137–51.

Parguez, Alain. 1988. "Avant-propos: Le fléau de la finance saine ou l'infortune des fourmis vertucuses." *Economies et Sociétés* 9:3–9.

Preiser, Erich. 1953. "Der Kapitalbegriff und die neuere Theorie." *Jahrbücher für Nationalökonomie und Statistik* 165:241–62.

Ranson, Baldwin. 1983. "The unrecognized revolution in the theory of capital formation." *Journal of Economic Issues* 17(December): 901–13.

Rousseas, Stephen. 1986. *Post Keynesian Monetary Theory*. Armonk, N.Y.: M. E. Sharpe.

Schumpeter, Joseph A. 1927. "Die goldene Bremse an der Kreditmaschine." In Kölner Vorträge, Band I, *Die Kreditwirtschaft* 1, 80–106. Teil, Leipzig: Gloeckner.

————. 1934. *The Theory of Economic Development*. Cambridge: Harvard University Press.

————. 1951. "The creative response in economic history." In *Essays on Economic Topics of J. A. Schumpeter*, Richard Clemence, ed. Washington, D.C.: Kennikat Press Port.

Tooke, Thomas. 1848. *History of Prices and the State of the Circulation from 1792 to 1856*. Vols. 3 and 4. New York: Adelphi Press.

Veblen, Thorstein. 1904. *The Theory of Business Enterprise*. New York: Charles Scribner's Sons.

Wray, L. Randall. 1990. *Money and Credit in Capitalist Economies*. Aldershot: Edward Elgar.

————. 1991. "Saving, profits, and speculation in capitalist economies." *Journal of Economic Issues* 25(December): 951–75.

Contributors

Zoltan J. Acs, College of Business and Management, University of Maryland, College Park, Maryland, USA and University of Baltimore, Baltimore, Maryland, USA

Esben Sloth Andersen, Department of Business Studies, University of Aalborg, Aalborg, Denmark

David B. Audretsch, Wissenschaftszentrum Berlin für Sozialforschung, Berlin, Germany

Jürgen Backhaus, Rijksuniversiteit Limburg, Faculty of Economics and Business Administration, Maastricht, The Netherlands

Mathias Binswanger, Institute for Industry and the Environment, University of St. Gallen, St. Gallen, Switzerland

Maria Brouwer, Department of Economics and Econometrics, University of Amsterdam, Amsterdam, The Netherlands

Uwe Cantner, Lehrstuhl für Volkswirtschaftslehre, Universität Augsburg, Augsburg, Germany

Bo Carlsson, Department of Economics, Case Western Reserve University, Cleveland, Ohio, USA

Anne P. Carter, Department of Economics, Brandeis University, Waltham, Massachusetts, USA

Nicola De Liso, IDSE-CNR, Milan, Italy

Domenico Delli Gatti, Istituto di Teoria Economica e Metodi Quantitativi, Università Cattolica, Milan, Italy

Elias Dinopoulos, Department of Economics, University of Florida, Gainesville, Florida, USA

Rinaldo Evangelista, Institute for Studies on Scientific Research, National Research Council, Rome, Italy and Science Policy Research Unit, University of Sussex, Brighton, U.K.

Michael Fritsch, Bergakademie Freiburg, Freiburg, Germany

Mauro Gallegati, Dipartimento di Metodi Quantitativi e Teoria Economica, Università "G. D'Annunzio," Pescara, Italy

Herbert Giersch, Institut für Weltwirtschaft an der Universität Kiel, Kiel, Germany

Christopher Green, Department of Economics, McGill University, Montreal, Quebec, Canada

Horst Hanusch, Lehrstuhl für Volkswirtschaftslehre, Universität Augsburg, Augsburg, Germany

Ernst Helmstädter, Westfälische Wilhelms-Universität Münster, Münster, Germany

Steven C. Isberg, University of Baltimore, Baltimore, Maryland, USA

Staffan Jacobsson, Department of Industrial Management and Economics, Chalmers University of Technology, Göteborg, Sweden

Brian J. Loasby, Department of Economics, University of Stirling, Stirling, Scotland

J. Stanley Metcalfe, School of Economic Studies, University of Manchester, Manchester, U.K.

Hyman P. Minsky, The Jerome Levy Institute of Bard College, Annandale-on-Hudson, New York, USA

Mark Perlman, Department of Economics, University of Pittsburgh, Pittsburgh, Pennsylvania, USA

Frederic M. Scherer, John F. Kennedy School of Government, Harvard University, Cambridge, Massachusetts, USA

T. Y. Shen, The University of California, Davis, California, USA

Gerald Silverberg, University of Tübingen, Tübingen, Germany

Roberto Simonetti, Science Policy Research Unit, University of Sussex, Brighton, U.K. and Faculty of Social Sciences, Open University, Milton Keynes, U.K.

Wolfgang Stolper, Department of Economics, University of Michigan, Ann Arbor, Michigan, USA

Bart Verspagen, Maastricht Economic Research Institute on Innovation and Technology, University of Limburg, Maastricht, The Netherlands

Georg Westermann, Lehrstuhl für Volkswirtschaftslehre, Universität Augsburg, Augsburg, Germany

Ulrich Witt, Institute for Study of Economic Evolution, University of Freiburg, Freiburg, Germany

Index